The Long Civil War in the North Georgia Mountains

The Long Civil War in the North Georgia Mountains

Confederate Nationalism, Sectionalism, and White Supremacy in Bartow County, Georgia

Keith S. Hébert

Knoxville / The University of Tennessee Press

Copyright © 2017 by The University of Tennessee Press / Knoxville.
All Rights Reserved.
Cloth: 1st printing, 2017.
Paper: 1st printing, 2021.

Library of Congress Cataloging-in-Publication Data

Names: Hébert, Keith S., author.
Title: The long Civil War in the north Georgia mountains : Confederate nationalism, sectionalism, and White supremacy in Bartow County, Georgia / Keith S. Hébert.
Description: First edition. | Knoxville : The University of Tennessee Press, 2017. | Includes bibliographical references and index. | Description based on print version record and CIP data provided by publisher; resource not viewed.
Identifiers: LCCN 2016053322 (print) | LCCN 2017011574 (ebook) |
ISBN 9781621903185 () | ISBN 9781621903192 () | ISBN 9781621903178 (hardcover)
ISBN 9781621906957 (paperback)
Subjects: LCSH: Bartow County (Ga.)—History, Military—19th century.
Georgia—History—Civil War, 1861-1865.
Classification: LCC F292.B3 (ebook) | LCC F292.B3 H43 2017 (print) | DDC 355.009758/36509034—dc23
LC record available at https://lccn.loc.gov/2016053322

For Inman Carter Hébert

Contents

Acknowledgments	ix
Introduction	1
Chapter 1: Antebellum Society, 1830–1860	9
Chapter 2: The Winding Road to Disunion	41
Chapter 3: "Let's Drink the Blood of thy Enemies"	69
Chapter 4: The Long Wait, 1862–1863	97
Chapter 5: The Atlanta Campaign	117
Chapter 6: Federal Occupation	141
Chapter 7: Bottom Rail Still on Bottom	171
Appendix A: Methodology	209
Notes	215
Bibliography	263
Index	277

Maps

1. Bartow County in 1860 — xii
2. Three Distinct Physiographic Regions in Bartow County — 2
3. Bartow County in the Atlanta Campaign — 124
4. Troops around Cassville, May 19, 1864 — 135

Tables

1. Cass County Home Manufactures, 1850 and 1860 — 35
2. Cass County Regions by Percentage Change in Household Manufactures, Corn, and Cotton, 1850–1860 — 36
3. Gubernatorial Election Returns, Cass County, 1833–1849 — 42
4. Cass County Secession Convention Delegates — 60
5. Cass and Surrounding Counties Final Vote on Secession — 62
6. Cass and Surrounding Counties Slave, Slaveowner, and Planter Population, 1860 — 63
7. Companies Raised in Cass County, 1861 — 72
8. Selected Agricultural Products of Bartow County, 1870 — 180

Acknowledgments

On my twelfth birthday my mother gave me a copy of Ken Burns's *Civil War*. The book became my constant companion. I probably read it cover to cover over one hundred times. Growing up in Bartow County, Georgia, I did not have to search long and hard to find the long shadow that the Civil War and Emancipation had cast over my boyhood home. Around that same time, two middle school teachers, Mrs. Casey and Mr. Smith, unknowingly set me on a course that ultimately produced this book. In Mrs. Casey's Georgia history class I first wondered if adults could make a living talking about history. Meanwhile, Mr. Smith's English course filled my imagination with his colorful "Grover" tall tales and led me to take my first steps toward becoming a writer.

As I entered my freshman year of college at the University of West Georgia, I could have never imagined how the history faculty would forever change my life. Elaine MacKinnon, Aran MacKinnon, Robert Claxton, Steve Goodson, John Ferling, Cita Cook, and Ann McCleary nurtured my love of history and helped transform what had been my favorite pastime into dreams of a future academic career.

Nearly two decades ago I walked into Ken Noe's Old South course and fell in love with southern history. Ken would become my mentor, friend, and colleague. What he ever saw in me I will never know but his encouragement and tutelage made me the scholar and person I am today. Privately, we amuse ourselves today by saying that I have "come a long way since that Longstreet paper."

Aspiring to emulate my mentor, I enrolled in the graduate program at Virginia Tech. For two years, I endured the bitter "Bleaksburg" winters and emerged prepared for doctoral work. At Virginia Tech, Randy Shifflett, Tom Ewing, Kathleen Jones, and Richard Hirsh taught me how to think and write like a historian. Under Shifflett's guidance I learned many of the local history research methods that I employed in this book.

As I completed my time in Virginia, I was blessed when Noe took a new faculty position at Auburn University. The chance to continue working with my mentor led me to the "loveliest village on the plains." Auburn surrounded me with a group of supportive faculty who stoked my dreams of becoming a college professor. Tony Carey, Kathryn Braund, Donna Bohanon, Guy Beckwith, David Carter, and Steve Murray all made significant contributions to this work.

Ironically, I did not realize how much I wanted to write about my childhood home until I found myself increasingly removed from it. The idea to write this book spawned from a conversation with Noe over a few rounds at The Cellar in Blacksburg, Virginia. Having published a history of his home, Noe understood the added value that such an undertaking would bring to my life and urged me forward. Noe's fingerprints can be found throughout the following pages. He taught me how to compile and analyze census data, identify local primary sources, and create a local history capable of addressing the dreaded "so what?" question. A gifted editor and patient advisor, Noe spent countless hours helping his sometimes struggling protégé turn my lifeless prose into a publishable work. Then, whenever it seemed that this book might never see the light of day, Noe nudged me forward.

Along the way, numerous archivists helped me locate valuable primary sources. I would like to thank the staff at the Georgia Archives, Emory University, Atlanta History Center, Alabama Department of Archives and History, Tennessee Archives, UNC Chapel Hill, Duke University, University of Georgia, Rice University, Huntington Library, and University of Tennessee–Chattanooga. Trey Gaines and Sandy Moore at the Bartow History Museum also helped me locate materials and personal contacts that enhanced my understanding of the local story. My friend and colleague Keith Bohannon welcomed me to West Georgia as a fellow faculty member and provided numerous sources and invaluable advice that improved this work. Together we spent hours discussing minute details of northwest Georgia history in the dimly lit halls in the TLC building and over lunch at The Border.

This book would not have been possible without the help of The University of Tennessee Press Director Scot Danforth who patiently guided this first timer through the publication process. Aaron Astor and an anonymous reviewer provided helpful comments. John D. Fowler tirelessly reviewed multiple versions offering suggested revisions that dramatically improved the book's quality. His attention to detail and efforts to refine my analysis transformed my drafts into a publishable manuscript.

While all of these scholars helped me along the way, I could not have made it this far without the love and support of my mother, Susan Hébert. Raising two boys as a single mother presented her with unimaginable challenges. Even in the most trying times, her support for our education pushed us to do great things. In my eyes, she is the strongest, bravest, and wisest person I have ever known.

My wife, Rebecca, has lived with this project from the start. Her unwavering support for my professional dreams made this book possible. Whenever I thought this book would never be finished, Rebecca urged me to persevere and gave me the time needed to see it through. Throughout all of the highs and lows Rebecca has been there steadfast. And finally, my son, Inman, has inspired me to continue my work. His constant love and enthusiasm motivates me in ways he will never know.

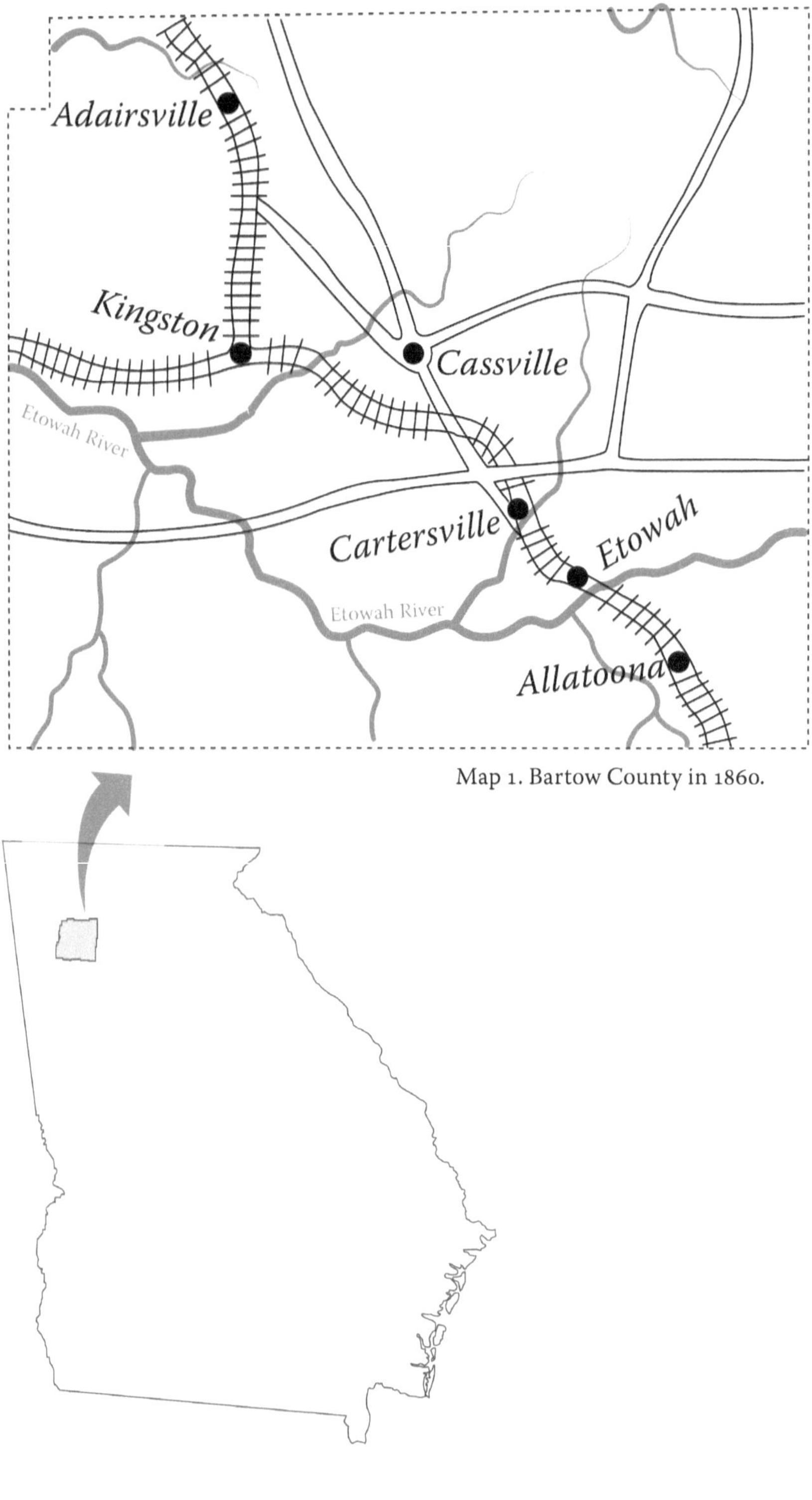

Map 1. Bartow County in 1860.

Introduction

In 1844, Moses H. Bunn, a land speculator from south Georgia, toured northwest Georgia in search of his next investment. As Bunn spent several days in Cass County (later renamed Bartow County in 1861), he recorded a journal filled with detailed descriptions of the local landscape and people. Bunn witnessed an environment where the rolling hills of the southern Piedmont gave way to the Great Appalachian Valley before rising sharply toward the Blue Ridge Mountains. At this crossroads of southern Appalachian and Piedmont regions sat Cass County, a land filled with enormous mineral, transportation, and agricultural potential. However, as Bunn predicted, some sectors of the local area offered greater financial rewards than others. Along the Etowah River valley, Bunn saw numerous plantations already in operation worked by hundreds of slaves under the management of a handful of wealthy planters. In the valley, Bunn saw lots of wealth but scarce opportunities because all of this rich farm land was already in the hands of affluent planters. The common folk that he encountered in the valley failed to impress him and seemed to toil away working for their wealthier white neighbors with limited potential for future growth.

Outside of the valley, Bunn rode the rugged paths that traversed the area's mountainous areas. Bartow County rests along the southernmost foothills of the Appalachian Mountain chain. While the maximum elevation of its mountains pale in comparison to mountains found in east Tennessee or western North Carolina, the foothills were steep enough to form a point of departure that visitors such as Bunn noticed. As travelers climbed the foothills, they left behind the southern Piedmont and entered a new environment where economic opportunity differed. Elsewhere in the county, Bunn reported vast opportunities to build new farms that could maximize the area's superior soils. In Appalachia, however, Bunn turned his attention to potential minerals, especially iron ore, and saw little chance for farmers to make it big in the mountains. Bunn saw Appalachia as disconnected from the Piedmont—a land isolated from the rest of the South. The people who lived there, according to Bunn, seemed to be people with few other options but to settle on some of the poorest lands that the speculator documented during his entire journey. Opportunity in the area, as seen through the eyes of an investment hungry land speculator, decreased the higher in elevation one traveled and the further one got from the fertile Etowah River valley.[1]

Bartow County, Georgia's geographic location—the intersection of three major southern subregions Piedmont, Appalachia, and the Great Appalachian Valley—makes this county more representative of a broader swath of the South than other counties located exclusively in just one of these regions. Bartow County is an ideal setting to examine broad questions in southern history. How did a society filled with enormous disparities in wealth and power keep internal division to a minimum? What role did geography play in influencing white intra-class relations? What relationship existed between Appalachian communities and the broader South and nation? If divisions among white households existed, how did the Confederacy manage to garner such widespread and persistent support? Why did some parts of Appalachia support the

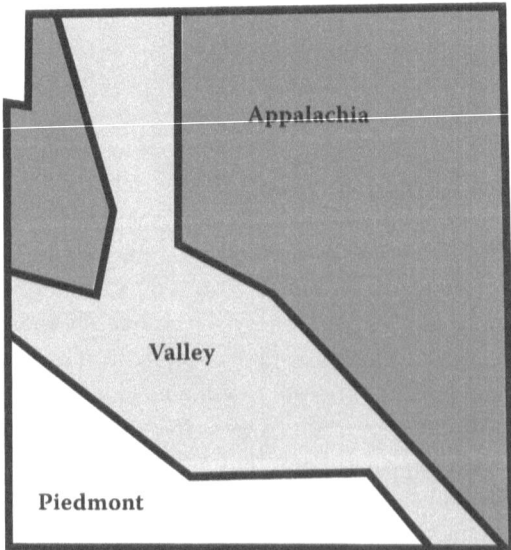

Map 2. Three Distinct Physiographic Regions in Bartow County.

Confederacy? And finally, how did the actions of Unionists and Confederate partisans living on the southern home front influence the Confederate war effort? My work argues that white supremacy—as expressed by local leaders and adhered to by poor whites—created a hegemonic white community where major differences in social, economic, and political status failed to create any lasting divisions or substantial societal changes that might have challenged the white men's democracy. Despite disruptions caused by the Civil War and emancipation, Bartow County society remained largely unchanged throughout the century as a prevailing conservative order never yielded power.[2]

Bartow County's geographic diversity created an antebellum society filled with internal divisions and massive discrepancies in wealth. However, despite these divisions, relations among white men remained peaceful. While a minority of locals protested secession and refused to accept Confederate authority, the majority of local residents, rich and poor, cast their support for the Confederacy. As in other locales throughout the South, the glue that held such a potentially divisive society together was a shared understanding of white supremacy, black inferiority, and optimism that the future protection of slavery might provide an avenue for upper mobility for all white men. These shared values, as well as kin networks and a desire to defend their homes from Federal invaders, convinced large numbers of local white men to enlist in the Confederate army.

The external pressures caused by the Civil War unraveled the appearance of white solidarity resulting in the rise of a small, vocal Unionist minority that opposed Confederate authority. While the county voted against secession in 1861, Unionists failed to gain an overwhelming mandate of support.[3] Local resistance to Confederate rule took a severe hit when many men who opposed secession either joined the Confederate military or sought out elected and bureaucratic positions in the new government. Hundreds of Unionists in the county rode out the war serving in the army, manning a government post, or working in a war-related industry. Such men saw themselves as neutral operatives who neither gave their all in support of the Confederacy nor actively resisted the new government.

Between 1861 and 1863, diehard Unionists resisted Confederate efforts to force them into the army and to impress their personal property and generally, along with other Unionists concentrated in north Georgia, remained a thorn in the side of state and national leaders. Always a minority of the total population, most Bartow County Unionists survived this period by arming themselves, staying close to home, and avoiding travel to market towns. Others sought refuge from Confederate agents by hiding in dense woods and caves and by leaving the area usually headed for east Tennessee. Nonetheless, a small network of Unionists managed to collaborate and were aware of one another's existence and political views. On occasion these Unionists banded together, often sharing quarters for extended periods, as a means of thwarting Confederate agents who came in search of trouble. The Unionist presence was loud enough in the county and region that Georgia Governor Joseph E. Brown had to dispatch state militia into the area on several occasions to disrupt Unionists activities.

The arrival of Union armies under the command of General William T. Sherman in the spring of 1864 only escalated local divisions as the remaining Confederate partisans worked to pester the occupying army while Unionists and slaves, emboldened by the arrival of Yankee soldiers, sought out ways to further erode local Confederate authority. Despite prolonged and widespread support for the Confederate government in Bartow County, a combination of internal divisions and external pressures combined to defeat local Confederate partisans in a manner that was symptomatic of widespread problems throughout the Confederacy.

Geography influenced Bartow County's Civil War era experience. Antebellum economic opportunity depended in large part upon access to rich farm lands located close to markets or railroads.[4] Where someone lived in the county suggested much about their socioeconomic standing in the region and biased their politics. Resistance to Confederate governance rose the higher in elevation and the farther from transportation networks and market towns one lived. Conversely, those who lived in rich valley lands close to transportation and market towns tended to offer steadfast support for the Confederacy. While small numbers of local Unionists were wealthy, mostly individuals who owned mercantile businesses or were employed in a number of professions, such as teaching or law, most were significantly poorer than the local pro-Confederate elite that dominated the county's economy, politics, and culture.[5] To be sure, significant numbers of poor white households also supported the Confederacy. They cast their allegiance to the Confederacy for a variety of reasons ranging from kin networks to shared notions of white supremacy.

Bartow County consisted of three distinctive geographic subregions that both divided the area's topography and created zones of extreme wealth and poverty. The county's wealthiest residents either lived in the Etowah River valley or in the southern end of the Great Appalachian Valley that extends from Bartow County in a northeastern direction for hundreds of miles through Tennessee, Virginia, Maryland, and Pennsylvania. Valleys accounted for about 40 percent of the land in the county. The Etowah River valley, which drained 80 percent of the county's water, gave rise to a booming slave society whose wealth rivaled some of the most affluent areas in all of Georgia and southern Appalachia. In the valley, approximately 90 percent of all land was cleared for agriculture by the start of the Civil War. Most planters and slaveholding yeomen farmers owned valley property. Here King Cotton reigned supreme. These valleys also provided suitable lands for the construction of a major railroad line, the Western & Atlantic Railroad, which in turn supported the growth of new towns with greater access to distant markets.[6] The centers of trade and political power were concentrated in valley areas. All of the county's major towns were located in the valley including Cassville, the county seat, and Cartersville, the largest antebellum community. However, while many valley residents held enormous personal fortunes, many less fortunate white households also struggled to survive surrounded by such opulence and power. Poverty in the valley could be extreme as many white households lacked real estate and were forced to either work rented farms or live a hand-to-mouth existence working as day laborers for their affluent neighbors. In the valley, both before, during, and after the Civil War, poor whites and their wealthier neighbors interacted frequently due to their close proximity. The potential for conflict was high and occasionally found expression prior to the war, but by and large a shared sense of racial unity and patriarchal home rule kept tensions from boiling over. The valley is where the Confederate government attracted its greatest support throughout the war as affluent slaveholders led their wealthy friends and poorer neighbors into battle. The Great Appalachian Valley also hosted the largest concentration of Union soldiers during the Atlanta Campaign and the ensuing Federal occupation. As Union soldiers tried to control the local pro-Confederate populace, the valley became a stage upon which scenes of internal division played out in a manner reflective of similar locations elsewhere in the South.[7]

Other subregions in Bartow County, such as the Piedmont region that covered the southern and western portions of the area, had broad, flat ridges and gently to moderately sloping hillsides that were not as conducive to growing cotton. The Piedmont comprised about 15 percent of the county. The altitude in this area is around 900 feet above sea level. Piedmont slaveholders tended to own fewer slaves and less land and often raised livestock and grew corn alongside plots of cotton.[8] Yeomen farms dominated this area.[9] Tenant farmers could also be found across the area. Migrations in and out of the Piedmont were commonplace as some families came and improved their fortunes while others remained for only a few years before looking westward for new and improved opportunities in places such as Alabama, Texas, Kansas, and California.

Few local political leaders hailed from the Piedmont. Based upon election results, it would appear that Piedmont farmers tended to cast their support behind Great Appalachian Valley planters whether those men belonged to the minority Whig Party or majority Democratic Party. The need for valley planters to maintain support among Piedmont yeomen likely drove antebellum political rhetoric toward adopting platforms that promoted yeomen economic growth and white solidarity and fostered consensus. At the start of the Civil War, Piedmont farmers sent scores of young men into the Confederate army. Georgia leaders understood that continued yeomen support for the war was critical and made some efforts to alleviate the suffering that their families experienced.

Support for secession and the Confederate war effort appeared to remain stable in this region at least until spring 1864 when many Confederate soldiers serving in the Army of Tennessee who came from this area deserted their ranks and returned home to protect their family and property. Confederate pension applications submitted by Piedmont families evidence the steep price Piedmont families paid for their Confederate support. Many limped away from the war scarred by their military service and uncertain if their economic prospects would rebound. After the war, yeomen in this area and throughout the county threw their support behind an independent Democratic Party movement that challenged the old guard's dominance of that party. Later, these same men cast ballots in support of the Populist Party who likewise challenged the dominant Democratic Party.

To the northeast and northwest of the Piedmont lies the hill country or Appalachia. About 45 percent of the land in the county was located in the hill country. The terrain here gets steeper and large-scale farming more difficult. The highest point in the county, Pine Log Mountain (altitude 2,000 feet), is located in this area. Common whites and small yeomen farms of fifty or less acres dotted this region. About 30 percent of the land in this area had been cleared for farming by 1860. Hill country farmers also received less rainfall annually than valley planters. Throughout the Civil War era, a number of severe droughts struck hill country farmers while larger farms located 20 miles away often received adequate rainfall amounts. Livestock herding and subsistence farming were more common in this section of the county than elsewhere. The number of household manufactured goods produced by Appalachian families here were also higher compared to Great Appalachian Valley and Piedmont families.

With substantially fewer crops to sell, Appalachian farmers were less connected to the county's towns and less dependent upon the railroad. Families were not entirely isolated, however. Informal exchanges of goods, such as bartering and other forms of trade, often required Appalachian families to travel into town or seek out wealthier farms in the valley to do their business. Compared to their Great Appalachian Valley and Piedmont neighbors, Appalachian households were politically marginalized. Few held elected office at any level and the dominant political rhetoric of the period rarely courted their support. Hill country farmers likely found the rise of planter and yeomen wealth throughout the rest of the county and region to be a limiting factor in their personal success. As slavery expanded, and cotton and railroads became central to the local economy, mountain households struggled to keep pace and generally experienced prolonged periods of financial stagnation.

Opposition to secession and defiance toward Confederate policies, especially conscription, was high in this region. Dissent was so pronounced that Governor Joseph E. Brown had to send state militia into the area to round up draft dodgers and subdue pockets of resistance that had organized to hamper Confederate efforts to collect materials for the war effort. Between 1861 and 1863, Unionists in this area continued to find ways to oppose Confederate authority and remained a consistent source of frustration for state and national leaders. Manuscripts penned by pro-Confederates elsewhere in the county routinely commented on anecdotal stories of dissent fomenting in the area. When General William T. Sherman led three major Federal armies in the county during the spring 1864 Atlanta Campaign, Unionists welcomed his arrival and at times worked closely with the soldiers in blue to provide information about Confederate troop movements and to identify pro-Confederate locals. Bartow County's hill country bore the brunt of the final months of the war as bands of guerrillas of varying allegiances and proclivities toward violence waged war upon the area. After the war, Appalachian families cast some support behind the Republican Party but as common throughout the South found it difficult to support a national party that seemed determined to extend civil liberties to freed slaves.[10] For the remainder of the nineteenth century, Bartow County's Appalachian families struggled economically and remained stuck between their unwillingness to support the dominant Democratic Party and their uncertainty about the state Republican Party's viability.[11]

Bartow County's history, much like the rest of Appalachia and the South, demonstrates a broad range of responses to the crises surrounding the Civil War era. This study joins a chorus of recent scholars who stress that one cannot paint with too broad of a brush stroke when depicting the motivations and responses of southern Appalachians. Bartow County, as a representative example of southern Appalachia, had a lot in common with the rest of the South. Bartow County, like east Tennessee, western North Carolina, and southwest Virginia, contained significant populations of both Confederate and Unionist partisans. Valley residents shared a similar economic and political outlook as did Black Belt communities elsewhere. As numerous studies have shown, Unionism and resistance to Confederate governance existed in many places across the South. At times, mountain men resisted Confederate authority much the same way that men facing similar conditions in Mississippi or along the Chattahoochee River valley in Georgia and Alabama acted. Meanwhile, mountain men, as well as men across the South whose neighbors resisted Confederate authority, clad in butternut and gray died on countless battlefields sacrificing their lives to serve the Confederacy. Others, from the same community, joined only to desert and returned home for a litany of reasons.[12] In Bartow County, members of the same household often disagreed resulting in some members staying at home and openly resisting Confederate attempts to secure their allegiance while close relatives remained with the Confederate army until its final surrender. If Bartow County's history represents a shared experience witnessed across the Confederacy then its story tells us much about the war's origins, Confederate defeat, and the enduring legacy of white supremacy in the postbellum South.

CHAPTER
1

Antebellum Society, 1830–1860

The internal divisions that existed within the Confederate States of America were rooted in antebellum inequalities among white households. During the decades that preceded secession, massive distinctions in wealth existed among Cass County residents as an elite group of planters and large slaveholding yeomen farmers rose to dominate the county's social, economic, and political life. This elite group controlled the best lands in the county, usually located in the Great Appalachian Valley subregion, and had the best access to local markets and transportation. They also possessed the wealth needed to influence local, state, and national political debates to ensure that their interests were always served by varying legislating bodies. Nearby, in the Piedmont subregion, enough yeomen farmers climbed the social and economic ladder that men from similar backgrounds believed in the possibility that one day their chance for success might arrive. Dreams of ascending into the ranks of the elite planter class aligned the interests of most yeomen farmers with their affluent neighbors. Meanwhile, those who lived in the Appalachian subregion struggled to achieve any form of upward social mobility. Without a cash crop and limited access to markets and transportation, the county's mountain folk relied heavily upon subsistence farming and played only marginal roles in shaping the county's social, political, and economic order.[1]

Despite discrepancies in wealth and power among Great Appalachian Valley, Piedmont, and Appalachian residents, relations among white households remained harmonious. Like other southern Appalachian communities, Cass County families formed interdependent communities bound by a shared kinship, economic desires, regional culture, and notion of white supremacy. Social and religious institutions and organizations, such as churches, fraternal groups, and agricultural associations, provided a place for residents to congregate and develop their communal bonds. While economic disparities existed among white households, a common sense of communalism, co-dependence, and attitudes regarding race and gender governed class relations. Culture tended to trump class and limit the latter's ability to sustain visible divisions among white men of varying affluence.

Economically, the completion of the Western & Atlantic Railroad in 1850 provided Great Appalachian Valley and Piedmont farmers with access to transportation technology that encouraged a greater participation in the market economy.[2] Flush times, however, were far from universal. Appalachian farmers and tenant farmers and poor whites who lived in the Great Appalachian Valley and Piedmont subregions, faced enormous pressures due to rising land prices, declining wage labor rates, and consumer inflation. Many left the county seeking better opportunities elsewhere.

On the eve of the greatest conflict in American history, a majority in Cass County society saw themselves as part of a booming community connected to an expanding market economy where economic winners overshadowed losers and relations among white households remained peaceful. These conditions created an environment in which large numbers of locals threw their support behind the Confederate government following secession. When the local interdependent white community, which had increasingly gained economic security through expanded market and transportation changes—movements that had brought the region even closer to its slaveholding southern brethren—felt threatened by an external enemy whose policies imperiled the very foundation upon which the system was constructed, slavery, most locals threw their support behind the Confederacy. Support for the Confederacy, however, was far from universal, and the roots of that dissent spread among those who had been marginalized during the county's golden age. The origins of Cass County's wartime divisions can be found within the inequalities of its antebellum society and were representative of broader trends found across southern Appalachia.

The Georgia General Assembly created Cass County on December 3, 1832, naming it in honor of Democratic Secretary of War Lewis Cass of Michigan. The legislature formed ten counties, including Cass, from Cherokee lands. Today, Bartow County, as it became known in 1861 when it was renamed in honor of fallen Confederate Colonel Francis S. Bartow of Savannah, who died during the First Battle of Manassas, is located in the state's northwestern region. It is bordered by Gordon County to the north; Pickens and Cherokee County to the east; Cobb, Polk, and Paulding County to the south; and Floyd County to the west. Cartersville, the modern-day county seat, lies fifty-seven miles south of Chattanooga, Tennessee, and thirty-five miles northwest of

Atlanta. The county encompasses 460 square miles or 294,400 acres. While the state altered the county's boundaries on several occasions, overall the current county closely resembles its original 1832 boundaries.

The best land in the county is located in the Etowah River valley and Great Appalachian Valley. The Etowah River is the county's largest river and flows in a northwestern direction from east to west across the southern portion of the county. The Great Appalachian Valley bisects the county running northwest to southeast. In 1860, landholders who lived in these valleys accounted for approximately 70 percent of the total wealth of the county's inhabitants. Eight out of every ten slaves that were held in bondage in Cass County lived along the Etowah River.[3] Three of the wealthiest planters in Appalachia lived within a few miles of one another on large Great Appalachian Valley plantations on the Etowah.[4]

Across southern Appalachia great disparities in wealth existed between those who lived in fertile river valleys and those who lived at higher elevations. Cash crops of varying kinds could be found throughout the Great Appalachian Valley. Wheat, cotton, and tobacco required a lot of labor to cultivate. Slavery took hold in the valley quickly as early settlers cleared large tracts of land and made plans to emulate wealthier landholders common in more established parts of the South. In southwest Virginia and east Tennessee, for example, an overwhelming majority of slaveholders lived in the valley. Valley slaveholders held numerous political offices throughout the Great Appalachian Valley. The valley supported the rise of major cities, such as Chattanooga, Knoxville, and eventually Roanoke. The valley's geography made it possible to build railroads that connected these cities to larger national and international markets. Portions of the Great Appalachian Valley, especially parts of northwest Georgia, resembled parts of the Deep South where large plantations and affluent planters dotted the landscape. Although Cass County slaveholders never achieved the level of wealth and power that their Deep South mentors enjoyed, they nonetheless aspired to reach such heights.

In contrast, the Appalachian region of the county located in Cass County's eastern section, around Allatoona, Stamp Creek, Adairsville, and Pine Log, and northwestern section, between Kingston and Rome, were home to only a few small slaveholders. Most of this area's residents were hardscrabble yeomen farmers and common whites whose total wealth represented about 10 percent of the county's totals.[6] In this region, tenancy rates climbed and persistence rates dropped compared to those who lived in the more affluent valley. Cotton and slaves, everyday sights in the valley, were rare in the hills. Without a staple crop to produce for the market or enslaved laborers to help expand their farms and production, hill country residents led a more localized existence compared to their elite neighbors who traveled and traded far and wide.[7]

Because Cass County contained a large fertile valley where plantations rivaled those found further south in the Black Belt and Coastal regions of Georgia, the county's Appalachian subregion struggled to exert any social, economic, or political influence upon local affairs. The vast majority of the county's elected officials and affluent citizens did not live in Appalachia. None of the major towns or transportation routes in the county existed in Appalachia. Nonetheless, mountaineers in the county were not isolated; in fact, many traveled into town regularly and some had kin who lived in other sections of the county. Mountain communities in eastern Kentucky, western North Carolina, western Virginia, and northeast Georgia, for example, were far more isolated geographically than Cass County. While geography alone did not make Cass County mountain men poor, the close proximity of substantially wealthier neighbors might have created a different kind of isolation. Without the best lands in the region, these Appalachian residents remained significantly poorer than their southern neighbors. The persistence of poverty in a region surrounded by wealth is one of many recurring themes in Appalachian history.

Cass County is situated where the Appalachian Mountains end and the Piedmont Plateau begins. The Piedmont sections of Cass County are located in the southwestern part of the county. The land in these areas is punctuated by a series of small valleys bordered by steep ridges. Yeomen farms of varying sizes dotted the Piedmont's landscape. Some of these farms were quite large and possessed small numbers of slaves while other farms were small and depended entirely upon household labor and white day laborers. Whereas many farmers in this area grew large quantities of wheat and corn and maintained sizable numbers of livestock prior to 1850, cotton gained popularity throughout the 1850s as many of these farmers reaped the financial rewards that staple crop market production offered. While yeomen only accounted for about 20 percent of the county's total wealth, they represented a majority of its citizens. Distinctions among Cass County's three subregions influenced the area's development and response to Civil War era crises.[8]

In Georgia, the Piedmont region cuts a large swath across the state running from the Appalachian foothills southward to the Fall Line. Most of this area had been settled by whites following the removal of the Creek and Cherokee Indians. Like Cass County, non-slaveholding yeomen farmers comprised a majority of Piedmont farmers. Despite their minority status, slaveholders, especially the handful of planters in the region, owned considerable amounts of land and controlled a disproportionate share of the region's total wealth. The Piedmont sections of Cass County resembled other Piedmont communities statewide.

Prior to the arrival of thousands of white settlers during the late 1820s and early 1830s, Cherokee Indians had controlled northwest Georgia. In the eyes of white settlers, the Cherokee were an obstacle preventing them from developing the region. While many white men married Cherokee women and formed tenuous trading relations with the Cherokee, most interactions between white men and Cherokee involved threats and violence. By the time that President Andrew Jackson signed the Indian Removal Act in 1830, the fate of the Cherokee Indians in the Southeast had been determined. Removal was a popular idea among most Georgia politicians and nearly all settlers saw it as a positive means of advancing the economic fortunes of all white men. With the Cherokee Indians out of the way, white men could transform the frontier into new white communities.[9]

Georgia developed a land lottery system to distribute Cherokee property among prospective white settlers. On the surface, the lottery appeared to offer all white men and their white dependents an equal opportunity to gain access to rich farm land at below market prices. The 1832 land and gold lottery proposed to parcel out property to large numbers of state residents, creating a region filled with yeomen farmers. Factors such as age, marital status, war service, past lottery draws, and state residency determined eligibility and the number of chances. Once winners learned of a successful draw, they paid a fee ranging from three to eighteen dollars to secure a grant providing them title to their allotment.[10]

Thanks to land speculators who eagerly purchased claims off of poor drawers and the poor's inability to pay the small lottery fees or finance the expense of a move from their current location to northwest Georgia, most of the lottery land ended up in the hands of men who had already owned property elsewhere and were looking to come to northwest Georgia to build their fortunes.[11] Lottery drawers accounted for a minority of early Cass County and northwest Georgia settlers. For example, of the 324 successful drawers in the Fifth District, Third Section, less than 20 percent moved to Cass County.[12]

In 1834, Georgia compiled a census of the free white population of Cass County. The official count listed the head of each household, omitting such information as the number of slaves in each household, the names of dependents, the ages of county residents, their real and personal property holdings, and the proportion of male/female inhabitants. Nonetheless, the census provides a basis for understanding the geographic origins and kinship networks of the county's early settlers.[13] In 1834, 235 households containing 1,388 people resided in six militia districts. About 60 percent of all heads of households who had moved to Cass County listed South Carolina as their birthplace.[14] An estimated 32 percent were natives of East Georgia counties, most notably Habersham (10 percent) and Gwinnett (12.6 percent). The remaining 8 percent originated in Virginia, North Carolina, Kentucky, and an array of New England and Mid-Atlantic states.[15]

During the late 1830s, Cass County's population rapidly expanded as Georgia reaffirmed the Treaty of New Echota and a statewide economic boom attracted out-of-state migrants. In 1840, 9,390 total inhabitants, including 1,995 slaves and fourteen free blacks, lived in the county. The average white settler was a forty-two-year-old non-slaveholding yeoman farmer whose household contained a spouse and five children. Approximately 27 percent of white heads of households owned slaves, while less than 1 percent owned twenty or more slaves.[16] The median slaveholder owned three slaves. John Rowland, a native North Carolinian and merchant who came to Cass in 1839 after moving from his home in Spartanburg, South Carolina, owned the largest number of slaves with fifty-four, while eighty yeomen held only a single bondsman.[17]

Although slavery existed across Cass County, much like the rest of the antebellum South it was more pronounced in the Great Appalachian Valley and Piedmont areas than in Appalachia. Approximately 80 percent of the county's slave population lived on plantations and large farms located in the valley. Plantations were large farms with over 200 acres worked by twenty or more slaves. In the valley, slaves accounted for about 40 percent of the total population. Here large cotton plantations lined the banks of the Etowah River and the various creeks that fed it. Colonel Lewis Tumlin's plantation was the largest in north Georgia and among the more expansive in southern Appalachia. Stretching for over a mile along the northern bank of the Etowah River, Tumlin's plantation eventually grew from fourteen slaves in 1840 to more than 162 by 1860.[18] The valley subregion also supported a number of large slaveholding yeoman farms such as those owned by the Brandon, Harris, and Garrison families. A majority of these men came from western South Carolina where they had previously owned land and slaves.[19]

Cass County's Appalachian subregion contrasted sharply with its valley neighbor. Along the eastern parts of the county, only a handful of farmers owned any slaves. Slaves accounted for less than 5 percent of the subregion's population. Samuel Adair Sr. was the typical hill country slaveholder. The son of a Cherokee woman and Scots-Irish trader, Adair had worked his farm for decades prior to white settlement. His white ancestry helped Adair maintain control of his land and determined the timing of his eventual relocation to Oklahoma.[20] Many white men, about one dozen heads of households, who lived in the Cass County hill country had Cherokee mothers. Their white kin networks and the poor quality of their land helped them to stall removal. By 1840, two years after Cherokee removal, Adair owned a small tract of land and a grist mill that were operated by his nuclear and extended family members and at least three slaves. Adair's holdings might have paled in comparison to county planters, but among hill country farmers he had few rivals. Wealth was relative to a farmer's immediate surroundings and kin networks. Adair's nearest neighbors, men who lived within a few miles of his farm, were mostly common whites who either owned small farms less than 50 acres or were landless day laborers with no real estate and little personal wealth. Several of Adair's relatives were planters. Some of them moved to central Alabama, southern Mississippi, and northeastern Louisiana during the 1820s where a few became planters.[21]

About one out of every five Cass County settlers came to the area involuntarily. While slavery existed throughout northwest Georgia, slavery represented a larger percentage of the county's total population than other counties such as Murray, Gilmer, Paulding, and Walker. The attractive and extensive lands along the Etowah River valley, the area first claimed by white settlers, likely explains slavery's faster rise in Cass County compared to other northwest Georgia counties. In fact, slavery in Cass grew at such a rate that the area compared favorably with slave holdings in large Black Belt counties located hundreds of miles to the south. By 1840 slaves comprised 21.2 percent of the total population. Most, like their masters, were native South Carolinians. Many came from farms and plantations in the western part of the state. Thomas Brandon, for instance, brought four slaves to Cass County during the early 1830s. Their labor helped to clear about 50 acres of farmland and construct housing so that Brandon's white family members could relocate.[22]

Most slaves frequently ate, worked, and slept in close proximity to their yeoman masters. John C. Aycock, a slaveholding yeoman who moved to Cass County from east Georgia during the early 1830s, owned two slaves, both women, who performed a variety of domestic duties and slept under the same roof as their owner. Living in close quarters, slaves and owners perhaps developed personal relationships that extended beyond the traditional master-slave dichotomy. Slaveholders who owned one or two slaves sometimes created last will and testaments allocating a small portion of their worldly possessions to their slaves. Aycock, for instance, left a slave a Bible. Others willed items such as furniture, pocket watches, clothing, and various family memorabilia. These actions, though unrepresentative, suggest that some small slaveholders developed bonds with their slaves that were expressed in terms of endearment that extended beyond a master's lifetime.[23]

Cass County possessed large iron ore deposits that fostered the rise of a number of iron manufacturing businesses. These iron forges relied heavily upon enslaved labor creating distinctive portions of the county where a local majority of slaves worked in furnaces rather than in cotton fields. Similar scenes could be found across parts of north Georgia. In Union County, northeast of Cass County, many slaves worked as miners.[24] Cherokee County, east of Cass County, also had several furnace operations worked by enslaved laborers. As was commonplace in many mountain South communities, Cass County slaves performed a wide array of domestic, agricultural, and industrial jobs. Most performed agricultural chores such as clearing, plowing, hoeing, and weeding fields. Many worked as domestics, especially female slaves who lived with small slaveholding masters. Some slaves, especially those held in the Appalachian subregion, acquired skills such as blacksmithing, carpentry, milling, or iron making. Iron pioneers Moses and Jacob Stroup, who built some of the first blast furnaces in western North Carolina, western South Carolina, central Alabama, and northeast and northwest Georgia, used slave labor, almost exclusively male, for a variety of industry-related tasks such as chopping wood, mining iron ore, smelting ore, and molding iron.[25] Several iron blast furnaces operated locally and in the surrounding counties. Each furnace required the harvesting of 400 acres of timber land annually to provide the needed charcoal. Large teams of slaves and white day laborers worked in small isolated logging camps scattered throughout the area's foothills.

At Etowah, a rare southern industrial village and perhaps the second largest of its kind in southern Appalachia, slaves worked in the furnaces as well as a number of associated manufacturing pursuits such as blacksmithing, wagon making, brewing beer, and small tool production. As many as 4,000 workers, one third of them enslaved, worked at Etowah during its late 1850s peak. Slaves were in such number at Etowah that its owner Mark A. Cooper reportedly opened a bordello run by enslaved females who provided sex to workers, enslaved and free, in exchange for the company town script.[26] Some of these skills allowed slaves limited opportunities to earn personal income based on the quality and quantity of their labor. At Etowah it seems likely that slaves and white laborers spent much time together both at work and during their free time. Cooper's industrial town frequently needed additional labor and provided a place where slaveholders, large and small, could lease out their slaves for some much needed cash or in-kind items such as nails, tools, or alcohol.[27] Whites and blacks, free and enslaved, formed the nucleus of a biracial slave society in which white masters enjoyed the fruits of black labor and the bonds of intra-racial supremacy.

While no slave rebellions occurred in antebellum Cass County and northwest Georgia, white residents lived in constant fear of a looming insurrection. Residents believed that full moons and rare cosmological occurrences such as eclipses and comets were events that slaves might use to trigger a planned assault. Editors filled local newspapers with reports of rebellious slaves in distant places setting fire to plantation houses or hiding stashes of edged weapons. These stories excited the southern white mind and produced a state of paranoia that must have been tiring. Sarah Clayton, the daughter of an affluent planter who lived east of the town of Kingston, remembered one particularly fearful time in the fall of 1860. For several days, armed white men patrolled the county seeking to extinguish a suspected plot among slaves. Word spread throughout northwest Georgia that slaves on an east Texas cotton plantation had set fire to a number of houses and murdered an unspecified number of whites. The reported incident never happened, but locals nonetheless worried that slaves across the region might be hatching an organized plot of their own. Clayton's home became a refuge for the plantation overseer's family as white families across the area sought safety in numbers. The threat passed without incident. Clayton believed that rumors of slave rebellions were usually started by poor whites who did not own slaves as a means of stirring up trouble. Similar accusations were also reiterated in other local family correspondence. These reports likely reflected the apprehensions that many slaveholders felt in areas where slaves and poor whites interacted frequently and had developed some form of social relations or bartering networks.[28]

Most slaves came to Cass County with their South Carolinian masters who by the 1830s comprised about 60 percent of all white heads of households. Of those who originated from the Palmetto State, 89 percent came from the state's Upcountry region. This exodus from western South Carolina included a number of planters and slaveholding yeomen farmers. Farmers had grown wealthy from their massive annual cotton crop, but their product slowly destroyed their lands and damaged the state's economy.[29] Upcountry South Carolina farmers produced so much cotton during the late 1700s that by 1820 most of the region's soil was unsuitable for staple crop production. As the situation worsened, the South Carolina legislature commissioned agricultural reformer Edmund Ruffin, a Virginia planter and the nation's leading agricultural scientist, to dissect the region's problems. Ruffin told leaders that cotton's survival depended upon the willingness of farmers to diversify their crops. In the long term, Ruffin's advice stabilized the state's cotton industry. In the 1830s, efforts to diversify local production and successive poor harvests convinced many landowners to immigrate westward.[30]

Most Cass County white heads of households owned real estate prior to coming to Cass County. Throughout the antebellum period, non-slaveholding yeomen farmers comprised a majority of Cass County heads of households. For example, out of a sampling of 300 heads of households who moved directly from western South Carolina to Cass County during the 1830s, 240 had owned at least 50 acres of land in the Palmetto state and sixty owned slaves. The average Cass County settler who relocated from western South Carolina, therefore, was already a landholding yeoman prior to their relocation.[31]

Throughout the antebellum period, kinship bound together many white households, helping reduce any possible intra-racial frictions. A wide array of consanguine, affinal, and fictive kin relationships held greater significance in the Old South since the region contained fewer public institutions than their northern counterparts.[32] Like other antebellum southern frontier communities, the extent to which settlers came to Cass County in association with their relations and established family and kin connections there played an important part in providing people with an essential support network. Among persistent heads of household, those who appear in the 1840 and 1850 census, 75 percent came to Cass County as members of kith and kin associations. Settlers who arrived without the support of extended family members, such as parents, siblings, in-laws, and cousins, or who failed to foster new relations through marriage typically left the county. As commonplace throughout rural America, families in association built Cass County.[33]

The experiences of frontier families who came to Cass County in the 1830s were similar to other communities across the antebellum South and northwest Georgia. Most settlers came as part of an extended family—a social and economic network of collaborative action that enabled individuals to group together resources. In the spring of 1833, for example, the families of Nathaniel and Lydia Wofford, some twenty persons residing in four households, packed their belongings onto wagons, left their homes in Habersham County, crossed the Etowah River near Canton, and rode west to their new mountain home in Cass County's 827th Militia District. The Woffords knew about Cass County since members of their family had lived in the hills near Pine Log among the Cherokee prior to their removal. One such relative, James Wofford, married a Cherokee woman, fathered several children with her, and then accompanied her westward during the Trail of Tears. After surveying their land—they had received draws from their father's Revolutionary War service during the 1832 land lottery—the party began clearing to grow corn, harvesting the timber to use in the construction of three separate dwellings. Initially, the four families of the Wofford settlement, similar to the settlers of Sugar Creek, Illinois, described by John Mack Faragher, pooled their labor, tools, and households' resources. Each season, the men cleared and planted another field until several years had passed and every household could work an independent plot. Through their communal efforts, these families managed to sustain one another during periods of illness or personal injury that might have otherwise doomed any individual effort to create and sustain a farm. The neighborhood gradually took the name of Wofford's Cross Roads, and the Wofford family emerged as local leaders.[34]

Cass County was a small part of a larger antebellum South governed by a patriarchal slave society filled with white male heads of households who despite real inequalities of wealth and status maintained peaceful relations. As Cass County's population expanded, the Great Appalachian Valley and Piedmont subregions emulated the places from which its settlers came, most notably Upcountry South Carolina. White male heads of households were "masters of small worlds" who exercised their authority over their household's women and slaves in general. A concept of racial distinction and supremacy separated all whites from all blacks creating a mudsill class of enslaved laborers. Planters, despite their relative small numbers in Cass County and southern society in general, wielded enormous social, cultural, and particularly political clout, but maintained various bonds of loyalty and communalism with their white neighbors that preserved a sense of interdependence that quelled many potential intra-white conflicts.[35]

White Cass Countians shared a common material culture. Most ate a similar diet of large amounts of corn and pork. Many white heads of households lived in log dwellings with their spouse and on average five children. Estate inventory records reveal that a majority of locals owned at least three common items: a Bible, a gun, and a bed. Both rich and poor usually possessed a few common household furnishings such as a dinner table, various pots and pans, a spinning wheel, a butter churn, and a lantern. Wealthier inhabitants could afford imported furniture, milled cloth, tapestries, carpets, and numerous other luxury items.[36]

In addition to sharing similar material possessions, some white Cass Countians belonged to a number of social and religious organizations that provided meaningful fellowship for rich and poor, black and white, male and female residents. As documented in other southern communities, churches and other social organizations provided a venue for planters, yeomen, and common whites to express some of their differences and work out their disagreements under the collective eye of church members. Clearly, planters dominated antebellum congregations, especially in the Piedmont and Great Appalachian Valley subregions, often funding the building, selecting its pastor, and holding numerous leadership positions. Yeomen and common whites, however, had a voice in local congregations and sometimes represented their church at regional conventions. When disagreements erupted, the church provided both parties with an established method of redress that usually resolved the issue before matters escalated. Plus, if church members disagreed with how the church handled matters, as many did throughout the period, those aggrieved individuals could remedy the problem by removing themselves from the congregation and seeking out opportunities to worship elsewhere or remain at home.[37]

Geography limited church membership. The average Macedonia Baptist Church member, for instance, lived within five miles of the church. By 1860, twenty-four churches held services throughout the entire county—eight Baptist, three Primitive Baptist, nine Methodist, and four Presbyterian.[38] Most of the country churches met once a month. Town churches usually congregated twice a month. While a majority of the county's population lived in rural households, a majority of church members resided in towns such as Cassville, Kingston, and Cartersville and hamlets such as Euharlee, Adairsville, and Stilesboro.[39]

To be sure, some unchurched Christians residing in Cass County held worship services in their homes for family, friends, and slaves. Godfrey Barnsley, for instance, organized a bi-weekly worship service for his children, white servants, and black slaves. Barnsley, a British citizen and a cotton broker with offices in Savannah and New Orleans, owned a plantation he named Woodlands, located halfway between the town of Kingston and the hamlet of Adairsville. Family correspondence indicates that slave preachers presided over these services on several occasions.[40]

Presbyterian churches in the county and throughout the state and southeast frequently requested that Barnsley's neighbor Reverend Charles W. Howard preach at their church, but he also worshiped at home during periods when his poor health prevented travel and inhibited his oratory abilities. Howard, a native of Savannah and a former Presbyterian minister, was a statewide religious and agricultural figure renowned for his orations and writings. Throughout the 1850s, he and his wife, Susan Jett Howard, operated a boarding school for girls. As part of their instruction, each student had to attend weekly church services and Sabbath school instruction provided by Howard or, during his absence, a church in nearby Kingston.[41] Like Howard, Mark A. Cooper, a devoted Baptist and affluent owner of the region's largest industrial town, Etowah, held regular worship services for his free and unfree workers.[42]

Slaves in Cass County, like in other parts of the South, also held services outside of established white churches. Julia F. Daniels recalled that on Sundays "Uncle Joe" held services in front of her master's home. Carrie Elder's owner constructed a small church on the plantation. There he held Sunday afternoon services and Wednesday evening prayer meetings. Easter Brown's master did not take his slaves to church, in part, as she explained due to the fact that they were so tired. While she did not attend church and it is unknown if slaves on her plantation held independent services, Easter believed in and prayed to God.[43]

As in most southern churches, women comprised a majority, approximately 62 percent, of Cass County's church membership. Of those members, 90 percent were either married or widowed. The typical Cass County congregation member was a married thirty-three-year-old female with at least four children. Women occupied several leadership roles within a typical antebellum church. They served on conferences and visiting committees, cast votes that determined church leadership and other related governance matters, represented their church at various state and local fairs, and most importantly helped spread the church's evangelical message. Women did not serve as ministers or preach but occasionally taught Sabbath school. While most women were married, a large number attended church without their husbands. Women attended church in greater numbers than men because it was one of the few opportunities for them to congregate with their neighbors.[44]

Though women outnumbered men, white males ruled church life in the same manner in which they were the earthly governors of dependent women, children, and slaves in their households. Male church members assumed the duty of maintaining church discipline, thus finding in church governance the legitimization of their household authority. While women outnumbered men, the latter ruled the church. Non-slaveholders also outnumbered slaveholders, but nonetheless repeatedly elected them to positions of congregational authority. Surviving church records indicate that 85 percent of pastors, deacons, and elders owned slaves. The church embodied the local community where approximately 17 percent of all heads of households in 1860 owned slaves.[45]

The dividing line between a majority of non-slaveholders and their slaveholding brethren was minimal. Most Cass County slaveholders between 1840 and 1860 owned a single slave. While prime field hands were valuable commodities worth potentially over a thousand dollars, approximately 65 percent of slaveholders who owned a single slave owned a middle-aged or older female whose value was considerably less.[46]

Slaveholders frequently doled out their slaves to neighbors, either in exchange for cash or simply as an act of neighborly charity. Godfrey Barnsley, for instance, hired out slaves in exchange for monetary compensation, as did Mark A. Cooper, Charles W. Howard, and Lewis Tumlin. The farm journal of slaveholder Dennis Johnson includes several accounts of providing slaves to his neighbors during non-peak times of the year to help them prepare their fields, mend fences, or herd livestock. In times of trouble, non-slaveholders also could depend upon the charity of local slaveholders such as Barnsley who provided them with sacks of flour and cornmeal. While it is uncertain how many slaveholders acted in such a charitable manner, it would be safe to assume that many devout church members did since their religious beliefs stressed the importance of aiding the poor.[47]

Primitive Baptist Churches and their evangelical neighbors, Baptist, Methodist, and Presbyterian, espoused a belief that slavery was a biblically sanctioned practice that reflected the natural order of the world's superior and inferior races. The state Baptist newspaper, *The Christian Index*, printed articles reminding church members that slave ownership created a "multiplicity of . . . new relationships." Some churches held masters responsible for the spiritual development of their slaves, while others seemed apathetic.[48] Slaveholders who worshiped at Euharlee Presbyterian Church regularly brought their slaves to Sunday services. Meanwhile, at Macedonia Baptist Church, located five miles from Euharlee, slaves attended services less regularly and their names were omitted from the church's membership rolls.[49]

Slaves comprised a sizable minority in at least two of the county's churches. The Euharlee Presbyterian Church identified their body's "colored" members. In 1860, eleven slaves became members in this church. Slaves constituted about 15 percent of Euharlee's total membership. Approximately 93 percent of slave members joined after providing the presbytery with a profession of faith. Malinda Franks obtained membership upon the reception of a letter transferring her membership from a church in South Carolina, where she had lived prior to her master's, R. H. Taylor, relocation to Georgia. While most southern churches regulated where slaves sat during worship services, the Euharlee Presbyterian Church's rules of order contained no such designations. The church building did not contain a balcony, nor does its architectural design or floor plan suggest that a separate "colored" sitting area had been installed. Slaves likely sat in a segregated portion located in the rear of the church.[50]

Slaves who worshiped at the Euharlee Presbyterian Church attended services with their masters. Since the church records only list the names of members, and not the names of their dependents or those who might have been too young to have been considered full church members, it is difficult to estimate how many slaves actually attended church services. The Milam family, Riley and Turner Milam, encouraged at least three of their slaves, Hal, Francis, and Chaney, to join the church. Meanwhile, local slaveholding families such as the Sproulls, Speers, Templetons, and Taylors also had at least one slave listed on the church's membership roll.[51]

Slave members at Nance Creek Baptist Church also attended worship services alongside their masters every fourth Sunday of the month. Most joined the church along with their masters after being baptized by immersion. In September of 1856, the church baptized 63 men and women, including "Virgil a servant of Col. Edwards," "Susan servant of Dr. Milam," "June servant of Mr. Todd," and at least six other slaves. During one ceremony, the church baptized thirty-three white men and women before four slaves entered the water. Mass baptisms were common in this congregation and throughout the South. The custom of allowing slaves to be baptized in the same ceremony as their masters, but only after all of the whites had been dunked, exhibits the bonds masters and slaves shared within an environment that reinforced the latter's inferiority.[52]

Mass baptisms perhaps reflected the hierarchical nature of antebellum southern society. In September of 1856, Nance Creek baptized twenty-three white men and forty-three white women. The first five men baptized owned slaves. The following fifteen owned real property. The final three men who entered the water were landless day laborers. One month later, the church baptized another fourteen white men and nineteen white women. Again, two slaveholders went first, followed by eight yeomen, and concluded by four laborers and tenant farmers. In each of these baptisms, women either followed their husbands or were dispersed among the yeomen. Mass baptisms at Macedonia Baptist Church and Euharlee Presbyterian Church also followed these general patterns. The ordering of baptism (slaveholders, non-slaveholding yeomen, non-yeomen, and slaves) reflected the hierarchical and deferential nature of antebellum society.[53]

Surviving church records reveal that slave members never engaged in white congregational business. They never represented churches during their local conferences and sessions, and they never served on white visiting committees sent to comfort members during times of trouble or to investigate a white member's transgressions. No record exists of a slave delivering a sermon in an organized church. White church members only mentioned a slave when they joined the congregation or when they were baptized.[54]

While slaves regularly attended some Cass County churches, whites interacted in a number of other social and cultural settings that were predominately segregated by race and usually by gender. By 1860, the county contained at least six Masonic lodges consisting of approximately 200 white male members. Masons prohibited women and slaves from joining their organization. No poor white men belonged, perhaps because of the ten dollar annual dues. Most lodges met twice monthly for closed door sessions that shrouded the body's activities. The Masons engaged in a social mission that benefited their immediate community by performing a number of anonymous charitable acts that reinforced the existing communal bonds. In January 1856, for instance, a poor man died in Cassville. His family could not afford a casket and could not locate a place in town to bury him. Local Masons responded by taking up a collection that paid for the casket and burial. Masons particularly cared for their own members. When a member lost a house to a fire or suffered an unexpected poor crop, the Masons found ways to provide relief to that member. If a member became injured, others helped to plant, harvest, or market his crop. In Cassville, Masons who owned gristmills regularly donated corn meal to local impoverished families regardless of their membership. Kinship influenced their communalism since many of their members were related to significant segments of the local population, but their organization's charity extended beyond the confines of familial relations. While the Masons prohibited slaves from becoming members, unfree laborers nonetheless helped perform many of the group's charitable deeds. Slaves rebuilt destroyed homes and barns and did much of the donated farm work. Masonic lodges fostered a communal spirit among its white members and non-members that strengthened the bonds of loyalty across their community.[55]

White Cass Countians belonged to several local and state agricultural societies. Reverend Charles W. Howard, a prominent local slaveholder and advocate for agricultural reform, helped to organize the Etowah Agricultural Society that participated in a variety of state and regional associations. Agricultural societies provided a venue for white male farmers to discuss their work with their peers and a chance to receive advice from the region's leading agricultural scientists. Topics at meetings included animal husbandry, crop rotation, fertilizers, labor management, and market prices. No complete membership roll exists for the county's agricultural society, but reports published by the Cassville *Standard* sporadically listed the names of members who attended the most recent meeting. Such reports identified ninety-five white men who attended society meetings throughout 1859 and 1860. Slaveholders comprised about 45 percent of these individuals, while less than three percent were common whites. Slaveholders dominated the group's leadership holding approximately 95 percent of all elected positions. These societies sponsored annual county fairs. At the fair white farmers competed for cash prizes rewarding the best livestock, garden produce, and field crops. Agricultural societies and fairs displayed and rewarded the talents of many white farmers, which fostered a community of farmers who shared a common base of knowledge and agrarian fellowship.[56]

Agricultural societies, like many northwest Georgians, eagerly anticipated the construction of "the State Road," the Western & Atlantic Railroad

(W&A). On December 21, 1836, four years after the creation of the county, the Georgia General Assembly passed an act authorizing the use of state funds to construct a railroad from a point near the Chattahoochee River (the eventual site of Atlanta) to the Tennessee border near Chattanooga. The W&A connected western farmers to Macon, Augusta, Savannah, and many smaller towns such as those located in Cass County. The notion of a state-funded railroad network attracted support from Democrats and Whigs alike during the flush economic times of the 1830s, but it became a divisive party issue as the state's economy fizzled during the late 1830s and early 1840s. In 1841, the state suspended construction. At that time, the State Road extended from the Chattahoochee River to the banks of the Etowah River along Cass County's southeastern border. Despite poor economic conditions, Whig politicians sponsored additional spending bills while a majority of Democrats—especially from the Black Belt—opposed those measures. In 1843, a coalition of eight north Georgia Democratic senators, including Cass County's largest slaveholder Lewis Tumlin, and statewide Whigs narrowly passed a W&A appropriations bill.[57]

Support for the W&A extended beyond a handful of Cass County Democratic legislators. While some Upcountry yeomen and townspeople alike protested the construction of the railroad because they feared that the trains would kill their livestock, escalate land prices, spark forest fires, and introduce undesirable elements such as saloons, vagrants, and prostitutes into their backyards, editorials published in the Cassville *Standard* and the actions of local leaders reflected a community that favored railroad construction. W&A surveyors determined during the 1840s that the steep rocky terrain, known as the gravelly plateau, around the town of Cassville would prevent the State Road from passing through the county seat. Initially, residents seemed unconcerned with this decision. Their newspaper published several editorials predicting that the State Road would be a mixed blessing for the region. Two years later, in 1852, editors changed their stance after witnessing the economic boom brought to railroad towns in the county including Kingston, Cartersville, and Adairsville. The town of Cartersville had scarcely existed before the W&A opened. By 1852, this rail town had surpassed the county seat of Cassville in total population, number of businesses, and overall wealth. Kingston and Adairsville too experienced a spike in population and number of businesses. A thriving hotel and resort industry developed in Kingston where none had existed only five years earlier. John Burke, Cassville *Standard* editor and proprietor, warned Cassville residents that if something was not done their town might decline as businesses and townspeople relocated to Cartersville. In 1852, a group of planters, merchants, and professionals from Cassville paid for a survey that proposed to reroute the State Road through their town. County representatives lobbied for the proposed changes, but due to the burdensome estimated cost, their efforts failed. If large numbers of Cass County farmers and townspeople had opposed the railroad, then no one would have borne the expense of conducting a survey.[58]

If yeomen farmers protested the railroad prior to 1850, economic trends during the following decade silenced those critics. During the 1850s, the W&A helped many farmers maintain and expand their existing landholdings. The railroad altered the county's agricultural production, racial composition, and economic foundation. Prior to 1850, Cass County farmers grew small amounts of cash crops. Most farmers devoted the bulk of their improved acreage to corn and raised livestock on the open range, eventually consuming those items within their household or bartering them among their neighbors. Most farmers were semi-subsistence producers with minimal contact with state and local markets. A typical yeoman during the 1840s might produce a single bale of cotton annually to sell for cash, but few grew more than that.[59]

The economic practices of antebellum Cass County farmers both reinforced local bonds of community and expanding interest in external trade networks. Like most rural American communities, approximately 80 percent of the county's heads of households were self-identified farmers and about the same percentage worked in an agricultural related occupation. Free laborers accounted for a majority of farm work, but slavery existed throughout the county and was especially prominent on farms located along the Etowah River. In 1860, 425 heads of households (17 percent of all heads of households) owned slaves compared to 302 a decade earlier. Masters who owned a single slave accounted for 19 percent (81 slaveholders) of all slaveholders. About sixty-two slaveholders owned 20 or more slaves, while only two owned more than 100. The median slaveholder owned seven slaves. During the 1850s, Cass County's slave population increased by over 1,200 slaves. The growth in the percentage change in the total slave population in Cass County between 1850 and 1860 outpaced the state of Georgia as well as the ten largest slaveholding counties in the state.[60]

The expansion of slavery in Cass County impacted some areas more than others. About 80 percent of the county's slaves were owned by planters and large slaveholding yeomen farmers who lived in the valley districts. In the valley, by 1860 farmers had cleared nearly 90 percent of available land to make way for growing farms that ranged in size from 200 to 1,800 acres. Most of the remaining slaves in the county were held in the Piedmont region. Only a handful of slaveowners in the Appalachian region of the county owned more than a single slave and a majority of white households did not own any slaves.[61]

While the total number of slaveholders increased during the 1850s, the number of farmer heads of households who owned the land they worked remained stable due to out-migration, population increases, and rising land prices. In 1850, approximately 65 percent of the county's farmer heads of households listed on both the manuscript and agricultural census owned their farms. Tenant farmers who rented their land accounted for the remaining 35 percent. One decade later, tenant farmers comprised about 33 percent of the county's heads of households.[62]

Throughout the 1850s the county's white population grew at a slow pace in part due to the large number of residents who migrated westward. The Cassville *Standard* focused much attention on the out-migration problem, running a series of letters from western correspondents that painted a mixed picture of out-migration. Hawkins F. Price, a local planter and politician, encouraged potential migrants to "remain among their friends and the enjoyments of home" rather than endure the hardships of California "and be swindled by crooks." Others painted a different scene. Nathaniel T. Wofford, local slaveholder and relative of local leader William T. Wofford, traveled to California during the early 1850s. In a published letter to the editor, Wofford told the *Standard*'s readers that "some Georgians here are making from 15 to 20 pennyweights per day." Those who moved to California, wrote Wofford, soon learned "that it is the finest country in the world" and the "greatest hog country I ever saw." Approximately 200 heads of households, 160 of whom were tenant farmers, listed in the 1850 manuscript census—as well as an undetermined number of dependents—moved westward during the 1850s. Arkansas, Texas, and California were the most popular destinations. Meanwhile, the county's white population increased from 10,271 to 11,433, a rate of 10.2 percent.[63]

Persistence and tenancy rates varied within the county's three geographic subregions. As valley slaveholders accumulated additional land and slaves and consolidated their near complete ownership of the area's best arable lands, poor whites and yeoman farmers were squeezed out of the region. Planters did not need to rent uncultivated lands to poor white farmers because the rising number of slave laborers provided as much labor as necessary to work the improved lands. Consequently, fewer than 10 percent of farmers in the valley were tenant farmers. Unable to find land to farm many poor white men resorted to seeking employment as a day laborer but such work offered minimal compensation because slavery depressed day laborer wages. Without land and facing declining wages poor white men left the valley often heading west in search of better opportunities. In the valley, the persistence rates of slaveholding heads of households hovered around 85 percent between 1850 and 1860. During the same period in the valley, persistence rates among poor white heads of households was about 37 percent between 1850 and 1860. The valley's 10 percent tenancy rate was significantly lower than most north Georgia counties. For example, about 35.2 percent of all Whitfield County, located northwest of Cass, farmers were tenants. Likewise, 22.9 percent of Cherokee County farmers were tenants. The valley's tenancy rates compare more favorably with similar numbers found in the Georgia Black Belt, eastern Piedmont, and Coastal Plain regions—places where slaveholders, slavery, and staple crop production dominated the local economy. Cass County's valley subregion shared more in common with more affluent regions of the South than with Appalachia.[64]

Conversely, persistence and tenancy rates were higher in Cass County's Appalachian subregion. Nearly 35 percent of all farmers in Appalachian Cass County did not own the land they worked. Great Appalachian Valley and Piedmont slaveholders held large tracts of land in the mountains. John Rowland, one of the county's largest slaveholders, owned nearly 1,000 acres of land in the mountains in addition to the large landholdings he possessed in the valley. Absentee landholders held large tracts. These men often lived several counties away or in another state. A survey of Appalachian subregion property deeds recorded during the 1850s found dozens of purchasers residing in North Carolina, South Carolina, and Tennessee. Most of these men owned large farms elsewhere and seemingly used their Cass County lands as either investment or rental property. The tenancy rates in the mountainous sections of Cass County mirrored those found in other north Georgia mountain communities. Whitfield, Fannin, Polk, Gilmer, Murray, Union, and White counties, as well as several others, had similar tenancy rates. As a whole this collection of counties housed the largest concentration of tenant farmers in the state.[65]

Surprisingly, despite relatively high tenancy rates, an indication of minimal economic opportunity in the area, Appalachian subregion residents were just as likely to remain in the county between 1850 and 1860 as their more affluent valley neighbors. About 75 percent of Appalachian heads of households remained in the county between 1850 and 1860. Kin networks likely contributed to stability in mountain areas. Many tenant farmers lived near relatives who owned small farms. Appalachian families, such as the Aycocks, Abernathys, Jones, and others, had both tenant and yeomen households as part of their extended kin networks. Family might have been enough to keep some tenant farmers from going elsewhere. Perhaps, while their opportunities might have been limited in this subregion, poor whites chose to remain because they saw some hope for advancement.⁶⁶

Westward migration gave those who failed to accumulate land and wealth in Cass County opportunities to realize their dreams elsewhere. Countywide, the movements of poor white households out of the county increased the percentage that landholding farmers represented of the total free population. In Cass County, the constant flow of tenant farmers out of the community likely reduced conflict among rich and poor white households because many of those who might have harbored resentment about the inequalities of this elite-dominated system left the county within a decade of their arrival.⁶⁷

Conflict was also ameliorated due to the symbiotic relationship that existed between tenants and landlords. A sampling of county land and census records revealed that most tenant landlords were planters and slaveholding yeomen. Others tended to be merchants, lawyers, doctors, and other professionals who lived in towns and rented out their country farms.⁶⁸ Tenancy during the antebellum period resembled many of the attributes of farm ownership, and tenants seemed to share the culture and outlook of yeomen. To be sure, some of the county's wealthier landholders looked down upon their poorer neighbors, but they rarely displayed this condescending attitude in public. George Barnsley, a son of a local slaveholder, for example, referred to tenants who rented land on his father's plantation as crackers, but he also developed friendships with them and on more than one occasion taught tenant children to read and write. When one of his tenants needed food during the winter of 1854, Barnsley donated several sacks of cornmeal and invited the family to dine with him.⁶⁹

The economic gap between a tenant and landholder varied greatly. Many sons of prominent landholders leased property until they received their inheritance. Nathan Land, a prominent Cassville jurist and planter, leased property to a man who owned a farm in Fulton County, but wanted to increase his cotton production by leasing improved acreage.⁷⁰ A sampling of heads of households who appeared in both the 1850 and 1860 census revealed that about half lived near landholding family members and some leased land directly from their family. Landholders routinely leased their unimproved acreage to tenants who in return cleared the land and built fences in exchange for any crops he produced. In a cash poor environment, tenants usually paid their lease agreements with their own labor.⁷¹

Most white farmers enjoyed the flush economic times of the 1850s. While slaves accounted for a higher percentage of Cass County's total population in 1860 than 1850, the economic position of the county's slaveholders diversified during the same period. Tenant farmers and farm laborers accounted for 15

(3 percent) of the county's 425 slaveholders. Only two tenant farmers and farm laborers had owned any slaves ten years earlier. About seventy-five yeoman farmers who lived in Cass County in 1850 and 1860 became slaveholders during that decade. Some large yeoman slaveholders, exactly 18, increased the number of slaves they owned to twenty or more. Meanwhile, the number of slaveholders who owned 20 or more slaves increased from 43 to 62. Three of the wealthiest planters in southern Appalachia lived in Cass County.[72]

During the late antebellum period, the number of and the wealth of slaveholders increased throughout southern Appalachia and northwest Georgia. By 1860, 40,370 heads of households owned slaves in southern Appalachia. Between 1830 and 1860, the percentage of Cass County landowners holding slaves increased from 29.6 to 41.5 percent of the total white population. In Cass County, the growth in the number of slaves and slaveholders measured by the total population and percentage of the total population outpaced the rest of southern Appalachia and northwest Georgia. In 1860, Cass County had northwest Georgia's largest slave population as well as the largest number of total slaveholders. About 107 more white men in Cass County, for example, owned slaves than its nearest rival Whitfield County. Cass County's number of slaveholders nearly doubled other northwest Georgia counties such as Chattooga, Cherokee, Polk, and Walker and tripled others such as Catoosa and Murray. Meanwhile, ten times the number of slaveholders lived in Cass County than its regional neighbors Dade and Gilmer counties. With the price of slaves rising by 20.5 percent between 1840 and 1860, those who invested in slaves substantially increased their personal wealth through capital gains. By 1860, Cass County truly was the "Deep South" of southern Appalachia.[73]

The increase in the number of slaves and slaveholders embodied the economic boom experienced in Cass County during the 1850s. Two principal and interrelated factors fueled the expansion of the local economy. In 1850, the state of Georgia completed construction on the W&A. Depots built in the towns of Allatoona, Cartersville, Kingston, Cass Station, Adairsville, and Kingston provided local farmers with greater access to state and regional markets. That same year, a second rail line opened that connected the town of Kingston to the city of Rome, Georgia, and its navigable rivers that allowed traffic throughout portions of Alabama and the Tennessee River valley. Second, throughout the 1850s the price of cotton increased by 22.5 percent from .089 to .109 dollars per pound motivating farmers to clear more land, reduce their livestock holdings, devote less acreage to corn and more to cash crops such as cotton, wheat, and, to a lesser degree, tobacco.[74]

Upcountry farmers seeking to reap financial rewards by planting larger amounts of cotton assumed enormous risks. While cotton production had been responsible for enormous profits in the Deep South, especially in the Black Belt region, growing it in north Georgia was often boom or bust, especially for small landholders. Upcountry farms experienced earlier seasonal frosts than their Black Belt counterparts. One early frost could be enough to push a farmer into the red. Railroads helped get cotton to Savannah and then on to international markets, but, as David Weiman demonstrates, the distance between their farms and the market increased transportation time and costs and sometimes prevented local producers from selling their crop at peak demand. Thus, while between 1850 and 1860 hundreds of Cass County farmers began growing larger amounts of cotton, a lot had to happen in favor of the producer in order to see maximum profits.[75]

While King Cotton reigned supreme throughout significant portions of the Deep South, King Wheat remained important in Cass County during the 1850s. In 1850, about 485 farmers produced 29,153 bushels of wheat or an average of sixty bushels per farm or 1.8 bushels per acre of improved land. Roughly half of all farms grew at least a few bushels of wheat. In 1860, farmers dramatically increased their wheat production to 136,694 bushels, a 368.9 percent increase compared to the county's 1850 totals. While wheat production soared, the number of farmers in the county who grew wheat fell to below 475. Yet three out of every four farmers grew at least twenty-five bushels of wheat in 1860. Railroad records indicate that at least 60 percent of the area's wheat crop was sold outside of the county. Much of it went North to distant urban markets where wheat was in great demand. A market for wheat also existed locally where slaveholders purchased food crops to feed their growing labor force.[76]

Farmers also grew more cotton in 1860 than 1850. In 1850, about 30 percent of farmers planted cotton producing 2,385 bales. That year slaveholders who owned more than twenty slaves accounted for 75 percent of the county's total cotton crop. Few non-slaveholding tenant and yeomen farmers grew cotton. One decade later, about 45 percent of farmers planted cotton producing 4,407 bales, an 84.8 percent increase compared to the county's 1850 returns. Slaveholders who owned more than twenty slaves grew more cotton but accounted for a lower percentage, 60 percent, of the county's total crop. Slaveholding yeomen raised 22 percent of the crop, while tenants and non-slaveholding yeomen grew the remaining 18 percent.[77]

The fact that in 1860 more farmers grew larger amounts of cash crops on an increased number of improved acres compared to 1850 does not prove that these products were produced for the market. Farm journals, W&A freight records, and newspaper accounts, however, indicate that by 1860 farmers dedicated more of their available farm land to staple crops rather than subsistence crops because of their eagerness to sell their goods for cash.[78] Freight records compiled by the W&A railroad reveal that local farmers shipped substantial amounts of wheat and cotton during the 1850s to state and regional markets. In 1860, Cass County produced 4,407 bales of cotton. That same year, 4,212 bales of cotton were shipped from the Cartersville depot alone. While it is possible that farmers from neighboring counties may have transported cotton to Cartersville to be shipped on the W&A, it is more likely that a majority of the cotton transported at this particular depot came from local producers. Cotton growers in neighboring Cobb County would have been more likely to use the Marietta depot to transport their bales rather than bearing the expense and trouble of transporting it several dozen miles to Cartersville. Gordon County, Cass County's northern neighbor, grew 432 bales of cotton in 1860 but their depot located in Calhoun transported 1,688 bales of cotton during that year. It is likely that some farmers from the Adairsville and Pine Log area might have found transporting their product to Calhoun easier than carrying it to Cartersville.[79]

Farmers brought their crops to market in a variety of ways. Many sold their crop to local planters who used factors to negotiate prices with state and regional brokerages. Factors provided planters access to an intricate worldwide marketing system.[80] Some farmers stored their cotton for months waiting for a spike in cotton prices before selling. Farmers routinely sold cotton outside of the county courthouse located in Cassville or at one of the county's railroad depots. Godfrey Barnsley, for instance, told his overseer John Connelly to visit the cotton market in Cassville, Cartersville, and Rome in search of a good price on some locally produced cotton. Barnsley, an affluent slaveholder and cotton broker, bought cotton locally at prices that were lower than those garnered in Savannah or overseas and then bore the transit costs to those markets earning a handsome profit. The role that local planters played in providing other farmers access to the market reinforced their existing communal bonds.[81]

Cotton and corn coexisted on most Cass County farms. Both were important crops that were sold to outside markets. Corn, however, was one of the main staple items in every household's daily diet. Cotton requires more labor in terms of the number of hours of work needed in order to produce each 400 lb. bale. As the amount of cotton increased during the 1850s, the amount of time farmers devoted to raising cotton rose, while attention given to other crops declined. Corn production declined by 13.6 percent. While 80 percent of farmers in 1860 grew some amount of corn, an overwhelming number grew less than they had in 1860. Wheat and cotton now grew where corn was once planted. Since most white household diets consumed large quantities of corn annually, the local decline in corn production was one sign that area farmers had become less concerned with producing crops for their tables and more concerned with growing cotton and wheat for the market. As historian Sam Hilliard demonstrates, the southern diet diversified during the late antebellum period as increased market relations introduced once isolated areas to fruits, nuts, seafood, and a variety of preserved meats that diversified local diets.[82]

While corn crops declined countywide, subsistence rates among farmers remained high. Subsistence agriculture is the use of household labor to produce enough goods to provide for that household annually. In economies such as the antebellum South where cash was scant, especially outside of towns and villages, subsistence gave farmers an added sense of security and independence. Even in subsistent households, small amounts of crops or products such as honey, candles, alcohol, or leather, were produced to be sold or traded for items that a family needed but could not produce themselves, for example, coffee, sugar, gunpowder, clothing, tools, fertilizer, etc. Corn yields might have decreased, but quantities remained well above the amounts needed to provide for local food needs. In 1860, county farmers grew about 430,202 bushels of corn.[83] Historians have estimated that in order to be sufficient local farmers had to produce about twenty bushels of corn per adult.[84] Cass County's 9,434 adults, slave and free, raised 45 bushels of corn each. A complete survey of area farms in 1860 revealed that the average farmer planted corn on about 40 percent of their improved acres. Farmers countywide yielded about seven bushels of corn per acre. Clearly, planters and slaveholding yeomen grew larger yields of corn than did their common white neighbors. Plantations alone accounted for about 40 percent of the county's total corn output.

Conversely, on smaller farms, especially those operated by tenant farmers, who typically worked lands owned by wealthy slaveholders, corn had been pushed aside by cotton and wheat. Tenants likely saw cotton and wheat as a better investment in their economic futures and hoped that one good crop might push them into the landholding class. Tenant farm owners also likewise pushed their tenants to raise larger amounts of cotton and wheat since both crops brought a higher cash value at market. Typically, tenants received about 66 percent of the total value of their crop once it had been sold. Landowners collected the remaining value. Market forces, and not a predetermined preference for maintaining self-sufficiency, seemed to have driven many farming decisions in Cass County during the late antebellum period.[85]

The farm journal kept by Oothcaloga Valley farmer Dennis Johnson from 1850 until 1859 reveals much about the county's efforts to maximize staple crop production. Johnson did not own slaves, but he frequently rented them to supplement his four full-time white laborers. Together his biracial workforce cleared fields, constructed fences, harvested timber, butchered hogs, and spread manure. In 1850, Johnson's farm produced a diverse number of crops: corn, oats, wheat, Irish potatoes, and cotton and included over 100 acres of unimproved farm land that supported his expanding herds of cattle and growing hog population. Five years later, in 1855, Johnson's farm had undergone a gradual transformation as he devoted less acreage for subsistence crops and livestock than previously.[86] His laborers had cleared an additional fifty acres of farm land. Johnson planted cotton on 55 percent of his improved acreage and wheat on 25 percent leaving only 20 acres for corn and potatoes. His journals mention the transport of cotton and wheat to the W&A depot in Adairsville as well as the sale of a portion of his crop to a local planter. While Johnson clearly sold wheat and cotton to local and regional buyers, he still produced a majority of the food that his family consumed. He spent a significant portion of his wheat and cotton profits hiring additional laborers and renting more slaves. That income also provided his family with some additional household items such as an imported china cabinet and mirror. Johnson's experience represents a sizable portion of the county's farmers who sought out the market economy but on terms they dictated by growing cotton and wheat after meeting their household's self-sufficiency.[87]

While the production of corn declined moderately during the 1850s, a majority of county farms maintained self-sufficiency. In 1860, approximately 60 percent of farm households were self-sufficient in grain and 55 percent were self-sufficient in meat. The percentage of farmers who achieved self-sufficiency in grain only fell from 66 percent in 1850 to 60 percent in 1860; meat figures experienced a similar decline. A 6 percent decline in self-sufficiency was minimal given the county's dramatic rise in cash crop production. Cass County trends matched similar happenings across Georgia. According to historian Numan V. Bartley, "Self-sufficiency in food declined during the 1850s as improved railroad transportation made low-priced midwestern foodstuffs available and thereby encouraged Georgia agriculturalists to place even greater effort on cotton cultivation and to make up any food shortages with imports."[88]

Table 1 shows similar patterns for other common products raised by Cass County farmers. The quantity of items manufactured at home declined sharply during the 1850s. In a related trend, the number of merchant businesses in Cass County tripled during that same period. Farmers made less products at home because they purchased more items from area stores and neighboring farms. Meanwhile, the production of wool, a product closely connected to household consumption, increased slightly between 1850 and

TABLE 1
Cass County Home Manufactures, 1850 and 1860

Select Agricultural Returns	Home Manufactures
1850	19,979
1860	15,025[a]

Note: [a]Represents a 25% decline from 1850 to 1860.
Source: Agricultural Returns, 1850 and 1860 Census.

1860. Census records fail to note that during that period Reverend Charles W. Howard, a local minister and agricultural reformer, labored hard to convince farmers to import Merino sheep into the county. Small numbers of local farmers became convinced that Merino sheep might provide their farm a financial safety net if cotton prices declined or yields dropped due to repeated overproduction. Dennis Johnson, for example, introduced Merino sheep into his livestock holdings probably following some convincing by his neighbor Howard. The fact that so many farmers heeded his advice prevented wool production from declining in the 1850s. Clearly, farmers sought the best of both worlds, a place within the market and a self-sufficient household.[89]

When agricultural returns are broken down by region within Cass County, the relationship between a farm's proximity to market and the production of household manufactures and other domestically consumed items suggests that the closer one lived to the railroad and the valley, the less likely they produced for home consumption. Appalachian farmers lacked the labor, land, and climate needed to grow large cotton crops. Many remained stuck producing for household consumption. In contrast, Piedmont and Great Appalachian Valley farmers clearly dedicated fewer resources to producing home goods and growing corn and shifted that time and energy toward larger cotton crops.[90]

A direct link exists between Cass County farmers who produced and sold crops for regional markets and men who in 1861 enlisted in the Confederate States of America military. In 1860, about 846 white men between the ages of 18 and 35 lived on farms in Cass County that produced surplus amounts of either cotton, wheat, or corn that would have been sold in either local or regional markets. Approximately 75 percent (635) of those men enlisted in a Confederate military unit during the spring and summer of 1861. Plus, many pro-secession advocates in the county were older white men from these same market producing households. Slaveholders such as Turner Goldsmith, John Hardin, Robert Young, John Rowland, and Lewis Tumlin led the county's pro-secession faction and produced crops for sale in local and regional

TABLE 2
Cass County Regions by Percentage Change in Household Manufactures, Corn, and Cotton, 1850–1860

Identified Regions	% Change Household, Manufactures 1850–1860	% Change Bushels of Corn, 1850–1860	% Change 400 lb. Bales of Cotton
Valley	-40	-11	+60
Piedmont	-10	-6	+22
Appalachia	+10	+3	+2

markets. Non-slaveholding market oriented farmers also joined or sent their sons off to fight at a higher rate than farmers who did not produce enough crops to sell in local and distant markets. Out of the 945 Cass County men who joined a Confederate military unit between the spring and summer of 1861, only 94 (10 percent) came from farm households that did not produce enough crops to sell in local and distant markets. Most of those men came from the valley and Piedmont subregion. In 1861, only a handful of the 945 Confederate volunteers came from the Appalachian subregion. In Cass County, market oriented farmers accounted for a majority of the local support given to secession and the early Confederate mobilization. Clearly, markets influenced local politics.[91]

For most Cass County farmers producing for the market was not an all or nothing proposition. The farm diary of James Washington Watts reflects how slaveholding farmers balanced their desire to sell crops on the market and to maintain their existing self-sufficiency and communal bonds. Of the hundreds of entries written by Watts between 1853 and 1857, a majority related to livestock. During that period, Watts devoted additional land to the production of cotton, while increasing his livestock holdings. His ledger reveals that Cass County herders bought, sold, and consumed their livestock in a variety of ways using an array of transactions. On average, Watts purchased calves for approximately twenty dollars. He subsequently raised these calves to adulthood, fattening them up by feeding them large amounts of corn immediately before exchanging them.[92]

Sometimes, Watts sold his cattle for cash to local residents. In February of 1854, he sold to Colonel James Sproull a heifer for $35.00. Watts purchased this heifer as a calf two years earlier for around $20.00. Minus the cost of feeding and raising the animal, he earned a tidy $15.00 profit. Cattle raising proved to be a profitable enterprise for Watts.[93]

Watts also continued the practice of bartering that had typified antebellum transactions in a cash poor region such as northwest Georgia. On February 24, 1856, he sold a milk cow and her calf to a local resident, who in return paid him $120.00 worth of sheep. When the local physician inquired about procuring beef for the upcoming winter, the herder traded sixty dollars' worth of beef for future medical and veterinary services. When Watts needed a lawyer, he routinely paid him in beef rather than cash.[94]

On occasion, Watts's transactions reinforced communal relations. When Reverend Charles W. Howard faced some trying hardships during the late 1850s, for example, Watts "freely" gave his old friend and customer some beef. Occasionally, he gave frequent customers or friends cattle as gifts. In October 1857, Watts gave Colonel James Sproull a cow worth twenty-five dollars. These donations and gifts created intense bonds of loyalty between generous herders such as Watts and his benefactors.

Watts's growing household additionally consumed a portion of his livestock. When Watts migrated to Cass County from Laurens County, South Carolina, on January 1, 1853, his household included his wife, four adolescent daughters, and six slaves. It soon expanded with four borrowed slaves. Watts's white family meanwhile grew with the birth of additional children and the occasional prolonged stay of friends and relatives. When Watts needed meat for his household, he typically slaughtered livestock from his herd that he believed would attract less money on the open market, cattle that were "too leggy" or "too fat." He estimated the value of these animals and entered them into his ledger as a net loss. On average, the Watts's family consumed livestock valued between ten and fifteen dollars.[95]

A relative newcomer to the county, Watts became involved in the local agricultural society and infrequently attended several local churches and informal services held at the home of Reverend Charles W. Howard. Watts soon developed a statewide reputation as one of the leading herders in the state. In 1848, he began raising sheep. In an effort to prevent dogs and humans from destroying his flock, Watts imported a limited number of Spanish sheep dogs, making him one of the first herders in the state to do so. In addition to helping introduce Spanish sheep dogs to Georgia, he was also one of the first to scientifically breed sheep. Through his research, Watts learned that Spanish Merino sheep were superior to all other breeds currently found in the state.[96]

* * * * *

Interdependence and collaboration described the ebb and flow of Cass County's economic life. Communities shared common patterns of exchange and communal organizations, forms common throughout rural sections of the

United States, which molded the core of their daily existence. The reciprocity of mutual obligations helped to diminish economic distinctions. Planters and slaveholders dominated county politics in part because of their white neighbors' support. Wealthier members of local society such as James W. Watts and Godfrey Barnsley fostered intra-racial bonds by extending credit to their neighbors, a necessity in a county without a bank, or by donating a sack of corn or small amounts of cash to their poorer neighbors. Mill owners such as E. V. Johnson and Charles W. Howard ground the corn of local tenants that earned them cash that could be used to purchase market goods or possibly land. Slaveholders Dennis Johnson, Thomas Brandon, John Crawford, William H. Stiles, and numerous others occasionally loaned slaves out to their neighbors during times of critical need. In return, their neighbors helped to build fences and clear fields and performed numerous other chores as a sign of their gratitude.[97]

While harmonious intra-racial relations were the norm, conflicts occurred creating temporary rifts within the community. Sometimes planters argued over matters such as the management of slaves. When a local slaveholder learned that George Barnsley had taught several of his slaves to read and write, he accused the young master of aiding runaways. Charles W. Howard and Godfrey Barnsley, despite their longstanding friendship, routinely sniped at one another in their private letters and journals, each believing the other to be unappreciative of their relationship. Arguments concerning the ownership of free range livestock or the destruction of a fence caused by a farmer's livestock were commonplace. James W. Watts confronted some of his poorer neighbors when he suspected them of stealing a hog. On several occasions, Watts extended credit to local families who never repaid their debt. While he might have pursued some form of legal recourse, it appears that he preferred to handle the matter by negotiating a labor contract that would satisfy the debt.[98]

Disagreements between local residents and the state government occasionally happened. During the 1840s, Colonel John Sproull, a local slaveholder, endorsed the construction of the W&A. During the following decade, Sproull grew hundreds of bales of cotton that he sold to factors and transported by rail. In 1854, Alfred a twenty-five-year-old field hand accompanied Sproull to the Cartersville depot. While there a slow moving train crushed Alfred's foot permanently disabling him. Sproull sued the W&A seeking $1,200—the average price an adult field hand garnered in Cass County in 1854. After a series of decisions and appeals, a Federal court ruled in Sproull's favor.[99]

Cass County's slave population resisted their bondage like others throughout the South. The Cassville *Standard* published numerous runaway slave advertisements posted by local slaveholders. Godfrey Barnsley's slaves resisted enslavement in a variety of ways. Activities such as religious services, weddings, and quilting parties strengthened the slave community. From the perspective of the Barnsley family and their overseers, slaves routinely broke tools, stole chickens and wine, and occasionally disappeared for days at a time. Resistance or at least the appearance of resistance led to confrontations between masters/overseers and slaves. Julia Barnsley, Godfrey's wife, died from consumption shortly after moving to Cass County. She frequently wrote to her husband, who frequently traveled while managing his New Orleans-based cotton brokerage, complaining about how whipping "disobedient" slaves had little effect on their behavior. When necessary she sent slave couriers to fetch a white male neighbor to give a field hand "ten lashes for [supposedly] stealing a ham."[100] The farm journals and personal correspondences of the Barnsley, Howard, Watts, and Johnson families reveal that Cass Countians, just like slaveholders across the South, anticipated slave rebellions. That lingering fear led to the creation of slave patrols and increased militia enrollments that at times healed white disagreements by forming additional communal bonds. Little evidence exists that would suggest that slavery in the northwest Georgia mountains was less harsh or more brutal than in other southern subregions.

Slavery was the foundation of Cass County's antebellum economy. By 1860, white farmers of all social classes desired to either acquire slaves for the first time or to expand their existing holdings. Some farmers were able to achieve significant upward social mobility as a result of acquiring slaves and raising cotton to sell in regional markets. While most white men shared the aspirations of affluent planters, the late antebellum economy also created a system of have's and have nots that produced tensions among white men. While these tensions were largely ameliorated by the unity created by white supremacy and a shared hope for future economic prosperity built upon the backs of enslaved black laborers, at times these feelings influenced antebellum politics.

CHAPTER
2

THE WINDING ROAD TO DISUNION

In 1861, Cass County voters narrowly elected a three-man delegation of cooperationists to the upcoming Georgia Secession Convention. The cooperationists' victory was hardly a mandate from the people. Only a few dozen votes separated the opposing sides. At the convention, the county's delegates unanimously rejected immediate secession in three separate votes, while a majority of Upcountry delegates supported immediate secession. This chapter explores the nearly three decades of political discussions and campaigns that preceded the secession winter of 1861. Antebellum Cass Countians usually voted Democratic, but at times they produced majorities for Whig and Know Nothing candidates. Local leaders routinely shifted party loyalties, citing a variety of local, state, and national concerns, but all defended the institution of slavery.

Changes in the county's economy and racial composition during the late 1840s and 1850s did not significantly alter the county's voting patterns. Ultimately, the political realm did not create any overriding animosities among Cass Countians. Instead, politics reflected a view shared broadly throughout the Deep South that tyrannical northern abolitionists and Republicans were far more threatening adversaries than Georgia Whigs, Democrats, or Know Nothings. While the county's secession convention delegates strongly believed that immediate secession was the wrong course of action, their opposition did not represent a lackluster commitment to preserving slavery, nor did they oppose the doctrine of secession. Their cooperationist stance mirrored nearly three decades worth of precedents that provided county and state voters, politicians, and parties some maneuverability.

The Democratic Party, in its multiple variations, served as the core of Cass County's antebellum political continuity. The county's allegiance to the

Table 3
Gubernatorial Election Returns, Cass County, 1833–1849

Year	Candidate	Party	% Total Votes Received
1833	Joel Crawford	Troup	54
1835	William Schley	Union-Democrat	56
1837	William Schley	Union-Democrat	61
1839	Charles McDonald	Union-Democrat	60
1841	Charles McDonald	Union-Democrat	42
1843	Mark A. Cooper	Union-Democrat	56
1845	George Crawford	Whig	54
1847	George Towns	Democrat	65
1849	George Towns	Democrat	62

Source: Milledgeville Federal Union.

democracy originated with the immense popularity of President Andrew Jackson, whom northwest Georgians credited for Indian removal. County organizers displayed their appreciation for Jackson's leadership by naming their county after his secretary of war, Lewis Cass. As shown in Table 3, in the nine gubernatorial elections that Cass Countians participated in between 1833 and 1849, the Union Democratic/Democratic Party received a majority of the votes cast in all except on two occasions. The average percentage of votes received among these candidates was 57 percent. Likewise, in five presidential elections, locals provided Democrats with a majority on each occasion with a similar margin of victory.[1]

The Democratic Party typically won more than half of the county's vote, but the Whig Party usually made a strong showing—44 percent on average—in defeat. They even managed to carry Cass in favor of George Crawford during the 1845 election. Although the Democratic Party dominated state and national elections, victory was less assured during local political contests. Between 1833 and 1849, roughly 15 percent of the county's state representatives belonged to the Whig Party. Meanwhile, Whigs routinely held judicial, bureaucratic, and law enforcement posts within the county government. Voters, for example, rejected Whig Turner H. Trippe's congressional and state house campaigns but supported his Cherokee circuit court candidacy.[2]

County Democratic and Whig politicians shared much in common. Both owned a considerable amount of real and personal property. They worshiped in the same churches, worked in the same law firms, belonged to the same social organizations, and supported many of the same moral crusades such as temperance. The sons of prominent Democrats married the daughters of well-known Whigs and vice-versa. When politically expedient, county Democrats attached themselves to ostensibly Whiggish programs such as state-funded transportation projects despite protests from within their state organization. The principal differences between these two parties on the local level revolved around their relationship with state and national bodies rather than any serious distinctions brought forth during face to face interactions.[3]

While distinguishing a Whig from a Democrat might have been difficult prior to 1849, a series of national events beginning with the Wilmot Proviso realigned the Jacksonian-era parties further blurred party lines. On August 8, 1846, Pennsylvanian Congressman David Wilmot proposed an amendment to an otherwise anonymous appropriations bill that would prohibit slavery in any territory acquired from Mexico. His amendment lacked enough support to become law, but the threat it posed to southern members of Congress permanently strained their relationship with their respective national parties. After the proviso, in Georgia, distinctions between Whigs and Democrats soon became secondary in importance compared to the growing rift between northerners and southerners.[4]

Following the 1849 gubernatorial election, Cass County Democrats backed Governor George Towns's efforts to draw a line in the sand between themselves and northern agitators. Towns's campaign adopted the old States' Rights Party platform that endorsed secession as a last ditch form of resistance against Federal tyranny. Cass voters responded positively to this message as he received more votes in that county than in any other county in the state. While the percentage of total votes cast for Towns decreased between 1847 and 1849, the emotion-filled campaign increased the local turnout by 47 percent.[5]

On the surface, the incumbent's strong showing might suggest that 62 percent of local voters endorsed the incumbent's Calhounite rhetoric; however, a clear difference of opinion can be seen between local voters and Towns's. His campaign benefited from Lewis Tumlin's unsuccessful bid to fill the state's Fifth Congressional District seat. The presence of a well-respected local candidate on the ballot directly impacted the county's increased turnout. Throughout its history, Cass County voters participated in greater numbers in elections that included local candidates running for state and national offices. As expected, a higher percentage of county voters cast their ballots in favor of Tumlin than the incumbent governor. His popularity, however, went beyond his local appeal as voters gravitated to his conservative stances.

While Towns drifted toward John C. Calhoun's beliefs, Tumlin's campaign reaffirmed his Union Democratic roots. He admitted that the Wilmot Proviso threatened southern rights, but he also sharply criticized members of his party who espoused the doctrine of secession. He worried that northern Democrats would view secession as a hollow threat thereby calling the South's bluff forcing it to either secede or to accept a humiliating submission. Whereas secession, warned Tumlin, offered the South a limited number of alternatives, their interests would be more credible if they remained in the Union and used the Constitution as their sword and shield. Ultimately, his Whig opponent prevailed in a district Democrats dominated.[6]

Cass County's two state legislators, William T. Wofford and Achelles Shackleford, exerted their influence as the assembly responded to the governor's request to draft a preemptive response to Congress's expected passage of the Wilmot Proviso.[7] The General Assembly's rejoinder included eight resolutions that, in concert, condemned the proviso, the abolition of slavery in the District of Columbia, the weak fugitive slave law, and the admission of California. As moderate Democrats and Whigs struck an alliance during the debate over the language used in the eighth resolution, their actions displayed a potential realignment in the state's parties. The original resolution stated that if the Wilmot Proviso received congressional approval that the people of Georgia would respond by calling a convention to voice their opposition.[8]

William T. Wofford protested the resolution's language and offered the assembly an alternate version that reaffirmed the party's 1847 and 1848 platform. He suggested that the first line of the resolution should read "the passage of the Wilmot Proviso *over territory south of . . . the Missouri Compromise Line.*" Wofford's proposal expressed a belief held among many Union Democrats that slavery could be protected within the Union as long as the North reaffirmed the boundaries established by the Missouri Compromise. Following several days of heated debate, a coalition of Whigs, southern-rights Democrats, and a handful of Union Democrats rejected Wofford's proposal.[9]

While Wofford's efforts fell short, national events soon led many into his camp. The question of whether or not to accept the terms provided by the proposed Compromise of 1850 recast the state's political parties, splintering the local Democratic majority into two principal factions. Democrats who supported the compromise and believed the region's interests would be served better under the umbrella of the existing Constitution and Union formed the Constitutional Union Party. This party also attracted support from former Whigs such as Alexander Stephens, Robert Toombs, and Allen F. Owen, who had split with their national party as well as Democrats such as Howell Cobb, William B. Wofford, John B. Lamar, and James A. Nesbit, who resisted the "fire-eater" rhetoric espoused by some of their former Democratic colleagues. The Constitutional Unionists formed an unlikely alliance among Black Belt Whigs and north Georgia mountain Democrats that could not have existed prior to the destruction of the Jacksonian party system.[10]

Meanwhile, those who initially protested the compromise established the Southern Rights Party. James Gardner, Charles McDonald, Hugh Haralson, and Herschel Johnson, among others, led this party. Southern Rights candidates received strong support from traditionally Democratic regions such as the Wiregrass, Piedmont, and Upcountry.[11]

In November 1850, Southern Rights and Constitutional Unionist partisans clashed in their first statewide contest as voters selected delegates for a December convention to debate the Compromise of 1850. Led by charismatic leaders such as Cobb, Toombs, and Stephens, a conservative electorate provided the Constitutional Unionists with a landslide victory. They captured 92 percent of the 264 convention seats while outdistancing their opponents in the popular vote by more than twenty thousand votes.[12] Cass County voters cast more than 60 percent of their ballots for the local Constitutional Unionist slate of candidates that included popular community leaders William T. Wofford and Lewis Tumlin.[13]

When the convention convened on December 10, Wofford and Tumlin vocally endorsed the Georgia Platform that had been drafted almost entirely by Charles Jenkins at an earlier date. The platform stated that in a "spirit of mutual concession" the state of Georgia and its northern agitators had reached an acceptable compromise that resolved many of the issues involving the acquisition of Mexican territory. The first three resolutions merely reaffirmed the state's support for the compromise. The fourth, however, drew a line in the sand as Constitutional Unionists forbade the Federal government from enacting any future legislation that infringed upon the rights of southern slaveholders and the institution's lawful expansion into the American southwest. Any hostile action, the convention declared, would be met with resistance and, if necessary, secession.[14]

In 1850, a majority of Cass County voters saw the Georgia Platform as an acceptable middle ground between outright submission and radical resistance to the issues decided within the compromise. The following year, Constitutional Unionist gubernatorial candidate Howell Cobb received more than 60 percent of the county's votes in route to a landslide victory over Southern Rights candidate Charles McDonald. Cobb's victory, combined with the recent convention vote, provided his makeshift party with a resounding mandate of authority. The victory for the Constitutional Unionists, however, did not guarantee any future party loyalties among hundreds of local voters. Their gains, however, would soon be tested throughout the upcoming presidential election.[15]

During the emotion-filled presidential campaign of 1852, the divisions between Cass County Southern Rights and Constitutional Unionists sharply divided the county. Cassville *Standard* proprietor and editor John W. Burke supported the Constitutional Unionist Party. In a series of scathing editorials, he labeled Southern Rights partisans as radicals who best served their own interests. Burke accused them of destroying the state's old party alliances with their overreactions and talk of secession. "If [Southern Rights men] are true Democracy," Burke sarcastically remarked, "we have long labored under a gross delusion as to the meaning of the term." Burke's rhetoric alienated some of his subscribers and cost him numerous friendships. After reading one of his editorials, local jurist and ex-Whig Turner H. Trippe stormed into the *Standard*'s printing office and demanded that Burke discontinue references to his fellow Southern Rights men as radicals. After knocking over a pile of papers in disgust, Trippe cancelled his subscription and ended his friendship with the editor.[16]

During the 1850 convention and 1851 gubernatorial election, the Constitutional Union Party's strength eroded as quickly as Burke and Trippe's friendship. The state's Whig leaders had reluctantly joined a party whose identity partially revolved around protecting the ideals of the old democracy. Cobb and Stephens worried that the state's Whig Party might disappear, trapped within the constraints of a new party dominated by Democratic intentions. By late April, the ties that bound this unlikely alliance had broken. During an April 22 party convention, ex-Whigs voted against sending Unionist delegates to the Democratic national convention to be held in Baltimore in June. Undeterred, Union Democrats and a handful of Whigs adjourned into a supplemental meeting. Cass County delegates Lewis Tumlin and John S. Rowland attended the "supplemental" meeting. Despite earlier Whig protests, this ancillary group selected twenty national convention delegates who would support the nomination of Lewis Cass and refrain from endorsing any candidate who did not support the Compromise of 1850.[17]

During the weeks prior to the Baltimore convention, the Cassville *Standard* published a series of articles, editorials, and biographical sketches that endorsed Lewis Cass's nomination. Burke tried to convince local voters and statewide convention delegates that Cass best exemplified the principles of the old Jacksonian democracy. Like "Old Hickory," Cass risked his national political reputation in support of Indian removal. He also supported the Compromise of 1850 when other northern Democratic leaders rejected the proposal. County delegates to the convention Lewis Tumlin and John S.

Rowland cast their votes for Cass, but, after forty-nine deadlocked ballots, the party nominated Franklin Pierce of New Hampshire for president.

Pierce's nomination further divided the Whig and Democratic factions within the Constitutional Union Party as both sides failed to agree upon a common candidate to endorse for president. Throughout the summer of 1852, the Unionist party splintered as many Whig members pursued establishing an independent party. Disenchanted by the prospect of advocating a Union ticket that did not attract the attention of the national Democratic Party, Howell Cobb and others decided to disband the party in favor of seeking a place on the Southern Rights slate of candidates.

John W. Burke and many other Cass County Unionists felt betrayed by Cobb's perceived treachery. They maintained their support for the Pierce campaign but could not bring themselves to join the Southern Rights Party. Following the lead of his uncle, William B. Wofford, William T. Wofford convinced Burke and others to support the "Tugalo" Pierce ticket. The Tugalo ticket struggled to distinguish itself as an independent and viable alternative to the Southern Rights Party. Nevertheless, the rhetoric of Tugalo editors such as John W. Burke and Hopkins Holsey castigated their opposition. "Will you return as slaves to your southern rights masters," Holsey wrote. "Submission now will key the yoke upon your necks." Burke criticized Cobb and others for "stifling the public voice" by disbanding the party without first advising its members.[18]

While the Tugalo ticket searched for an identity, William H. Stiles struggled to find a conservative position within the Southern Rights Party. Born in 1810, in Savannah, Stiles attended Yale University prior to returning home to start a legal practice. In 1832, he married Savannah socialite Eliza Mackey. When Mackey's brother attended West Point, she had developed a congenial relationship with her brother's roommate, Robert E. Lee. During the Jackson administration, the president appointed Stiles attorney general for the state of Georgia. After a term in the United States Congress, Stiles served as charge d'affaires to Austria. He published a history of Austria shortly after returning to the United States that was widely read during his lifetime. Politically ambitious and socially astute, Stiles, a wealthy planter with homes in several counties and along Savannah's prestigious riverfront district, dreamed of becoming governor or a United States senator.[19]

Stiles held the precarious stance of rejecting both secession and the Compromise of 1850. Henry Clay's plan, according to Stiles, violated the constitutional guarantees afforded to slaveholders. If secession meant war, he argued, than the South should reject secession. Rather than secede, he tried to convince audiences throughout Georgia and South Carolina to remain in the

Union and to use the powers given to the states by the founding fathers to protect their sectional interests. "Perish Democracy, perish Whigery, perish all party, perish everything political except the constitution of our country," he said. Stiles suggested that extending the Missouri Compromise to the Pacific Ocean would prevent future sectional squabbles.

During a Kingston speech, Stiles made a concerted effort to identify a middle ground between "disunion" and "submission," but his remarks only produced confusion. Following his address, an Augusta and Milledgeville newspaper printed separate editorials commenting upon the speech. One described it as a submission address, while the other applauded his secessionist rhetoric. At a later date, the Milledgeville *Federal Union* described his position as an "awkward and unenviable predicament."[20]

While Stiles's opinions confused many audiences and editors, he expressed a philosophy espoused by many Cass Countians. Hawkins F. Price, for example, joined the Southern Rights Party sometime in 1850 after losing confidence in the national Whig Party. A few months later, he reconsidered his decision and rejoined the Whig Party, determined to remain independent if that national party afforded no protection to southern slaveholders. One year later, he campaigned for a seat in the state legislature on the Winfield Scott ticket. Likewise, Reverend Charles W. Howard, a lifelong friend of Stiles and local planter, rejected both secession and the Compromise of 1850 and therefore felt uncomfortable in either party. They, like many, stayed away from the polls.

Voter turnout on Election Day in 1852 was abysmal. Only 1,342 Cass Countians voted. Three years earlier, 2,366 voters participated in the state governor's race. Despite an increase in population between 1849 and 1852, 1,042 fewer residents went to the polls. The Southern Rights Party received 49 percent of the vote, while the Tugalo ticket ran a surprisingly competitive second, with 41 percent. Exactly one in ten county voters supported Winfield Scott. The Southern Rights Party carried the state for Pierce earning 56.1 percent of the vote. Scott's 27 percent showing placed him in second. The Tugalo ticket and Daniel Webster both carried about 8.5 percent of the vote.[21]

Following the 1852 presidential election, the Southern Rights faction of the state Democratic Party dominated the democracy, absorbing into their body many of the Constitutional Unionists' former leaders such as Howell Cobb, Hopkins Holsey, and John Lamar. The 1853 gubernatorial campaign pitted the reunified Democratic Party against another hastily constructed anti-Democratic Party filled with ex-Whigs and a scattering of old Union Democrats and dominated by Robert Toombs and Alexander Stephens. The anti-Democrats nominated longtime state legislator Charles J. Jenkins to run against Democrat Herschel V. Johnson. During the campaign, the men commonly shared the same hotel rooms and freely engaged in hours of amicable debate. Statewide, Johnson won in one of the closest contests in state history, 47,638 to 47,145. The final gubernatorial tally in Cass closely resembled the statewide results. Johnson won by a narrow 66 vote margin. Voter turnout, however, declined by 44 percent compared to the 1849 election. Meanwhile, in the Fifth Congressional District race, local voters overwhelmingly supported local candidate Lewis Tumlin's candidacy providing him with a 64 percent majority over Union County Democrat Elijah W. Chastain. Chastain, the incumbent, won his seat two years earlier when he ran as a Union Democrat. By 1853, he had reconciled with the Southern Rights factions within the state party and chose to run as a Democrat. Tumlin, however, maintained his Union Democrat loyalties during the 1851 and 1853 elections. The overwhelming majority he received among Cass voters, compared to the small majority they provided Johnson, suggested that many local voters crossed party lines during that election. The differences between Democratic and anti-Democratic candidates did not convince local voters of the necessity of casting a straight party ballot. Despite their support, Tumlin's campaign suffered defeat as Chastain edged him by 257 votes.[22]

During the 1855 gubernatorial election, Cass Countians responded to a series of local events by casting a majority of their votes in favor of American Party candidate Garnett Andrews. Many ex-Union Democrats, including Andrews himself, and Whigs formed the base of the American Party's support within the state. Locally, the American Party attracted support from the lasting remnants of those Jacksonian-era parties. Reverend Charles W. Howard, for example, had previously belonged to the Whig, Union Democrats, and Constitutional Unionist Party but, in 1855, cast his influence behind the American Party. The party's nativist rhetoric—combined with members' opposition to the southern rights dominated state Democratic Party—convinced him to switch parties. Likewise, Lindsey Johnson, a lifelong Democrat and one of the county's pioneer settlers, cast aside his old allegiances and became an American Party member. The American Party's platform differed from northern Know Nothings in its unwavering support for the Kansas-Nebraska Act. Members declared that anyone who opposed the act held incendiary values that violated southern rights.

The American Party platform attracted the attention of many Cass County voters. A series of events related to Governor Herschel V. Johnson's management of the Western & Atlantic Railroad pushed a large number of Democrats into their camp. Fire had destroyed the State Road's Etowah River Bridge, temporarily severing the county's connection to southern commercial centers. Many residents blamed the governor and Superintendent of the State Road James F. Cooper for the accident. The Cassville *Standard*, a pro-Johnson newspaper, attempted to heal any existing wounds prior to the 1855 election, but, as usual, its ringing endorsement of the governor's record proved unconvincing to many of its readers. Cooper's bungled efforts to repair the bridge fostered additional resentment. In February 1855, he negotiated a contract to build a new bridge across the river, but, according to locals, the contractor underestimated the span causing an inestimable delay in the project's completion. For months, locals endured transportation delays as goods shipped south by rail had to be unloaded on the north side of the river, reloaded onto horse-drawn wagons, carried across a temporary wooden bridge, reloaded onto a southbound engine, and placed on a turning table before finally steaming toward Atlanta.[23]

As Election Day neared, American and Whig Party newspapers throughout the state printed a series of scathing editorials accusing Cass County iron producer Mark A. Cooper, a Democrat and father of the current superintendent of the State Road, of paying Governor Johnson a handsome bribe in return for reducing freight rates on the W&A. To make matters worse, Cooper's brother-in-law, Joel Branham of Eatonton, Georgia, published a letter to the editor confirming the bribery charges.[24] In his rebuttal, Cooper denied the charges, but his efforts only fueled additional criticism that discredited Johnson's leadership. "If this road," attacked Cooper, "belonged to any good man, a wise economist, he might double the value of it in ten years.... The excessive charges on the road have been the greatest drawback to the influx of both capital and population in this country."[25]

On Election Day, Cass voters voiced their reaction to the alleged mismanagement of the W&A by casting a majority of their votes in favor of a slate of American Party candidates. Garnett Andrews won a tightly contested gubernatorial race receiving 106 more votes than Johnson. Whig candidate Basil H. Overby finished third receiving a total of seventy votes. The total number of votes cast declined by 13 percent compared to the 1853 election and by 5 percent compared to the 1849 returns despite the county's experiencing substantial increases in its population during that same period. The continued decline in voter turnout, perhaps, illustrated the voting populace's dissatisfaction with the dissolution of the Jacksonian-era Democrat and Whig parties.[26]

Lewis Tumlin's 1855 congressional campaign further illustrates the continuous shifting of party loyalties among Cass Countians during the 1850s. Two years earlier, Tumlin lost his bid to win the state's Fifth Congressional District seat running as a Union Democrat and as part of an anti-Democratic Party movement. In 1855, the Cassville *Standard* and the Calhoun *Southern*

Statesman reported that he had joined the American Party.[27] The Cassville newspaper vilified American Party candidates refusing to use their local party name and, instead, drawing their readers' attention to the party's affiliation with northern Know Nothings who advocated abolition. On Election Day, 58 percent of Fifth District voters cast their ballots for Tumlin. Of the sixteen counties who cast votes for the Fifth District congressional seat, only three—including Cass—provided a majority for the American Party. Tumlin again lost his congressional bid to his Democratic challenger, John H. Lumpkin.[28]

While the Democratic and American parties in Georgia blamed one another for the situation in Kansas, state party allegiances continued to shape Cass County politics throughout the late 1850s. In 1857, only 1,750 county voters cast ballots in the gubernatorial election that pitted Democrat Joseph E. Brown against the American Party candidate Benjamin H. Hill. The low turnout represented a 17 percent decline in voter participation since the last governor's election and a 26 percent decline compared to the last Jacksonian-era party statewide race in 1849. Brown's yeoman background and north Georgia origins supposedly made him a favorite among mountain voters. While he won local majorities in almost every north Georgia county, his appeal failed to attract additional voters to the polls. In 1849, fire-eater George Washington Bonaparte Towns of Wilkes County, an eastern Black Belt county, received 1,461—or 42 percent more—votes in Cass than Brown earned eight years later. Two years later, local voter turnout increased from 1,750 to 1,918, or 9 percent, but that race included Cassville attorney Warren Akin as a Whig gubernatorial candidate. His presence on the ballot accounted for the bulk of that increase as many die-hard Whigs and anti-Democrats supported his campaign.[29]

The Fifth Congressional District returns from 1857 and 1859 further evidence the county's affection for local candidates regardless of their party. In 1857, the Democratic gubernatorial candidate earned 57 percent of the total local vote, while the same party's congressional nominee, Augustus Wright of Rome, lost in a bitterly fought contest to American Party candidate John Hooper. The son of a prominent Cherokee circuit judge and a member of one of the county's earliest pioneer families, Hooper received more votes than his party's candidate for governor. Out of the seventeen counties who cast Fifth Congressional District ballots, only Cass supported Hooper, who lost the election by almost 4,000 votes. In 1859, the congressional election lacked a local candidate. Consequently, the Democratic nominee John Underwood defeated his Whig opponent in one of the largest landslides in county history. Underwood received more votes from Cass Countians, 1,236, than Brown, 1,051, but still one hundred votes fewer than Towns won in 1849.[30]

Nearly two months elapsed from the time of John Brown's capture at Harper's Ferry, Virginia, and the 1859 governor's election. Cass resident Andrew Jackson Cone recorded in his personal memoirs a brief account of Brown's raid upon local political beliefs. History, according to Cone, would always falsely claim that the first shots of the Civil War were fired at Fort Sumter by the Confederate military. Such claims, as he described, were completely false. The Confederates fired on Fort Sumter because "the first shot of the War was fired by Old John Brown, Kansas' Jayhawker, nearly two years before, at Harper's Ferry." According to Cone, northern abolitionists had funded Brown's planned slave rebellion. These abolitionists pretended to be agents of God Almighty, but, in reality, "truly [were] the vicegerents of His Satanic Majesty."[31]

Whereas events such as the publication of Harriet Beecher Stowe's *Uncle Tom's Cabin* and the controversy over the Kansas constitution concerned many Cass Countians, John Brown's raid pushed several of the county's prominent former Union Democrats, Americans, and Whigs into the southern rights fold. American Party member Charles W. Howard, for example, abandoned his party and began delivering a series of speeches defending southern society and by extension slavery. Howard had always supported southern rights but disdained secession. His views on slavery cost him a place within the national Presbyterian Church, but that separation had not created any lasting animosities. He labored as a prolific antebellum writer who published and edited many journal articles. As an accomplished orator, he delivered numerous political speeches and sermons, including a memorable evening long public debate against the formidable Governor Herschel V. Johnson. Yet, nothing within that large body of work, prior to 1860, gave but scant attention to the defense of slavery. Howard also never directly mentioned Brown's raid nor spoke publicly on that subject, but the change in his rhetoric that suddenly desired to defend slavery and glorified the endowments of the southern gentleman began in the months following Harper's Ferry.

An address delivered before the Alpha Phi Delta and H. H. H. societies at the Cherokee Baptist College in Cassville characterized Howard's rhetoric. The speech analyzed the education and characteristics of the southern gentleman. That body of characters, he commented, faced challenges that no one in the world had to endure. Their dual role as both a southern gentleman and an American citizen complicated matters. All Americans, he argued, believed in liberty, but southerners must be aware that such virtues were subject to the abuses of the national majority. The relationship, therefore, should be approached with great apprehension. In order to protect the nation's liberties, southerners must remain firmly attached to their espoused conservative values. Northern society, he claimed, rushed to judgments and entertained extremists who threatened the nation. The South, however, acted in a state of constant deliberation that served to uphold the true democracy established by the founding fathers.

Minutes into the speech, Howard focused his attention on the future preservation of slavery. The slave, according to him, represented a vital part of southern society, one necessary to foster the ideals espoused by southern gentlemen. "We all deeply deplore the moral evils which are connected with our slave system," he stated:

> But are these evils less in any other country.... Compare the North and the South as to purity of public sentiment, soundness of public morals and sacred observances of public faith. ... The negro is one whom, while we would not be so cruel as to make him free, because God and nature have not designed him for freedom, we feed, clothe, protect, and defend him as we defend our hearth-stones, our wives and children. Nor is it a confession of unworthy weakness to acknowledge that our social organization is dependent upon the inferior African.... Our conservative strength ... is based upon the connection of our slave system with our whole internal political economy.

Howard's words earned him the unceasing praise of all those who listened or read his speech. The Alpha Phi Delta society sent him a letter expressing their sincere appreciation to a speaker whose message exalted "the youth of the country." His speech equated the preservation of liberty with the continuation of slavery. Few orators expressed the unity that slavery brought to white southern society better.[32]

* * * * *

Following the aftermath of Brown's raid, the triumph of the Republican Party during the 1860 presidential election propelled Georgia toward secession. During that election, the Republican candidate Abraham Lincoln of Illinois managed to win despite not receiving a single electoral vote from the nation's slaveholding states. The 1860 election's turning point came a few years earlier when Democratic Party presidential hopeful Stephen A. Douglas broke with southern Democrats when he opposed passage of the Lecompton Constitution, a document that would have protected the rights of slaveholders in Kansas.

Douglas's siding with Republicans on the question of the expansion of slavery in Kansas combined with statements he made during the 1858 Illinois Senate debates, led many Cass County voters, as well as others across the South, to distrust Douglas's commitment to slavery. Only Douglas could have successfully unified the national Democratic Party's northern and southern factions, but the Lecompton Constitution and the Freeport Doctrine ruined Douglas's presidential aspirations and permanently placed the nation on the road toward secession.

On April 23, 1860, during the 1860 Democratic Convention held in Charleston, South Carolina, the southern delegation, minus Georgia, stormed out of the convention in opposition to Douglas's nomination. Most of the Georgia delegation left the convention the following day. The southern Democrats later regrouped at Baltimore and nominated their own presidential candidate, John C. Breckinridge of Kentucky. To compound matters further a fourth party emerged, a new Constitutional Union Party, comprised largely of ex-American and Know Nothing Party members who nominated John Bell as their presidential candidate.

Cass County voters, during the 1860 presidential election, split their votes among three candidates: Breckinridge, Bell, and Douglas. Douglas attracted strong support among Cass voters despite lackluster appeal throughout most of the state. The county's largest newspaper, the Cassville *Standard* (joined by the Augusta *Constitutionalist* as the only pro-Douglas newspapers in the state) strongly endorsed Douglas and the National Democratic platform. Douglas's support in Cass County derived from the inclusions of Herschel Johnson as vice-president on his ticket and the sizable number of old Union Democrats, especially in the town of Cassville, who distrusted the Democratic Party's southern rights wing. Union Democrats and Southern Rights Democrats shared much in common. Both sought to defend slavery and saw secession as a viable response but disagreed over how to best defend slavery: in the Union or out of it. The newspaper printed weekly propaganda pieces lauding the Illinois senator's virtues. An article entitled "Douglas at Twenty–An Example for Young Men" appeared on August 30, 1860. The article mirrored Benjamin Franklin's *Autobiography* in that Douglas received constant praise for his hard working pragmatic approach to life and politics.[33]

The Cassville *Standard* also ran a series of unflattering biographical sketches of Breckinridge. The newspaper predicted that there was "no Chance for Breckinridge" to win the election; therefore, a vote for him would be a wasted vote that would only guarantee a victory for the "Black Republicans." On September 6, 1860, an article filled with false statements of fact appeared chiding Cass County voters for supporting Breckinridge because he was not a slaveholder. Only a slaveholder, declared the newspaper's editor James R. Wykle, could understand the South's need for moderation not radicalism. True slaveholders, according to Wykle, understood that the region's best interests would be served by Douglas and a unified national Democratic Party.[34]

In the same issue that Wykle incorrectly questioned Breckinridge's support of slavery, the editor blasted the secession faction's motivations for running a sectional candidate. Wykle reasoned that had the southern delegation remained at the Charleston Convention and participated in the nomination and balloting process that a unified South, along with a handful of sympathetic outsiders, could have successfully ended Douglas's bid in favor of Georgian Alexander H. Stephens. Wykle greatly exaggerated Stephens's chances. The editorial continued by stating that even if the South had been unable to prevent Douglas's nomination, the national Democratic Party did not plan to adopt a platform that would have been adversarial to southern interests.[35]

Cass County's other newspaper, the Cartersville *Express*, like most Georgia newspapers, supported Breckinridge's campaign. They portrayed Douglas as the wedge that divided the national party. His stance on popular sovereignty led editors to question his southern loyalties. The paper called for Cass Countians to abandon their old party allegiances and cast their ballots for Breckinridge because only his campaign promised to defend southern liberty. The differing opinions expressed in the county's newspapers were predictable. In 1860, Cassville and Cartersville contained a shared desire to defend slavery and southern rights, but factors such as party loyalties and demographic differences created friction. Cassville contained a larger number of former Whigs, American Party, Union Democratic Party, and anti-Democratic Party loyalists. Whigs and American Party supporters likely cast their support behind Bell, while Union Democratic and anti-Democratic Party advocates chose Douglas. Statewide most Democrats loathed Douglas, but in Cass County, strong Union Democrat leaders such as William T. Wofford, James R. Wykle, Joseph Bogle and Hawkins F. Price persuaded many to support Douglas. In Cartersville, and to a lesser degree Kingston and Etowah, southern rights supporters such as Abda Johnson, Mark Hardin, and Mark A. Cooper as well as the influential Goldsmith and Young families saw Breckinridge as the only option for southerners interested in preserving their liberty. Age and the railroad clearly played a role in the divisions that existed between these towns. In Cassville, their leaders were wealthier, but considerably older than those in Cartersville. In 1860, Cartersville's population included a significant number of small slaveholders whose wealth had grown during the 1850s and perceived the current election as a threat to their continued prosperity.[36] The best way to preserve liberty, according to the *Express*, was to exercise personal freedom. Cassville's leaders differed only in degree. They too wanted to preserve liberty, but as the *Standard* proclaimed, the Constitution must remain intact and secession should be considered as a final solution only once all other options had been exhausted.

During the campaign, Douglas, his wife, and his brother-in-law stayed overnight in Kingston. Trains stopped in Kingston to take on water and to allow passengers a chance to eat or book an overnight room in one of the town's four hotels. At the time, Douglas was traveling throughout the South, making his way toward Montgomery, Alabama. While at Kingston, Douglas actively campaigned. At a large outdoor gathering, Douglas addressed a crowd that included local residents and individuals from neighboring counties. By the time Douglas spoke, people from as far away as Atlanta had arrived to hear the "Little Giant."[37] While most voters disliked Douglas's stance on issues such as popular sovereignty, many saw the inclusion of former Georgia governor Herschel Johnson on the party ticket as a sign that, if elected, Douglas would not threaten southern interests.

Local lawyer, newspaper editor, and Mexican War veteran William T. Wofford actively campaigned on Johnson's behalf. The two men maintained a strong friendship that had developed during their law school days. Alexander Stephens's brother, Linton, also campaigned on Douglas's behalf in Cassville, attracting large crowds during his extended evening address. The county's Breckinridge partisans responded with a flurry of their own campaign stump speeches and scathing newspaper editorials. In an effort to ensure a county-wide victory, Goldsmith and Smith arranged for a campaign stop in Cartersville by popular Georgia senator and Breckinridge supporter Robert Toombs.[38]

Neither of Cass County's newspapers endorsed John Bell's campaign. Former Whigs, American Party members, and anti-Democrats such as Charles W. Howard, Turner H. Trippe, James Parrot, and Warren Akin supported the Tennessean nonetheless. They agreed with the Milledgeville *Southern Recorder*'s assessment that a vote for Breckinridge was a vote for disunion, anarchy, and bloodshed. While Bell supporters hoped for an improbable victory, they cautioned the electorate that if Republicans won and disunion was inevitable than the future of this government should be placed in the "hands of *moderate men*."[39]

Statewide, Douglas fared poorly, receiving 11,581 votes out of 106,717 cast. Breckinridge won the largest percentage of votes garnering 48.89 percent compared to Bell's 40.26 percent.[40] Breckinridge attracted support from Georgians who saw the states'-rights wing of the Democratic Party as the true national party. Speeches by some of his more radical supporters such as

Robert Toombs and Howell Cobb perhaps weakened his position during the final weeks of the campaign. After Republicans won majorities in many state elections, Toombs and Cobb told audiences that when the Republicans won the presidential election the South would leave the Union. Their assertion that a Republican victory and by extension a vote for Breckinridge would lead to secession perhaps pushed some of his supporters into the Bell and Douglas camp. In Cass County, Douglas finished a strong third, receiving 332 votes. Breckenridge received 1,055 votes and Bell earned 613. The charged election significantly increased, for the first time since 1859, the number of ballots cast.[41]

When Cass Countians learned of Lincoln's victory, they began debating Georgia's options. County resident Tom Dowtin informed his mother that in Cassville "there is a great deal of excitement here on account of Lincoln's election. Some are for doing one thing, some another, I hardly know what will be done." According to the local town residents with whom Dowtin had spoken with following the election, Georgia would choose to remain in the Union as long as possible. "The people here," Dowtin commented, "have no notion of fighting as long as they can keep from it."[42]

In addition to creating an air of excitement, Lincoln's election closed the local slave market. "Negoes," reported Dowtin, "have fallen very much. They can not be sold at any price as nobody wants to buy."[43] Potential buyers feared that once in office the abolitionist-friendly Lincoln might free the slaves. Those who had wanted to purchase slaves thus waited to see what Georgia and the rest of the slaveholdings states would do before making any new transactions.

South Carolina's secession in December 1860 created another stir among county residents. Local leaders called for a meeting to be held to discuss secession. It eventually took place at the Presbyterian Church in Kingston. There several members of the crowd openly expressed their concern that if the Federal government attacked South Carolina than they would be forced to respond whether or not Georgia chose to do so. Native South Carolinians comprised a majority of the people who attended the meeting. Those individuals anxiously waited to see if Georgia too would secede.[44]

In Georgia, political leaders led by Howell Cobb and Robert Toombs also called for immediate secession. While Mississippi and Florida followed South Carolina, the Georgia General Assembly refrained from declaring secession. Instead, the assembly determined that, January 2, 1861, the people of Georgia would elect delegates to serve at a state convention that would commence a fortnight later. Voters chose between delegates advocating immediate secession and those supporting a cooperationist platform. Cooperationist candidates hoped to resolve the nation's sectional divisions while remaining in the Union and establishing a convention of southern states. Cooperationists believed that in order for the slave states to wield political power over the newly elected administration, they must form a united coalition that could serve as a sounding board for their protests. The secession of individual states, according to the cooperationists, only weakened the region's chances of influencing the new administration.

Cass County voters remained evenly divided on the issue of immediate secession throughout December and January. During the convention election, the cooperationist slate of candidates escaped with a narrow victory of a few dozen votes over their immediate secessionist opponents, hardly an authoritative mandate. Cass County joined seventeen other north Georgia counties that had voted for Breckinridge and now rejected immediate secession. In Cass, Douglas and Bell supporters united in their disdain for immediate secession which they viewed as a tool of the Southern Rights Party and state Democrats.[45]

The state's cooperationist faction lacked any firm ideals that might have resolved the crisis without resorting to secession. Their platform proved contradictory. On one hand, cooperationists rejected immediate secession in favor of seeking further political compromise. On the other hand, cooperationists agreed with their immediate secessionist opponents that the chances of meaningful compromise were slim. Therefore, while Cass County voters narrowly favored the cooperationist platform, it would be incorrect to suggest that county residents rejected secession altogether or that residents carried any overarching Unionist sympathies. Cass County voters, like other Georgia voters, firmly believed that secession remained a viable option due to the continued threat posed by Republican and northern hostility toward slavery. If those parties would not refrain from undermining slavery, Georgia would be forced to dissolve all political ties to the existing Union.

While cooperationists struggled to define their message, some ardent secessionists in the county used violence to intimidate and silence those who sought compromise. On Election Day, Cassville resident and Massachusetts-born inn keeper James McGee traveled into Cassville where he cast his vote in support of the cooperationist candidates. Secession supporters did not think that northern born men such as McGee should participate in this election. McGee later told Federal officials after the war that large numbers of armed "secesh" men loitered around the county courthouse on Election Day to intimidate cooperationist supporters. One of those armed men, James Morrison, pointed his Colt revolver at suspected cooperationists as they moved about the town square. When one of McGee's friends confronted

Morrison, a fight broke out, and Morrison shot and killed the unarmed man. As McGee's friend lay dead in the street, Morrison strutted around town threatening cooperationists, especially northern born men, to "keep quiet if they knew what was good for them." Local officials never prosecuted Morrison, and months later his peers chose him to serve as an officer in a Confederate cavalry company. The threat of violence likely kept many cooperationists away from the polls.[46]

Despite the Election Day violence, cooperationists won a narrow majority that sent three cooperationist candidates to serve at the upcoming statewide convention.[47] The county's senior delegate was Turner H. Trippe, who turned sixty years old shortly after the secession convention. He was the prototypical Cass County professional. In addition to earning a living as a jurist, Trippe owned and managed one of the county's largest farmsteads. In 1860, his farm, Linden, was worth $9,750, placing Trippe among the county's wealthiest landholders. Trippe, like many Cass County residents, aligned himself with the Whig Party. Despite that party's collapse, he called himself a Whig. During the election of 1860, Trippe had supported the Bell campaign.[48]

Cass County's second delegate was Hawkins F. Price. He was twenty-one years younger than Trippe. Originally from North Carolina, Price moved to Cassville during the late 1830s. He soon accumulated a substantial amount of real estate. He owned one of the largest plantations in northwest Georgia. By 1860, Price had accumulated $15,000 in real estate and $22,800 in personal property. Only a handful of individuals in the county could match or exceed his personal wealth. Unlike the county's other two delegates, Price did not practice law. He operated a mercantile business in Cassville.[49]

Cassville lawyer William Tatum Wofford served as Cass County's third delegate. He belonged to a family whose lineage included several prominent Revolutionary War veterans and were among the first inhabitants of western South Carolina and northeast and northwest Georgia.[50] Wofford graduated from the University of Georgia law school. A highly successful lawyer, he also had co-owned and co-edited the Cassville *Standard*.[51] A lifelong friend of Herschel V. Johnson, Wofford had supported Douglas for president.

Table 4 compares some of the vital statistics of the county's secession convention delegates. All three men claimed professional class membership. When asked by the census enumerator about their profession, all three responded with occupations that revolved around village life. In 1850, Trippe and Price owned a significant amount of property and slaves and held title to two of the county's most valuable farms. Yet, neither man listed farmer or planter as their primary occupation, despite earning most of their income from agriculture rather than their professional trades.

TABLE 4
Cass County Secession Convention Delegates

Name	Age	Occupation	Origin	No. Slaves 1850	Value of Real Estate 1850 ($)	No. Slaves 1860	Value of Real Estate 1860 ($)
Turner H. Trippe	49	Lawyer	GA	31	7,000	< 31[52]	9,750
Hawkins F. Price	43	Merchant	NC	14	8,000	26	15,000
William T. Wofford	21	Lawyer	GA	3	0	10	7,500

Source: Seventh Census.

Between 1850 and 1860, the future delegates, along with a majority of the county, saw their personal wealth increase. The number of slaves owned by this group increased at least by twenty or more. Price's personal wealth in particular experienced a tremendous amount of growth. In 1860, he owned almost twice as many slaves as he did ten years earlier. During that decade he went from slaveholder to planter while watching his real estate nearly double. When county voters selected Price, his combined real and personal estate totaled almost $50,000. Only a handful of Cass County residents owned as much property and controlled as much wealth as did Price. Likewise, Trippe too saw his fortune expand. While the 1860 slave census failed to list Trippe as a slaveholder—probably due to human error—his real estate increased by $2,700 and his reported personal estate exceeded $24,500.[53]

As did Trippe and Price, Wofford's personal wealth increased during the 1850s. Despite his relative youth, Wofford had earned a reputation as one of the region's leading attorneys. While Wofford was the only one of the three delegates who was not a member of the planter class, judging his socioeconomic status based on slave ownership proves misleading. Although Wofford owned only ten slaves, members of his immediate family, including his aging mother, owned a substantial number.[54]

Overall, Cass County's cooperationist delegates shared common ground, not only with one another, but with their immediate secession opponents. Collectively, their social, economic, and political lives revolved around the defense of a white men's republic that was inextricable from a need to protect the institution of black slavery. Economically and socially, the divide between the average county voter and their elected delegates was as large as the division splitting apart the nation's sections. The sole unifying factor, the glue that held together multi-class allegiances, was a determination to protect slavery and the economic expansion and white unity that it provided. Those desires ultimately trumped any ideological divisions separating cooperationist and immediatist factions.

The convention election determined which slate of candidates voters trusted to guide the state through the secession crisis and defend black slavery. Ultimately, in Cass County, more local voters trusted Trippe, Price, and Wofford than their fire-breathing opponents, Lewis Tumlin, Turner Goldsmith, and Mark A. Hardin. In 1861, most county voters believed, as did Rebecca Felton, that secession was inevitable, but voters remained cautious and leery of any politician or faction who might seek to champion that cause for the sake of political gain. Trippe, Price, and Wofford represented the majority of Cass County voters who had enjoyed some degree of economic and social prosperity during the previous decade and now wanted to take extra precaution before allowing their state to voluntarily secede from a Union that had been so profitable. Most voters saw secession as a viable option although many hoped that it could be avoided.[55]

In the seven counties that border Cass County, voters responded at the polls in mixed fashion. Pickens and Polk County voters elected delegates who unanimously rejected the immediate secession platform. The fact that both counties rejected secession was quite paradoxical because the two counties' demographic composition differed. Pickens County was a mountainous area with only a handful of valleys suitable for large-scale agricultural production. Out of the eight counties listed in Tables 5 and 6, Pickens contained the fewest number of slaves, slaveholders, and planters. Their decision to reject immediate secession appears logical if slavery had been the single most divisive issue separating the two sides. But Polk County voters also rejected immediate secession despite maintaining an expanding slave population. Almost ten times more slaves lived in Polk County than did Pickens. Over two hundred slaveholders and thirty-six planters comprised a sizable minority within the county's overall white population. Despite being more characteristic of a prototypical antebellum southern slave society, Polk County rejected immediate secession for many of the same reasons as did Pickens, a county where slavery was almost nonexistent.[56]

Five of the counties listed in Tables 5 and 6 supported immediate secession: Cherokee, Cobb, Floyd, Gordon, and Paulding.[57] Only Gordon County's delegates split their votes.[58] Sixty-six percent of the total slave population in the counties neighboring Cass lived in those five counties. Almost 1,700 slaveholders and 138 planters resided in those counties. As a voting block, these counties advocated immediate secession but differed demographically. For example, Paulding County voted in favor of immediate secession yet their white population owned significantly fewer slaves than the other four counties.

TABLE 5
Cass and Surrounding Counties Final Vote on Secession

County	Total Delegates	Cooperationist	Immediate Secession
Cass	3	3	0
Cherokee	3	0	3
Cobb	3	0	3
Floyd	3	0	3
Gordon	3	1	2
Paulding	2	0	2
Pickens	2	2	0
Polk	2	2	0
Total	21	8	13

In 1860, only two slaveholders in the county owned more than twenty slaves. Four of the counties that supported immediate secession—Cherokee, Cobb, Gordon, and Paulding—had fewer slaves and planters than Cass County, yet Cass voters rejected immediate secession. The statistical data gathered from these eight northwest Georgia counties suggests that there was no direct correlation between the number of slaves a county owned and their support for immediate secession.[59]

During the secession convention numerous counties presented the convention with resolutions passed in support of immediate secession. While Cass County never adopted such a resolution, a faction existed within the county that advocated immediate secession and actively sought a platform from which they could express their opinions. They worried that the state as a whole would doubt whether anyone in the county supported immediate secession. In an effort to rectify this situation, a delegation of immediate secession advocates met in Cassville before the state convention convened. At this meeting, Mark A. Hardin, a prominent slaveholder and local businessman, read a resolution passed by immediate secession advocates in neighboring Floyd County. That resolution blamed the ongoing national crisis on the rising "abolition sentiment of the Northern States." Abolitionists, the resolution declared, "prompted the armed invasion of Southern soil" by John Brown "for the diabolical purpose of inaugurating a ruthless war of the blacks against the whites throughout the South." The Floyd County residents who adopted this resolution believed that the Republican Party was dominated by abolitionists who had plotted to destroy southern society. Hardin and his Cass County delegation agreed.[60]

TABLE 6
Cass and Surrounding Counties Slave, Slaveowner, and Planter Population, 1860

County	No. of Slaves	No. of Slaveowners	No. of Planters
Cass	4,282	425	62
Cherokee	1,199	207	6
Cobb	3,819	529	33
Floyd	5,913	529	79
Gordon	2,106	297	18
Paulding	572	136	2
Pickens	246	37	2
Polk	2,440	226	36
Total	20,577	2,386	238

Cass County's three cooperationist delegates also believed that the threat of abolitionism had created the current crisis, but unlike Hardin, they saw the threat of secession as a powerful bargaining tool that could be used to subdue abolitionism and protect slavery's future. When the convention convened in Milledgeville, Cass County's delegates unanimously supported a resolution presented by Johnson of Jefferson County that called for a meeting of slave state delegates in a congress at Atlanta, Georgia, on February 16, 1861.[61] The gathering of a slave state congress was the cornerstone belief of the cooperationist faction. During this convention, delegates would determine a course of action. The cooperationists also proposed a series of demands that if met by the North, they would remain in the current Union. Each revolved around the future preservation of slavery. Cooperationist delegates wanted to restrict Congress's power to abolish or prohibit slavery. They also wanted the Federal government to tighten its current enforcement of the fugitive slave law. Anyone who was found guilty of aiding and abetting runaway slaves would be subject to prosecution under Federal law. The resolution's third declaration reinforced the cooperationists' states' rights advocacy. They demanded that Congress allow newly formed states to decide through popular sovereignty slavery's legality and that no state or federal agency could rightfully interfere with the interstate slave trade. Individual states, asserted cooperationists, could not prohibit slaveholders from carrying their slaves into free territory. They also wanted to prevent Africans from voting or holding federal office regardless of whether or not they resided in a free state. The resolution warned the North that rejection of their platform would force them to secede from the Union.

Once Johnson finished reading the cooperationist resolution, debate began. During that debate, none of the Cass County delegates rose to voice their cooperationist sympathies.[62] Once the debate ended, the convention chair moved that the body vote on a previous resolution presented by James A. Nisbet, which called for the state's immediate secession. The immediate secession resolution passed 166 to 130 despite not receiving a single vote from among Cass delegates. After the resolution passed, Benjamin H. Hill of Troup County demanded that the convention vote on Johnson's cooperationist resolution before moving forward. The convention rejected the cooperationist resolution on a 133 to 164 vote. Cass delegates unanimously supported the cooperationist resolution. After Johnson's resolution failed, Nesbit called for a final vote on immediate secession. The measure carried on a 208 to 89 vote. Again, all three Cass delegates voted against immediate secession.

Once the secession ordinance passed, Cass County delegates had to decide how far they were willing to carry out their opposition. Wofford, Trippe, and Price remained at the convention. None of them made a last ditch plea urging caution and condemning immediate secession. Instead, they engaged in the business of secession. Their peers selected all three men to serve on various committees. Wofford served on the Committee on the Relations with Slaveholding States of North America. Trippe received an appointment to the Committee on the Constitution of the State and Constitution and Laws of the United States. Price worked on the Committee on Printing. If any of these Cass Countians held any long-lasting discontent regarding what had occurred during the secession convention, they failed to express it, at least in the surviving documents.[63]

Once the secession ordinance passed, the county's secessionist faction became more vocal and widespread. Tom Dowtin wrote to his cousin, Nan L. Dowtin, who lived in Rocky Hill, about his overall displeasure with local voters. Following the convention vote, Dowtin was not "in a very good humor with cass . . . because the yunion ticket beat" the immediate secessionists. His anger however was soon to be replaced with joy and an overall haughty attitude once the state convention elected to secede. "Thank goodness," wrote Dowtin, "it did not do them [cooperationists] any good Georgia is gon out of the yunion & glad am I if it had not of went out I would of went out myself." Dowtin's letter further commented how he had longed to return to his home state of South Carolina: "I am not a Georgian and I am glad of it."[64]

Dowtin's enthusiasm for secession was not shared among all Cass County residents. While a majority of cooperationists accepted immediate secession and demonstrated loyalty to Georgia whether it remained in or out of the Union, a sizable minority existed, especially in the northeast portions of the county, that remained steadfast in their allegiance to the republic. The violence that surrounded the secession convention election, however, led many Unionists to silence themselves. After being threatened at the polls, Unionist Shem Carnes, a farmer outside of Adairsville, returned home and began keeping a watchful eye on his property. When his sons did not enlist in the Confederate army during the spring of 1861, Carnes became concerned that someone might show up at his farm and force the boys into the army. To draw less attention upon himself, Carnes stopped going into town and socialized with a small group of Unionists such as James McDow and Sarah Crow who lived near his farm. Often forced into seclusion, what historians know about Cass County's Unionists was only made possible after the war when dozens of locals testified before the Southern Claims Commission. From the start, their Civil War would be a fight to keep their family and property safe from overzealous Confederates.[65]

* * * * *

In later years, Rebecca Felton remembered the evening hours of January 21, 1861, as the calm before the storm. That night, the then twenty-five-year-old Felton sat resting on her front porch outside of Cartersville, Georgia. The crisp night air relaxed her into a state of semi-consciousness until cannon fire resonating from Rome disturbed her peaceful state. As alarming as the noise was, Felton became even more disturbed upon realizing the sound's meaning. At the state capital in Milledgeville, the state secession convention had ratified an ordinance of secession. When the news reached Rome, many of the townspeople celebrated the joyous and historic occasion by pouring into the streets. Many men carried pistols that were discharged into the night sky. In front of the courthouse, the local militia had begun firing blank rounds from their cannon intent on announcing the ordinance to the surrounding community.[66] Felton did not need to travel into town to learn that her state had seceded. As she stared into the sky toward Rome, sadness descended upon her. She had hoped that the crisis might be resolved through a last minute political compromise. The cannon fire she heard meant that compromise was lost.

Felton did not have to travel far to hear the fiery rhetoric of secessionists. Her beloved husband, Dr. William H. Felton, strongly advocated secession. They maintained a close partnership in all matters throughout their marriage. On most issues, the couple agreed, but on whether or not the state should secede from the Union, the two diametrically disagreed. Nonetheless, Felton uncharacteristically refrained from openly expressing her views. While throughout her lifetime she frequently spoke out as a woman on numerous occasions for a myriad of causes, in 1861, Felton remained quietly opposed to her husband's politics.[67]

Unlike Rebecca Felton, United States Military Academy Cadet and Cass County resident Pierce Manning Butler Young experienced a rush of excitement upon learning of Georgia's secession. The twenty-four-year-old cadet had previously graduated from the Georgia Military Institute. Young decided to resign the second he received the news. He could no longer remain at West Point "with honor & duty." In a letter to Governor Joseph E. Brown, Young expounded upon his voluminous military resume. "My class," wrote Young, "has finished infantry & cavalry tactics, a system of strategy & outposts & I am also prepared upon heavy & light artillery."[68] Young wanted a war, an opportunity to command soldiers to a valiant victory in defense of southern rights. In route to his Cass County home, Young stopped in Washington, DC to solicit an appointment from a group of Georgia congressmen. When his lobbying seemed ineffective, Young boarded a train to Montgomery, Alabama, where he received a military commission from Jefferson Davis.[69]

Harold Barnsley learned of Georgia's secession while completing some family business in Hong Kong. Barnsley's father Godfrey owned one of the nation's most prosperous cotton brokerages. Upon learning that his brothers intended to enlist for military service, Harold worked feverishly to complete his remaining business while making plans for a return voyage home. Harold spent weeks visiting clients and accumulated an enormous amount of cash. He believed that he would be unable to return to Hong Kong for a while and therefore needed to settle as many accounts as possible before departing. When his business affairs were complete, Harold loaded the cash into a large sea trunk in anticipation of his voyage. A few hours after his ship left Hong Kong, Chinese pirates attacked the vessel. During the ensuing struggle, pirates shot Harold several times. When the pirates occupied the ship, they began dumping the bodies of the dead and wounded overboard. Harold struggled to swim back to shore but succumbed to fatigue and drowned. Before the first shots were fired at Manassas, the Barnsley family received word of Harold's murder, a tragedy that occurred because he wanted to serve in the Confederate army, alongside his brothers, and return home before the war was over.[70]

Secession postponed one of Reverend Charles Wallace Howard's lifelong ambitions. Howard was a well-educated minister with a keen interest in Georgia's colonial history and agricultural science. As a scientific writer, Howard published *A Manual of Grass and Forage Plants for the South* that was widely read among the region's livestock producers. In 1838, the state had sent him to London, England, to comb the archives for materials relating to Georgia's colonial past. An avid writer, Howard intended to produce a history on this subject.⁷¹ During the late 1850s, Howard wrote Governor Joseph E. Brown requesting access to some of the state's vital documents. Brown complied with his demands and allowed for several boxes of original colonial era documents to be transported to the aspiring historian's home. While it is unknown how far Howard had progressed in his writings, it is certain that he had begun the task prior to 1861. Secession and the ensuing war forced Howard to postpone his plans. He opposed secession. During a December 4, 1860 meeting held in Cassville, Howard distributed anti-secession pamphlets. He believed that secession would never resolve the state's quarrels with the national government.⁷² In 1863, Howard's wife Susan voluntarily returned the state's colonial records to the governor because she "did not think prudent or safe to keep them.... When this section of the country is in a measure opposed to Yankee invasion." He never wrote his history, an undertaking that might have been completed had it not been for secession.⁷³

For some Cass County residents, secession meant reassessing existing friendships. Elizabeth Mackay Stiles had developed close bonds with many of the East Coast's elite families. As Georgia's secession loomed, some of their friends living on Staten Island grew concerned over the Stiles's possible political views. While these elite New Yorkers vehemently disagreed with secession, they did not want to see politics stand in the way of continuing decades of friendship. As a Christmas gift, Elizabeth sent a package of fruit preserves made on her plantation to the Mayer family in New York. Given the tense political situation that had grasped the nation following the presidential election, the Mayer's were almost shocked to discover that their southern friends had sent them such a "kind and thoughtful" gift. In a thank you letter, Agatha M. Mayer reassured her friend "Whether you are *Secessionists* or not, it will never change the feelings of affection and interest which I have cherished for years . . . notwithstanding our being *Republicans*, these feelings will never cease to be reciprocated by you." Later in the same letter, Mayer attempted to plan a visit by one of the Stiles children "as soon as she comes North."⁷⁴ This letter indicated that some northerners—even staunch Republicans—hoped that some form of quick and peaceful resolution might be achieved before matters spiraled out of control. For Elizabeth, secession meant years of isolation from her dearest friends. While the Mayer family reaffirmed their continued desire to remain friends, other families were less forgiving. During the ensuing war, the circle of friends Elizabeth had relied upon during the antebellum period shrunk to a mere handful of individuals much smaller in number than her once voluminous social life had allowed.⁷⁵

In Cartersville, men who shared Tom Dowtin's views gathered around the Western & Atlantic Railroad depot eager to receive news regarding secession.

During a public meeting in said city the mayor announced to a secessionist audience that he was prepared "to drink every drop of blood that secession will bring to this country." After a wave of applause, the mayor continued by declaring that "Yankees will not fight; one Southern man could whip a dozen anywhere."[76] Like a scene stolen from the pages of Margaret Mitchell's *Gone With the Wind*, many exuberant Cass County males truly believed that the North would simply allow secession to occur without repercussions, if there was a war it would be short, and the Yankees lacked the masculine qualities necessary to engage in warfare. Rebecca Felton witnessed this public meeting. Afterwards she was in a state of shock that such "bravado" dominated the discussion. Worst of all, her husband shared those beliefs.[77]

Antebellum Cass County politics, and Georgia politics in general, revolved around party loyalties, intra-class relations, and an overarching defense of slavery. While strongly Democratic, the county's anti-Democratic forces maintained a presence in numerous elections and managed to band together during the secession convention vote to defeat immediate secession. While county voters disagreed over the means of removing the state from the Union, they found common ground on the right of secession and the need to defend slavery. Cooperationists and immediatists alike feared that northern tyranny threatened to enslave the South. The preservation of white privilege and their slave society, the central tenets of a white men's democracy, pushed these men toward secession and war.

CHAPTER
3

"Let's Drink the Blood of thy Enemies"

If Cass Countians questioned the wisdom of secession, most resolved those doubts when President Abraham Lincoln issued a call to raise 75,000 soldiers to suppress the rebellion following the Confederacy's attack upon Fort Sumter. Most white Cass County residents responded to the impending war with enthusiasm. War fever spread throughout Cass County. In 1861, despite favoring a slate of cooperationist candidates during the secession convention vote, most military service aged Cass Countians volunteered for duty. The debate over secession that had divided the county primarily centered on questions of timing and hopes for a last-minute compromise rather than objections to secession itself. Cooperationists, who represented at least half of the county's white male population, supported secession, but disagreed on questions of timing. They believed that the South should wait until Lincoln took office and a few more compromise measures be explored before Georgia broke from the Union. When Georgia seceded in January, Lincoln took office in March, and Confederates fired upon Fort Sumter in April, a great majority of cooperationists abandoned compromise. Instead, they threw their support behind the Confederate government because it stood in defense of a southern society threatened by black Republicans who challenged slavery's legitimacy and future place in American society. Convinced that they were an abused minority being trampled by a misguided majority, Cass Countians, like many white southerners, believed that the Confederacy would protect their way of life, a social order built on the backs of an enslaved black labor force that fostered unity among white men. While soldiers enlisted for many reasons stemming from their sense of honor, duty, and political beliefs, they all wanted to preserve a way of life that was under assault. A shared culture—whose political rights and economic opportunities were tethered to common notions of white supremacy and racial privilege—bound together large numbers of white households in support of the Confederate cause. The Civil War, however, tested their resolve in unexpected ways placing enormous pressure upon white households, particularly women. The pains of physical separation, material hardship, sickness, disability, and death impacted soldiers as well as civilians with such severity that many partisan rebels found themselves doubting if independence was either possible or worthwhile. Between 1861 and 1863, despite the trials and tribulations of war, a majority of Cass Countians, rich and poor, remained committed supporters of Confederate nationalism and hopeful that independence lay ahead.

At 4:30 a.m., April 12, 1861, Confederate forces located in Charleston, South Carolina, opened fire on the federal installation Fort Sumter situated in that city's harbor. "The shedding of blood," predicted fire-eater Edmund Ruffin, "will serve to change many voters in the hesitating states, from the submission or procrastinating ranks, to the zealous for immediate secession." In Georgia, the inauguration of military action cast aside lingering disagreements between cooperationists and immediatists. Six days later, Governor Joseph E. Brown called for military volunteers to defend their homes and country. By the fall of 1861, the state had raised almost 25,000 troops for service in the Confederate army. Twelve months later, the total number of Georgians serving in the army had tripled. By 1865, roughly 120,000 Georgians had completed some form of military service.[1]

In 1861, Cass County organized ten infantry and cavalry companies and accounted for numerous enlistments in companies raised in neighboring Floyd, Gordon, and Cobb counties. Approximately 940 Cass County males volunteered for military service. About 45 percent (834) of the county's 2,086 households had at least one soldier serving in the military. Of the 1,459 households that had at least one male member between the ages of 18 and 35, about 85 percent had at least one man in the army. Their companies left Cass County with colorful nicknames, such as the Bartow Yankee Killers and the Fireside Volunteers. Most companies identified themselves with a local leader or their community: the Rowland Highlanders (named after John S. Rowland) and the Kingston Volunteers. The average 1861 volunteer was a 5 foot 7 inches tall twenty-two-year-old male. Many volunteers, 376 or 40 percent, still lived in their parents' household or were not listed as the head of household at their residence. Of the 546 volunteers who were listed as heads of households in the 1860 census, 137 or 25 percent owned slaves, 328 or 60 percent owned land, 33 or 6 percent were planters, and 9 percent were non-yeomen. The number of non-yeomen included in these figures is misleading since many of those volunteers absent as heads of households in the 1860 census lived in non-yeomen households. While poor whites probably represented more than 9 percent of all local 1861 veterans, their share of all 1861 enlistments fell far short of their 45 percent share of the county's total population. In 1861, many poor white men chose to remain at home rather than get caught up in the excitement of war. Overall, Cass County provided an estimated 4 percent of the state's 1861 volunteers.[2]

Enlistment patterns varied within the county's three subregions. Households located in the Great Appalachian Valley and Piedmont sections contributed nearly 87 percent of all Cass County 1861 volunteers. In the valley, nearly 90 percent of all households with at least one male member between the ages 18 and 35 had at least one man enlist. Among the sixty-three planter households located in the Great Appalachian Valley and Piedmont regions, 90 percent of households with at least one male member between the ages of 18 and 35 had at least one man enlist and nearly 75 percent of those same households had two or more men enlist. Non-slaveholding households in the Great Appalachian Valley and Piedmont also contributed large numbers of men to the Confederate military.[3]

Cass County men, at least those who lived in the Piedmont and Great Appalachian Valley subregions, responded to secession and the formation of the Confederate army like most Upcountry Georgia communities. As documented by Steven Hahn, many Upcountry farmers were "ambivalent" toward secession yet rallied to defend their homes and join the excitement of the war by enlisting in the Confederate army. Piedmont communities sent scores of men into the army in 1861 bolstering national hopes that the conflict might unite all white men against a mounting federal threat.[4]

Conversely, fewer households (about 15 percent) located in Cass County's Appalachian subregion sent men into the Confederate military.[5] As seen in other southern Appalachian communities, households in isolated regions disconnected from major transportation networks tended to either oppose or remain ambivalent toward the Confederacy at a higher rate than others who lived closer to major roads and railroads. Sometimes neighboring communities expressed very different opinions toward the Confederacy. In isolated communities such as Fannin County, Georgia, located about 80 miles northeast of Cass County, most white men offered the Confederacy little support and worked hard to keep themselves and their sons out of the Confederate army. Meanwhile, as Jonathan Sarris documented, neighboring Lumpkin County, a place with greater connections to regional trade with a small but powerful number of slaveholding farmers, aligned themselves with the Confederacy. Likewise, Keith Bohannon found that north Georgia families had "kinship, social and economic ties to other portions of Georgia and the South" that "fostered strong state and sectional loyalties that proved important during the secession crisis and Civil War." While Bohannon describes north Georgia as a decidedly pro-Confederate region, pockets of unionism and anti-Confederate sentiment could be found throughout the area. In northeast Cass County, significantly fewer white men supported the Confederacy than white men who lived in other more regionally connected parts of the county. Similar distinctions between market oriented and economically isolated mountain communities have been documented across the South.[6]

The distinctions among Cass County's three geographic subregions mirrored trends across the Confederacy. Compared to other Appalachian communities, Cass County ranked among the most pro-Confederate in the region. However, only a third of the county's terrain resembled Appalachia and in this hill country support for the Confederacy lagged behind the rest of the county. The mixed actions of Cass County white men in 1861 evidence that antebellum distinctions extending from proximity to markets, transportation, and slavery carried over into the war and likely impacted who did and did not support the Confederate government.[7]

The Confederate army and Governor Brown depended upon local leaders to recruit, organize, and, at times, equip military companies that were later formed into regiments and assigned to duty. Elite men such as Mark A. Cooper, John Rowland, and Mark A. Hardin helped to organize several companies. Most Cass County soldiers enlisted in the town nearest to their home. During

Table 7
Companies Raised in Cass County, 1861

Company	Regiment	Army	No. of Volunteers
1st Co. E	1st CSA	Army of Tennessee	88
Co. K	14th Georgia Infantry	Army of Northern Virginia	87
Co. F	18th Georgia Infantry Regiment	Army of Northern Virginia	92
Co. G	18th Georgia Infantry Regiment	Army of Northern Virginia	101
Co. H	18th Georgia Infantry Regiment	Army of Northern Virginia	117
Co. K	18th Georgia Infantry Regiment	Army of Northern Virginia	123
Co. K	19th Georgia Infantry Regiment	Army of Tennessee	104
Co. G	22nd Georgia Infantry Regiment	Army of Northern Virginia	104
Co. A	23rd Georgia Infantry Regiment	Army of Tennessee	90
Co. B	Phillip's Legion	Army of Northern Virginia	39

Source: Henderson, Confederate Muster Rolls.

the spring of 1861, volunteers filled the streets of Kingston, Cartersville, and Cassville eager to enlist, but frustrated by unforeseen delays. A lack of adequate numbers of weapons and equipment hampered mass enlistments. Many volunteers wanted to join cavalry units but neither they nor the government had enough horses available to meet this demand. Some men returned home if they could not serve in the type of unit of their choosing.

A myriad of reasons motivated Cass County males to volunteer for military service. Most desired to protect their homes and families from a perceived enemy that threatened their personal liberty and independence. Soldiers identified the Republican Party and abolitionists as a principal cause of the conflict and therefore the defense of slavery while not explicit motivated these volunteers. Large percentages of the Confederacy's 1861 volunteers owned slaves. Many soldiers identified the need to defend a southern way of life as a major reason to fight. Ideology aside, many soldiers also enlisted because of their friends and family members joining up.[9]

In the fall of 1861, Cassville slaveholder William Augustus Chunn, a native of North Carolina, volunteered to defend his masculine notions of honor and duty. Victorians conceived notions of honor that revolved around masculinity. Sometimes a soldier's honor conflicted with his family duties. Initially Chunn's wife questioned why he wanted to fight when she needed him at home. In a letter to his wife, he lectured her about his decision. "I am . . . a man," he wrote, "determined to forgo the pleasures of home & friends for a while to benefit the interest of my country." William's letters displayed his heartfelt love for his wife and family. Before the war, the thought of leaving his home for any extended period seemed unbearable. But as with many things, war changed his perspective. In 1861, military service gave a man the best means to protect home and family. Victory would bring independence followed by tranquility and prosperity. Many soldiers such as Chunn saw honor as a means of expressing their family duties.[10]

Other factors encouraged enlistment. Wherever Confederate soldiers prepared for duty, flocks of young adoring women appeared. Many Cass County men soon discovered that southern women adored a man in uniform. At every train station located along the Western & Atlantic Railroad, young females waited with anticipation for the arrival of another carload of traveling soldiers. While the train stopped for water, women showered volunteers with flowers, cool drinks, and sandwiches to ease their journey. A soldier traveling from Cassville to Savannah might make a handful of similar stops. Upon recounting his initial journey to camp, William Chunn told his wife about the throngs of beautiful women who showered the men with flowers, lemonade, and food. He wrote: "I never saw a group of boys enjoy themselves better in my life, they were hollering & waving hankerchiefs the whole time." While stationed in Virginia, George S. Barnsley of the 8th Georgia Infantry Regiment likewise wrote that "it was a pleasure to strut about when one could get a leave." Young women in town, he wrote, treated him like a celebrity. Likewise, upon arriving in Richmond, John Bentley told his parents that young women visited their camp bringing so much food and treats that they were forced to share the excess with other nearby companies.[11]

Cass County recruits less cosmopolitan than Barnsley saw enlistment as an opportunity to see the world. Many had never traveled much farther from home than the nearest market town, which for many Cass farmers would have been Cartersville or perhaps Rome. The prospect of seeing new places added to the excitement. While traveling by train to his post located along the Georgia coast, Chunn enjoyed every sightseeing opportunity. When he stepped off the train in Macon, that city was probably the largest he had ever seen. While the train's engineer stopped to make a few minor repairs and acquire some water, Chunn casually strolled Macon's "beautifully laed off" streets, gazing upon the city's numerous large dwellings. Having never been to Savannah, he eagerly anticipated traveling through Georgia's oldest city. It, however, proved disappointing. "There is no wonder that there is so much sickness," Chunn wrote, "for all the filth of the houses is thrown into the streets."[12]

Private John F. Milhollin eagerly anticipated seeing Richmond for the first time. He pictured a pristine town sitting atop some lofty hill overlooking the tranquil Virginia countryside. When his unit, Co. B, Phillips Legion Georgia Volunteer Cavalry, received orders to report to Richmond, he wrote his wife about his exciting upcoming trip. The soldier's next letter home, however, told a much different story. Richmond apparently disappointed Milhollin. "This city stinks worse than a dead horse," wrote Milhollin, "I never visited such a filthy place before."[13] For Chunn, Milhollin, and others, seeing the world turned out to be a disappointment.

Parents viewed their children's enlistment differently. Rebecca Hood of Cartersville remembered experiencing mixed feelings upon learning that her oldest son had enlisted in the military. She prided herself for rearing a child so willing to sacrifice his own life for a greater cause. She equally fretted about his personal safety. Each passing day seemed to shrink in size as the moment of his departure neared. When the morning came, she awoke with a "troubled heart." She "prepared him some lunch" and despite her sorrow "tried to appear to him composed." Silently weeping, Hood packed the last of her son's belongings and "placed a small Bible in his pocket," giving him all that he would need on his upcoming journey. "With a 'God bless and protect you, my son' [Hood] kissed him goodbye, not knowing that [she] would ever" see him again. The time between a soldier's departure and the arrival of their first letter seemed like ages. A degree of Hood's anxiety vanished upon receiving her first letter. In the letter, her son told her that he was doing well and not to worry for they had plenty of good food and water. Comforted, Hood reread each letter a thousand times to help pass the time before the next letter's arrival. Fortunately, for Hood, her son returned home physically unscathed from the war four years later.[14]

Fathers too worried about their children's impending mortality. Mark A. Cooper served in the Seminole War. When his three sons, Thomas, John, and Mark, volunteered for military service, he applauded their decision. Cooper's political sympathies aligned with the region's most ardent pro-secessionist sympathizers. He felt that everyone needed to contribute to the war effort if the South were to emerge victorious. As his sons prepared to leave for northern Virginia, Cooper secretly wrote President Jefferson Davis a letter with the intent of aiding his sons' transition into military service. He mentioned that all of them lacked any combat experience, but the emotions associated with defending their homes would carry them into battle. Cooper requested that Davis assign a West Point officer to his sons' regiment because "These are all the sons I have."[15]

Religious faith undergirded both recruits and their families. They believed that God held sovereign power over all of humanity. God created the world. Once He accomplished this unimaginable feat, God did not merely set the world into motion without supervision as suggested by Deist philosophers who argued, according to John F. Milhollin, "that God made all things and made laws by which they are ruled and then left them." Instead, God's hand touched the daily lives of all of His creatures. At times, this influence could produce positive effects, while during more trying moments, His intervention allowed evil to triumph over mankind's best laid plans. Both the good and the bad comprised God's larger plan.

Again, the period's zeitgeist not only influenced how soldiers saw themselves but also how they explained their relationship with their creator. In the eyes of most volunteers, God ordained secession. This degree of personal faith was woven into a much larger social fabric that in the spring of 1861 bolstered Confederate nationalism and ultimately justified the impending war. Milhollin instructed his wife to make sure that his children attended Sabbath school and church and routinely read the "word of God." If he were to perish in battle, then at least his soul could rest at ease knowing that his mortal family would carry on the individual and communal values that had convinced him to enlist. God, family, and country motivated Cass County soldiers to fight. Soldiers equated family and country in terms that paralleled their deeply held religious convictions, therefore, no one believed that any part of this triumvirate conflicted with the rest.[16]

Others ached for the chance to fight the enemy. Soldiers such as John Milhollin romanticized death in battle as a sign of unending personal glory. If fate determined that a soldier must die, most prayed they would fall in battle leading their company with their face toward the enemy. In a literary period dominated by romanticism, soldiers aspired to assume the hero's role in their chosen adventure. "Should I fall on the field," Milhollin cautioned, "tell my dear children to be kind to their mother. . . . Remember too that I go with a bold heart strong in opinion of the success of our cause, believing that we will with our cause succeed it being a holy one." Soldiers such as Milhollin wanted to become heroes who earned the respect and admiration of their local communities. Their death in battle secured their eternal place within local history.[17]

Making the transition from civilian to military life proved difficult for many Cass County soldiers. Life in the 8th Georgia Infantry Regiment transformed George and Lucien Barnsley. Before the war, the brothers lived lives of luxury thanks to their father's vast shipping fortune. They received the finest education that money could afford including expensive private tutors, many of whom had previously held teaching positions in some of Europe's most prestigious universities. The boys' lifestyle included a summer home, Woodlands, in northwest Georgia, built far from the coastal heat and disease, and principal residences in Savannah and New Orleans.[18]

Many volunteers in early 1861 tried to maintain a sense of home and family while serving in the military. Soldiers who came from planter households were able to afford luxuries that most soldiers could have only dreamed. While in training camp at Rome, Georgia, the Barnsley brothers brought with them dinnerware and food supplies and purchased any other items, such as alcohol, that they needed from town. After drilling for hours, the brothers returned to their four-walled tent, rested comfortably on cushioned chairs, sipped brandy, and smoked cigars and pipe tobacco. A slave washed their clothes routinely, and both men enjoyed the comfort of new soft leather boots.[19] During the summer of 1861, however, the Barnsley brothers experienced a much different side of military service. Gone were the fine wines, enslaved servants, and hearty meals. Dust-filled roads, long marches, wet bedding, brackish water, and insect-polluted meals replaced those luxuries.[20]

Some soldiers, such as Tom Dowtin of the Rowland Infantry and John W. Bentley, adjusted more easily to military life. Unlike the Barnsleys, Dowtin and Bentley came from humble roots. Dowtin's family did not own slaves and generally represented the typical Cass County household. A zealous supporter of secession, Dowtin was one of the first men in the county to enlist. While at Camp McDonald, located at Big Shanty in Cobb County, Dowtin informed his mother that he "was perfectly delighted with camp-life." The soldiers at Camp McDonald were suffering from a "considerable rage of dysentery" at the time of Dowtin's letter, but despite the arduous circumstances, he reaffirmed his military commitment. "We are under the strictest discipline here being compelled to undergo the hardest duties of the camp life," reported Dowtin. "We have to rise quite early and have to go through a perfect series of drilling." Things were good except that Dowtin would have liked "it better if [he] were nearer the enemy." In the letter, Dowtin informed his mother that he intended to stay with the army "for the whole length of time." In closing, Dowtin reiterated his desire to finally confront the Yankees because the extended wait had made him "thirsty for their blood."[21]

Like Dowtin, John W. Bentley arrived in Virginia eager to face the enemy. His early letters reflect how most soldiers saw enlistment as an adventure. He recounted in detail the train trip he took from Roswell, Georgia, to Richmond. Despite uncomfortable travel caused by riding in open air cars, Bentley described the trip with enthusiasm. In Richmond, as well as during his first two years of military service, Bentley comforted concerned family members by complaining that he and his mates ate too much and had grown fat. The variety of foods that Bentley described as part of his routine diet illustrate that some soldiers ate as well if not better in the army compared to the homes they left behind. Bentley had little money prior to the war. Working as a day laborer on white farms in the Cassville area, Bentley certainly did not represent that town's social elite. Beyond writing about food and travel, Bentley filled his letters with reports about the health of his fellow soldiers. Visits to army hospitals to comfort his friends were commonplace. Bentley often instructed family members to pass word along to neighboring families at home regarding the condition of their loved ones. With his material needs provided for by the army, Bentley felt a bond of loyalty and comradery among soldiers that made the experience not only manageable but enjoyable.[22]

Notions of masculinity influenced Civil War service. In Victorian America, two competing versions of masculinity existed: the hard-drinking, fighting, and swearing man among men and the sober, dutiful son or husband. The Cherokee Baptist Association worried that military service might turn sober men into immoral sinners. In response to these fears, the Cherokee Baptist Association and Mark A. Cooper organized a campaign to promote the moral condition of their beloved soldiers. Cooper owned the Etowah Mining and Manufacturing Company and was one of the wealthiest men in northwest Georgia. Through private donations, he acquired hundreds of copies of the New Testament. When Cass County soldiers boarded trains, Cooper and other volunteers handed each man a copy of the New Testament. They encouraged the men to read the New Testament daily and observe the Sabbath as often as possible. Local clergymen also always led departing soldiers in communal prayer prior to boarding their train. These prayers asked God to return these soldiers safely to their homes and to guard their religious sanctity from the immoral temptations that accompanied military life.[23]

Parents worried about how their sons would behave away from home. John W. Bentley's father penned his son a special letter filled with instructions for how he believed his son should act while serving in the army. The father urged his son to refrain from foul language, gambling, and alcohol and to focus his attention instead on God and upholding his family's reputation. Such writings demanded soldiers to be morally upright in camp and courageous in battle. In response to his father's pleas for him to remain steadfast in combat, Bentley replied, "if I fall in battle I will fall with my face towards the foe." Such words reassured parents that their sons would behave in a manner that would prevent others from labeling the family as cowards or drunkards.[24]

The Etowah Infantry was among the first companies from Cass County. Peter H. Larey served as the company commander and principal recruiter.[25] The company's original muster roll contained the names of sixty men, the majority of whom lived in Cass County and previously served in a militia unit organized by Larey during the civil war in Kansas. Volunteers from neighboring Gordon, Cherokee, Floyd, and Cobb counties were also on the roll. As evidenced by their previous attempts to thwart Federal jurisdiction during the conflicts in Kansas, the men who comprised the Etowah Infantry were among the county's most avid states' rights supporters and secessionists. The average age of the Etowah Infantry was twenty-four. A majority of the soldiers were not the head of their household. As expected, the largest occupation among these soldiers was farming although a significant number of professional class members served as regimental officers. Most of these volunteers had migrated from western South Carolina and North Carolina to Cass County sometime during the previous two decades. Overall, these initial volunteers represented a wide array of the county's population. Rich planters and day laborers volunteered for duty with little concern for their obvious economic differences. If the war was truly a rich man's war and a poor man's fight, Cass County's 1861 enlistment patterns did not resemble such a state of affairs. In March of 1861, Captain Larey informed Governor Brown that his unit was "ready and anxious to be ordered to whatever point you may see proper."[26] The Etowah Infantry eventually became part of the 1st Confederate Infantry Regiment and was assigned to the Army of Tennessee.

Material shortages hampered the mobilization of Cass County's volunteers. Like all Georgia infantry companies, those raised in Cass County struggled to locate enough small arms to effectively equip an effective fighting unit. Governor Brown had confiscated a large store of weapons from various Federal arsenals located throughout the state, but the amount collected could not properly arm the massive number of volunteers. The state executive office received a flood of letters from local recruitment organizers demanding that the governor supply their units. Brown simply lacked enough muskets and rifles to fulfill those demands. Consequently, many volunteers who wanted to enlist and go off to war in the spring of 1861 were forced to wait until an unspecified future date to serve because their unit needed armaments.

The experience of John Frederick Cooper, Mark Cooper's son, illustrates the difficulties of recruiting, equipping, and brigading a local military unit. Weeks before secession, Cooper initiated plans for organizing a volunteer unit known as the Etowah Rangers. Like most unit organizers, he could afford to privately fund a significant portion of his unit's outfitting, but despite his best efforts, he had difficulty acquiring all of the necessary items. On January 3, 1861, Cooper wrote Governor Brown requesting a shipment of arms. Among the items Cooper requested were weapons suitable for equipping a cavalry unit. "We now ask that no time shall be lost in supplying us," wrote Cooper. "The Crisis of the Country demands instant preparation and as far as we are concerned it seemed to us hard to be kept back by the mere want of arms and thus deprived of an opportunity of taking the post of danger which we so ardently desire."[27] One month later, he grew frustrated as the items he requested never arrived. Brown wrote Cooper informing him that he would help to equip the unit. Again, the materials never arrived. Impatient with Brown's delays, he wrote the governor repeatedly soliciting supplies. When a shipment finally arrived, Cooper erupted in anger on discovering that the crate contained sabers unfit for cavalry service.

Immediately after Fort Sumter, Mark E. Cooper, John's brother, informed Brown that "your old and true friends the Etowah Rangers . . . [seek] an opportunity they have *so long desired* to serve their country at any point whatever."[28] By April, John Cooper had equipped his unit with private funds. Discouraged by Brown's slow response, he decided to play upon the governor's sense of loyalty by stressing the executive's friendship with his father. Brown remained steadfast. A week later, on April 27, 1861, Cooper criticized him in a letter stating that "it is in your Excellency's character to abandon old friends for the sake of those who have never ceased to slander you at a distance."[29]

In addition to frustrating small arms shortages, Cass County volunteers struggled to acquire proper outfitting. Besides guns, soldiers required uniforms, blankets, shoes, socks, tents, and numerous other material items. The state and Confederate government held individual companies responsible for obtaining these items. Routinely, volunteer companies left for camp or the front lines before the necessary equipment could be produced. Wealthier volunteers quickly placed orders with the county's few professional tailors. These tailors, however, became inundated with requests that their small cottage industry operations could not fulfill. Cass County women responded to this need by organizing the county's first Soldier's Aid Society. Ladies formed this society during a meeting held at the Presbyterian Church in Kingston. The society worked under the loose supervision of a Reverend J. Telford, who ensured that the women's conduct remained appropriate. Most of the women in this group were slaveholders but a significant number belonged to yeomen households. When selecting its leaders, the group chose elite women. The aid society located in Kingston appointed Mary Ann Woolley as president, and Josephine Beck, Mrs. Telford, and Mrs. Erastus V. Johnson as vice-presidents. With the exception of Mrs. Telford, whose husband served as the local Presbyterian minister, all of the women's husbands had volunteered for military duty during the spring of 1861. They, like their spouses, volunteered for duty eager to serve the new government's cause while simultaneously protecting and caring for their loved ones.[30]

A majority of Soldier's Aid Society members in Kingston and Cass County came from the planter class or slaveholding households who had the ability to alter their household to better serve the needs of the military. Whereas many of these women owned female slaves who worked a variety of domestic chores, in the spring of 1861, most of that slave labor became focused on knitting socks, stitching blankets, and repairing damaged clothing for the soldiers. The aid society president, Mary Ann Woolley, used her large slave workforce to produce Confederate uniforms. When her husband marched onto the field of battle, the clothes on his back more than likely were the fruits of slave labor and not necessarily the product of his wife's loving hands. These materials went to soldiers, rich and poor, from Cass County. The aid societies, as well as a number of other charitable wartime activities, carried on antebellum traditions of mutual aid among white households thus preserving the existing social order.[31]

The Soldier's Aid Society came together during a period when hundreds of local men were leaving to join the Confederate army and those who remained at home experienced increasing apprehension about the loyalty of local slaves. In May 1861, Kingston residents hanged a slave on charges of inciting a slave revolt.[32] An unidentified poor white man was also convicted and sentenced to death for supposedly aiding the revolt. Similar fears spread throughout the Confederacy creating uncertainty and a heightened state of vigilance as slaves came under the watchful eye of whites. Kingston resident Sarah Clayton described scenes of local slaveholders moving to the city of Atlanta to distance themselves from a feared impending slave rebellion. Other slaveholders, Clayton believed, began moving their slaves to southwest Georgia to distance them from any potential Union army incursion that might enter north Georgia and reduce the potential for violence by decreasing the local slave population.[33]

* * * * *

Perhaps as important as the large number of volunteers the county sent off to war was the thriving local economy that now became a vital part of the new government's military-industrial complex. The Civil War propelled an economic growth that had started in antebellum Cass County. Agricultural and non-agricultural industries both grew steadily throughout the 1850s. In 1860, the county lacked any city or town that could be considered urban, but during the 1850s, towns such as Cassville and Cartersville had experienced significant growth. The Civil War and Confederate policies enhanced these trends.[34]

The Confederate Ordinance Department depended on materials produced in Cass County mines and iron works. Cass County contained the Confederacy's largest saltpeter cave. Located outside of Kingston, the cave had once been used by Cherokee Indians who converted the raw potassium nitrate into gunpowder. During the antebellum period, local resident Mark A. Hardin purchased the property and developed the cave's production capacity. The production of gunpowder depended on obtaining vast quantities of potassium nitrate. Throughout the war, Confederate blockade runners managed to import potassium nitrate, but shipments were expensive and sometimes unreliable. Ordinance department officials realized during the first months of the war that the Confederacy needed new domestic sources. In the spring of 1861, speculators and entrepreneurs invested large amounts of capital to aid in further tapping the cave's vast resources. In May, several interested parties led by Colonel John D. Gray formed a gunpowder manufacturing company at Kingston. Engineers constructed the production facility within close proximity of the cave, thereby reducing transportation expenses. By the summer of 1861, the saltpeter cave produced over 1,000 lbs. of potassium nitrate daily. Once this material was transported to manufacturing facilities, workers turned 1,000 lbs. of potassium nitrate into 1,400 lbs. of gunpowder. Local citizens invested money in the facility hoping to profit from the increasing demand for gunpowder. These investments placed the county firmly within the ever expanding Confederate military-industrial complex.[35]

In the spring of 1861, Mark Cooper, owner of the Etowah Iron Works, sought out purchase orders with the Confederate government. While at Montgomery, he arranged for a private meeting with President Jefferson Davis and several cabinet members. Cooper proposed that the government construct a national arsenal located at Etowah. The "Iron Man of Georgia" offered the Confederate government complete control over his two iron blasting furnaces in exchange for $300,000.[36] Confederate officials declined Cooper's offer. Undeterred, Cooper immediately wrote Governor Brown seeking a similar arrangement with the state of Georgia. Brown also rejected Cooper's proposal. Intent on profiting from the war, Cooper increased his labor force and began accumulating massive quantities of raw materials needed to produce pig iron. By the time the first Georgia troops arrived in Virginia, he had negotiated several lucrative iron contracts with the state and national government.[37]

The Etowah Iron Works played an instrumental role in supplying the Confederate war effort. Cooper's manufacturing center spanned some twelve thousand acres in four counties and by some accounts was the second largest iron production facility in southern Appalachia. The center housed a furnace, forge, foundry, rolling mill, flour mill, grist mill, and sawmill. Prior to the war, Cooper employed over 1,000 laborers and owned 200 slaves. The town of Etowah, which Cooper owned, functioned much like a northern antebellum factory town complete with a post office, churches, worker housing, and merchant stores. The town also included a brewery and bordello that housed a dozen enslaved prostitutes. While the employment of 200 slaves might seem extraordinary, similar facilities in Botetourt County, Virginia, employed nearly 3,000 slaves during peak production periods. In 1861, production at Cooper's works suffered due to the loss of dozens of workers who enlisted in the army. After that, Cooper's wartime workforce included larger numbers of slaves and fewer white laborers. The facility contained "two pig iron furnaces, one rolling mill, and a nail factory; they not only could provide railroad bar iron, but represented the only facility south of Richmond capable of turning out car axles."[38]

Like Mark Cooper, Godfrey Barnsley recognized that he too might profit from the war. Barnsley owned several oceanic ships and had European contacts at banks and brokerage houses. With the blockade of southern ports and the disappearance of northern manufactured goods, individuals such as Barnsley who understood the intricacies of international trade proved to be a valuable asset to the Confederate government. Prior to enlisting in the Confederate army, Godfrey's son George debated how he might best serve the Confederate war effort. Perhaps he could transform some of his father's ships into blockade runners? Godfrey frowned upon the thought of one of his son's becoming a pirate and participating in raids on unsuspecting vessels. Such action, believed Godfrey, lacked honor and was beneath the family's elite social standing.[39]

Godfrey Barnsley nonetheless saw blockade running as a potentially profitable enterprise. Samuel Smith, one of Barnsley's cotton brokers in Liverpool, England, contacted Barnsley in March informing him that "textile mills in his area are still obtaining large amounts of cotton. . . . Some Manchester spinners and manufacturers worry about 'short time' but little has been impacted as of yet." The mobilization of two large American armies benefited the British economy. Investors poured money into British textile firms and banks hopeful of cashing in on this boom period. Union and Confederate forces required a substantial amount of textile goods, some which would be imported from England. Smith told Barnsley that British banks were paying out 6 percent returns on all foreign investments. Barnsley ordered his British agents to invest with the hope of making a quick profit once "Lincoln . . . freely recognized Southern independence."[40]

In addition to investing in British textile manufacturers, Godfrey Barnsley saw Confederate and state bonds as an appealing investment opportunity. Confederate bonds promised a high return on every investment paid out once the bond matured. Confident that the Confederate States of America would defend its independence and subsequently develop beneficial trading partnerships with other major world nations, he sunk tens of thousands of dollars into Confederate bonds. Within a year after Fort Sumter, Barnsley's investments included over $40,000 worth of Confederate bonds. Initially, he profited from reselling these bonds on the open market. For example, Barnsley would purchase a $100 bond and two months later sell that same bond for a 100 percent profit. As long as investors believed in Confederate victory, his investments seemed safe, secure, and highly profitable.[41]

Barnsley's shipping business, in contrast, suffered dramatic losses during the Civil War. As early as the summer of 1861, Barnsley's coastal agents informed him that due to the presence of the Union blockade fleet, none of his ships could leave their harbor. Most of Barnsley's ships were harbored in the ports of Mobile, Savannah, and New Orleans. When New Orleans fell, Barnsley lost several ships. Without a reliable source of income, Barnsley watched as the war slowly drained his massive personal fortune.

Upon rushing off to war, George Barnsley left his personal finances in a state of disarray. Before the war, Godfrey rarely visited Woodlands more than once or twice a year and usually only during the summer. The rest of the year, George managed Woodlands. Willing to take risks, George had borrowed from local merchants and banks in order to support his various ventures. Shortly before the war, he borrowed several hundred dollars from Kingston millwright Erastus V. Johnson. George enlisted in the Eighth Georgia Infantry and went to Virginia without repaying his debt. Johnson expected to receive payment during the spring of 1861, but upon learning that George had left Woodlands, he became concerned. If George died in Virginia, how would he get paid? Meanwhile, during the winter of 1861, Johnson opened a mill in the town of Kingston. The mill's initial start-up costs were high, forcing Johnson to borrow $657 from a Rome bank. The bank demanded that the note be paid in full within six months. In June, Johnson wrote Godfrey informing him of his son's substantial debts. Godfrey knew nothing about the debt but was not surprised to discover that his son owed yet another local businessman money. In order to avoid the humiliation of having a delinquent debtor as a son and a possible lawsuit, Godfrey responded to Johnson's request. One day after receiving Johnson's letter, Godfrey and his agent traveled the fifty-four mile round trip into Rome where he personally paid off Johnson's bank note. That night, Godfrey wrote George and informed him about how disappointed he was that his son had allowed his personal finances to become questionable. He cautioned his son that once the war was over, the two would have to sit down and map out the young man's economic future. The war, Godfrey advised his son, could not serve as a hiding place from a man's domestic concerns.[42]

George Barnsley meanwhile had already grown tired of military duty.[43] In a letter written in July while stationed at Camp Washington near Winchester, Virginia, he told of the uncertainty that existed within military life. "Our force here," wrote George, "is estimated about 18,000 men—6,000 militia included, who cannot be expected to do much fighting." He also complained about his declining diet: "we don't see any vegetables.... I often long for some of those at home. I have not eaten any fruit this season.... Sometimes we feel unwell from eating irregularly too much dough and fat meat." Months earlier, he had dined on imported caviar and mutton while in camp at Rome. Now the harsh realities of military service had begun to set in.[44]

To make matters worse, George now believed that the army was retreating. The commanding officer, General Joseph E. Johnston, abandoned the army's position at Harper's Ferry without a fight. Afterwards, Johnston moved his forces south near the city of Winchester to avoid engaging the enemy. George, a private with no prior military training or experience, disagreed with Johnston's decisions. To retreat in the face of the enemy, in his mind, equaled cowardice. "We are greatly chagrined," he wrote, "that we had to retreat by orders the other day and I am sure if any retreat from this place was made *without a fight* it would have a very demoralizing effect upon the army." Despite George's mounting concerns, his letters reiterated his belief that "this is a glorious cause of ours. Its sacredness seems to pervade every breast. We're ready to a man to lay down our lives if necessary to the promotion of the cause."[45]

Driven by impatience, Godfrey Barnsley and some other Cass County reactionaries had concluded that the Confederacy was losing the war because it was unwilling to fight. Godfrey worried that his sons might miss the opportunity to prove their honor on the battlefield. In contrast, Charles Howard saw Johnston's retreats as a positive delaying action. Howard feared "that the two armies will meet before Congress goes into session." Once Congress meets, Howard assured Barnsley, they would most likely "let the South go without a fight."[46] Of course, Congress intended no such action. Johnston's retreat proved to be little more than a maneuver designed to draw his forces closer to Confederates stationed outside of Richmond in anticipation of a large-scale battle.

In July of 1861, Cass Countians serving in the Army of the Shenandoah stationed in northern Virginia became the first soldiers from the county to engage in battle. George and Lucien Barnsley; Mark, John, and Thomas Cooper; Jett Howard; Benjamin Stiles; and others were among the Cass County residents who fought at First Manassas. Most of these Cass Countians served in Colonel Francis S. Bartow's 8th Georgia Infantry Regiment.

The 8th Georgia Infantry Regiment fought in the First Battle of Manassas, July 21, 1861, as part of General Joseph E. Johnston's 12,000 men Army of the Shenandoah. Days before the battle, Johnston managed to board his force onto the Manassas Gap Railroad and transport them to Manassas Junction (a distance of 50 miles) where they would support General P. G. T. Beauregard's 20,000 men confronting Union General Irwin McDowell's 35,000 soldiers. During the Civil War's first major battle, confusion reigned supreme as two amateur armies, led by inexperienced commanders, endured scorching temperatures and a hilly terrain that hampered communications.

During the battle, Colonel Bartow died and his second in command received a debilitating wound. Command passed to Major Thomas Cooper, who lacked any previous military experience. He eagerly embraced the task before him. Modeling himself after Bartow, Cooper reorganized his men and gave them a speech to fortify their resolve. A shell exploded beneath his horse's head before he could finish his speech. The shell "exploded" wrote Mark Cooper, "totally hiding him [Major Cooper] and the horse in a cloud of dust and earth." John and Mark Cooper stood alongside their infantry companies only a few feet away. Had their brother died? As the dust cleared, Thomas Cooper spurred the nervous horse forward and raised his sword as if to challenge the federal battery who had fired the shell. Under Cooper's leadership, the 8th Georgia Infantry Regiment reformed their lines on Henry Hill, helping to halt the federal advance in the area of the battlefield.

During the fighting, John Cooper received two musket ball wounds in his knee and thigh. The severely wounded Cooper nevertheless urged his men forward until a commanding officer ordered him to retire from the field. His bravery under fire did not escape the attention of his men, who after the battle and for subsequent decades recalled their commander's epic courage. As Cooper lay on an improvised stretcher awaiting transport, he told passing men to fight "for your country, my boys. For your country. For your country."

The diary of George Barnsley provides an excellent account of the experiences of a Cass County private caught up in the whirlwind of events that surrounded the First Battle of Manassas. While Barnsley grew up in an elite household and enjoyed greater educational opportunities than all but a few Cass Countians, he, like most local soldiers, lacked any military experience. For these men, the first battles of the war were a time of exhilaration and fear. Barnsley's writings provide a glimpse into how many soldiers would have experienced "seeing the elephant" for the first time. "All I recollect" wrote Barnsley, "is that we came after a long march into a large old field, and we rushed up a small hill." As Barnsley moved up the hill, the unit was greeted by the sound of federal artillery shells bursting high above their heads. The sound of the cannon "aroused" George's "enthusiasm and energy." Barnsley recalled how Bartow rode on a white horse in front of the ranks in defiance of the federal cannons. He was inspired to move forward because Bartow "was not afraid." As he steadily moved forward, Barnsley remembered how his father had told him that when in battle "to keep your powder dry and trust in the Lord." Shells landed around the unit, creating small holes that they had to climb in and out of. For the first time, fear crept into Barnsley's mind: "I confess that I did wish that I was a ground-squirrel, or a possum so I could get into that hole." Those fears, however, proved fleeting as he became "baptized" under fire. In later years, he proclaimed that after those initial moments of doubt that he "never had any more fear, keeping cool and in some [illegible] way enjoying the sport or excitement" of engaging in battle.[47]

After falling back due to the constant barrage of "six guns in the front," George came upon a thicket of young pines and blackberry bushes. Still hungry, Barnsley and others grabbed handfuls of blackberries as their lines moved directly through the bushes. The unit then proceeded to move up a steep incline. "I remember being much amused at Schofield, who was in the rank ahead of me," he recalled. While hurrying up the slope, he stepped several times on the back of Schofield's heels. Annoyed by Barnsley's repeated missteps, Schofield "became angry and still advancing turned his head and shouted to me that if I trod on his heels again he would knock me down with the butt of his gun."[48]

Soon thereafter Barnsley and his unit encountered an "old sedge field" that had a split rail fence running across its length. Having moved up into the front ranks of his advancing unit, Barnsley was among the first soldiers to run into this fence. Barnsley dropped his gun and began to disassemble the fence. Before he could remove a single rail, the ranks of men behind him pushed forward causing Barnsley to tumble head first over the fence into a thick patch of thorny briars. He struggled to emerge from the briars. After rejoining his ranks, he still had to climb over the same fence that he had minutes ago tried to tear down. After getting one leg over the thigh high fence, a "short, chunky, red-faced ... good [natured man] we all called 'Coon Mitchell'" climbed onto the same rail Barnsley was attempting to cross. Mitchell's weight caused the split rail to break, which in turn made Barnsley fall backward yet again into a patch of briars. Mitchell also fell into the patch. During the fall, he scraped his head, causing it bleed profusely. Dazed and unaware of what had occurred, Mitchell stood up and began shouting that he had been hit. As Barnsley lay in the patch for the second time in less than ten minutes, he laughed aloud as Mitchell scurried about thinking that he had been wounded by a Yankee rifle.[49]

Once Barnsley caught up with his unit, he finally saw the enemy standing in line some fifty yards away. For the first time in the war, Barnsley fired his weapon toward the enemy. Remembering his drill instruction, he fired his weapon while in a kneeling position. After firing, he laid flat on his back along the ground while he reloaded before again returning to a kneeling position. At a range of fifty yards, even Barnsley's old smoothbore musket proved capable of damaging the enemy line. His gun's barrel became increasingly hot as Barnsley fired numerous rounds.[50]

Barnsley remembered the first federal soldier that he knowingly killed. The enemy began to advance upon his position. A split rail fence stood between the Union and Confederate lines. Barnsley watched as a big Union soldier grabbed hold of the rail fence and pushed it into the ground. As that soldier crossed over the rails, now lying on the ground Barnsley aimed "at a bright brass button on his bluecoat" and fired. "There were others shooting," he recalled, "but I think I killed him." As he reloaded his musket, he shouted to the men in his unit "boys I got one anyway." Suddenly, he realized that he was alone. The unit had fallen back while he had been preoccupied with shooting the large enemy soldier. Barnsley quickly jumped to his feet and began sprinting toward the retreating unit's lines that were now several hundred yards away. Along the way, he ran into an old friend who had frequently dined with he and his family at Woodlands, Jett Howard, the son of Reverend Charles W. Howard, one of Godfrey Barnsley's closest friends. Howard needed Barnsley's assistance carrying their "badly wounded" colonel back to their lines. The men used Barnsley's gun to carry the wounded colonel to safety. They loaded the colonel on top of the gun and picked him up and carried him by each man lifting one end of the weapon. Barnsley carried the musket from its stock while Howard carried the barrel end. When the two soldiers dropped the colonel within their lines, they learned that Barnsley had left the weapon loaded and cocked to fire. The soldiers had carried the colonel through a dense thicket. Barnsley realized that he "might have shot Jett if a twig or briar had caught and pulled the trigger."[51]

Jett escaped unharmed but would not escape the battle unscathed. Minutes after the two friends rejoined their unit, "Jett got a ball and fell backwards." Barnsley wanted to stay with his friend, but Jett told him to continue moving forward. As he moved onward, he encountered a deadly cross fire directed from two Yankee lines. "It was not from any bravery or foolhardiness on my part," remembered Barnsley, "that I walked through this cross-fire of musket balls and cannon balls. The fact was I had lost all consciousness of danger. I suppose from physical fatigue." His officers informed him that he "had to win the fight or die." During the battle, Barnsley lost all sense of self. His dire hunger and fatigue that he had bitterly complained about hours prior to the fight had vanished. As he followed orders on that day, he felt as if he "were treading on air." Barnsley daydreamed about dying in battle in service to his country. Those moments propelled him forward for he knew how proud his family, community, and nation would be if he should per chance fall in battle. Barnsley always remembered Manassas as the single greatest adventure of his life.[52]

The Confederate victory at the First Battle of Manassas had a profound impact on the country. During the battle, the Federal army suffered 2,393 dead, wounded, and missing soldiers compared to Confederate losses of 1,969 men. To the Confederates, their display of military might proved their assumptions that northerners were inferior fighters. The defeat spread a lingering sense of inferiority among the Federal army. Cass Countians cheered news of the victory. The same church bells that had rang months before announcing secession sounded again in celebration of the battle.[53]

The following day, the army transported John Cooper to a temporary hospital set-up in the Culpeper, Virginia county courthouse. While recovering, he received the rank of major for his courage in battle. Initially, physicians informed his family that his condition would gradually improve even to the point that he might return to active military duty. Upon receiving word of John's wound, Mark and Sophronia Cooper, his parents, and Hattie Cooper, his wife, left their Holly Springs home bound for Virginia. There, the concerned parents stayed at John's bedside. During those moments, his father prayed for his son's recovery. His prayers went unanswered as John's condition worsened due to mounting internal infections. John died on September 6, 1861, with his parents, wife, and brothers at his bedside.

Hattie returned home a twenty-four-year-old widow with two small children and pregnant with her third. The exuberance of John's departure only a few months prior had disappeared. She remained haunted by his sudden death. She had been assured that he would not die. After all, he was an upstanding Christian man, and those kind of men did not die young. While recuperating in the Confederate hospital, John had experienced a religious reawakening. During his prayers and conversations with Hattie, he expressed an interest in becoming a preacher if only God allowed for him to recover from his wounds. The two planned to return home to Cass County and build a church. His death ended those dreams. On October 31, 1861, Hattie gave birth to her third and last of John Frederick's children. She named the boy Frederick after his fallen father.[54]

Anxiety followed the First Battle of Manassas as Cass County families awaited word regarding their loved ones. On July 22, Charles W. Howard rushed to the Kingston Post Office hoping to find his copy of the Charleston *Mercury* waiting. On receiving the paper, Howard poured through the newspaper searching for any mention regarding Bartow's regiment. Howard cried upon reading a report that the regiment had been nearly annihilated. The hundreds of miles that separated Howard from his son Jett never seemed as great as on that day. As Howard returned to his home at Spring Bank, he desperately wanted to go to Virginia and find his son. Seeking a companion for the voyage, Howard sent Godfrey Barnsley a hastily written note via a slave courier. From Howard's message, Barnsley first learned of the regiment's destruction. Howard offered to take Barnsley along with him. While they were gone, Howard's wife would remain at Spring Place in order to tend to Barnsley's daughter Julia and her young nephew Forrest. Barnsley too grew concerned about the fate of his two sons, but unlike the always emotional Howard, he tended to make decisions based purely upon logic. Barnsley declined Howard's kind offer in favor of waiting a few more days and seeing what news might arrive from either of his sons.[55]

Two days later, Barnsley received a letter from his son George, informing him that both he and Lucien had survived the battle. George's letter painted a triumphant picture of the recent Confederate victory. During the battle, George and a group of others had helped a wounded colonel receive medical attention that saved his life. George saw Bartow fall while in front of his regiment leading them forward. The death and carnage of battle surprised George, but overall, his letter glorified the war and his actions. He proudly told his father that he believed that he had killed a Yankee while in battle. The letter also contained mention of the wound received by Jett Howard. Barnsley, unsure of whether or not Charles W. Howard had learned of his son's wound, quickly boarded a horse-drawn carriage headed for the neighboring Spring Bank. Whether or not Howard had previously learned of Jett's wound prior to Barnsley's arrival remains unknown, but soon after hearing of his son's injury, Howard made arrangements to travel to Virginia to be by his son's bedside.

The Confederate victory at Manassas bolstered local morale. Newspaper accounts of the victory reflected the confidence that the Confederacy held in the summer of 1861. While the battle instilled a degree of confidence and bravado among county residents, the events that transpired following the battle tempered the celebration. Critics such as Godfrey Barnsley and Mark Cooper believed that the inept Confederate government and military had bungled a once-in-a-lifetime opportunity to capture the Federal capital, Washington, D.C.

Surviving records created by members of the Barnsley family provide a window through which the wartime lives of Cass County elite households can be viewed. The Barnsleys were far from a representative example of the typical local household. They were wealthy slaveholders who had traveled widely prior to the war. However, by 1861 the family fortune had declined sharply due to the start of the war as well as a number of financial reverses during the late 1850s. The Barnsleys' story tells us much about how the war impacted the households from which Confederate soldiers came. Their story also tells us a lot about how the household roles of elite women changed when most of the men in the family left to fight. As early as July 1861, members of the Barnsley household began expressing mounting frustrations created by their prolonged physical separation. With George and Lucien Barnsley serving in the 8th Georgia Infantry Regiment, their sister Julia was left at Woodlands along with her father Godfrey, her adopted son Forrest, and the plantation's slave population. Godfrey proved to be an astute businessman but a poor plantation manager. He grew tired of the daily details of managing such a large estate. Godfrey would rather work in the garden pruning his beloved roses and dreaming of his deceased wife than supervising his slaves constructing fences or gathering the harvest.

To make matters worse, Godfrey spent most of the summer in bed due to a debilitating cough, which had prevented him from doing various plantation tasks. In July, shortly before the First Battle of Manassas, Julia Barnsley wrote to her brother George explaining her poor circumstances. "I am sorry to say Papa is quite sick," wrote Julia, "and I am alone. . . . The Howards have turned the cold shoulder to my repeated invitations but they ignore me. They are so gay."[56]

The Howard family had maintained a long relationship with the Barnsleys. They lived in nearby Spring Bank only a few miles from Woodlands. Julia had once been a student at Charles W. Howard's school. During the antebellum period, the Howard and Barnsley families regularly dined with one another. Alone and weary from her extra duties, Julia needed the familiar interaction with the Howard family in order to release some of her pent-up anxieties. The Howard family, however, had their own struggles to bear and could not spare much time with Julia. They spent hours instead working their own plantation now that their son Jett was in the army. Charles had his own slaves to manage and his own crops to harvest. Also, he lived in constant fear that something might happen to his son. He spent hours traveling to and from the Kingston Post Office hoping to receive a letter or news about his son's condition. The war, even during its earliest phases, had already isolated many individuals from one another who had in previous years enjoyed the constant presence of friends and family members. Extended absences of friends and family created a sense of isolation from their local communities and the war in general. Julia certainly confronted bouts of depression during this period as she watched her life suddenly transform from that of a local socialite to that of an aging spinster. She needed help. Her letters repeatedly asked for assistance from her neighbors and brothers serving in the military. Unfortunately for Julia, they, like her, were preoccupied with adjusting to their new lives, lives that had been transformed by the war.

When the fall of 1861 came, it would be one of the first times since Godfrey Barnsley had constructed Woodlands that he remained in Bartow County during the winter. Due to her father's ambivalence toward managing the plantation, Julia assumed the daily duties of plantation management. Those duties included ordering supplies for the slave and white population such as food, tools, and clothing. Without the assistance of an overseer, Julia coordinated the work schedules of the plantation's slave population. She decided whether the slaves would spend the day mending fences or working in the fields and if the slaves needed to split up into small groups so that each task could be completed simultaneously. More importantly, Julia inspected their work to ensure that the slaves were indeed completing their assigned tasks and not just idle now that the plantation lacked any strong white male presence. While Godfrey signed the checks, balanced the plantation ledger, and negotiated prices with both slaveholders and markets, Julia worked to prevent Woodlands' decline.

In addition to her increased plantation duties, Julia faced mounting domestic responsibilities. With her brothers serving in the military, it became her assumed duty to sew their Confederate uniforms. During the antebellum period, Julia might have hired a local tailor to complete this task or perhaps used one of the plantation's domestic slaves. During the war, the local tailors had more orders than they could handle. At night, when most of the other plantation and domestic tasks had been completed, Julia sat down and worked on her beloved brothers' uniforms. The work was slow. The materials required were difficult to purchase since the demand for wool cloth had increased sharply during the summer months. With all of her other duties, Julia lacked the time and energy needed to complete their uniforms.

In northern Virginia, Lucien and George anxiously awaited their uniforms. Many of their fellow comrades of the 8th Georgia Infantry Regiment had already received theirs. As their anxiety increased, so did their letters home to Julia. Neither of the brothers seemed to realize or perhaps did not care about their sister's increased workload. They assumed that their father was taking care of Woodlands and that, as in olden times, Julia spent her days working in the garden.

From Julia's perspective, their repeated questions concerning the completion date of their uniforms wreaked of ingratitude. Their letters informed her of how grand it was to be defending their home and family and how fortunate she was to have such honorable men fighting for such a noble cause. Sometime in late October, George's repeated requests provoked Julia's wrath. George had wondered why his uniform had not arrived when he had asked his dear sister to complete the work several months beforehand. In her response, Julia made it clear just how displeased she was with her brothers and attempted to inform them exactly what her current situation resembled. "I will try to send for your clothes," wrote Julia. "Don't blame me for not having sent them, as I have done all I can for you and am still doing everything that a person can do."[57]

After reading several of Julia's letters written during the month of October, her brother Lucien decided that it might be time to alleviate her stressful situation. He worried that her health could not withstand the constant workload required to manage a plantation. He considered hiring an overseer or some white laborers to help manage the plantation but soon realized that finding someone would be difficult due to the war and that the addition of another stranger into the Woodlands household might only create additional problems for Julia. Lucien's solution was to convince his brother George to resign from the military and return home. On November 4, 1861, the same day that Julia wrote to George describing her pitiful circumstances, Lucien suggested to George in a letter that "if you can stay at home I think you ought to as Pa had no one there. I can fight."[58] In Lucien's mind, this seemed like an honorable solution. As long as one of the brothers remained in the military, no one in the community could dare say that Barnsley family was scared to fight. Once George returned home, he could relieve his exhausted father and sister from their tiresome daily chores. George could hire and manage additional white and enslaved laborers to work at Woodlands. Meanwhile, Lucien would continue serving in Virginia and upholding the family's sense of duty and honor.[59]

Lucien's plan failed to gain George's support. During the antebellum period, George had made it abundantly clear that he had little intention of ever assuming Woodlands' daily management. He did not want to be a farmer but instead desired to live in a city or at least a large village where he could enjoy various cultural events and be around a wide array of people. He longed for Savannah, his birthplace and where most of the Barnsley's elite social connections remained. Woodlands to George seemed like a million miles away from those ambitions. Moreover, he did not want to be seen as a coward for returning home while his brother remained at the front. George rejected Lucien's offer and informed his sister that he intended to stay and fight regardless of his brother's wishes.[60]

Tragedy meanwhile struck the Cooper family again in late December of 1861. While examining a potential place for winter quarters, Colonel Thomas Cooper's horse was startled by an unknown source and ran wild through the dense thicket with its rider in tow. Lucien Barnsley of the 8th Georgia Infantry Regiment watched the tragedy unfold before his horrified eyes. Cooper fell from the "very fiery" steed striking his head against a tree. "He was never conscious," wrote Lucien, "after he received the blow. Although we all more or less disliked him we must say we will miss him."[61] Another soldier, Tom Wragg, wrote that Cooper "was an awful sight to look at. His face was so swollen that you could not recognize him at all."[62] Cooper died shortly after being transported back to camp. His promotion to the rank of colonel was opposed by the majority of the regiment. Most believed that he was too inexperienced to command such a large body. His premature death, while sad and tragic, came as a bit of welcomed relief to many of the regiment's soldiers.

At Etowah, Mark Cooper grieved the loss of a second son who died in Confederate service. Of the three sons Mark Cooper proudly sent off to serve in the Confederate military during the spring of 1861, only one remained by the end of the year. Anxious to ensure that Mark E. Cooper, the sole surviving son, would not suffer the same fate as his brothers, Cooper petitioned Confederate President Jefferson Davis for his son's discharge from active military duty.[63]

The death of local men at the Battle of Manassas inspired other local soldiers to fight bravely in honor of their fallen comrades. John Brantley, a private serving in the Bartow Yankee Killers stationed in Richmond, responded in writing to a letter penned by his father in which the elder Brantley advised his son to remain steadfast in front of the enemy. The son replied, "Be assured that I will never disgrace you by acting the coward for if I fall in battle I will fall with my face towards the foe." At that time, wounded Confederate soldiers had been transported to Richmond and placed in buildings and home across the city. Brantley saw firsthand men who returned from battle mangled by bullets. Such sights inspired Brantley to make similar sacrifices when it was his unit's turn to fight.[64]

While most locals supported the Confederacy, small numbers of Unionists existed in Cass County, especially in the Appalachian subregion. During a meeting of a Home Guard unit being organized in the village of Fairmount in neighboring Gordon County, L. R. Ramsaur notified Governor Brown about the "existence of some things in this District." Part of this Home Guard district overlapped into northeastern Bartow County near the village of Pine Log. In that village, Ramsaur reported, lived a man who stood opposed to "our southern cause." This unidentified man had a son who had volunteered for Confederate military service. After receiving instruction, the son obtained a brief furlough that allowed him time to travel home and be with his family before finally being assigned to a post. When the son arrived home, the Unionist father supposedly told him how disappointed he was that the son had chosen to volunteer. After a brief argument, the father ordered the son to leave his home and never to return as long as he wore a Confederate uniform. The soldier went to the local justice of the peace and requested his aid in calming down his father. When the two men returned to the home, the father walked out onto the porch armed with a loaded double barrel shotgun. The father ordered his son and the justice of the peace off of his property. He chided the justice of the peace for having the nerve to interfere in a family squabble that was none of the government's business. The justice of the peace swore that he would soon return with some men and arrest the father.[65]

According to Ramsaur, news of the old man's impending arrest spread throughout the countryside. By the next morning, Unionist sympathizers in the area had banded together willing to defend the old man from any attempts made by local Confederates to seize him or his property. "His friends," reported Ramsaur, "now swear if he is arrested they will fight for him." The Home Guard commander then informed Brown that the local Unionists had held secret meetings to discuss a strategy to resist conscription. Even worse than evading the draft, the Unionists, according to him, intended to arm local slaves.[66] If these Unionists remained, declared Ramsaur, they would either join the Federal army or sabotage the Confederate war effort. The Home Guard unit contemplated arresting the suspected Unionist leader, but such an action was prevented because the guard feared that the Unionist forces far outnumbered their meager unit. Ramsaur wanted Brown to dispatch a large number of state troops into the area and arrest all known and suspected traitors. Brown ignored Ramsaur's request.[67]

Cass County's decision to rename itself in honor of Colonel Francis S. Bartow shows the county's level of Confederate nationalism. In November, Cass County representatives in the Georgia General Assembly Samuel Sheats and Warren Akin introduced a bill to change the county's name. "Deeming it the duty," they wrote, "it is always the pleasure of a brave and free people to perpetuate the memory of those who have fallen upon the field of battle in defense of the honor, rights, and liberties of our common country." The bill also changed the name Cassville to Manassas.[68]

Yet by the end of 1861, some of the exuberance of war had been blunted by its reality. Men seeking an adventure of a lifetime and an opportunity to display their manhood by defending their homes had marched off to war and soon discovered that war was not as glamorous as they had once believed. Despite fading dreams of a bloodless revolution, locals remained committed to the Confederate military and government and all that its independence represented. The bonds of whiteness that had existed during the antebellum period remained largely intact as rich and poor white men struggled to defend the South's interests against what turned out to be a dogged foe. White men showed their support by joining the military, fighting in battles, working for Confederate industries, planting food crops for civilian and military use, and through a number of actions that held out hope for the preservation of a society they believed faced possible eradication if their dreams of victory went unfulfilled. The years 1862 and 1863 tested local support for the Confederate government as a series of external and internal pressures undermined the war effort and created great skepticism among even the most devoted rebel partisans. Few Bartow Countians would have predicted at the end of 1861 that their worst days lie ahead.

CHAPTER
4

THE LONG WAIT, 1862–1863

Lucien Barnsley volunteered in the spring of 1861 to defend southern rights and to experience some adventure. After nine months of war, his initial zeal had faded. In January 1862, he wrote to his brother, "I hope that this confounded war will stop soon."[1] In 1862 and 1863, the Confederacy's failure to achieve victory resulted in the unexpectedly prolonged absences of more than 2,000 white men from Bartow County. The Confederacy's survival depended on maximizing the number of white men serving in the army. The government's demands for greater numbers and longer enlistments placed an enormous strain on civilians. Internally, uncertainty spread throughout the populace as citizens and soldiers alike combated separation anxiety, material shortages, increased governmental intrusions, death and disease, and contentious slaves. Externally, repeated military setbacks—particularly in the western theater—led some to question the government's viability and many to wonder when federal soldiers would show up on their doorstep. By the winter of 1863–1864, Bartow Countians had good reason to doubt the Confederacy's viability, yet despite these problems Confederate support remained high locally, especially among families living in the Great Appalachian Valley and Piedmont subregions.

Inhabitants in Bartow County's three distinctive geographic subregions (Great Appalachian Valley, Piedmont, and Appalachian) responded differently to the problems that beset the Confederacy between 1862 and 1863. The existence of an increasingly vocal number of Unionists in the Appalachian subregion began to concern Confederate partisans in the neighboring Piedmont and Great Appalachian Valley areas. The situation in Appalachian communities such as Pine Log and Wofford's Crossroads resembled northeast Georgia mountain counties such as Fannin and White where local Unionists resisted Confederate authority. In Bartow County, elites living in the Great Appalachian

Valley and Piedmont equated Appalachian men who had avoided Confederate military service with bands of vagabonds, robbers, and thieves that roamed the countryside from their base of operations deep within the county's mountain foothills. While local Unionists remained a minority in an otherwise pro-Confederate community, their existence concerned local partisans and contributed to growing fears that home front violence and lawlessness might escalate the longer the war lasted.

As the war entered its second year, a majority of Bartow County, as well as northwest Georgian, civilians and soldiers remained committed to the Confederacy. With more than 2,000 local white men serving in the Confederate military, approximately 75 percent of men in Bartow between the ages of 18 and 35 were in the army. An additional 10–12 percent of men between 18 and 35 who remained at home had received some form of exemption because they were employed in industries such as railroads and iron production that supported the Confederate war effort. While a handful of soldiers deserted the ranks, about 97 percent remained.[2] Some chanted "rich man's war, poor man's fight," but rich and poor alike served in the army, protested various government intrusions, and suffered from the physical and psychological travails of war.

Nonetheless, the prolonged absence of many husbands, fathers, sons, and brothers threatened to undermine local Confederate support. Lila Chunn expressed such concerns. Her husband Willie's absence altered her mood. Her mind wandered throughout the day as she dwelled upon past events or imagined what he was doing at that moment while the routine chores that accompanied domestic life went unattended.

Most afternoons, Chunn spent hours walking along the several paths that encircled her Cassville home. Years ago, Willie had courted her there. She now recalled the way he looked at her during those youthful days, as well as how much she anticipated those planned encounters. "I think of you and sigh for your company," she wrote. As she allowed her mind to slip into the past, Chunn grasped the thin air where her husband's hand had once been. "I want to take your hand as I used to do." If only, the war was over.[3]

Lila Chunn, daughter of a Great Appalachian Valley slaveholder and wife of a slaveholding attorney, experienced a different war than women from less privileged backgrounds. While Chunn eventually volunteered to work as a nurse in the various hospitals that operated in Cassville and Kingston, her ability to do so was afforded by the continued labor her family received from their slaves. Poorer women had little time to dream away afternoons in the garden missing their husbands. In the Appalachian subregion, a large number of households struggled to produce enough food to feed themselves prior to the war. While many men in this area remained at home during the war, significant numbers whether by choice or force entered Confederate service leaving their wives, children, and elder family members at home to plant and harvest crops or locate cash paying jobs to make up for the lost income. Whereas valley women such as Chunn often published pleas in local newspapers asking "ladies" to donate goods and time to provide relief efforts for Confederate soldiers, poorer Appalachian women neither had the time nor surplus resources to give. Unfortunately these poor women left behind few records. What we know about them in Bartow County largely derives from their absence from ladies aid society rosters and an occasional postwar claims commission or pension application narrative.[4]

Other family concerns further challenged local Confederate support. The 1870 Federal Census reveals that the county experienced a "baby boom" period between 1861 and 1864.[5] Most of these children arrived during their father's absence. News of a newborn child stirred emotions among soldiers. For William Chunn, remaining in the army while his newborn child slept several hundred miles away required all of the loyalty that he could muster. Already remorseful that he could not see his beloved wife more frequently, the thought of having a child at home that he had never seen reduced him to tears. During lonely hours spent in the doldrums of camp life, he dreamed of home and imagined his daughter's face.[6]

The death of a newborn baby was a routine part of mid-nineteenth-century life. Local cemeteries such as those in Kingston and Euharlee served as constant reminders of the fragility of life. Most family cemetery plots contained a headstone bearing a lamb that represented the death of an infant child. As several letters indicate, the wives of absent soldiers frequently refrained from naming their newborn child until several months had passed or upon the arrival home of the child's father. Until such time passed, the newborn was simply referred to as "the baby."

Kingston resident William Hardin never saw his infant daughter. His wife delivered the child after his 1863 capture aboard a blockade runner outside of Nassau. Hardin spent the remainder of the war at Fort Warren in Boston, where he corresponded with his wife and family. The news of his daughter's birth lifted his sagging spirits. He remained hopeful that Federal officials would exchange him soon allowing his return home to see his daughter. The exchange never came, however, and in the fall of 1864, Hardin's daughter died of fever.[7]

In 1862, soldiers and civilians came to the realization that the war would last far longer than they had originally anticipated. "It seems that we constantly have something to mourn over," wrote Lila Chunn. "Our reverses and misfortunes are becoming frequent." Likewise, Julia Barnsley believed that "our darkest hours are yet to come. . . . Papa known for a certainty that we will be whipped at Richmond." By early summer, Godfrey Barnsley had lost all hope that a decisive victory would be achieved. "The loss of New Orleans is disastrous. . . . There seems to have been a great want of energy and industry on our side. . . . I often think the War may destroy all I have accomplished."[8]

The attitudes displayed by Bartow Countians between 1862 and 1863 did not reflect a disdain for combat or for the Confederate government but rather a mounting frustration compounded by cold, hunger, disease, military discipline, and loneliness. The thrill of battle remained a popular topic for soldiers. Letters written following a battle were much longer in length and detail than ones penned during periods of prolonged encampment, resembling those written following the Battle of First Manassas. Upon receiving one such letter, a father congratulated his son for "escaping being killed or wounded," for in the future, such tests would "silence envious tongues."[9]

Inadequate supplies of food exacerbated a soldier's susceptibility to war weariness. Soldiers and civilians alike carped about both the quantity and quality of food. Warren Akin, a prominent local politician, informed Governor Brown that Charles Howard's regiment, the 63rd Georgia Infantry, lacked sufficient foodstuffs due to the inefficiency of the state government. In their tattered condition, he warned, the soldiers could not withstand a fight against the Union army.[10] Hungry, a soldier serving in Phillip's Legion told his family that he could not afford the additional supplies of rations that were available in Richmond due to extreme inflation. He "[hoped] the government [would] act at an early day and impress all surplus corn in GA." This action, he believed, would curtail inflation and greedy speculators seeking to profit from hoarding agricultural products.[11] A local officer serving in the Army of Tennessee likewise grew increasingly frustrated that many of his requisitions for additional food went largely ignored due to "bureaucratic red tape."[12] Most soldiers looked toward home for relief. They asked family members to forward crates of biscuits and preserves that would supplement their meager diet of coarsely ground corn meal and fat portions of salt pork. Few camp events made a soldier lonelier than when his comrades received a box from home while he received nothing. Soldiers from poorer non-elite households likely received few packages from home.[13]

While many blamed the government, the blockade, or the quartermaster department, the conduct of soldiers also created problems with obtaining enough food. Shortly before the start of the Peninsula Campaign, the 18th Georgia Infantry Regiment became the target of a series of pranks orchestrated by the 4th Texas Infantry Regiment. While stationed at Camp Wigfall, located outside of Fredericksburg, the Texans raided the Georgians' camp while the men were away on picket duty. They stripped the camp bare, stealing anything that was not nailed down. Colonel William T. Wofford, commander of the 18th Georgia, reported the incident to Major General John B. Hood, who soon thereafter ordered the Texans to return the stolen items. Several weeks later, as the 18th Georgia endured brutal conditions during a forced march, the men grew increasingly angry that the Texans still neglected to return the regiment's cooking utensils. As the regiment huddled around their camp fires trying to protect themselves from a cold rain and to secure the first hot meal they had in days, frustrated and hungry, the Georgians according to Gerald Smith "improvised by mixing dough in bark trays and cooking it on boards leaned against the fire."[14]

Colonel Wofford exerted great energy to prevent his men from stealing. His policies fostered resentment among some 18th Georgia soldiers who passively watched as soldiers from the 4th and 5th Texas Infantry regiments freely stole from local farms and subsequently taunted the Georgians with their captured harvest. Finally, even the stern condemnation of a highly respected commanding officer could not curtail foraging. At the conclusion of the Peninsula Campaign, it became apparent that many of the 18th Georgia had indeed helped themselves to an assortment of stolen goods. Fearful that such behavior might embitter people on the home front, the commander purchased large quantities of interest bearing bonds, the proceeds of which were used to support indigent soldier families who he considered susceptible to theft.[15]

Foraging created a strong sense of guilt and remorse among some Bartow County soldiers. Most soldiers decided to steal only after serious deliberation. During the Battle of First Manassas, Private George Barnsley of the 8th Georgia worried that he might be executed by his commanding officer after commandeering some honey from a local farmer's property. As a practical joke, members of his company had prodded the young private into believing that stealing a small portion of honey would not seriously damage neither the property owner nor the soldier's soul. Plagued by guilt and the stinging of hundreds of angry bees, the reward for his dubious efforts proved bittersweet.[16] Likewise, Noble Brooks confessed his wrong doings while attempting to offer some degree of justification: "No telling what a hungry man will do, Esau like, he will sell his very birthright for a mess of pottage. I thought I never would take anything, but I pressed a pint of good milk, yesterday for dinner from an old cow that came up into camp."[17]

Camp conditions varied widely depending on where a Bartow County soldier was stationed. John Brantley's unit remained in Savannah throughout 1862. There, he told a concerned sister, "I have no doubt . . . I have gained several pounds." In addition to their standard rations, Brantley received regular supplies of fresh oysters and fish as well as baked goods and smoked meats from nearby Savannah families. Brantley joked that if he lost weight here it would only be because he was too lazy to cook.[18]

The lack of respect that many soldiers held for private property deeply disturbed many morally conscious soldiers. While serving in east Tennessee, William Chunn witnessed the devastation that both Union and Confederate soldiers inflicted upon vast amounts of personal property. "Never did I see such recklessness in people and government," wrote Chunn, "while on our tour in East TN I was compelled to witness a destruction of private property that made my heart turn sick and involuntarily loathe such an age and such a government." The government he was referring to was his own. In an effort to punish Unionists in the area, Confederate soldiers committed numerous criminal acts against "unarmed civilians." They destroyed farms, stole cattle, and assaulted women. Chunn pitied these people who seemed trapped between two armies, unsure of whom to turn to for aid. In subsequent letters home, he increasingly became concerned that the Confederacy would indeed lose the war because so many of its combatants had ignored God's supreme authority. He also grew in his conviction that one day soon a similar fate might befall his own family. If it could happen in east Tennessee, he wrote, there was little to prevent such atrocities from being committed at home.[19]

While the utter disregard for personal property troubled some soldiers, the absence of proper clothing also affected morale. Local women exerted a great deal of energy providing clothing for their soldiers. Their best efforts failed to overcome statewide cloth shortages. Desperate for help, local women petitioned the governor for aid, but their requests went unanswered. In October of 1862, the "ladies of Bartow County" tried to provoke a response from Brown. "The intelligence which we receive of the destitution of our soldiers in Virginia appalls us. They are our husbands, sons, brothers and friends. We suffer when we know they suffer unable to help since stony hearted owners of factories placed materials of clothing beyond our reach. We call upon the governor to protect us from unnatural extortion by seizing the cotton and wool factories of the state, and working them for the public benefit." The petition contained the signatures of 157 ladies and "would have been signed by all the women of Bartow Co. had it been possible to reach them all."[20]

As expected, most of the women who signed the petition were from slaveholding households. Roughly 85 percent of the women who signed the petition lived in a household that owned at least one slave. The group's leaders belonged to the more affluent planter class. Consequently, all of the women identified here lived in either the Piedmont or Great Appalachian Valley subregions. No woman from the Appalachian subregion signed the petition. Like many newspaper advertisements urging "ladies" to organize aid for Confederate soldiers, the petition also referred to this group of women as "ladies"— an indicator that beyond a shared gender these women saw themselves as representative of a better class of women.[21]

As some elite women petitioned the state to organize relief efforts, other women began letting their husbands in the army know about the declining situation at home. Like many soldiers, private George W. Carter, Co. A 23rd Georgia Infantry Regiment, received troubling letters from his wife. She complained bitterly about the lack of provisions in the area as well as the uncontrolled inflation. Without salt, she warned, the family might have a hard time making it through next winter. Theft had become commonplace. "I wish you could send me a repeater," she wrote, "to kill tories and niggers with I think they was kild this war would stop."[22]

Georgia newspapers echoed Carter's fears that "tories" might prey upon Confederate families. The Rome *Tri-Weekly Courier* printed a number of editorials in support of Confederate conscription measures as a means of decreasing the presence of "vagabonds, robbers, and country murderers" found in northwest Georgia. A large class of military age men, according to the editor, had remained at home in defiance of Confederate authority. Seeking to avoid conscription agents, these "vagabonds" fled to the woods and caves of the region seeking shelter. From these hidden locations these men struck out at night robbing local Confederate farms and generally creating panic among area residents.[23]

Unionists and men seeking to avoid conscription found refuge in Bartow County's Appalachian subregion. Here the densely wooded foothills and hidden caves shielded these men from capture. One such group inhabited a cave located near the small hamlet Pine Log. When Georgia militia entered the area intent on arresting the men, the group of "vagabonds" armed themselves and resisted arrest. These "tories," according to postwar Southern Claims Commission records, received support from likeminded farmers in the area who provided them with food, clothing, and information. Despite receiving reports from Confederate partisans that this group of "tories" presented a real threat to local security, Governor Joseph E. Brown failed to make a concentrated effort to halt their activities. As shown by Jonathan Sarris and Keith Bohannon, Brown believed that Unionists were more common in northeast Georgia and devoted a great deal of energy in those counties trying to preserve order. While the number of Unionists in northeast Georgia counties such as Fannin and White likely exceeded those found in Bartow, northwest Georgia Confederate partisans had a "tory" problem of their own.[24]

Locals also lived in constant fear of a possible slave rebellion. In 1861, Kingston residents had lynched a slave and a white man for allegedly conspiring to arm slaves. Rumors of distant slave violence spread throughout the county. George Carter, Co. A 23rd Georgia Infantry Regiment, reported to his father that "up in Tennessee 5 negroes kild a famley of white folks and they burned four of them and cut the other one up in to mins meat." The letter continued with a supposed conversation between Carter and a group of slaves who had entered his Confederate camp. The slaves, according to Carter, said "they would be able to waid through white mens blood to there knees for there freedom." Those same slaves ranaway that night in search of nearby Union lines. Heightened suspicions of slave conspiracies and tales of violent murders certainly heightened stress levels among Bartow County families.[25]

While the varying physical and emotional hardships experienced by Bartow Countians challenged Confederate support, other contributing factors such as the proximity of the war in relation to the home front created similar trials. The large numbers of convalescing soldiers sent home for medical care enabled family members to see the horrors of war firsthand. During the Battle of Fredericksburg, William H. Stiles Jr. received a life threatening wound to his right arm. The bullet smashed into his side with such force that it drove a toothbrush located in his breast pocket through his arm. For weeks, his life hung in the balance. Finally, officers granted Stiles permission to return home to the care of his mother. The long train ride from northern Virginia to Bartow County nearly killed the wounded soldier. Loaded into a drafty freight car that lacked any heating source, Stiles endured intense discomfort as his blood soaked dressings froze to his skin. By the time the train pulled into Cartersville, the young lieutenant had developed a severe cough that doctors worried might develop into pneumonia. Once home, Stiles recuperated under the constant care of his mother and the family physician. When naked, Stiles' right side seemed grossly out of proportion with his left side. His mother wrote that it was as if it had caved in. The family doctor told the patient that his "wound . . . is so wonderful not to have produced death, that he intends writing and publishing an account of it."[26]

Wounded soldiers affected more than kin as their numbers expanded. In January 1863, Confederate officials established hospitals in Cassville and Kingston. At Cassville, the army occupied the closed male and female colleges. Local hospital directors constantly searched for additional space due to the ever increasing number of sick and wounded. They easily found homes to use as temporary medical facilities since many residents had already left the county seeking refuge further south. As the county developed into a major medical center for the Army of Tennessee, locals grew concerned that the wounded would introduce epidemic diseases into their community. Several thousand soldiers received treatment in Kingston hospitals. Cassville's hospitals also treated large numbers of Confederates.[27]

During the winter of 1863, a smallpox epidemic broke out in Bartow County. The situation became so bad that Cassville resident Nathan Land commented that the presence of convalescing soldiers annoyed locals and caused depredations which encouraged many elite families to "refugee." By the late fall of 1863 he wrote, "many of our best citizens are selling out and leaving."[28]

Military conscription and increased governmental intrusions throughout portions of the county also challenged support for the Confederate government. Less than a year after the firing on Fort Sumter, some Bartow Countians began to reconsider whether or not Confederate military service served their best interests. Unionists and other disaffected people advised their friends and relatives to resist the temptation to enlist. Most of these individuals lived in the northeastern portions of the county in the Appalachian subregion. John Addington "advised [his] son to go north to the Union army." The son took heed and fled to east Tennessee where he promptly enlisted. Nathaniel Guyton likewise told his two sons not to enlist in the fall of 1861. Aware of rumors that the Confederate government would soon enact conscription, his sons decided to wait until agents forcibly enlisted them. Joel Maxwell's two sons enlisted despite his protests, and as early as the winter of 1861–1862, he began harboring draft evaders and deserters while vocally criticizing the state and national government. When conscription agents attempted to enlist David Mostetter, he informed them that he refused to "fight for a rich man's slaves." He managed to escape the draft by keeping a shotgun close by throughout the war.[29]

Confederate partisan newspapers in north Georgia painted a negative portrayal of Unionists that likely represented how many Confederate households viewed suspected "tories" in their communities. The Rome *Tri-Weekly Courier* described Unionists as "traitors to save their own property, the poor who have nothing to fight for, and the ignorant . . . tools of tyranny."[30] Similar editorials accused "tories" of harboring resentment toward their wealthier slaveholding neighbors.[31]

Local organizers of new military companies now struggled to fill their ranks because a large number of men had already volunteered. Some local leaders demanded that the state do more to enforce the Confederate conscription acts. Reverend Charles W. Howard recognized during the winter of 1862 that local support for the Confederate government had lost much of the momentum it had gained during the previous year. It seemed to him that all of those residents who supported the new government and the war had left the county to serve in the military. Those who remained at home, according to Howard, lacked the same zeal for war. In a letter written to Governor Joseph E. Brown, Howard expressed a sense of urgency due to local fears that an invasion by northern forces seemed imminent. Yet while invasion concerned him, he found the attitude of local residents more troubling. He complained to Brown that "a sad apathy" had spread among hundreds of local men who were of sound physical health and the appropriate age for military service but seemed intent on shirking military service.[32] The Rome *Tri-Weekly Courier* echoed his sentiments when its editors declared that "in every town and village in the Confederacy, there are 'gentlemen of leisure' who sit on the corners and stroll on the streets talking but doing nothing."[33]

As one of the county's most well-respected citizens, Howard hoped to use his popularity to raise an infantry company in response to Brown's call for thirty new units. He scoured the county searching for volunteers, only to discover to his chagrin that most men he encountered already belonged to one of several local militia units and therefore did not feel the need to volunteer for military service outside of their county. The local militia system, according to Howard, was "worse than a farce." County militia units met monthly for a few hours of drill instruction. Members frequently skipped meetings, and officials rarely punished these absentees. "If the enemy should reach Chattanooga & make a demonstration on this part of Georgia," worried Howard, "we are in the worst possible condition to meet them." Even if the Federals invaded, he believed most of the militia would remain at home content with "making money" and acting "as if no war existed."[34]

While recruiting volunteers, Howard grew especially disappointed with the large number of "young & middle aged men, who have land & negroes & who can leave their families in comfort," yet remained at home. "Few of this class have gone, unless they held an office," complained Howard. The state militia also contained a disproportionate number of officers. Howard advised Brown that if a draft was instituted that "[he] for one would be glad to see it confined to men, who return more than $500 worth of property." Few military aged poor men remained at home, and the minister empathized with the circumstances of their families. "The poor have already done their share. They refuse to do more until their richer neighbors do theirs." Howard thus advised Brown to resolve these problems and annihilate the hypocrisies of privilege by instituting a universal conscription law as soon as possible. Failure to do so would be a crippling blow to the state's future.[35]

Godfrey Barnsley supported conscription as well but increasingly believed that the Confederacy was doomed anyway due to a combination of internal and external factors. Internally, the planter grew impatient with local whites who had protested the draft chanting "rich man's war, poor man's fight": "There is a large party in this State, with the government at the head who are placing all the obstacles in their power in the way of Confederate conscription. ... We are ... under the rule ... of unprincipled demagogues and are not likely to gain much by secession. ... The troops have been poisoned by the insidious rumor that the poor are fighting the battles of the rich."[36] Mention of a "rich man's war, poor man's fight" angered Barnsley, whose two sons served in the 8th Georgia.[37]

Like Barnsley, Pierce Manning Butler Young, a Lieutenant Colonel serving in Cobb's Legion, applauded the Conscription Act's passage. Young claimed that Confederate soldiers supported the measure and believed that the addition of new recruits would help tip the scales in favor of a southern victory. "I begin to believe," he wrote his father, "that all the patriotism is in the army and very little out of it." Conscription, Young asserted, assured soldiers that the home front was willing to give their all to support the cause. He also argued that conscription might force men into the army who had previously wanted to do so but could not pry themselves away from their family farm. Such statements were easy for wealthy men such as Young to say. A member of a wealthy slaveholding family, Young could leave the family farm for years without a significant loss in production since slaves remained to do the work. Young could not understand why all southern men of military age did not sell their farms and elect for the glory of serving in the Confederate army. His writings shed light on the lack of empathy and understanding that many elite white men had for their poorer white neighbors. Young lived on a large family estate located on choice lands in the county's valley subregion. Most of his friends that had joined the Confederate army did so with an officer's commission or election. These men, like Young, could afford to enlist in part because their families owned slaves that would be expected to maintain the farm in their absence. Young's letters indicate that he had little connection with non-slaveholding families in the area and failed to see how military service might negatively impact a poorer soldier's family.[38]

Perhaps many non-elite soldiers, such as George Carter, serving in the Confederate army disliked the Conscription Act. In August 1862 Carter advised his Bartow County relatives to change the dates of birth for some of his male kin so that they would be too old to be forced into service. "I am not in favor," Carter wrote, "of this conscription bill all poor men has to go and rich and contemptuous speculators can hire substitutes and stay at home and impose on our families the very men that voted up this thing is the very men ain't going to fight." Carter closed by declaring that he could whip any man who might come to force any of his kin into the army.[39]

George Carter's writings reflects the tensions that existed among wealthy and poorer white men in the Georgia Piedmont. Carter and his kin lived in an area east of Cartersville where some men owned small farms but most worked as day laborers. Few of Carter's relatives owned any property. Most rented from local yeomen. On one hand, Carter blamed local elites for starting the war. He also saw them as doing less than their share of the fighting. On the other hand, Carter supported the Confederacy and expressed enormous satisfaction whenever his unit gave "the Yankees and good whipping." After volunteering to serve in the army in the spring of 1861, Carter remained in the army until his unit surrendered four years later. Carter, like many poor white soldiers, stayed because they believed in Confederate victory and feared the consequences of a Union victory. They also believed that no Confederate victory could be achieved without their support. Carter saw himself as an important cog in the Confederate war machine. The fact that he felt that many elite men had failed in their duty gave Carter, as well as other poor soldiers, great pride as well as a heightened sense of their superior masculine attributes.[40]

Other men in northwest Georgia, likely Unionists, resisted conscription by forming into armed groups that resisted Confederate agents and plundered pro-Confederate farms and households. In Cedartown, located in Polk County southwest of Bartow County, a band of armed men fired shots at Confederate conscription agents and pitched a skirmish when state militia moved into the area to halt their behavior. Meanwhile, across northwest Georgia men stole Confederate uniforms and robbed farms pretending to be conscription officers. Pro-Confederate households opened their doors to these disguised thieves who preyed upon their support for the war effort and made life generally anxious for those unsure of a Confederate officer's true identity. Such tactics were commonplace across north Georgia as Unionists and others who resisted Confederate authorities devised all sorts of devious methods.[41]

In Bartow County, the Civil War was both a rich and poor man's fight. While Reverend Charles W. Howard accused local elite of neglecting their duty to serve in the military, an abundance of available records indicate that by-and-large the local elite had made enormous sacrifices while supporting the Confederacy. Howard's frustrations likely stemmed from some of the men he encountered on farms located near his home Spring Bank, near Kingston. Some of the farmers in this area held Unionist loyalties throughout the war. Among those Unionists existed a small number of men who owned slaves. Howard, who prior to the war equated states' rights ideology with defending the natural order of white supremacy, likely could not understand how a slaveholder could not support the Confederacy. Often prone to exaggeration, a fault that his neighbor and friend Godfrey Barnsley privately complained about, Howard might have overstated the difficulties he experienced recruiting soldiers. Many of the young white men Howard would have encountered in either Kingston or Rome would have likely received some form of exemption from military service due to their employment in an industry considered vital to the Confederate war effort. Both Kingston and Rome were important rail centers that required white men to supervise freight and maintain locomotive engines. Outside of Kingston, there was a major salt peter cave that supplied the Confederacy with nitre used to produce gunpowder. This industry required a number of young white men to supervise its large slave force.[42] Meanwhile, Rome had developed into one of the Confederacy's critical manufacturing centers producing iron, wagons, and an assortment of military accouterments. Howard's claims that the war was becoming a "rich man's war, poor man's fight" likely stemmed from his lack of understanding of the Confederate war effort as a whole.

In 1862 and 1863, approximately 85 percent of all white households who owned slaves had at least one member of their family serving in the Confederate army or state militia. Some of those households paid dearly for their support. Mark A. Cooper, for example, lost two of his three sons in 1861. Likewise, John Addington's youngest son, William, died at the Battle of Fredericksburg. Joseph P. Burge of the 14th Georgia Infantry Regiment and son of prominent planter Nathaniel Burge died from exposure in the army in 1861. Thomas B. Connor of the 61st Georgia Infantry Regiment died at the Second Battle of Manassas. In sum, approximately 25–30 percent of all Bartow Countians who died while serving in the Confederate army belonged to a family who owned slaves. Large percentages of local elites served in the military thus ensuring that the war would not be a poor man's burden to bear alone but rather a white men's fight.[43]

In Bartow County, men of wealth and property also fought alongside rather than against their poorer neighbors. Local soldiers from elite backgrounds rarely deserted. Most who joined remained in the army either in the field or serving in some administrative capacity for the duration of the war. Conversely, dozens of elite soldiers resigned from the army; some hired substitutes; and even fewer signed the Union oath of allegiance. Most elite soldiers remained in the army until their unit officially surrendered, until they were furloughed due to disability or illness, or until their death. Soldiers from elite households comprised approximately 46 percent of Bartow County soldiers who surrendered as part of the Army of Northern Virginia or Army of Tennessee in 1865.[44]

In 1862 and 1863, approximately 998 Bartow Countians joined the Confederate army—either by choice or by force. By the end of 1862, nearly 2,000 local white males had served in the Confederate army and state militia units.

An overwhelming majority of the county's households (approximately 83 percent) had at least one family member serving in the army. In May of 1862, 126 soldiers enlisted in what became 2nd Co. E, 1st Confederate States of America Regiment. The unit included eighty-two non-slaveholding and fifteen slaveholding yeomen, four planters, fifteen common whites, and ten unskilled laborers. The average age of soldiers who joined in 1862 was older than their 1861 counterparts, twenty-six compared to twenty-four. Like their 1861 counterparts, 2nd Co. E, 1st CSA Infantry's muster rolls contained the names of white men (rich and poor, slaveholder and non-slaveholder, yeoman and non-yeoman) who risked their lives to fight a white men's war.[45]

External pressure created by military setbacks beginning in the spring of 1862 and extending through the winter of 1863 further challenged support for the Confederate government among Bartow Countians. No actual military action took place in the county during this period, but the threat of a Union invasion deeply concerned Bartow Countians. The ease with which federal forces captured the city of New Orleans, as well as Fort Pulaski near Savannah, and occupied northern Alabama troubled men such as Godfrey Barnsley who believed that the government had not exerted enough energy in the defense of its territory. Private John Brantley tried to console his sister who had expressed some concerns about the Confederacy's recent losses. "The Yankees," he wrote, "have not won the day yet. Although we have suffered several defeats recently we should not become discouraged. I do believe our cause is righteous.... We are all in fine spirits and think of nothing but success ahead of us."[46] Informed residents knew that the loss of Forts Henry and Donelson, Island Number 10, Nashville, and reverses at Shiloh exposed northwest Georgia to a potential offensive against the valuable W&A. The same rails that had previously ushered in an era of prosperity now appeared to be an avenue that would soon destroy all that was gained. Locals heard accounts from refugees who flooded the county during much of 1862 and 1863 about how occupying forces mistreated civilian property in western Tennessee, northern Alabama, and Georgia's coastal islands. By the spring of 1862, most had accepted the realization that the longer the war continued, the more likely that Union soldiers might one day be at their doorstep. Pierce Manning Butler Young, for example, wrote his parents that he "would not be at all surprised if the Yankees get down among you, so you better hunt you a nook and have it ready."[47]

A few soon arrived. In April of 1862, a small band of Union soldiers and spies infiltrated northwest Georgia to sabotage the W&A. James Andrews, a spy hired by General Ormsby Mitchell, and twenty-one co-conspirators slipped into Confederate lines with the intention of capturing a locomotive somewhere between Atlanta and Chattanooga and using the engine to destroy track, equipment, and communication lines, in anticipation of a simultaneously planned offensive launched by General Don Carlos Buell's forces in occupied northern Alabama. The raid's overall plan disintegrated as costly delays and second thoughts combined to persuade Buell and others to abandon their large-scale invasion. Nonetheless, the raiders went about completing their mission. On the night of April 11, Andrews and his party reached Marietta, a bustling town located south of Bartow County in neighboring Cobb County. Early the next morning, the raiders boarded a northbound engine named the *General*. That morning, as was customary, the train's engineer stopped the *General* at Big Shanty station where he and passengers ate breakfast at the local hotel. Using this distraction to their advantage, the raiders occupied the locomotive and successfully pulled away from the station before their activities attracted attention.[48]

Steaming northward, the raiders paused at various points long enough to cut telegraph wires and sabotage small sections of track. Captain William Fuller, the *General*'s engineer, along with the aid of a handful of men, aggressively pursued the captured train. Their efforts comprised some of the most dramatic moments in the state's history. Initially, the men chased the train on foot for several miles until they commandeered a small push cart. Dodging missing rails and debris, the party crossed into Bartow County where it encountered a small engine, the *Yonah*, at Etowah. At this point, the pursuers acquired a flat car loaded with tools and rails before heading northward toward Kingston. The raiders had briefly stopped at the Kingston Depot. Andrews explained to the depot engineers and agents that the Confederate army had placed him in charge of transporting a vital load of ordinance to troops located in Corinth, Mississippi. After some brief delays that involved placing southbound trains on alternate sidings, the *General* left the small town shortly before Fuller's men arrived. The pursuers abandoned the *Yonah* in favor of the more powerful *William R. Smith*. Locals who had heard that Union spies had captured an engineer joined the pursuers as they headed toward Adairsville. Between the two towns, the raiders had removed several portions of track and piled small loads of railroad ties in an effort to derail their adversaries.[49]

Andrews's Raid had little chance of success. The raiders did not anticipate delays caused by southbound traffic and wood shortages that slowed their movements. They also did not expect to be actively pursued by the captured engine's crew. After leaving Bartow County, the party ran out of fuel near Ringgold. "They jumped off the car and took to the woods," reported W&A superintendent John Rowland. Confederates managed to capture the raiders.

"One of them took 150 lashes . . . before he would acknowledge" his orders and the number of his men.[50]

The raid had little impact upon the overall course of the Civil War. In an effort to protect the railroad from future attacks, the State Guard and many local Home Guard units were ordered to maintain regular patrols and encampments near the state road's vulnerable bridges. This action evoked the ire of some locals who resented spending much-needed time away from their family and farms to patrol the railroad. Farmers bitterly complained to Governor Brown that protecting the railroad would cause their crops to fail. If northwest Georgians failed to produce a surplus of wheat and corn, what use would the railroad be? These fears, combined with drought-like conditions that in the summer of 1862 threatened to destroy much of the annual wheat crop, caused great anxiety as locals wondered if they would be able to feed themselves or their troops.[51]

Bartow Countians increasingly feared the arrival of federal soldiers. The enemy by late 1863 had developed a reputation among some residents as a highly courageous fighting force dedicated to restoring the Union. Julia Barnsley admired the fact that "every time we whip the Yankees they appear only more determined to whip, subjugate, and exterminate us."[52] When Confederate forces achieved a great victory at Fredericksburg, Godfrey Barnsley respected the tremendous amount of "discipline" and "courage" that the Federals displayed as they repeatedly advanced on ground where so many before them had faltered. Such an adversary, he warned his overconfident son, should not be easily discounted when even in the throes of hopeless defeat they remained dedicated to their central purpose.[53]

While serving in the 40th Georgia Infantry Regiment, William Chunn also developed a healthy respect for the enemy. In 1861, he had bragged to his wife about the assurance of victory. Two years later, he no longer predicted such a positive outcome because, in his opinion, the enemy would never leave the Confederacy alone. At battles such as Baker's Creek and Vicksburg, Chunn and the soldiers of the 40th Georgia had yet to taste the fruits of victory. The regiment spent the end of May, all of June, and the beginning of July 1863 trapped within the lines at Vicksburg, enduring the hardships that accompanied a prolonged siege. "The soldier," wrote Chunn, "is now truly drinking the bitter dregs of war. But notwithstanding the hardships you would be surprised what degree of endurance they display and the cheerfulness they exhibit."[54] On July 3, 1863, he and 30,000 other Confederates—among them nearly one hundred Bartow Countians—surrendered to Union forces.[55]

The 40th Georgia's surrender and parole at Vicksburg was a critical moment in the history of the regiment's three Bartow County companies. After receiving their parole, the regiment returned to their homes in piecemeal fashion with orders to reorganize their companies in the coming weeks. This provided soldiers with an opportunity to visit their families and a chance to avoid further military service. Despite this opening, approximately 78 percent of those parolees returned to duty and re-formed their companies in time to participate in the Confederate defense of Chattanooga, and another 10 percent joined other Confederate, state, and local units. The return of these men to their ranks evidenced the devotion that most still felt for the Confederacy.[56]

Other Bartow County companies displayed a similar fighting resolve. Of the nearly 2,000 locals who served in the Confederate army between 1861 and 1863, only sixty-two deserted. Approximately 675 soldiers died in battle or from disease during that same period. Soldiers perished on battlefields scattered throughout the country from Malvern Hill to Baker's Creek, Gettysburg to Chickamauga, and Antietam to Shiloh. An additional 150 soldiers returned home permanently disabled and physically incapable of serving in the army. Nonetheless, a sizable number of these disabled soldiers joined local militia units, volunteered as railroad guards, or found some other means of contributing to the war effort. These numbers suggest that between 1861 and 1863 thousands of Bartow Countians remained devoted to the Confederate war effort.[57]

The sole victory that the Confederacy could tout in the Western Theater prior to the start of 1864 was the Battle of Chickamauga. In the fall of 1863, the Federal Army of the Cumberland penetrated northwest Georgia in pursuit of the retreating Army of Tennessee. For two days, September 19 and 20, 1863, the armies collided producing some of the bloodiest fighting seen during the war. After the timely arrival of portions of General James Longstreet's corps from Virginia, the Confederacy held the field while the Federals hastily fled to Chattanooga.

What followed sorely disappointed and unnerved Bartow Countians. With federal troops bottled up in Chattanooga and surrounded by Confederate defenses located along Lookout Mountain and Missionary Ridge, the Army of Tennessee appeared to be on the verge of producing a major victory that might reverse the course of the war. The federal position, however, benefited upon the arrival of their new commander General Ulysses S. Grant and his subordinate General William T. Sherman. Under their leadership, along with the aid of 37,000 reinforcements dispatched from the Army of the Potomac and Army of the Tennessee, the situation at Chattanooga steadily improved during the fall of 1863.[58]

Meanwhile, the Army of Tennessee wasted a golden opportunity to follow up their major victory largely due to infighting among the army's high command. In an effort to resolve conflicts between Bragg and his division commanders, President Davis personally visited the army's headquarters. The disgruntled division commanders informed Davis that they would no longer be willing to serve with Bragg and strongly urged the president to immediately replace him. After offering the command to Lt. General James Longstreet, who supposedly rejected the proposal in favor of returning to the Army of Northern Virginia, Davis was left with few viable alternatives. Longstreet recommended that Joseph Johnston be given the command, but Davis still blamed him for the loss of Vicksburg. The only other option was P. G. T. Beauregard, whom Davis also disliked and who had proven to be an unreliable theater commander. Davis instead extended Bragg's tenure as commander and reassigned many of his dissident divisional commanders. When Davis left for Richmond, the Army of Tennessee was in no better position than it had been prior to his arrival.[59]

While the Army of Tennessee remained at Lookout Mountain and Missionary Ridge, Chunn eagerly anticipated an opportunity to gain a forty-day furlough. "Just think of it," he wrote, "I am only about sixty miles from home." Bragg had issued an order granting a forty-day furlough to every noncommissioned officer and private who could muster in a new recruit. Chunn instructed his wife that "if you hear of anyone willing to join the army tell them to come to the 40th Georgia and I will liberally reward them."[60]

When three divisions of General Joseph Hooker's corps drove three Confederate brigades from Lookout Mountain's northern slope, Chunn's chances for obtaining a furlough vanished. In two days, the seemingly impregnable Confederate defenses crumbled on Lookout Mountain and Missionary Ridge. The routed defenders retreated southward for thirty miles toward Dalton. The situation seemed dire. General Braxton Bragg correctly assessed that the loss of Chattanooga was in part due to the demoralized state of his army.[61]

Chunn's letters to his wife reflected the low morale that plagued some soldiers serving in the Army of Tennessee. "When I contemplate the deplorable state of our country," he wrote a week after the fall of Chattanooga, "the bright hopes of the future are dispelled."[62] The demoralized soldier blamed the nation's troubles on his poor relationship with God. He lamented the fact that his experience in the army had been one of repeated defeats and embarrassing setbacks.[63]

William Chunn believed that the Army of Tennessee would not make a concerted stand at Dalton. On December 12, 1863, he advised his wife and family to make preparations to move to south Georgia. The soldier heard rumors swirling through the ranks that the army commanders intended to retreat to the Etowah River shortly after New Year's. Such a movement would place his home and family within enemy lines. Fearful that a retreat might permanently damage his personal property, he reminded his family to take their slaves with them when they fled south. Once they located a place to live, his family could then rent out as many of the slaves as possible in order to obtain cash and other supplies.[64]

As 1863 came to a close, the Army of Tennessee had abandoned Tennessee and portions of northwest Georgia. Their winter quarters at Dalton were located a mere forty miles from Bartow County. General Joseph E. Johnston replaced General Braxton Bragg as commander, but his appointment did nothing to relieve local anxieties. Many families were familiar with Johnston's reputation; after the Battle of First Manassas, Godfrey Barnsley labeled Johnston as the true "king of spades" because the commander lacked the fortitude to engage the enemy in combat.[65] Those who served with the general during the Battle of First Manassas and the Peninsula Campaign—such as the 8th Georgia and 18th Georgia—had experienced firsthand the commander's willingness to surrender large portions of territory without a fight. Most Bartow Countians predicted that 1864 would be their darkest hour.

Despite the hardships and setbacks that many Bartow Countians experienced between 1862 and 1863, most remained committed to the Confederacy, although some began to express serious doubts about the government's viability. Civilians worried about the physical condition of their family members in the army while soldiers grew concerned about the impact that their prolonged absence had upon their households. Conscription, military defeat, inflation, drought, death, and wild rumors combined to create a heightened level of uncertainty that left the region vulnerable to the enormous external pressures that would be applied by invading federal armies in the spring of 1864. Looking back upon their wartime experiences, many Bartow Countians remembered 1862 and 1863 as a harsh prelude to the even more desperate times that followed. What happened next would be seared into the community's collective memory for generations.

CHAPTER
5

THE ATLANTA CAMPAIGN

The Atlanta Campaign placed an enormous amount of external pressure on the residents of Bartow County. The line that had separated the home front from the front lines disappeared in May of 1864 as General William Tecumseh Sherman's Federal army and General Joseph E. Johnston's Confederate army maneuvered through the county. The Atlanta Campaign tested the loyalties of Bartow County soldiers serving in the Army of Tennessee and elsewhere. As the home front collapsed, they had to decide if they should remain in the army and fight or return home to protect their families and property. Many went home, but more remained determined to continue fighting and optimistic that the course of the war might turnaround.

With the Army of Tennessee in winter quarters at Dalton, the somber shadows of war began to descend on Bartow County. "Our poor country," wrote Eliza Stiles, "seems in such a deplorable condition, and men so wicked that we dare not expect the Almighty to help us." Notably, the Confederate army's presence in towns such as Cartersville, Kingston, and Adairsville increased throughout the winter of 1864. Army quartermaster agents also scoured the countryside commandeering food and supplies. Confrontations between local residents and hungry Confederates created much animosity. When soldiers visited Robert Montgomery's farm outside of Adairsville, they took several bushels of corn and questioned the farmer why he had not joined the military. He claimed that he received an exemption because he worked for the railroad. The next day, the soldiers returned, intent on arresting Montgomery and forcing him into the army. As they approached his small, double-pen home, Montgomery "narrowly escaped through a back door." Convinced that he could no longer remain in the county, he fled to the northeast Georgia mountains in search of Unionist sympathizers. Within a few days, Montgomery found employment gathering firewood for the Federal army.[1]

The close proximity of the Army of Tennessee created other problems for both Bartow County residents and the Confederate military. Foremost, the army struggled to prevent soldiers from leaving their camp at Dalton to visit their families without a furlough. Between September and December of 1863, seven members of Co. I, 40th Georgia Infantry Regiment, deserted their ranks. Private John R. Tucks, a yeoman farmer, left the army in September, perhaps traveling home, and returned sometime prior to the Battle of Missionary Ridge. In Co. B of the 40th Georgia, 1st Lieutenant Edward B. Ford deserted, but then enlisted in Co. C. Baker's Regiment Georgia Militia Cavalry. Private Charles Culver did not immediately report to his regiment following his parole at Vicksburg. Local militia captured and arrested him as a deserter sometime in the early fall. On his return to the army, Culver deserted and traveled to Chattanooga, Tennessee, to the Federal army where he promptly took the oath of allegiance. While nearly 100 soldiers deserted the ranks permanently, about 25 percent of those deserters went home for a few weeks and then unceremoniously returned to their unit or subsequently volunteered for service in local militia companies.[2] Kingston Provost Marshall Captain James Baltzelle informed his superiors that there were so many deserters in the area that it would require an entire brigade to capture them. In March, pickets stationed at Hardin Bridge arrested two cavalrymen who had been reported as absent without leave from the 4th Georgia Cavalry. The two men were attempting to cross the Etowah River in route to their home located near the small town of Euharlee. Per orders, Baltzelle dismounted the deserters, stripping them of their guns and equipment before sending them, as well as a group of about one dozen other deserters, back to the front under an armed guard.[3]

Prior to the Atlanta Campaign, desertion was not a major problem among Bartow County soldiers. Of the approximately 2,000 soldiers who served in the army prior to 1864, only 5 percent deserted before the Atlanta Campaign, and most of those desertions occurred while the Army of Tennessee was in winter quarters in Dalton. Of the roughly 100 soldiers who deserted, 67 percent of them had joined after 1861, and 90 percent of them served in the Army of Tennessee.[4]

As provost marshall, Baltzelle not only dealt with deserters, but also had to prevent unauthorized civilians from traveling to the front. By March 1864, Confederate officials no longer allowed civilians to travel on the W&A to any station north of the town of Kingston. Nevertheless, many women attempted to circumvent local authorities in order to visit loved ones at Dalton. On April 15, for example, Baltzelle arrested Lou Magnis and Emma Miller who had donned Confederate uniforms in an attempt to go to the front.[5]

Deserters and Unionists only accounted for a small number of military aged white men who could be found in Bartow County in the winter of 1864.

The 1864 Georgia Militia Census (also known as the Joe Brown Census) documents the number of military aged men in the county. The census enumerators identified approximately 840 white men whose ages ranged from sixteen to fifty-nine years old and lived in one of eight county militia districts. Roughly 10 percent of these men had once served in the Confederate army but at some point either resigned, received an exemption due to their occupation or disability, or furnished a substitute.[6] The roll does not identify any known deserters who might have been lurking about the county or hiding out on the farms since many of them would have avoided detection. A majority of the men had received an exemption from either the Confederate or state government. James M. Broughton, age thirty-four, received an exemption to continue his work as a millwright. Likewise, a William Wooten, age forty-four, remained at home working as a miller rather than fighting in the army. Three industries—the W&A Railroad, the iron works, and the saltpeter mine—accounted for approximately 67 percent of all exemptions. Occupations such as minister, wagon maker, brick mason, schoolmaster, cabinet maker, mechanic, blacksmith, and farmer also received exemptions based on their work. Ailments such as dropsy, heart disease, myopia, tuberculosis, and arthritis earned medical exemptions and accounted for about 15 percent of the total number. The 1864 Georgia Militia Census reveals that while a large body of military age men had remained at home for significant portions of the war, most worked in occupations that contributed to the war effort or suffered from a disability that prevented them from military service.[7]

Bartow Countians fully expected the Army of Tennessee to retreat southward during the upcoming campaign season. In late January 1864, Andrew Jackson Neal traveled through the northern portion of the county in route to Kingston. His commanding officer ordered him to locate forage for his unit's horses. On horseback the soldier passed through what he considered to be "the best part of Georgia." Rich farms surrounded the road between Adairsville and Kingston. The locals seemed to be doing well. Their barns contained an "abundance of provisions." As Neal moved from farm to farm, he quickly learned that a majority of the population had abandoned their land seeking refuge south of Atlanta. He recorded that every resident he encountered believed that Johnston would retreat to the Etowah River by early spring. With all of the farmers gone, Neal predicted that few provisions would be "raised about here this year." Apparently, General William J. Hardee advised Kingston residents to remove all property south of the Etowah River.[8]

William Chunn, encamped outside of Dalton along with other members of the 40th Georgia, likewise warned his father-in-law that once the weather improved and campaign season began that General Joseph E. Johnston would execute a planned retreat to the Allatoona Mountain range. Citizens reacted to such news by leaving Bartow for points south. In January, Cassville attorney and Confederate congressman Warren Akin relocated his family to Oxford, Georgia. Unable to find a suitable residence in Oxford, the Akins moved again, this time to live with family members in Elberton, Georgia. Godfrey Barnsley wrote that "most of the wealthier families have either left or are about leaving, under the belief that the army will fall back here long." In March, Rebecca Felton finally convinced her husband to abandon their Cartersville home in favor of Macon.[9]

While many Bartow Countians sought refuge, others remained at home. Godfrey Barnsley notably refused to abandon Woodlands because he feared that Confederate and Union soldiers, as well as the irregular bands of deserters who roamed the area, might ransack his beloved estate. He and an Irish housemaid Mary Quinn remained at Woodlands even after his recently married daughter Julia and grandson Forrest Reid traveled to Savannah.

The Howard family also refused to abandon Spring Bank. During the winter, Captain Charles W. Howard of the 63rd Georgia Infantry Regiment tried to convince his family and the Barnsleys to move southward. During the previous year, Susan Howard had seen the poor living conditions that confronted most refugees. The captain returned to Dalton fearful of what might happen to his family.[10]

Many Unionists stayed, assured that the arrival of federal soldiers would afford them some protection from their pro-Confederate neighbors. Unionists had lived in the county since the beginning of the war, but the proximity of blue clad soldiers made some more willing to openly express their views. Prior to 1864, however, they had good reason to stay quiet. James McGee, for example, had moved to Bartow County in 1860 after purchasing a hotel and boarding house located in Kingston. When the outsider allowed a Massachusetts-born physician to rent a room after every other establishment in the county had refused to accept the doctor's money, McGee's neighbors accused him of being a Yankee. For almost four years, locals harassed McGee by breaking windows, stealing items from his storehouse, and chasing away potential customers. As Kingston residents fled southward to escape the Federal army, the entrepreneur felt a sense of temporary relief. He hoped that any invading army would offer him some degree of protection from hostile rebel sympathizers.[11]

William Collins meanwhile remained in Bartow County in anticipation of receiving a visit from his brother, Dossius M. Collins, who had joined a Union regiment organized in east Tennessee that now served in General William T. Sherman's command. The Adairsville area farmer had passed through both the Confederate and Union lines at Dalton visiting his brother on several occasions. As spring approached, Collins continued his normal farm work and never seriously considered abandoning his home. When several local slaveowners sought refuge elsewhere and needed a place to keep their domestic slaves, the farmer volunteered to supervise them during their master's absence. Collins opposed slavery and knew that once the Federals arrived, the slaves would be freed.[12]

Slaveholders like the ones who left their slaves with Collins encountered the additional burden of caring for slaves in an unfamiliar setting. The Rome *Tri-Weekly Courier* published numerous advertisements during the winter of 1864 placed by local slaveholders attempting to hire out their slaves or sell them. With the enemy so close, the local slave market virtually collapsed as prices and demand declined sharply. Likewise, Warren Akin's efforts to hire out his slaves prior to leaving Bartow County failed. Rather than abandon his property, he, like many slaveholders, took them with him. Feeding, clothing, and finding shelter for as many as fourteen slaves proved to be too much of a burden for the Akin family. Unable to endure these hardships, the Confederate congressmen agreed to hire out several slaves to local farmers and businessmen at rates that were far below their antebellum market value.[13]

Despite the fact that many white residents believed that Johnston would retreat south of the Etowah River without a fight, most, and especially women, remained active supporters of the Confederate war effort. For those who remained, there were few idle moments. Many white women spent nearly every second of daylight dutifully working on endeavors that directly benefited the Confederate war effort. Those who lived within walking distance of one of the county's hospitals frequently spent their early morning hours milking cows and gathering eggs. In the afternoon, they walked miles in order to personally deliver the much needed provisions. As Anne Elizabeth Johnson recalled, "there were no idle hands. . . . [Women gave what] their limited storehouse could furnish, as the times were growing harder and harder." Once a woman delivered the provisions, she typically remained at the hospital for hours nursing wounded soldiers. Many had fathers, husbands, and sons fighting in the Confederate army. They developed caring relationships with many of the soldiers. Physically exhausted from continued labor, the woes of these women were frequently compounded by news about their loved ones who had perished in battle or on discovering that one of their convalescing soldiers had perished. As Johnson remembered, these were sad times when women needed to stay occupied with other matters in order to avoid being overcome by fear and sadness.[14] "Some of the most tragic episodes of my life," recalled Rebecca Felton, "happened in trying to relieve the distress of the time."[15]

Day and night, citizens of Kingston worked feverishly to sustain the war effort. The Confederacy impressed the local grist mill from its private owner, Erastus V. Johnson. Livestock herds brought southward from Kentucky and

Tennessee filled the town's streets. Cattle grazed on local farms and forests until fattened enough for slaughter. At night, women carded wool and cotton to prepare clothing for their loved ones, refugees, and convalescing soldiers.[16]

Other Bartow County residents were less assured of the Confederacy's future prospects. "I am more anxious now," wrote Nathan Land, "for the war to end than ever, I want to go to Texas or some other country where I can have new views and different feelings from what I can ever have here." Land hoped for a Confederate defeat as the Union army began pushing southward.[17] When he received Land's letter, William Chunn replied with an extended response that attempted simultaneously to encapsulate the condition and morale of the Army of Tennessee and dismiss some of Nathan Land's dire predictions: "Everything now is remarkably quiet along the lines but this is ominous. It is but the lull of a gathering storm that pauses before it snaps the earth with all its fury. It is but the premonition of the viper, before it gives the fatal stroke. This part of the country will not long be blessed with quiet but in less than one month it will be theatre upon which will be acted the strategic scenes of a young nation struggling for independence." He further informed his father-in-law that the Confederate cause was not a "desperate" one. The soldiers in his company understood "the importance of stubborn resistance and realized the meaning of subjugation." The soldier admitted that the Army of Tennessee had recently experienced a number of "disgraceful" reverses but reported that the "spirit of our soldiers was never so buoyant as it is now."[18]

William Chunn's letter correctly assessed the ramifications of the impending campaign. He understood that, in November, northern voters would go to the polls to elect a president. If the Army of Tennessee could reverse the Federals and push them out of Georgia and back into Tennessee, Chunn predicted that northerners would become tired of the war and elect a "conservative" candidate in lieu of Abraham Lincoln. "The manner [in which] the campaign is conducted," he wrote, "will determine the election of the next president of the United States." Realizing that his father-in-law had expressed doubts as to whether or not it would matter who served as president, he emphasized that "we have nothing to fear as there is no party that can put forward a worse man in every sense of the word than Abraham Lincoln." But if Atlanta fell before the enemy, so too would the hopes of the Confederacy.[19]

Chunn expected the Union army to launch a series of frontal assaults upon the Army of Tennessee's prepared defenses. He did not worry about Sherman flanking those lines, for he incorrectly assumed that the Federal army would suffer from a dire lack of provisions once they separated themselves from the W&A. A student of world history, Chunn finally compared the upcoming campaign to Napoleon Bonaparte's 1812 invasion of Russia, with Atlanta becoming the Confederate Moscow. He neglected to add that prior to their defeat the French had occupied and destroyed much of that city.

Braxton Bragg's removal from command and Joseph E. Johnston's arrival brightened Chunn's hopes that the Army of Tennessee might be victorious on the field of battle. For as much as the men of the 40th Georgia despised Bragg, they adored Johnston. A skilled quartermaster, the new commander fed, clothed, and housed his army better than any of his predecessors. "I have of late," wrote Chunn, "had an instinctive impression that the time for the beginning of our success is at hand. God grant that it may be." Johnston, according to the soldier, would be the difference. He would not yield valuable territory to the enemy without a fight. Johnston would never allow Sherman to outflank him without going on the offensive. The Virginian would always keep his army better supplied than his opponent. When Nathan Land told his son-in-law that he was considering seeking a refuge south of Atlanta, his son-in-law chided him declaring that the Confederate army would not "yield another inch of territory." Chunn's confidence in Johnston did not reassure either his father-in-law or many other Bartow Countians familiar with the commander's lackluster military record. Certain that his son-in-law was wrong, Nathan Land fled to Brooks County prior to the beginning of the Atlanta Campaign and promptly sold all of his slaves.[20]

On May 5, 1864, General Ulysses S. Grant received a telegram from General William T. Sherman informing him that the latter would, as ordered, take to the offensive tomorrow. "Everything is quiet with the enemy," wrote Sherman, "Johnston evidently awaits my initiative. I will first secure the Tunnel Hill, then throw Major General James B. McPherson's Federal Army of the Tennessee rapidly on his communications, attacking at the same time in front cautiously and in force."[21] Thus began the Atlanta Campaign. Unwilling to attack the Confederates' fortified position at Rocky Face Ridge, Sherman ordered the Federal Army of the Tennessee to swing around Johnston's left through undefended Snake Creek Gap. This action forced the Confederate Army of Tennessee to abandon their fortifications and retreat ten miles south to the small town of Resaca. There Sherman spent three days probing Johnston's lines, searching for a nonexistent weakness. On May 14 and 15, he launched several frontal attacks against the Confederate lines while the Army of the Tennessee again outflanked Johnston's defensive position. When McPherson's army crossed the Oostanaula River, the Army of Tennessee retreated along the W&A, moving through Calhoun and entering Bartow County.[22]

While moving southward toward Adairsville, Joseph E. Johnston debated his options. He could have launched an attack on the divided Union army, but as indicated by Major William H. Stiles, "both man & beast" were "broken

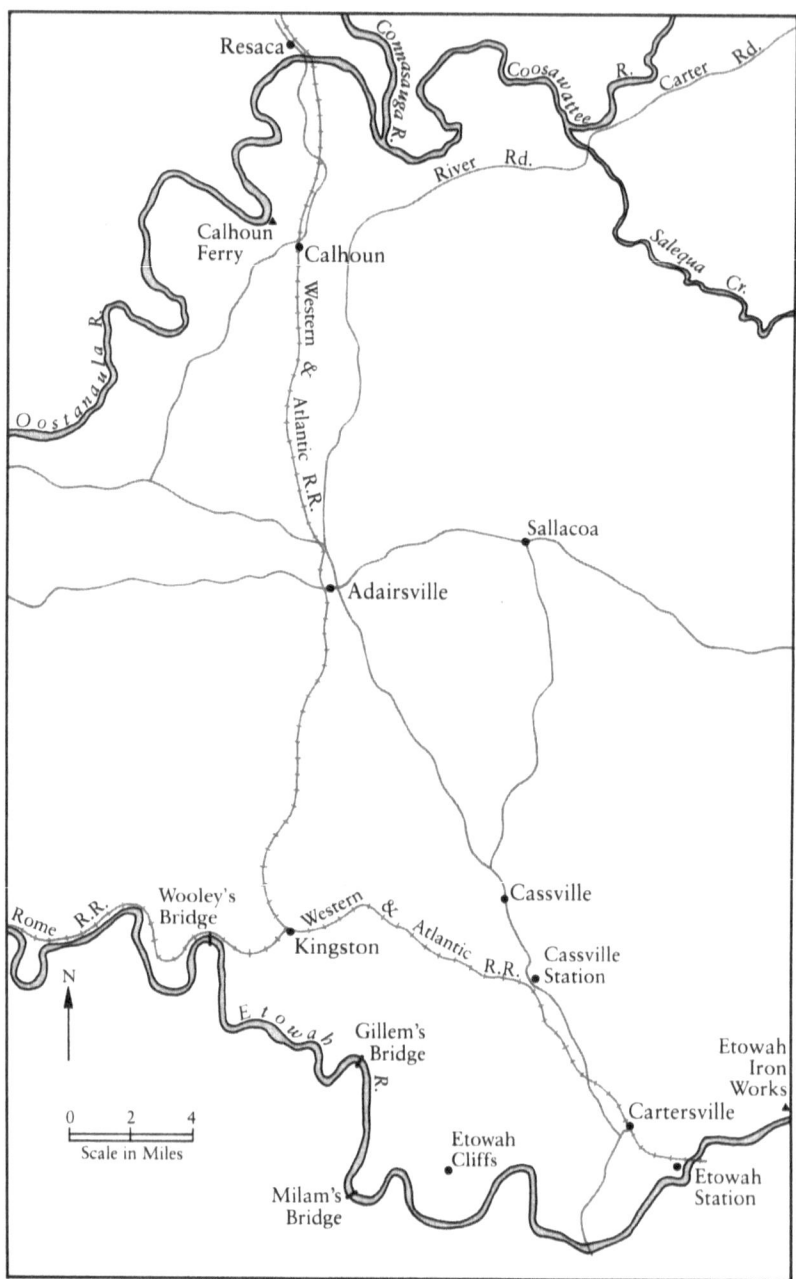

Map 3: The Atlanta Campaign. As McPherson's army crossed the Oostanaula River it entered Bartow County. From Albert E. Castel, *Decision in the West: The Atlanta Campaign of 1864* (Lawrence: University Press of Kansas, 1992). © Board of Trustees, University of Kansas, all rights reserved. Reproduced by permission.

down" from the previous week's movements. The Confederate Army of Tennessee could have moved into Alabama, forcing Sherman to choose whether to pursue the army or to advance on Atlanta. This plan lacked the support of the Confederate government, however, which wanted its principal manufacturing and rail center to be defended at all costs. Johnston instead planned to retreat slowly waiting for an opportunity to strike a divided portion of Sherman's army. The Confederates then retreated seven miles farther to Adairsville, hopeful that reports of a narrow valley with high flanking ridges located outside that town held true.

The Army of Tennessee won a foot race to Adairsville, which enabled them to improve their defensive position. Johnston discovered upon his arrival that his maps had been incorrect. The valley proved too wide for the front of his army. Reinforcements significantly increased his strength, that ordinarily might have enabled the commander to hold it, but scouts informed him the federal units had flanked the town to the east and the west thereby threatening his rear. Again, Johnston decided to retreat.

The heading of a letter written by an Alabama soldier, "on the skeddadle," thus summarized the Confederate Army of Tennessee's actions during the first weeks of the campaign. The constant flanking maneuvers of the enemy frustrated Confederate soldiers. One wrote, "it is generally believed that we got the best of the fight 'that is' we killed more of the enemy than we lost." To have faced the enemy and hold the field only to subsequently retreat disheartened soldiers who had placed such confidence in Johnston's command.[23]

At 6:00 p.m. on May 17, Johnston and his corps commanders—John B. Hood, William J. Hardee, and Leonidas Polk—met to debate the Army of Tennessee's next move. Initially, Johnston proposed moving the entire army southeast eleven miles to Cassville. The road proved to be too narrow to efficiently transport an entire army. At this point in the discussion, Hardee recommended that the army make a stand at Adairsville. Johnston rejected his proposal in lieu of diverting his retreating army along two separate roads, one leading to Kingston—a distance of seven miles—and the other heading toward Cassville.

Using two roads resolved two of Johnston's problems. An army moving along two roads could retreat at a much faster pace and without the risk of being overtaken by their federal pursuers. Moreover, the multiple roads provided Johnston with an opportunity to set a trap for the enemy, much like Robert E. Lee had done during the Battle of Chancellorsville. Facing a numerically superior foe, "Old Joe" boldly divided his army and dispatched the two disproportionate halves in separate directions. He hoped that by sending Hardee and his cavalry down the Kingston road and the rest of his army toward Cassville,

Sherman too would split his forces in order to maintain the pursuit. Hardee's orders were to march to Kingston and then to head immediately east to rendezvous with the main army at Cassville. Once the Army of Tennessee reformed at Cassville, Johnston proposed to pounce upon the portion of the divided Union army moving along the Cassville road before those at Kingston could arrive in time to support the fight. In order for Johnston's plan to work, the enemy would have to split its forces while his divided force moved swiftly toward their prescribed destinations. Any delay might jeopardize the plan, leaving a part of the Confederate army vulnerable to attack. After the conference concluded, Polk, who was an Episcopal Bishop, baptized Johnston upon the commander's request.[24]

Meanwhile, Sam Watkins and other soldiers of Company H, 1st Tennessee Infantry Regiment helped to slow the federal advance with a well-fought rear guard action. On the evening of May 17, Watkins had begun collecting firewood to cook their supper when quite unexpectedly, a large mass of cavalry hurried past him. A cavalryman informed Watkins that the "Yankees" were coming. Soon thereafter, the company received orders to occupy a nearby octagon-shaped house that could be used as a temporary fort to impede federal progress. By the time that the Confederates reached the cement-walled dwelling portions of Brigadier General John Newton's 2nd Division, the 4th Corps, Army of the Cumberland were in plain view, only a few hundred yards distant. Once inside, men stationed themselves at every available window firing their rifles as fast as possible toward the oncoming skirmishers. The rebels, convinced that they would not survive this fight, began to sing in unison. As their supplies ran low, three soldiers raced outside of the Octagon House to retrieve some ammunition. During the early morning hours of May 18, the Confederates abandoned the Octagon House and hurriedly rejoined their retreating comrades along the Kingston road. Colonel Francis Sherman's 88th Illinois Infantry Regiment suffered 167 casualties. All in all, the Federals suffered about 400 casualties in skirmishes fought around Adairsville.[25]

Marcus Woodcock, a "Southern Boy in Blue" serving in the 9th Kentucky Infantry Regiment, entered Adairsville on the morning of May 18. Their commanders and newspapers had told union soldiers that northwest Georgia contained vast farms and bustling towns that helped to sustain the Confederate war effort. While marching from Dalton to Resaca and then toward Adairsville, Woodcock had seen little that matched such descriptions. Had it not been for a number of soldiers in his regiment who had visited Savannah and other locales throughout the state, he wrote, he would have held the opinion that "Georgia ain't much."[26] There, Woodcock met a ten-year-old boy who appeared to be unafraid of the invading Federals. He asked the boy if any Unionists lived in the area. The boy responded that there were "union men" in the town, but few of them dared to express their political beliefs. Upon further questioning, the child revealed that local Confederates threatened Unionists with physical violence. In fact, just days prior to the federal occupation, local secessionists had lynched two Unionists.[27]

Sherman meanwhile believed that the entire Army of Tennessee had retreated southward along the Kingston road, which ran parallel to the W&A. During the early morning hours of May 18, a domestic slave burst into the bedchamber of Susan Howard as the Confederate army passed through Spring Bank in route to Kingston. Alarmed by the news, Howard awoke her slumbering daughters. Once dressed, the women ran to the estate's upper gate, which opened onto the Kingston road. Initially, fog prevented the women from seeing the flow of butternut clad soldiers. When the morning sun rose through the early haze, it unveiled an astounding procession.[28]

A sense of joy overcame Susan Howard when she realized that the soldiers belonged to Lieutenant General William J. Hardee's Corps. Her husband Charles and son Jett served in the corps along with several dozen Bartow Countians who comprised Co. I, 63rd Georgia Infantry Regiment. This regiment only recently had joined the Army of Tennessee after being reassigned from their post in the Department of South Carolina, Georgia, and Florida, where it had defended the coastline in the vicinity of Savannah. As the Howard women began questioning passing soldiers about the whereabouts of the 63rd Georgia, Lieutenant Jett Howard appeared and told them that his father would meet them at Spring Bank's lower gate. When Susan arrived at the gate, a barely recognizable figure stood waiting. Charles warned his family that within a few hours the enemy would arrive. If they acted fast, they might be able to save the family's large livestock holdings from being stolen. Time was short. After a brief conversation and a hug and kiss goodbye, the elder captain rejoined his company, knowing that soon his family and home would be overtaken by the Federals.[29]

That morning, a well-executed rear guard action slowed the Federals' advance from along the Kingston road as Major General Joseph Wheeler's cavalry ensured that Brigadier General John Newton's division did not overtake Hardee's withdrawal. The Alabama cavalryman obstructed the federal army's path by felling trees along the Kingston road. As enemy skirmishers approached the logs, small detachments of dismounted cavalrymen, infantry, and an artillery battery opened fire from behind the safety of their temporary stronghold. Skirmishers lacked the firepower to dislodge the well-protected Confederates. The Federals then lost valuable time sending artillery to the front to oust the defenders. Once it arrived, the Confederate rear guard retreated several hundred yards to their next prepared breastwork. Wheeler's efforts thus prevented the IV and XIV Corps from reaching Kingston until 5:00 a.m. May 19, well after Hardee's Corps had safely passed through the town.[30]

Sometime before noon on May 18, 1864, skirmishers detached from four companies of the 17th Indiana Cavalry reached Spring Bank with orders to cut the telegraph wire. While the rest of the Confederate army continued towards Kingston, a small detachment of cavalry remained at Spring Bank with orders to slow the Union army advance. The detachment had installed a battery atop a small hill located directly across from the W&A and Spring Bank's upper gate and placed dismounted cavalrymen in front of the house. As soon as Federal skirmishers appeared along the crest of the road, the battery opened fire, scattering the enemy into a roadside thicket. Within minutes, Union reinforcements arrived and overwhelmed the Confederate defenders. Federal cavalry cut the telegraph wire and proceeded northwest toward Woodlands to probe for Confederate cavalry that might be operating on their flank.[31]

While the 17th Indiana Cavalry fell back, seven companies from the 4th Michigan Cavalry, Colonel Robert H. G. Minty's brigade, received orders from Brigadier General Kenner Garrard, commander of the 2nd Cavalry Division, "to proceed" toward Kingston "as far as he could, and drive everything before him."[32] Sherman's horsemen managed to get within a mile of the town before encountering the Confederate rear guard. Confederate cavalry officer Samuel Ferguson had anticipated that federal commanders would send reconnaissance units toward Kingston. He accordingly stationed his soldiers along both sides of the Kingston road, using the forest for cover, and behind an improvised breastwork that blocked the enemy's path. When the men of the 4th Michigan Cavalry encountered the well-protected Confederates, they quickly realized that they were outgunned and outnumbered. Sergeant Albert Potter, Co. B, described the scene: "I had my men deployed as skirmishers on the left on a hill our attention all directed to the front when a regiment of rebels came charging around to my left and rear. Yelling like incarnate fiends."[33]

The Confederates had outflanked and "nearly surrounded" the 4th Michigan. Lieutenant Colonel J. B. Park ordered companies F and L, under the command of Major Richard Robbins, to charge in order to break through the rebel lines. Robbins's men crashed into the Confederate cavalry pushing them back 200 yards. This enabled the remainder of the 4th Michigan to fall back and reform their lines. After an exhausting push, Robbins's men slowly fell back; however, as the enemy cavalry reformed and again advanced, companies F and L, without orders, again charged into the rebel lines, again forcing them to retreat. For five miles, the 4th Michigan rapidly formed their lines, fired a single volley, and then retired several hundred yards, only to repeat the entire process. When the retreating Federals reached Woodlands, their numerical deficiencies disappeared as they rejoined their division. During the five mile retreat, their regiment suffered twenty-five casualties.[34]

At Woodlands, Godfrey Barnsley had spent the morning listening to federal artillery dislodging Wheeler's rear guard along the Kingston road. Hoping to convince the enemy that he was a neutral British citizen innocently caught in the midst of a foreign rebellion, he raised a British flag over his mansion. Barnsley's efforts to proclaim his neutrality, however, were quickly spoiled when Colonel John T. Wilder's scouts spotted the Englishman talking to a group of Confederate cavalry officers and offering them spring water.[35]

By mid-afternoon, Confederate and Federal armies surrounded the entire estate. As Confederate cavalry pursued the 4th Michigan, they slammed into Garrard's 2nd Division, Cavalry Corps, which had arrived at Woodlands around noon. Along the lower valley situated west of the main house, remnants of two Confederate cavalry brigades fought a prolonged action against a vastly numerically superior foe. The Confederates managed to capture 135 prisoners and kill approximately twenty-eight enemy soldiers. Outnumbered and without artillery support or possible reinforcements, the Confederates withdrew from Woodlands southward toward Kingston.[36]

During the fight, Colonel Richard Earle of the 2nd Alabama Cavalry Regiment attempted to warn the Barnsley family to seek shelter in the wine cellar. While returning to his unit from the mansion, the colonel encountered federal soldiers who were pushing toward the Confederate lines. Unable to flee the pursing enemy, Earle stood his ground. After an intense period of hand-to-hand combat, during which time the officer was apparently shot several times, the Alabamian died at the hands of his enemy. The following day, Barnsley received permission from Union commanders to bury the fallen colonel.[37]

Federal Army of the Tennessee commander Major General James B. McPherson arrived at Woodlands shortly after the skirmish ended. He met with Barnsley and guaranteed him that his home would not be disturbed. That night, according to Clint Coker, "McPherson rested quietly in the cottage on Godfrey Barnsley's prominent hill." While the general slept, federal soldiers broke into the Englishman's wine cellar and stole more than 2,000 bottles of wine, brandy, and whiskey. Others stripped the upper kitchen bare, stealing food, utensils, and imported china. Soldiers indeed took everything from Woodlands' nine cellars except several barrels of rice. "If you ever have any friends about to fall into [enemy] hands," advised Jane Howard, "advise them to lay in a stock of rice, for a Yankee cannot be induced to touch it." While Barnsley suffered a tremendous loss of property, by remaining at his home, his estate escaped catastrophic damage.[38]

While events at Woodlands unfolded, the Confederates evacuated Rome. On May 17, 1864, Brevet Major General Jefferson C. Davis's 2nd Division, XIV Corps, attacked Rome. Ordinarily, a division might have easily overtaken the city's small garrison, but on that day, three brigades—two infantry, one cavalry—sent to reinforce Johnston from Polk's command in Mississippi were filing through the city when Davis attacked. Brigadier General Sul Ross's brigade of Texas cavalry staved off Davis's attack, while the remaining Confederates prepared the city's evacuation. The last train left the depot destined for Kingston loaded with munitions, soldiers, and civilians an hour before fleeing rebels burned the bridges over the Etowah and Oostanaula Rivers. Rome's loss hindered the Confederate war effort because it housed the Noble & Co. Ironworks and Machine Shop. Federal soldiers entering the city discovered that the facility had been left behind intact and operational.[39]

On the night of May 18, 1864, the women of Spring Bank hurriedly prepared for another visit from Union soldiers. After the skirmish at Woodlands, several Confederate cavalrymen fell back to the Howard residence, a distance of approximately four miles. The Howard women welcomed the soldiers, who helped them carry most of their home's furniture and valuables upstairs in exchange for some food. Early the next morning, most of the Confederates left the area, but three pickets remained behind stationed on a hill overlooking Spring Bank. Another dense morning fog created limited visibility as the pickets and women could not see the approaching federal lines a mere fifty yards away. Aware of the pickets' presence, Sarah and Francis Howard brought them breakfast. The group sat atop the hill listening to the echoing conversation of some nearby Federals. When Sarah Howard overheard an enemy soldier's plans to kill one of the family's roosters, she exclaimed, "no they won't" before rushing down the hill toward a fence upon which a white rooster had perched itself. As she snatched the rooster, one of the pickets yelled "Run, run! The Yanks have heard you." Hurrying toward the house, Howard watched as the pickets mounted their horses and fled while dodging a hailstorm of bullets unleashed by the nearby enemy.[40]

Within a few minutes, Major General Oliver Howard, along with his staff and escort, rode up to Spring Bank, eager to question the women about the Confederacy's movements. He asked them to estimate how many Confederate soldiers had passed their home yesterday. The women evaded his questions, acting as if they knew nothing. Their efforts annoyed the general.

Frustrated, he stormed out of the home's veranda while exclaiming "Madam, when you meet a gentleman, treat him as such!"[41]

Following Howard's hasty departure, Union soldiers invaded Spring Bank. The women remained indoors, Francis and Jane Howard staying downstairs hopeful of preventing the soldiers from entering the house, while their mother and sisters hid in an adjoining bedroom. Encountering a soldier staring through a parlor window pane, Francis fled into the bedroom seeking comfort from her mother. At that moment, the women heard the loud "crash of a falling door." A mob of soldiers had entered the kitchen. As the women sat silently listening for any sign of their movement, they heard the "tramp of many feet running across the laundry floor" as yet another door came crashing down as the men moved through the home. The frightened women fled to an upstairs bedroom locking the door behind them as "each was nerving herself for the coming storm." "Yankees" filled all of the upstairs rooms breaking glass lamps, windows, and carrying off any item of value. "At last there was a pause, followed by a tremendous blow upon our door, which instantly flew open." A group of soldiers entered the room eyeing the women. Fortunately, a lieutenant arrived soon thereafter who ordered the soldiers to exit the home. When one soldier refused, the officer lifted him by his collar and kicked him down a flight of stairs. Slowly, the soldiers abandoned the home, leaving behind the Howard women and a path of destruction.

Federal soldiers ransacked Spring Bank, stripping the home of almost every item light enough to carry. A trail of "valuable old books in all stages of mutilation" stretched from the family's library out into the front yard. The mob placed six bonnets—heirlooms from the family's ancestors—into a batch of lard. Men smeared lampblack on the doors, windows, and walls. One soldier fled from the house carrying a beaver hat and its decorative case. In his effort to elude both the women and his commanding officers, the thief stumbled over a stone wall face first onto the ground causing his nose to bleed profusely. Federal soldiers likely did more than steal the family's treasured valuables and desecrate their beloved home. According to accounts shared with family friends, federal soldiers had sexually assaulted the women before vacating the property.[42]

The Howard women were not the only women to be accosted by federal soldiers. At Woodlands, Godfrey Barnsley's Irish housemaid Mary Quinn endured a harrowing encounter with the enemy. A soldier approached Barnsley on the evening that McPherson's Corps arrived at his estate and asked the Englishman for the time. When he pulled a gold pocket watch from his coat, the soldier snatched the watch from his hand and fled toward the basement. Quinn pursued the soldier. When the maid demanded the soldier return the watch, he threatened to burn down the home. The soldier proceeded to pick up a shovel full of smoldering coals from the basement furnace with the intent of scattering them across the upstairs carpets. When the Irish woman blocked his path, the soldier, according to Quinn, "jist slung me back agin the wall so hard it knocked ivery bit o'breath out o' me body." Heading upstairs, the soldier began spreading the coals as Quinn regained her strength to stand up to the enemy. As she grabbed his coat, the soldier spun around grasping his revolver and struck the maid in the chest with the gun's stock. In retaliation, the dazed maid clawed the soldier's face with her long nails. "He sqaled like a pig," she reported, "an' called me a shedivil, an' ran clane out o' the house."[43]

While scores of Federals stole private property and made threats toward civilians, a number of officers made a concerted effort to prevent and recoup these losses. Soon after the initial group of Union soldiers left Spring Bank, a "Lieutenant Randolph" promised Susan Howard that he would help to recover their stolen valuables once she provided him with a list of the missing items. True to his word, the officer returned the following day with a wagon filled with the family's articles. Mary Quinn had a similar experience when dealing with federal officers. After Barnsley's watch was stolen, she traveled to McPherson's headquarters, intent on locating the thief and recovering the item. During the melee between her and the soldier, the attacker had dropped a letter revealing to Quinn the name of his infantry unit. McPherson apologized for his soldier's poor behavior and immediately sent for the company so that she could identify her assailant. The soldier's scarred faced singled him out. Once the thief returned the watch, McPherson asked Quinn if he should execute the soldier. The woman declined because she did not want his blood to stain her hands. As a punishment, the general ordered the soldier to be removed from the unit and sent to Chattanooga in ball and chains where he would serve a period of hard labor digging trenches around that city.[44]

As the Confederate Army of Tennessee meanwhile converged upon Cassville, the overwhelming majority of the town's remaining population evacuated. Some residents lacked a place to go. Many hid in the woods for several days while the armies passed. Lila Chunn and her family barely escaped. On the morning of May 18, she along with her mother-in-law and two small children boarded an Atlanta-bound train. When the family arrived in Atlanta, they encountered numerous other Cassville and Bartow County families huddled at the train depot awaiting transport further South: "Atlanta was perfectly thronged with people and they all panic stricken, everything was fuss and confusion."[45] She, like most refugees, moved several times before returning to Bartow County. The Chunn family eventually moved in with family in Coweta County.[46]

While Bartow County civilians endured the hardships of being left in the wake of their retreating army, the Army of Tennessee committed a series of blunders that further compromised the county's security. Internal squabbles among their general commanders created missed opportunities for the army to take the offensive and repel the invaders.

By the morning of May 19, 1864, the Army of Tennessee had abandoned the towns of Adairsville and Kingston, as well as the city of Rome, to the enemy. The weather proved "painful[ly] hot through the day" exhausting soldiers who marched as much as eight miles.[47] With most of the army now amassed slightly west of the county seat, Cassville, in a defensive line stretching from the southwest of Cass Station to a position northeast of the town cemetery, Johnston grew determined to fight. At dawn, the commander issued a general order proclaiming his resolve.

> Soldiers of the Army of Tennessee you have displayed the highest quality of the soldier-firmness in combat, patience under toil. By your courage and skill you have repulsed every assault of the enemy. By marches by day and marches by night you have defeated every attempt upon your communications. Your communications are secured. You will now turn and march to meet his advancing columns. Fully confiding in the conduct of the officers, the courage of the soldiers, I lead you to battle. We may confidently trust that the Almighty Father will still reward the patriots' toils and bless the patriots' banners. Cheered by the success of our brothers in Virginia and beyond the Mississippi, our efforts will equal theirs. Strengthened by His support, those efforts will be crowned with the like glories.

Johnston's general order temporarily bolstered his army's morale as the men anticipated a fight. "I never saw our troops happier or more certain of success," recalled Sam Watkins, "a sort of grand halo illuminated every soldier's face."[48]

The Battle of Cassville never happened. What could have been one of the largest collisions in the western theater turned into yet another retreat. On May 19, after receiving permission from Johnston to probe for Union forces along Marsteller's Mill road, Major General John B. Hood, at the head of his corps, encountered Brigadier General Edward McCook and Major General George Stoneman's federal cavalry moving westward along the Canton road. Hood could no longer advance toward Sallacoa with the enemy operating in his rear. After briefly skirmishing the enemy, Hood fell back to Cassville.

McCook and Stoneman unknowingly saved the federal lines from a potentially devastating attack.⁴⁹

When Hood returned to Cassville, the Army of Tennessee lost its best opportunity to strike Sherman's divided army. With each passing hour during the morning of May 19, the severed armies congregated around the county seat. Sherman assumed that Johnston had already retreated from this position. The commander ordered Major General David Stanley's 1st Division, IV Corps, to move toward the town expecting to find it abandoned. Instead, after "severe skirmishing" along the Cassville road, Colonel William Grose's 3rd Brigade encountered Hardee's Corps drawn into three battle lines west of the town.⁵⁰ The Confederates attacked, then withdrew. Constant withdrawals frustrated soldiers such as Watkins who wanted to engage the enemy in battle and to stop retreating. Hardee's slow withdrawal, however, played a critical role in Johnston's new plan.

Unable to pounce on an isolated segment of the Federal army, Johnston retreated to a position east of his original lines, intent on drawing Sherman into battle against a prepared position along a ridge overlooking Cassville. Had the Federals launched a series of frontal assaults on those lines, the results might have resembled those of Fredericksburg. The attack never occurred because, by the next morning, May 20, the Army of Tennessee had retreated. Johnston's three mile defensive line proved vulnerable to federal artillery fire. By the late afternoon of May 19, the federal lines—XIV, IV, and XX Corps from right to left—had deployed in a position near the Army of Tennessee's original breastworks. The town of Cassville rested between the XX Corps and Hood's Corps. In an effort to provide cover for his advancing infantry, Sherman ordered an artillery barrage upon the Confederate center and right flank. The first proved devastating to Hood's Corps. Fire landed upon his lines scattering the men and preventing any Confederate battery from silencing the enemy's guns. The 1st Ohio Light Artillery took a position atop a small hill located next to the Cassville Female Seminary. From this vantage point, they enfiladed Hood's exposed position. Confederate engineers had failed to account for this hill thus foiling Johnston's best laid plans.⁵¹

As night descended upon the two armies, the situation from both Polk and Hood's vantage points seemed dire. If their corps remained in this defensive position, then at morning's first light the Union artillery—that would have been significantly strengthened during the night—would resume their fire and decimate their ranks. Around 9:00 p.m., Johnston, Hood, Polk, French, and Captain Walter Morris—Polk's Chief Engineer—met at the bishop's headquarters located at the McKelvey house. Polk and Hood, along with Morris, urged Johnston to reconsider the army's current position. The

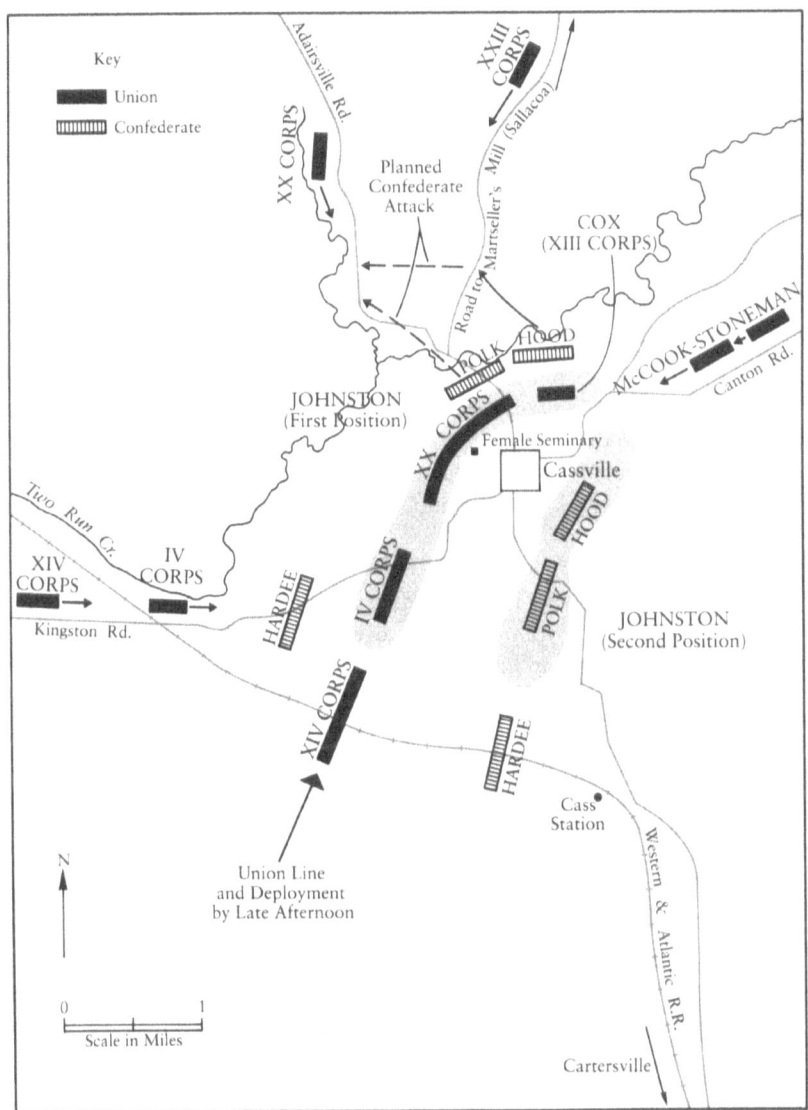

Map 4: The Atlanta Campaign. Union and Confederate troops mass around Cassville, May 19, 1864. From Albert E. Castel, *Decision in the West: The Atlanta Campaign of 1864* (Lawrence: University Press of Kansas, 1992). © Board of Trustees, University of Kansas, all rights reserved. Reproduced by permission.

commander initially resisted any recommendation to retreat or to reform his lines. Just that morning, Johnston had told his soldiers that they would stand and fight the enemy at Cassville. Approximately seventeen hours later, he stood at the McKelvey house and listened as two of his corps commanders advocated abandoning their current lines. Hood offered Johnston an opportunity to stay and fight but rather than be on the defensive, he recommended that, at daybreak, the army conduct a flanking maneuver along the enemy's left side that would disable their artillery. Polk hesitantly agreed with Hood's recommendation.

After listening to Hood and Polk for several hours, Johnston decided to retreat southward toward Allatoona Pass's impregnable defenses. His decision has been the subject of an intense amount of scrutiny from ex-Confederate commanders, politicians, and historians. Who was to blame for the Confederate retreat at Cassville? During the postwar period, Johnston and Hood waged a bitterly contested battle concerning their meeting at the McKelvey house. Each blamed the other for the retreat. Polk's death shortly after the meeting robbed historians of his account of what occurred. French's account of what transpired exists, but its credibility was compromised both by his postwar disdain for Hood as well as the fact that he left the meeting prior to its final conclusion.

Rather than cast blame on Johnston and Hood for the debacle at Cassville, it would be more useful to recognize the achievements of Sherman and his commanders. Johnston's original plan to strike an isolated portion of the Federal army went asunder once segments of cavalry threatened Hood's rear. The movement of these units was timely and their encounter with the enemy accidental. Nevertheless, their presence possibly saved the Union's left side while staving off the impending Battle of Cassville.

Later that same day, Hood and Polk advised Johnston to either engage the enemy or retreat. Johnston chose to retreat because, prior to arriving at the McKelvey house, he had received a report from his cavalry that portions of Sherman's army had crossed the Etowah at Woolley's Bridge and were in position to potentially cut-off his supply line. Had Johnston insisted on following through with his original intention of fighting at Cassville, his action would have jeopardized his vital connection with the W&A and would have placed an enemy force between himself and the city of Atlanta. Nothing guaranteed that an offensive assault upon a unified and significantly larger Federal army would have wielded any positive results. Had Hood's flanking movement failed, Sherman could have moved virtually uncontested toward Atlanta preventing the Confederates from arriving first and defending its prepared fortifications. The situation at Cassville proved to be a double-edged sword. Johnston simply decided to accept the duller of the two blades. By maintaining his Fabian tactics, Johnston sustained his army and lived to fight another day.[52]

When Sergeant Rice Bull, 123rd New York Infantry Regiment, awoke on the morning of May 20, 1864, a dense fog surrounded the Federals' position. Initially, the mist hid the fact that the Army of Tennessee had vacated their prepared lines. As the morning sun pierced through the murk, Bull smiled as he realized the enemy had retreated without a fight. He described Cassville as a "fine little town with four churches, a female seminary, courthouse, many stores and at least 100 residences, some of which were quite pretentious." Few residents remained in the town. After breakfast, the men from his company strolled the local streets. On a normal Friday morning, the stores in Cassville would have been bustling with customers. On that day, the only people seen in town wore federal uniforms. Prior to their arrival, Confederates had "ransacked and wrecked" all of the local businesses while leaving many of the private dwellings undisturbed. "The village," wrote Bull, "did present a deserted, deplorable sight."[53]

Locally, much debate surrounds the amount of property damage inflicted on Cassville during Sherman's initial occupation. While it is difficult to pinpoint precisely which structures were damaged or destroyed by the Federals, letters from Union soldiers indicate that the army did not inflict "total war" upon the town. Colonel Warren Parker, 5th Connecticut, marched his regiment into Cassville on the morning of May 20, 1864. He acknowledged that passing soldiers, both Confederate and Federal, had looted many of the homes and stores. At 9:00 a.m., Parker and his men responded to a call for help from a New York regiment who were fighting a "heavy fire [that] broke out in some large wooden buildings." After several tiring hours spent battling the blaze, soldiers spared most of the town. Had the Union army intended to destroy the town in May of 1864, they would not have exerted so much energy fighting a fire set by one of their own looters. Without the efforts of Parker's unit, as well as a New York company that contained a large number of firefighters, Cassville probably would have been consumed by fire in May, several months prior to the town's ultimate destruction.[54]

While the Federals attempted to save portions of Cassville, observers could retrace the army's path by following a number of trampled crops, blackened fields, dead livestock, and burned homes and barns. A German-born soldier fighting in Sherman's army wrote that "burning and burned houses marked our path" as we moved from along the Kingston road. The soldier admitted to stealing food from civilians and witnessing fellow soldiers slaughter chickens, pigs, and cattle without a thought given to their rightful owners. Hiram Smith regretted the fact that when his regiment reached Cassville, the thousands of soldiers who had passed through the town and countryside prior to his arrival had stripped all of the peach trees bare.[55]

Food was not the only item sought after by soldiers. When a German-born soldier arrived at Kingston, and his regiment was ordered to rest, he hoped to catch a glimpse of some of the local women. While his intent might not have been to sexually assault a local woman, he was greatly disappointed when after scouring the town he found "it [was] deserted, except for a fat dirty woman. She knew quite well that the filth on her would be her security."[56]

Slaves recalled that the federal soldiers they encountered treated them in a variety of ways. In route to Kingston, a member of Wilder's cavalry confiscated a mule from a slave working on William Collins's farm. The slave pleaded with the soldier to allow her to keep the animal since it was the only thing that she owned. Her tears did not persuade the soldier to change his mind. As he carried off the mule, the slave cursed the Union army whose arrival brought both emancipation and deprivation. Sarah Jane Patterson also watched as Federals stripped her master's plantation of food and valuables, but, according to her, they treated her and other slaves "nicely." Her master had told her wild stories about federal soldiers who murdered slaves. Initially afraid to even look in the eyes of a Union soldier, Patterson soon realized that her master's stories had been just that, stories. Callie Elder's master sent one his slaves into the woods with his prized stallion in the hopes of keeping the animal out of federal hands. Elder's grandmother had earned a ten-dollar gold piece. She decided to hide the coin in the bottom of a butter churn. Her plan failed, however, as soldiers hoping to find some freshly churned butter were surprised to discover a ten-dollar gold piece. Most slaves, like Easter Brown, never saw a federal soldier during the entire war.[57]

A few days later, several Union soldiers and commanders inspected the Confederate lines. The soldiers had never seen such well-prepared defenses: "they were the finest we had seen up to that time and it must have taken much labor to build them." They questioned how the enemy could have constructed such elaborate "fortifications" that contained "redoubts" and "abates in front" in such a brief period. And why they would "abandon such a line without making a defense." While these soldiers might have been completely unaware of the exact reasons why the Confederates had retreated, the presence of such well-prepared defenses led some to believe that the enemy was unwilling to fight.[58]

Twenty-four hours after retreating from Cassville, the Army of Tennessee crossed the Etowah River. Hoping to lure Sherman into a frontal assault, Johnston positioned his army along the Allatoona Mountain range. The Union commander, however, would not assault such an impregnable position. Before the war, Sherman had traveled through Bartow County and had surveyed the deep railroad cut known as Allatoona Pass. Rather than attack the Army of Tennessee, the Federal army again swung around the Confederate left threatening their supply line and forcing Johnston to abandon his prepared defenses. In less than one week, the Confederate army had passed through Bartow County and abandoned it to the enemy without a major fight.

In May 1864, the arrival of thousands of Union and Confederate soldiers in Bartow County erased the dividing line that had separated the home front and the front line. As Bartow Countians serving in the Army of Tennessee passed through their home county during the retreat many deserted. Approximately 30 percent of all Bartow County soldiers serving in the Army of Tennessee deserted during the Atlanta Campaign, most in May of 1864. Union soldiers arrested dozens of deserters hiding in the woods or roaming about the county. About 60 percent of those deserters signed the oath of allegiance thereby symbolizing their loss of will to continue the fight. Regiments such as the 40th Georgia that contained large numbers of Bartow Countians fought poorly throughout the campaign due to their dwindling numbers and plummeting morale. While William Chunn maintained his steadfast patriotism until after the fall of Atlanta, he witnessed firsthand during the battles around Atlanta scores of men in his regiment surrendering to federal soldiers without giving much of a fight. The external pressure applied by Sherman's invasion crushed the morale of many Bartow County soldiers. Nonetheless, while scores deserted and fled the county certain of a Confederate defeat, a larger percentage remained in their posts clinging to their fledgling nation and willing to continue the fight.

CHAPTER
6

Federal Occupation

In the summer of 1864, Maggie Branson, a resident of Cassville, wrote a letter to her aunt seeking relief. Branson's family was not among the wealthy elite. She had remained in the county during the Atlanta Campaign because she had nowhere else to go. Friendly and charitable toward others, Branson began taking in refugees who had left their homes elsewhere in northwest Georgia and Bartow County and seeking shelter from the invading Union army. To make matters worse, as Confederates moved through the county in May 1864, conscription agents carried off her fifty-one-year-old father and fourteen-year-old brother. Months had since passed since she had received any news of their condition. She did not know how much longer she could hold out. If the Confederacy managed to persevere and keep Sherman's army from capturing Atlanta, the Confederate victory might be for nothing as hundreds of families, such as the Bransons, saw themselves on the verge of defeat.[1]

Residents caught in the path of an invading army, as Stephen Ash maintains, did not impede the enemy's movements for three reasons: a lack of local leadership, disillusionment with the retreating Confederate army, and the psychologically crippling shock that a large mass of blue-clad soldiers moving through the local countryside created among the general populace.[2] Women dominated the opposition as men either fled in fear of being captured or maintained a low-key presence to avoid arrest for being a Confederate supporter. Bartow County's minority Unionist population meanwhile voiced their opinions in a far more aggressive manner because of the occupying army's presence and the utter disorganization of local Confederates. Slaves embraced the occupation but soon discovered that they were caught in the middle of a conflict that delayed many of the tangible benefits of emancipation.

When General William T. Sherman's army resumed its march south of the Etowah on May 23, it left behind Colonel William Lowe's 3rd Division,

Cavalry Corps, to protect his extended supply lines. "Uncle Billy" created the District of the Etowah to administer the territory from Bridgeport, Alabama, to Allatoona, Georgia, "including Cleveland, Rome, and the country east as far as controlled by the federal troops." General James B. Steedman established district headquarters in Chattanooga. He created three garrisons in Bartow County at Cartersville, Cass Station, and Kingston.[3] On June 28, Brigadier General John E. Smith, commander of the 3rd Division, XIV Army Corps, received a transfer from his post in Huntsville, Alabama, to Kingston, Georgia. Smith placed his headquarters at Cartersville and ordered Colonel Jabez Banbury of the 5th Iowa Infantry to man the Kingston post. In Bartow County, the Union garrison's principal responsibilities would be to guard the W&A from an array of potential saboteurs ranging from Confederate cavalry to hostile civilians.[4]

Union occupation disrupted the daily lives of Bartow County civilians in a number of different ways. Church stood at the heart of the local antebellum community. The "Yankees" hoped to use the persuasive influence of clerics to convince the remaining populace to take the oath of allegiance. This tactic was not successful since most ministers were either serving in the military or had fled prior to the occupation. Indeed, by March of 1864, every congregation in the county had ceased worship services in anticipation of a federal invasion. The absence of proper church services troubled residents who already felt a loss of community when many of their neighbors sought refuge elsewhere. Lizzie Gaines organized a weekly Sabbath school that met in her home for several weeks. When Union soldiers discovered her flock, they disbanded the meeting, informing the women that no such congregations were permitted until they had taken the oath of allegiance. Due to the Union presence, most of the county's churches did not hold regular Sunday services until the summer of 1865.[5]

Bartow County residents further lived in constant fear that foraging soldiers might rob their homes, stealing their ability to survive. Southerners in federal occupied territory lived in three distinct worlds: garrisoned towns, Confederate frontier, and no-man's land. Those caught in a garrisoned town came into constant contact with federal soldiers. Those who lived on the Confederate frontier avoided contact with federal soldiers on a regular basis. Those who lived in no-man's land were "beyond the pale of Confederate authority and endured frequent Yankee visitations, but did not experience the constant presence of a federal force." In Bartow County, any family who lived along the W&A lived in no-man's land since the army maintained regular patrols along this valuable supply line.[6]

In August, federal soldiers stripped Rebecca Hood's fields of several bushels of corn and stole three sheep and eight hogs. On October 23, several local women confronted a band of Union soldiers collecting corn in a field located in "no-man's land." The women swore at the men, telling them that their actions were starving their families. The soldiers quietly continued gathering the crop.[7]

In contrast, Cassville residents experienced constant contact with Union foragers. Lizzie Gaines had remained during the occupation in order to care for her invalid mother. When the Union army arrived, she watched with abject horror as the invading horde "set Mr. J. Terrill's house on fire" followed by "Col. Warren Akin's house." Despite these shocking sights, she "felt comparatively secure while they remained." Her sense of security diminished a few days later, however, when a second foraging party visited her home. The soldiers demanded that Gaines give them her cow. After destroying the lot fence, the soldiers began herding the cow away from the home. Gaines rushed into the yard, blocking the cow's path and urging it to return. When the commander demanded the cow, Gaines placed herself between the cow and the officer uttering something to the effect of "over my dead body." The officer ordered his men to drive the cow over the woman if necessary. As they prodded the cow with their bayonets, Gaines stepped aside, unable to prevent the theft from occurring. With the cow, the soldiers paraded the animal in front of the family home as the invalid mother cried from her doorstep "gentlemen, please don't take our cow." The soldiers laughed at the woman and continued toward Cartersville.[8]

Undeterred, Gaines hitched "an old poor horse" named Bragg given to her by some Confederate soldiers and headed toward Cartersville in pursuit of the foraging party. Due to the poor condition of her mount, the ten-mile trip took two days to complete. In town, Gaines promptly petitioned the provost marshall for the return of her cow. He told her that he would gladly return her cow provided that she take the amnesty oath. Gaines refused and stormed out of his office, convinced that she would never see her cow again. When she noticed that several Cassville women were also in town to recover cattle, she offered to help drive them home. When she reached the slaughter pen where she expected to gain her friends' cattle, much to her surprise, the soldier on duty returned her cow along with a calf that had been stolen during a prior raid. The sharp contrast between the generosity and cruelty of federal soldiers puzzled Gaines, who never knew what to expect when the "Yankees" came.[9]

The level of distrust conditioned by such inconsistent behaviors led to numerous incidents as each side probed the other for information. Civilians routinely visited federal garrisons and professed their loyalties to the Union while clandestinely collecting information for Confederate soldiers and guerrillas. The Federals knew that such activities occurred and made limited efforts to discourage such espionage. After receiving a visit from an "old rebel gent," for example, several soldiers from the Kingston garrison donned Confederate uniforms and paid the man a visit. They questioned him about "how the 'Yanks' were fixed, and he replied that they had 'stacks of rations at Kingston.'" He divulged the number of Union soldiers at Kingston, at the Etowah River and in the different block houses." The following morning, the garrison commander escorted the man outside of Union army lines, warning him that he would be executed if caught within the lines again.[10]

Federal soldiers correctly believed that the Howard women at Spring Bank also provided information to Confederate scouts. They made several attempts to trick the women into revealing their sympathies. A Union train of sutler's wagons had camped one evening along nearby Connesena Creek. A man wearing a Confederate uniform then arrived. He told the women that Confederates were going to attack the wagon train that night and needed to learn how many soldiers were guarding the wagons. Suspicious, the women said they knew nothing. Francis Howard remembered, "his accent was unmistakably Southern, but his perfect unconcern [for the Federals nearby] made us doubtful. If he were a Confederate, this was as foolish as it was dangerous; still it was hard to distrust one who wore that uniform." The following day, they discovered that the soldier was actually a Georgia-born Confederate deserter who had enlisted in the Federal army prior to the start of the Atlanta Campaign.[11]

Lizzie Gaines experienced a similar act of deception. Three armed Illinois cavalrymen threatened to burn down her home after they failed to locate any tobacco or whiskey. She and her invalid mother faced countless sleepless nights thereafter. They worried constantly that a drunken mob of soldiers might destroy their property or assault them. Late one evening, five men wearing Confederate uniforms and claiming to belong to a local militia unit knocked on their door. The men wanted to know the location of a known Unionist sympathizer. Gaines quickly gave the men the information they requested, bidding them farewell as they vanished into some neighboring woods. Minutes later, the same men returned to her home. Instead of knocking, the men kicked open the door shouting, "we are Yankees and you have told us enough to hang you. What will you give us not to tell on you?" Frightened and confused, the woman handed the men a handful of Confederate currency, as well as a few greenbacks. She watched as the men fled her yard and traveled a half mile distance to her neighbor where they repeated their charade. When their next victims refused to surrender any cash or valuables to the raiders, the men placed a rope around an old man's neck, nearly killing him, and knocking his wife to the ground when she tried to rescue him.

In this case, the presence of federal soldiers nearby both created and resolved the problem. Fearful that the man would return, Lizzie Gaines informed the provost marshall that a series of night raids had occurred upon defenseless civilians. She reported that the men wore Confederate uniforms but clearly exhibited an allegiance to the Union cause. After a brief investigation, the provost arrested and punished the leader of the gang. Gaines later came to believe that the leader belonged to a Home Guard Unit comprised of local Unionists.[12]

On June 28, 1864, after pro-Confederate guerrilla units orchestrated several attacks upon the W&A, General Steedman issued General Order No. 2, which stated:

> The frequent depredations committed upon the communications between Bridgeport and the army in front as well as the barbarities practiced by placing torpedoes under the track to blow up trains containing sick and wounded soldiers and citizens demand the most stringent measures to suppress these crimes and atrocities. To this end all citizens except Government employees found within three miles of the railroad from Bridgeport to the Federal Army in Georgia, outside of the picket lines of any post or station of troops after the first day of July, 1864, will be arrested and forwarded to these headquarters to be tried before a military commission as spies "found lurking" within the lines of the armies of the United States.[13]

According to Lizzie Gaines, General Order No. 2 affected forty families in Cassville. Residents protested and on July 23, a group of women traveled to Kingston to petition Colonel Banbury to rescind the order. The federal officer told the women that he would ignore the order as long as he was in command, but he warned them that he would soon be replaced. A week later, two Union lieutenants arrived in Cassville with orders to remove the remaining civilians. Many balked, while others gathered their remaining belongings into the wagons furnished by the army for the removal. Much to the civilians' dismay, soldiers plundered the wagons robbing them of many of their valuables. The following morning, three elderly men traveled to Cartersville to see General Smith. Upon hearing their complaints, he reprimanded the soldiers and rescinded the removal order.[14]

General Order No. 2 also affected the Howard family since the W&A's track was located a hundred yards from their Spring Bank home. Initially, the women ignored the order, despite the constant harassment of patrolling Federals who repeatedly reminded them that they would have to relocate soon. Fortunately for the Howard family, Colonel Benjamin Dean, the new post commander at Kingston, befriended them and decided to overlook their continued presence. Had it not been for an unexpected inspection by General Steedman—who discovered much to his surprise a pro-Confederate family living within a hundred yards of the army's principal supply line—the Howard family might have remained in their home throughout the occupation. His discovery, combined with a threat to remove the Kingston post commander, forced their removal. Previously, the family had refused to become refugees because they feared the uncertainties that accompanied life away from home. Hard-pressed by federal officers to relocate, the Howards turned to Godfrey Barnsley for help. On August 5, the family moved to Woodlands, thankful that their longtime friend had remained during the occupation.[15]

While General Order No. 2 could have potentially affected hundreds of Bartow County households, in reality, the order influenced only a handful. The Macon *Daily Chronicle and Sentinel* reported that: "Sherman's order requiring all disaffected persons living within three miles of the railroad to remove, had been applied only to those whose education, station, and known sentiments, rendered them, in the enemy's opinion, dangerous. Where they have been quiet they have not been disturbed. Between Kingston and Adairsville but a single family of females has been compelled to remove up to the middle of August."[16] The Federals' reasons for removing the Howard women were sound. Their father and brother served in the 63rd Georgia. Several Confederate scouts had been seen leaving Spring Bank. Sallie Howard provided information to scouts on two occasions. The women possessed a high level of education and sophistication that would have allowed them to organize, plot, and direct attacks against the railroad or conduct various espionage missions. Yet, despite the family's obvious pro-Confederate sympathies and actions, the federal commander of the Kingston garrison allowed the household to entertain guests and receive passes to visit their friends in and out of the lines. Until receiving a direct order from the district's commanding officer, the colonel had allowed the women to remain within his lines despite knowing about their activities.[17]

In her memoir, Frances Howard fondly remembered Colonel Dean. His generosity helped ease the stress that accompanied occupation. Ordered to relocate the women, he graciously outfitted them with six wagons and a guard for transporting their effects. After their removal, the Howard family still received preferential treatment. On August 10, Frances and Jane asked the colonel for permission to travel southward to care for their wounded father. Not only did Dean grant their request, he refrained from examining their baggage, provided them with an escort, and transported them via an ambulance to the front lines. In the span of a few months, the Howard family had experienced the best and worst that the Federal army had to offer in their conduct toward noncombatants.

Similar relationships between Union soldiers and local citizens sometimes proved beneficial for both parties. A black market developed in Union-occupied territories. Goods, such as coffee, soap, and candles that could not be purchased prior to the occupation, suddenly appeared on the market as Union soldiers traded them for fresh foodstuffs and home-cooked meals. Cooking meals for enemy soldiers provided civilians with another opportunity to communicate with their conquerors in an intimate setting that consequently made the affair more human. After giving one hungry Federal a glass of buttermilk, Rebecca Hood noticed that the boy was not much older than her son. The enemy suddenly seemed less foreign and more familiar. Following the war, occupying soldiers such as Jenkins Lloyd Jones fondly recalled friendly "rebel" women such as "Grandma William's," who lived in Allatoona and earned a small income by selling hot meals to passing soldiers for fifty cents.[18]

In contrast, soldiers described the "ladies of Cassville" as "the strongest secesh ladies they had met." Women shouted insults toward passing soldiers that questioned their masculinity and courage while promising that the Confederate army would soon return to punish them. When physically assaulted, women slapped, bit, kicked, and clawed their assailants with a ferocity that repelled most attackers. Yet in a world where masculine identity revolved around the protection of white women, the absence of large numbers of males fostered a new environment where women invented new survival methods that asserted their own sense of femininity. While women assumed new roles within the household, often becoming its principal provider and protector, their lives remained constrained by their gender and a debilitating sense of defenselessness. During the occupation, women thus treated enemy soldiers as both friend and foe, depending upon the circumstance. As long as soldiers conducted themselves in a manner that allowed women to feel a sense of safety, their relationships could be quite beneficial. When soldiers acted inappropriately, however, women reverted to their antebellum gender expectations. They frequently resolved their problems by soliciting aid from a male authority figure who could either offer protection or provide justice. Trusted federal officers such as Colonel Benjamin Dean and privates such as Jenkins Jones provided local women with a masculine safety net that, when needed, could be brought to bear in an effort to address concerns that their husbands and fathers had once assumed. The "softening" of hostilities noted by a northern journalist reflects the void that some occupying soldiers filled within the lives of many female civilians struggling to strike a balance between their current and former gender roles.[19]

Keeping respectable company with Union soldiers also provided isolated women with added protection from raiding parties as well as access to valuable goods. In the weeks after a federal soldier became infatuated with Godfrey Barnsley's maid Mary Quinn, the number of stragglers who violated his property declined, in large part, due to his increased presence at the estate. Sensing the value of this relationship, Barnsley welcomed the soldier into his household, offering him peach brandy and access to his expansive library. The Englishman extended similar luxuries to a number of other federal officers in return for additional protection from stragglers.

* * * * *

Bartow County slaves welcomed Union occupation. By the spring of 1864, the master/slave relationship no longer resembled its antebellum form, which depended upon physical proximity, as well as an owner's ability to maintain a paternal influence over their property. Material shortages prevented masters from providing for their slaves' physical well-being. Many local planters had hired out large numbers of their slaves to the Confederate government or had them impressed to work on defenses around Atlanta. While many owners took their slaves with them when they fled southward, a significant number still remained during the Union occupation. As slavery weakened, the appearance of Union soldiers offered local slaves their best chance at obtaining freedom.[20]

The proximity of the Federal army emboldened slaves to run away. Easter Brown lived on a plantation with 110 other slaves. As the Federal army approached, most of them ran away never to be seen again. Her master, "Marse Frank," had brutally punished runaway slaves before the war but now made no effort to recover them since he believed that the war would soon end. All of Charles W. Howard's slaves, except enfeebled Mary, fled. Older slaves were more likely to remain with their masters only because their physical condition inhibited their flight. The large number of runaway slaves surprised many slaveholders, who had convinced themselves that their "property" would remain loyal during the occupation. General William T. Wofford's mother, for example, lamented the fact that her entire slave population ran away in June. Only two slaves, Dick and Charlotte, remained at Woodlands. Godfrey Barnsley's slave Houston revealed to Union soldiers the location of hidden valuables scattered throughout the plantation. A soldier from Colonel John T. Wilder's brigade tried to encourage Dick to run away, but he remained because he feared receiving ill-treatment from federal soldiers.

During the occupation, Dick purposely dressed in rags in order to convince those he encountered that he did not have anything worth stealing.[21]

Scant evidence exists documenting the fate of Bartow County's runaway slaves. Many headed to the federal garrison in Rome. In June 1864, that garrison sent approximately 300 black refugees to Pulaski, Tennessee. One hundred and sixty freedmen enlisted in the 44th U.S. Colored Infantry, stationed at Dalton. Surviving regimental records do not indicate the place of origin of these volunteers, but it would be reasonable to assume that some of the men came from Bartow County.[22]

Federal soldiers treated slaves in mixed fashion. While ransacking Spring Bank, soldiers stole the only possessions that slave Mary had managed to accumulate during her lifetime. After complaining to her master, the owner sarcastically replied, "why we thought the Yankees loved you, and would rather give you things than take away the little you had." Slaves who accompanied Union columns soon discovered that the soldiers sometimes treated them with as much contempt and disrespect as their prior owners. After the war, a federal soldier wished that the "war [had] continued for seven years longer, if only to kill the negroes off." When Sherman began his March to the Sea, he took along only those slaves who were physically fit and willing to work. Many older slaves and slave women with children had no other place to go except to return to their former masters.[23]

The presence of Union soldiers combined with the potential threat of their running away without notice or recourse, nonetheless, destroyed the last vestiges of the master/slave relationship. Masters frequently commented that their slaves were acting "high and mighty" since the Yankees came. At Spring Bank, the Howard family had grown dependent on the labor of their slaves. In 1864, for the first time in her life, Susan Howard had to cook her own meals. At Woodlands, two "loyal" blacks remained, but it was clear to both them and Godfrey Barnsley that they were slaves no more. Nancy Wofford awoke one morning to discover that her domestic slaves had run away. On the way out, the slaves cut the rope to the well bucket, forcing the elderly woman to carry water from a branch.[24]

* * * * *

In May 1864, Unionists, who had remained fairly quiet throughout the war, became more vocal and active in their resistance to the Confederacy due to the protection afforded by federal troops. Unionists who testified before the Southern Claims Commission overwhelmingly claimed to have voted for Stephen Douglas during the 1860 election while a few stated that they would have voted for Abraham Lincoln had he been on the ballot. Unionists defy easy characterizations.

Some Bartow Countians who remained during the occupation held Unionist and anti-Confederate sympathies. Most of the county's ardent secessionists were either in the army or lived as refugees scattered throughout the region. In their prolonged absence, Unionists began to openly support the federal government. They served as an invaluable ally. Unionists worked as guides, laborers, spies, cooks, and nurses. Their knowledge of the local terrain aided federal cavalry in apprehending Confederate guerrillas, scouts, and deserters. They also gathered intelligence by spying on their neighbors. Unionists frustrated Confederate recruiters and scouts by hiding deserters and leading draft evaders northward.

Nonetheless, identifying Unionists proves problematic. Their membership represented a wide array of socioeconomic classes. While most owned land, some were tenants. By-and-large, known Unionists owned roughly the same amount of land—50 to 100 acres—as did most local farmers. A majority of Unionists were farmers, but, then again, so were most Bartow Countians. In addition to farmers, Unionists worked as ministers, lawyers, day laborers, railroad workers, woodchoppers, teamsters, blacksmiths, and in numerous other skilled and unskilled occupations.

Most did not own slaves, but some did. The minority of Unionist slaveholders espoused a belief that the Union needed preservation but frequently resisted emancipation. Slaveholder John McDow was a known Unionist in Bartow County. In May, McDow took his slaves southward to prevent their capture. Willis McDow, John McDow's slave, testified that he "was off from home with my young master to keep me from the Federal army." Like McDow, Nancy Russell sent her slaves southward with an overseer to avoid capture. After the war, some Unionists slaveholders petitioned the Southern Claims Commission to compensate them for the loss of their slave property.[25]

A majority of Bartow County Unionists lived in the county's northeastern Appalachian subregion. After the war, Unionists who testified before the Southern Claims Commission revealed a large network of Unionists families living around Adairsville and Pine Log. Of the forty-five Unionists identified within the Southern Claims Commission records, all but four lived in the county's Appalachian subregion. Most of these individuals either owner small farms or had worked as day laborers prior to the war. Few owned slaves or any other significant amounts of personal property. Some had relatives that fought in the Confederate army, while many had worked tirelessly throughout the war to prevent their kinfolk from being forced into service. Countless other Unionists likely existed in this subregion, but since the Union army neither marched through this area during the Atlanta Campaign nor placed occupation forces there after the campaign most of these anti-Confederates escaped notice.[26]

Bonds of kinship tied together many Unionist households. When Southern Claims Commissioners questioned William Collins about his wartime experiences, the yeoman slaveholder who lived near Adairsville revealed that he had a brother who served in the Union army. Eight self-identified Unionists testified on Collins's behalf. Of those eight individuals, six were related to Collins including a couple of brother-in-laws, a sister, and a sister-in-law. Thanks to the support of his family, Commissioner A. A. Beck referred to Collins as "one of those unflinching, uncompromising, Union men such as are few and far between in this country and yet is respected as a man by his worst enemies."[27]

While the Southern Claims Commission records reveal that kin linked Unionist sympathizers, even those associations had its limits. Sarah Crow and her husband vehemently opposed secession, yet her brother and two nephews expressed an interest in joining the Confederate army in the spring of 1861. She pleaded with them to reconsider, but her protests fell upon deaf ears.[28] Edmund Cook owned a small farm located four miles east of Adairsville. He hoped to avoid serving in the military because he did not support secession. Cook's overbearing "secesh" brother-in-law reported him to conscription agents who forced the Unionist into the Confederate army.[29]

Generational tensions played an additional but limited role in determining Unionist sympathies. Parents might have disapproved of their children's decision but could do little to prevent them from enlisting. Mary McDonald warned her two sons that their deceased father would not have approved of their enlistment and neither did she; nevertheless, they enlisted. A few months later, some "secesh" women from Kingston invited her to join their soldier's aid sewing society. She firmly told them that her sons had made their own decisions and that she would not be party to treason.[30] Samuel McDow of Adairsville refused to join the Confederate army and advised his two son-in-laws to do the same. Despite his advice, the men enlisted.[31] William Corbin of Cartersville feared that if his son enlisted that he would die. His consternation came to fruition when he received word that his son had fallen during the Battle of Missionary Ridge. Thereafter, Corbin "damned" the Confederacy and began openly displaying his Unionist sympathies.[32]

Likewise, children harbored Unionists beliefs that were ignored by their parents. In 1862, William Law's father and two brothers joined the Confederate army—it is unclear whether they volunteered or were conscripted. In 1864, when federal troops occupied Cartersville, he enlisted in the Union army, despite knowing that his family was serving in the Army of Tennessee.[33]

Prior to the occupation, some Unionists had developed a reputation among their friends and neighbors for their pronounced criticism of the Confederate government. Loud speeches, however, attracted unwanted attention. Grandison Vaughn liked an audience. Numerous individuals testified before the Southern Claims Commission that he had said that he "wished the Confederacy was in the bottomless pit of hell."[34] His emotion matched that of a handful of local Unionists such as Miles and Sarah Crow who also earned a reputation for criticizing the national government. Most maintained a low profile whenever possible in order to avoid possible retribution by pro-Confederate zealots. Nancy Russell, for example, rarely proclaimed her sympathies in public while privately she helped to organize an "underground railroad" that transported Unionists to east Tennessee.[35]

During the initial occupation of Cassville, someone burned the home of three prominent secessionists. While many accounts blame the Federal army for these fires, circumstantial evidence suggests that Unionists played a major role in determining which homes were destroyed. In a letter to her husband, Lila Chunn complained of "Tories" living in Cassville. She mentioned a Mr. Bohannon who "had taken the oath and was fixed up in a Yankee wagon ready to move farther north." While raiding a federal supply train, Confederate cavalry captured Bohannon and sent him to Atlanta with sixty-three other prisoners. In prison, he was visited by Will Patton who later informed Chunn that Bohannon and several Unionists had claimed responsibility for setting fire to three homes.

Concerned that Confederates might exact retribution, Unionist Oliver Vaughan organized a company of Union men to serve as a home guard during the occupation. The Home Guard unit preyed upon Confederate stragglers and deserters. After capturing two soldiers who were absent without leave and who attempted to cross the Etowah River to visit their families, Vaughan led the men to the Cartersville garrison where they were placed in shackles and transported northward to a military prison. Scouts scoured the Confederate frontier searching for Vaughan. The Home Guard commander eluded capture by rarely traveling beyond no-man's land.[36]

Some civilians embraced the Union for the sake of self-preservation. Berry Houk, who had never expressed any Unionist sympathies prior to 1864, led a party of sixty people who traveled to Calhoun to take the amnesty oath. In Cassville, two old men who remained during the occupation but had previously maintained their neutrality suddenly proclaimed their allegiance to the United States in an effort to avoid any possible conflict with nearby Union soldiers. Some former secessionists hoped to receive special privileges from the occupying army in return for taking the oath. Women whose property had been stolen by soldiers frequently took the oath in order to curry favor with the local provost marshall. Lizzie Gaines discovered upon arriving in Cartersville that she was not the only woman with such a request. Dozens of other women under similar circumstances had already entered the garrison but had already taken the oath. The provost marshall demanded that women who were seeking their property present documentation proving they had taken the oath. Gaines observed the "air of exultation" and excitement as women waved the required document to retrieve their stolen property. As Gaines moved to the head of the line, the officer requested her papers. She replied "I am a Southerner by birth and principle and would not take the oath for all the cows in the United States." Much to her dismay, another woman scolded her, saying that her defiance was putting everyone at risk of not having their cattle returned.[37]

* * * * *

Federal soldiers particularly warned civilians such as Gaines not to harbor or aid Confederate scouts, but citizens regularly violated these orders. Scouts received food and shelter from many Bartow Countians who still supported the Confederacy. Sometimes, civilians engaged in acts of sabotage that targeted the W&A. Locals joined guerrilla bands comprised of many regular army deserters and state militia members but, in general, lacked any formal military authority. Guerrillas and scouts differed according to their relationship with the national military. Scouts, such as the 1st Georgia Cavalry, received orders directly from Confederate authorities. Guerrillas, such as John Gatewood's band, did not.

Scouts and Federals fought a protracted struggle that revolved around the W&A. A federal officer once told Frances Howard that "he would rather be the leader of the forlorn hope, in storming the strongest fort in the Confederacy, than to make the trip from Chattanooga to Atlanta."[38] District of the Etowah commander Steedman issued General Order No. 2, in large part, in an effort to curtail sabotage efforts.

Guerrilla activity frustrated federal troops. Following an attack, Union soldiers interrogated suspected saboteurs, typically threatening to burn their homes or towns if they did not reveal the culprit's identity. The Cartersville garrison temporarily jailed dozens of citizens accused of aiding and abetting guerrillas. Most returned home after a brief period of confinement, but military officials banished several hundred civilians to north of the Ohio River for the duration of the war.

Women engaged in a wide array of illicit activities that attracted attention from federal authorities. In July, soldiers garrisoned at Kingston arrested Julia and Jane Murchison. They had enjoyed a great deal of freedom during the early months of the occupation. They regularly received passes from the Kingston provost marshall allowing them to visit the Howard and Barnsley families. On the morning of July 19, the sisters walked into the Kingston train depot to request a pass to visit Spring Bank. Lieutenant Colonel Ezekiel Sampson, 5th Iowa Infantry, rejected the women's request, in part, because of Julia's chosen attire, a gray Confederate jacket adorned with a captain's insignia. The sight of the uniform annoyed Sampson, who ordered the young woman to remove the coat. He believed it was part of the uniform that belonged to a suspected guerrilla. A few days earlier, while in pursuit of this renegade, Union cavalry found a pair of gloves that had been dropped by the fleeing guerrilla. Grabbing the woman's jacket, Sampson placed it on his desk and promptly removed the gloves from a nearby drawer presenting it to the women as evidence of their deceptions. Intent on further aggravating the situation, Julia picked up the gloves and kissed them.

After leaving Sampson's office, the sisters traveled to Spring Bank without a pass. Upon their return, federal pickets arrested the women and charged them with aiding and abetting guerillas and violating General Order No. 2. The District of the Etowah's commanding officer sentenced the women to serve time in a military prison located in Louisville, Kentucky. On July 22, the Murchison sisters along with fifty other Georgia women arrived in Louisville.

While imprisoned, the Murchison sisters endured harsh conditions that weakened their physical health. During their first six weeks, the women stayed at Barracks One which lacked any proper sanitary facilities as well as adequate bedding. By the time the sisters were transferred to the Female Military Prison, Julia had developed pneumonia. Jane begged her to take the amnesty oath rather than risk death by remaining in prison. As her condition worsened, Julia consented, took the oath, and was released to remain north of the Ohio River for the remainder of the war. After living in Ohio for several weeks, she decided to return to Bartow County anyway. The journey required slipping through numerous federal checkpoints while avoiding detection since her parole banned her return. While moving through a picket line in Tennessee, soldiers mortally wounded Julia. As she lay dying, she wrote her sister a tearful farewell letter. Jane remained in prison for the remainder of the war, unwilling to take the oath. She did not return to Bartow County until May of 1865.

In August 1864, General Joseph Wheeler dispatched Co. I of the 1st Georgia Cavalry, under the command of Lieutenant James Gilreath, to strike the W&A for three months. The general handpicked the company, meaning that a majority of soldiers hailed from Bartow County and therefore knew the terrain well. His unit grew in size while operating in the county since many deserters were willing to ride with a cavalry detachment to avoid persecution. O. P. Hargis's brothers, Henry and Dick, left the Army of Northern Virginia to join the 1st Georgia Cavalry. Their orders included tearing up the railroad, cutting telegraph wires, derailing trains, and disrupting supplies traveling between Calhoun and Cartersville. Wheeler instructed the soldiers to refrain from firing upon the enemy "unless [they] were compelled to to keep from being captured."[39] The Federal army immediately felt their presence. In August, Sherman ordered the revival of the old visual signal system since enemy scouts continued to severe their telegraph wires.

Many civilians provided the cavalry and guerrillas with intelligence and supplies that benefited their operations. O. P. Hargis recalled that "the people would find out where we were camped and cook a basket full of rations and bring them to us, and we would get feed for our horses from them. . . . We had a good time out there."[40] Warren Akin believed that most locals would have gladly surrendered their "last mouthful of bread" to feed a "rebel" scout. The county contained loyal Confederates who were "as full of rebel blood as a tick." A network of support designed to foil federal attempts to track the movements of suspected supporters developed. Federals were especially suspicious of women whose husbands and sons served in the Confederate army. They knew that numerous deserters had returned to the county and had joined guerrilla bands or else were hiding out in the countryside near their homes. Any woman who traveled into the woods to visit their family members risked compromising both herself and their loved ones because Union soldiers and Unionists commonly watched their every move. Women therefore gave food and supplies to other local women who were not under enemy surveillance who in turn carried the items to the men.

Federal scouts routinely searched Spring Bank and Woodlands in search of Confederate soldiers. A Union officer once questioned Jane Howard if she had harbored Confederates. She responded that "we, like all true Southern women, will aid our soldiers whenever and wherever we can." Cassville sheltered Confederate scouts, guerrillas, and deserters that attracted the nearby garrison's attention. After soldiers ransacked Lizzie Gaines's home looking for a suspected guerrilla, she told the intruders that "if they did not want the Rebels to visit the place, they must be more vigilant themselves, that we would not make it our business to keep them away."

Federal soldiers often killed captured guerrillas. While on a mission to destroy a bridge over the Etowah, a partisan known only as Hutchison detoured from his objective to make an unannounced visit to his mother. Federal scouts tracked his movements. While crossing back over the Etowah River, the Federals attacked Hutchison, who fled on foot into some nearby woods with the enemy in close pursuit. One week later, federal soldiers knocked on Hutchison's mother's door. They told her that her son had drowned in the river while attempting to reach Confederate lines. Upon recovering his body, the mother was shocked to discover that his head was covered in blood and his skull badly fractured. Moreover, his hands were tied with his halter. He still had his hat, which would have been unlikely had he drowned. The mother claimed that Union soldiers caught and interrogated him hoping to learn the identity and location of his companions. The soldiers beat Hutchison to death after he refused to cooperate with their demands.[41]

The proximity of large numbers of scouts and guerrillas instilled a sense of paranoia among federal soldiers. They feared that attackers lurked around every corner. During the summer, for example, a small band of foragers impressed several cows from the residents of Cassville. While herding the cattle toward Kingston, the soldiers noticed that they were being followed by two girls. Initially, the soldiers ignored the girls, but upon reaching an isolated stretch of road, their insecurities overwhelmed their emotions. The girls had stopped fewer than a hundred yards from the soldiers when they began clapping their hands while shouting "here they are, catch them, catch them." Surrounded by a dense thicket, the soldiers panicked and "skedaddled," believing that the girls were signaling nearby guerrillas. Later that evening, the stolen cows wandered back into Cassville.[42]

Federals lived in constant fear of such ambushes. On July 8, Jenkins Jones's commanding officer ordered him to graze their artillery unit's horses. Ordinarily, this duty would have been considered light, but Jones knew that grazing the horses would isolate him from the rest of his unit. After traveling as short of a distance as possible, he located an area suitable for grazing. A few minutes later, he was startled by a passing Unionist who warned him that a band of guerrillas were lurking in some nearby woods waiting to capture his horses. Jones appreciated the warning and returned to his post as soon as possible. Two weeks later, he recorded in his diary that a squad of about one hundred fifty guerrillas overran a picket post and then vanished into thin air. A month later, he reported "troublesome" rebels between Allatoona and Acworth. At this time, he suspected two missing comrades had been murdered, but he learned a few days later that these men had been taken prisoner and were in "humane hands." On September 1, bushwhackers killed a Union soldier, whom they "stripped of all valuables, boots, and hat, leaving his corpse in the road, taking two others prisoners."[43]

Unionists and Confederates used the occupying army and roaming guerrillas to exact revenge upon one another. Martin Chumler was a Unionist who lived in Wolf Pen, a small community near Pine Log. He was known to have led Union soldiers on foraging expeditions. Upon discovering that a local secessionist was harboring an ill Texas soldier, Chumler arrested the soldier and attempted to transport him to the Cartersville garrison. Guerrillas found this out and intercepted him before he reached Cartersville. Chumler ran but was later captured and hanged.[44]

The strategy employed by General John B. Hood after the fall of Atlanta directly impacted Bartow County. His plan involved marching the Army of Tennessee into northwest Georgia to strike Sherman's supply lines. If successful, Hood would force the Federals to abandon Atlanta and pursue him into northern Alabama. If Sherman did not take the bait, the Army of Tennessee could then attack his rear.

Sherman fell back to secure his lines. Hood's movements pulled additional federal troops into Bartow County. Sherman moved his entire army, minus the XX Army Corps, into northwest Georgia, reinforcing garrisons scattered along the W&A. On October 4, Confederates captured the Big Shanty garrison. Moving northward, they captured Acworth, destroying several miles of track between the two garrisons. General Samuel G. French received orders from Hood to take his division and capture the federal fortifications located along Allatoona Pass, fill the railroad pass with debris, and then march northward to burn the Etowah River bridge. The federal position at Allatoona Pass was strong. During the occupation, Sherman had ordered the construction of two forts situated on the east and west ridges that overlooked the steep railroad pass. The western Star Fort sat along the Alabama Road. The eastern fort blocked the Tennessee Road. A wooden planked footbridge extending across the pass connected the two positions.

Observing Confederate movements from atop Kennesaw Mountain, Sherman believed that Hood would strike Allatoona and then move toward Rome. If he could stop the Confederate advance at Allatoona, he believed that he could avoid any subsequent confrontations in front of Rome. Therefore, he ordered Brigadier General John Corse's 4th Division, XIV Corps, garrisoned in Rome, to reinforce the 976 soldiers who currently held the pass. Through the use of two railroad lines, Corse arrived with a single brigade at Allatoona one hour before French launched his assault.[45]

At 1:30 a.m., Confederates advanced upon the federal picket lines consisting of men from the 93rd Illinois Infantry Regiment. French's assault pushed the pickets back into the main body of their regiment and successfully drove it into the fort. Corse ordered the 18th Wisconsin Infantry Regiment to reinforce that line. The 18th Wisconsin, minus two companies who were stationed at the Etowah Bridge block house, took heavy fire from the enemy but delayed the enemy advance until dawn. As the day's first light appeared above the horizon, the Confederates outflanked the 18th Wisconsin's position, forcing the regiment to retreat into well-prepared earthen fortifications. At 6:30 a.m., Confederate artillery bombarded the fortifications with little effect. Confident that his forces would prevail, French sent a message to Corse under a flag of truce demanding the fort's surrender. After briefly reviewing French's demands, Corse "respectfully" refused to surrender. Anticipating the coming assault, Corse hurriedly redistributed his command throughout the two forts.[46]

Two hours later, the Confederates resumed their advance from the north and the west. Young's brigade of Texans—approximately 1,900 strong—charged the 39th Ninth Iowa and 17th Illinois Infantry, stationed along the Alabama Road. The Texans pushed the Federals several hundred yards into a prepared redoubt defended by Colonel Richard Rowett, 7th Illinois Infantry Regiment. Protected by the redoubt, the reformed Federals fired a series of volleys into the hastily advancing Texans causing numerous casualties and temporarily checked their movements.

While Rowett's men slowed the Confederate's advance along the Alabama Road, a new threat soon revealed itself as another brigade of Confederates attacked the western portion of the pass from the north. Two infantry companies and an assortment of pickets fell back as the Confederates pressed the Federals. The situation looked dire as the advancing brigade threatened to overtake the Federals before they could retreat into the Start Fort. Flanking fire from the 4th Minnesota Infantry Regiment, however, briefly stalled the advancing rebels who had never realized that their rapid advance had exposed their left flank. While the rebels regrouped, Corse sent a staff officer across the foot bridge with orders to receive reinforcements from the eastern fort.

Meanwhile, along the Alabama Road, Confederate units reformed and slammed into Rowett's redoubt, engulfing its defenders before the much-needed reinforcements arrived. Fierce hand-to-hand combat broke out in this section as the 39th Iowa Infantry sacrificed numerous casualties in a last ditch effort to buy the western fort time. Due to their efforts, the 7th and 93rd Illinois Infantry and what was left of the 39th Iowa were able to retreat into the relative safety of the Star Fort. Under intense fire, these outnumbered units successfully staved off a series of rebel advances for nearly three hours. In his report, Corse commented that "the extraordinary valor of the men and officers of this regiment and of the Seventh Illinois" had won the battle. [47]

Disorganized due their repeated and unsuccessful frontal assaults, the Confederates failed to take the fort. Unable to fully retreat, many remained in small groups or individually hiding behind tree stumps and in hollows firing upon the fort with great effect while taking advantage of their improvised cover. Fire from the north, south, and west completely enfiladed the fort making it nearly impossible for the Federals to seek cover behind their parapets. With their men pinned down, "officers," wrote Corse, "labored constantly to stimulate the men to exertion, and most all that were killed or wounded in the fort met this fate while trying to get all the men to expose themselves above the parapet."[48] At 1:00 p.m., a rifle ball struck Corse, knocking him senseless for nearly an hour. The bodies of the "dead and dying" soon filled the fort as the situation seemed hopeless. Only the overwhelming fire of the 12th Wisconsin Artillery prevented the charging rebels from overtaking the position.

While regaining consciousness, Corse heard his men shouting "cease fire! cease fire!" It appeared to him that some of his men intended to surrender. As he looked around him, most of his soldiers were hiding behind the parapets refusing to expose themselves to the enemy fire. The artillery had been silenced due to a lack of ammunition. Corse ordered his few remaining staff officers and a handful of privates scattered around him to renew the fight. To their peril, the staff officers raised their guns above the parapets exposing themselves to the enemy. Their example helped to rally the troops as Corse encouraged the men that Sherman would soon join the fight. Meanwhile, the commander sent a brave artillerist across the foot bridge to secure ammunition. Upon his return, the battery resumed its murderous fire slowly thinning the enemy's ranks. The Confederates attempted to reform their lines for a last ditch assault, but the artillery fire from the fort caused "great confusion" that made "it impossible for the enemy to rally." After more than twelve hours of heated battle, the Confederates withdrew toward New Hope Church, fearing the imminent arrival of federal reinforcements.[49]

The Battle of Allatoona Pass was "a useless effusion of blood." Approximately, 30 percent of the 5,300 Union and Confederate soldiers engaged in the battle were either killed, wounded, or listed as missing. The Confederates suffered greater casualties—900—than did the Federals 703. French's division failed to achieve any of the battle's original objectives. In fact, even had he managed to capture the pass, it would have unlikely that he would have had time to either fill it with debris or burn the Etowah Bridge due to the close proximity of federal reinforcements. For Hood, the Battle of Allatoona Pass proved to be the first in a long line of poorly planned and executed strategies employed after the fall of Atlanta.

* * * * *

On October 6, Sherman established his headquarters in Kingston at the Hargis house, located near the train depot. As during the previous May, tens of thousands of federal soldiers poured through the county, looting civilian homes wherever they passed. For four days, from October 10 until the 13th, the bulk of the Union army marched through Cassville, stripping the already decimated town bare of all livestock, feed, and horses. On October 12, soldiers pushed aside the federal guard that had been placed at Woodlands to protect Godfrey Barnsley's property and proceeded to ransack the estate causing more damage than the Army of the Cumberland had done six months earlier. The depressed owner lamented the fact that the wealth that he had worked a lifetime to build had vanished over the course of a single afternoon.

In October, the number of guerrilla attacks upon federal soldiers increased. Irregulars targeted Union foragers who frequently operated miles from their fortified garrison. On October 9, bushwhackers attacked a detachment of the 100th Indiana sent into the countryside to gather firewood. The partisans surrounded the men forcing them to surrender. As the attackers began executing the soldiers, Private Charles Ellis, Co. B, dropped his rifle to the ground and pleaded with the guerrillas to spare his life. They shot him at point blank range despite his pleas. The following morning Theodore Upson of the same regiment discovered the bodies of several civilians hanged for the attacks. Their executioners pinned a placard on each corpse which read: "This done in retaliation for the unwarranted attack made upon my foragers yesterday. Any repetition of this offense will be similarly punished, and in addition, all buildings upon ten square miles of the adjacent territory will be destroyed. W. T. Sherman, General Commanding."

The violence escalated throughout October. On October 12, a federal ambulance passing through the town broke down. Unable to repair the wagon, the driver set up camp for the night. As the evening progressed, nine Union stragglers joined the driver, drawn toward his camp by its warm fire. That night, an unidentified band of guerrillas killed the ten men while they slept. The following morning, the advanced guard of the XVII Corps found the driver with a bayonet protruding from his chest. Federal personnel stationed at the Female College awoke to find the bodies of nine soldiers that had been dumped over a fence onto the grounds.[50]

The way the ten soldiers died deeply angered federal commanders. Members of the Brigadier General Kenner Garrard's 2nd Division Cavalry burned the Cherokee Baptist and Female colleges and the homes of Nathan Land and Dr. Thomas Rambant, president of the college, in retaliation for these murders.[51] On October 29, federal soldiers informed the residents of Cassville that they would have to relocate. The following morning, Colonel T. T. Heath and the 5th Ohio Cavalry arrived with wagons to help three families move their belongings. The 5th Ohio's orders demanded that they "permit the citizens to remove what they desire, and burn the town, after which you will proceed to Cassville and make the same disposition as at Canton."[52]

On the afternoon of November 5, the 5th Ohio ordered the remaining civilians to leave town immediately and then proceeded to burn Cassville. The soldiers watched as towering flames spewed a dark black smoke into the clear blue sky. Frightened residents pleaded with soldiers to put out the blaze before it reached their home, but the cavalrymen followed their orders and refrained from aiding any civilians. Fire claimed the property of every Cassville resident, regardless of their political beliefs, except three. Indeed, one of the first homes destroyed belonged to Unionist William Sylar.[53]

As flames consumed the town's structures, soldiers plundered homes and businesses, often running into smoke filled buildings searching for remaining valuables. Glass from broken lamps, dishes, and windows littered the town's streets. Most residents who remained behind to watch the blaze, according to one account, conducted themselves "with the greatest composure. Some made no attempt to save anything, but with the reckless calm of desperation, sat quietly and watched their homes go up in smoke."[54]

As the sun set upon a blackened sky, a chilling rain mixed with sleet descended upon the smoldering town. Lizzie Gaines watched as "dark threatening clouds, which hung suspended for a while over the doomed spot, and then seemed to melt away in tears of grief. It appeared as if nature were weeping over the sad fate of Cassville."[55] Most of the town's women and children endured the rain and sleet while remaining outside of their charred homes guarding their few remaining possessions. A few stables and churches survived the fire, but few wanted to sleep in stables because they feared that the soldiers might return and set fire to them while they slept. A few other families sought refuge from the storm in the town cemetery. Six months before, the center of the Confederate line stretched across this ground, abandoned breastworks marked the site. The desperate civilians occupied the abandoned entrenchments.

In the spring of 1861, Cassville resident John F. Milhollin had enlisted in the Confederate army, confident that God had ordained secession. He died in combat while serving in the Army of Northern Virginia. On November 5, his wife and her six children watched as Union soldiers torched their home. That night, the family huddled together in the cemetery using planks from their father's fresh gravesite and several heavy quilts to construct a makeshift shelter against a wrought iron fence. As the family endured the cold and rain, they could see the glowing embers of their decimated home glittering a few hundred yards away. The soldier's fourteen-year-old son spent the next morning searching the countryside for a suitable dwelling. Four miles outside of town, the boy located an abandoned slave cabin on the Saxon plantation that would function as the family's home for months.[56]

Sherman watched the smoke rise from Cassville from his Kingston headquarters. He had not personally ordered the town's destruction; Brigadier General John E. Smith wrote the order. Indeed, four days later, Sherman demanded that guerrillas return Union prisoners, or else Kingston, Cassville, and Cartersville would be burned. Cassville already lay in ruins. The commander included the town to provide "post facto" validity to Smith's October 30 order.

The Federal army ultimately destroyed Cassville because the town actively aided and abetted guerrillas. A majority of people in town supported the Confederacy. Union soldiers regarded Cassville as "a hot bed of saboteurs." According to Warren Akin, only two Unionists lived in the town. Since the town lacked a garrison and was located along several critical roads, partisans and Confederate scouts moved in and out of the area with little resistance. A member of the 1st Georgia Cavalry reported that locals regularly fed, hid, and provided information to both scouts and irregulars.

Three days after the burning of Cassville, Captain Abraham Tate's scouts struck a squadron of foragers belonging to the 74th Indiana Infantry Regiment. They captured seven and wounded two Union soldiers. The ambush took place near the home of Unionist Berry Houk who afterwards carried one of the wounded men back to his command. Upon learning of the attack, Sherman, believing it was the work of guerrillas, ordered the arrest of six to eight suspected partisan supporters. After their arrest, he released two of them to warn guerrillas to either release the soldiers, or Kingston, Cartersville, and Cassville would be burned, as well as the homes of those arrested. On November 9, XIV Corps dispatched a regiment into the area. Their orders included seizing some citizens, and then releasing one of them to warn to return the soldiers by noon the next day. If the soldiers were not returned by that time, the regiment was instructed to burn a dozen homes.

Anxious to capture the irregulars, Sherman instructed Lieutenant Colonel Thomas Morgan of the 74th Indiana Infantry to conduct a "guerrilla hunt." Unionists provided him with a list of suspected partisans as well as a hand-drawn map showing their residences and hideouts. Within a few hours, Federals arrested six men—a Mr. Kelly, William Crow, Berry Houk, Wash Henderson, Lindsey Hendricks, and Captain James Hendricks. Soldiers interrogated Hendricks, who admitted that he belonged to the First Georgia Cavalry and that his unit had been involved in the ambush. He subsequently confessed that his men had killed two soldiers and a "Negro" during the fight. Hendricks also revealed that the seven prisoners-of-war had been transported to Athens. In an effort to secure his release, he promised Morgan that if he was freed he would travel to Athens and secure their release. He also promised to free thirty-one prisoners scattered throughout north Georgia. Morgan rejected the offer.

Morgan's "guerrilla hunt" continued to scour the countryside searching for a partisan named Madison Denman. Like many irregulars operating in Bartow County, Denman had once served in the Confederate army. When Federals failed to locate him, they burned his house along with those of neighbors Lindsay Hendricks and Washington Henderson. In a thicket a few hundred yards from his blazing home, Denman and several of his men watched and waited for an opportunity to pounce upon Morgan's troops. As the Federals returned to their garrison, partisans attacked their passing causing minimal damage before quickly returning into the dense woods. For several miles, the Federals could hear Denman's horsemen shadowing their movements, but as the troops moved closer to Kingston, the likelihood of an attack decreased.

At Kingston, Morgan questioned five of the six men that had been captured earlier that day. He soon realized that his soldiers had mistakenly arrested Berry Houk, a known Union man who had previously supplied the Federals with information. Morgan tried to hide the Unionist's loyalties from his fellow inmates, but these efforts failed. After his release, Warren Akin questioned Houk's devotion to the Confederacy and hoped that scouts would hang him. Fearing for his personal safety, Houk headed toward east Tennessee, leaving his wife and children behind. Weeks later, some of the irregulars who had been arrested with Houk accused the Unionist's wife of leading the Federals to Denman's house.[57]

* * * * *

On November 2, Grant approved Sherman's March to the Sea proposal. The beginning movements of this campaign marked the end of the federal occupation of Bartow County. Ten days later, Sherman abandoned his Kingston headquarters. As the last train passed through the county, Union soldiers destroyed the railroad and telegraph lines. The following morning, Federals burned Kingston and several homes in Cartersville. A soldier ordered to spread the blaze commented that "most of the families have either gone north or south, but a few, from some cause, have failed to get away and now they are weeping over their burning homes. The sight is grand but almost heartrending."[58]

The Athens *Southern Banner* called upon refugees from northwest Georgia who had settled in that city to return to their farms and plant a substantial wheat crop.[59] Julia Barnsley, living in Augusta, resisted the urge to return because her father's letters had emphasized the devastation. Rebecca Felton missed her Cartersville home but did not know whether or not her house had been destroyed. Mary Akin wrote her husband about her plans to come back to Cassville despite the loss of her home. He told her and other refugees to refrain from returning since a majority of the homes and mills had been razed. "I have learned," wrote Akin, "that many persons have returned to our section of Georgia, and I fear have gone too soon. . . . I have no idea of seeing where my house once stood until the war is over, if I do then. From all I can learn there must be great destitution in that section of Georgia. No hogs, cows, or sheep. How are the people to be fed?"[60] Colonel Hawkins Price, who had served as a county delegate to the state secession convention, regretted coming back to Cassville since he could not locate any place to purchase much-needed supplies in the decimated town.[61]

Starvation threatened the lives of all who remained in Bartow County. The county had raised little corn or wheat during that year's harvest. Most of what had been planted had been impressed by Federal, Confederate, or partisan forces. A few mills escaped the torch, but most residents had nothing for the grindstone. As the spring planting season approached, farmers lacked seed and draft animals capable of breaking the soil. Only a handful of cows, swine, chickens, and sheep remained in most of the towns. Shortages of salt curtailed winter slaughtering. Residents depended upon trapping rabbits and hunting opossums, deer, and squirrels for food.

The end of the federal occupation removed the sole source of local authority, creating a power vacuum as the county spiraled dangerously toward anarchy. In the wake of the occupation, a lawless consortium of thieves, ruffians, and deserters descended on the populace like locusts upon a wheat field. They preyed upon vulnerable, female-headed households and unarmed travelers. Hiding in nearby wooded areas, caves, and swamps during the day, they used the cover of darkness to conceal their actions. A scheme commonly employed involved donning Confederate uniforms and presenting themselves to women as malnourished soldiers in desperate need of a "Good Samaritan." Many of the women had husbands, sons, and brothers serving in the Confederate army. From their letters, they read horrifying depictions of the poor conditions that existed within camps or defensive lines such as those surrounding Petersburg. Eager to help a soldier in need and hopeful that women elsewhere were doing the same for their loved ones, women opened their homes to these deceptive wolves in sheep's clothing. Once inside, the outlaws held the women and children at gunpoint, demanding money, jewelry, and food in exchange for not burning the home or physically assaulting its inhabitants.

Numerous partisan groups also operated in Bartow County during and after the occupation, including Jack Colquit's scouts, Aycock's scouts,

J. Woodville Baker's scouts, Abraham Tate's scouts, Matt Moore's scouts, John Gatewood's scouts, John Prior's scouts, Woody's scouts, Lillard's scouts, Benjamin McCollum's scouts, and Jordan's Gang. Dozens of others small bands of deserters, stragglers, and vagabonds existed within the area, but their names are unknown. Additional research is necessary in order to reconstruct the rosters and scope of activities of north Georgia's irregular units.[62] Captain Charles W. Howard returned to Spring Bank in January 1865 after recovering from a wound received during the Battle of Atlanta. Shortly after his arrival, a small group of men dressed in Confederate uniforms stormed into his home after his wife offered them some food. The men claimed to be cavalry scouts, but they probably belonged either to John Gatewood or to Jack Colquitt's partisans, who had been active in the area. Unaware of Howard's presence, the thieves began emptying drawers in the family's parlor searching for valuables. When the veteran entered the room still wearing his captain's uniform from the 63rd Georgia, the robbers fled into the night. Their flight was short-lived, however, as they stumbled upon a tenant home located on Howard's property. The miller who worked at Howard's mill, along with his family, lived in the former tenant farm house. The irregulars broke into the home at gun point startling the residents. Panicked, the miller's wife offered to do anything for the men in exchange for the safety of her family. The partisans calmly sat at their dinner table and ordered the woman to cook them dinner. That night, the supposed scouts slept on the family's beds while the miller and his wife spent a restless night on the floor.[63]

Jack Colquitt's partisans preyed upon the residents of Bartow, Polk, and Floyd counties. Colquitt had connections to the region. Prior to the war, he had married the daughter of a Polk County merchant, Jerry Isbell, but nothing else about Colquitt's early life is known. His tactics frequently included mock executions designed to force their targets to reveal hidden valuables. When Judge Lewis D. Burwell of Rome supposedly refused to reveal the location of a stash of gold he had hidden for a local Jewish merchant, Colquitt tied a noose around the jurist's neck and hanged the man until he finally disclosed its whereabouts.

Colquitt's reign of terror eventually cost him his life. Shortly after the incident with Judge Burwell, his company murdered H. M. Prior of Cedartown. Prior's three sons swore revenge. After several weeks spent tracking Colquitt across portions of northwest Georgia, they ambushed the scouts, killing the leader and seven others. Had the Prior boys not caught up with the guerrilla leader, he would likely have been killed by members of J. Woodville Baker's scouts, whose leader he killed "over the ownership of a mule" weeks earlier.[64]

Partisans regularly targeted Unionists. Cartersville resident Richard Chitwood initially supported secession. Four of his brothers enlisted in the

Confederate army. Sometime during the war, he became disenchanted with the Confederacy and developed a reputation for being a Union man. During the last weeks of the federal occupation, Benjamin McCollum's band raided Chitwood's farm, stealing two horses. Through the use of a courier, the guerrillas notified him that if he traveled to their camp located near Canton that he could recover his property. Desperately in need of those horses, Chitwood made the twenty-plus mile journey only to be detained by the scouts who tried to persuade him to join their ranks. He refused but negotiated his release in exchange for a suit of clothes.[65]

Unionists who had served as guides, scouts, informants, and foragers for the occupation army lived in constant fear of pro-Confederate guerrillas. McCollum's partisans routinely executed their victims. Jim Pitts served as a guide for federal cavalry during the occupation. When the irregulars captured him, they transported him several dozen miles to Pine Log where they lynched him while forcing a local minister to read the 23rd Psalms. On several occasions, McCollum's men captured Unionists, carried them to their camp located along the Etowah River, and placed their hostages on horseback before shooting them off the horses, watching the dead body fall down the riverbank into the water.[66]

In defiant gasps of devotion, hundreds of Bartow County soldiers remained with the Confederate army. In Virginia, Brigadier General William T. Wofford maintained his loyalty to the cause. Since the beginning of the war, Wofford had experienced tremendous personal tragedy. While commanding the 8th Georgia Infantry and eventually Wofford's Brigade, he watched as dozens of young men fall in battle or succumb to disease. Personally, he and his wife dealt with the tragedy of losing two infant children to disease. On November 6, the 5th Ohio Cavalry burned his home leaving his wife temporarily homeless. At that time, Wofford had been granted an extended medical leave to recover from wounds while serving in the defense of the Shenandoah Valley and was staying with friends in Murray County.

Wofford traveled to Cassville shortly after the end of the occupation. After a few days, he informed Akin of the situation: "Bands of robbers are going through the country and taking anything they want and killing who they please. . . . There is no law of any kind in that section. . . . There is corn on the Etowah River, in Cherokee County, but there is no way of hauling it. The horses are all gone, and nearly everything else, and the people are suffering much."[67] Robbers with blackened faces stormed into Samuel McDow's home. While holding him at gunpoint, they took his wife into every room in the house forcing her to empty all of her drawers removing any money or valuables. Wofford believed that the thieves who had robbed McDow and numerous other families were primarily Confederate deserters who were roaming the countryside in small independent bands. Throughout 1864, according to Mark Weitz, "when soldiers from [Bartow County] were faced with the choice of going home to help families and communities ravaged by war or moving on to continue the Confederacy's war, they went home."[68] Some deserters did not go home. Some remained in northwest Georgia. For example, Jack Colquitt's scouts consisted of stragglers from the 11th Texas Cavalry who had served in Major General Joseph Wheeler's Cavalry Corps during the Atlanta Campaign. Regardless of their origin, Wofford knew that roaming deserters damaged both the Confederate war effort and local morale. If given an opportunity, he believed, that "he could likely reclaim many of these men for the military."[69]

In late December, Wofford returned to the Army of Northern Virginia, trapped in the trenches outside of Petersburg. After bidding farewell to his officers and men, he left for Richmond where he petitioned President Jefferson Davis for an independent command in north Georgia. The overcrowded capital lacked any available hotel or boarding house vacancies. Fortunately for Wofford, Warren Akin, who at the time was serving in the Confederate House of Representatives, had secured a room at George Washington Gretter's boarding house.[70]

On January 4, Wofford and Akin met with Davis in order to discuss the organization of a new department to protect the people of north Georgia against bands of thieves and deserters. Davis agreed with the men that the region needed a permanent force that could discourage crime and arrest deserters but required that Wofford get permission from his commanders in the Army of Northern Virginia before creating the department. General Robert E. Lee reluctantly accepted his request, commenting that "I do not know what duty is designed for Gen'l Wofford. He is a brave and gallant officer & I regret to part with him. If the duty in which he is to engage in is considered of more importance than with his brigade I make no objection."[71]

In late January, Wofford returned to Bartow County to assume command of the Department of North Georgia. His army consisted of numerous officers and soldiers that had previously served under him in the 18th Georgia Infantry Regiment and Wofford's Brigade. Soldiers who had received a furlough from the Army of Northern Virginia but found themselves cut off from their unit were allowed to remain in Georgia by joining Wofford's command. The general approached his new command with the same level of discipline that he had administered while serving in the Army of Northern Virginia. As soon as his force converged upon Atlanta, he promptly organized them into more efficient units and began an intense period of drill instruction.

The Department of North Georgia's mobilization attracted criticism from Brigadier General G. T. Anderson, who feared that Wofford's force might increase the number of desertions among Georgia regiments. Since its inception, Anderson felt that the department's commanders had abused their authority and mandate by inducing soldiers to desert their original units in favor of serving closer to home.[72] Lieutenant General James Longstreet also worried about increased desertions among Georgia soldiers:

> The impression prevails among the Georgia troops of this command that persons at home, having authority to raise local organizations, are writing and sending messages to the men in the ranks here, offering inducements to them to quit our ranks and go home and join the home organizations. The large and increasing number of desertions, particularly amongst the Georgia troops, induce me to believe that some such outside influence must be operating upon our men. Nearly all of the parties of deserters seem to go home, and it must be under the influence of some promise.[73]

Neither Longstreet nor Anderson accused Wofford of inciting mass desertions. The new command, nevertheless, presented a significant number of Georgia soldiers serving in Virginia with an honorable alternative to their current service. After all, if a soldier rejoined a unit closer to home, was he truly a deserter? By 1865, thousands of Georgia soldiers, including over 200 Bartow Countians serving in the Army of Northern Virginia, questioned the logic of defending Virginia while their homes and families required their attention.[74] Nationally, desertion hastened the Confederacy's eventual defeat. Locally, the return of large numbers of military-aged males to their homes and families helped to rescue Bartow County from being conquered by the "bitter dregs of war." Ultimately, Bartow County benefited from the Confederacy's loss.[75]

The formation of the Department of North Georgia and the return of numerous deserters to their homes combined to diminish the impact of lawless bands preying upon Bartow County civilians. Wofford divided his force into small units that patrolled major roads in the area. Informants provided these soldiers with the intelligence necessary to track down guerrilla outposts and hideouts. Capturing guerillas and deserters proved to be an arduous undertaking. While his command arrested several hundred of these individuals, a much larger number remained beyond their reach. The force's presence, nevertheless, helped to keep most of these outlaws running rather than attacking civilians.

While Wofford scoured the countryside searching for deserters and criminals, he maintained amicable relations with Union Major General George H. Thomas, who commanded the closest enemy forces stationed in east Tennessee. After arresting a member of John Gatewood's partisans in northeast Georgia, Wofford learned that this band planned to strike the railroad near Knoxville. The commander became concerned that if the raid took place, Thomas might retaliate by raiding north Georgia. Rather than face that scenario, he dispatched, under a white flag, a courier to Union headquarters to inform the "Rock of Chickamauga" of the raid. His decision proved wise, as Thomas had become concerned that Wofford might have been planning a raid into east Tennessee. If that occurred, the Union commander promised north Georgia citizens he would "so despoil Georgia that 50 years hence it will be a wilderness." Wofford's forthright sharing of intelligence assured that the Union commander would not carry out those threats.[76]

Wofford lacked the will to fight the Union army when so many north Georgians were on the verge of starvation. According to official reports, during the spring of 1865, 62 percent of the inhabitants of Bartow County lacked enough food and supplies to get through the spring. The state of Georgia had purchased $800,000 worth of corn during the previous fall specifically intended to be distributed to north Georgia civilians. Much of this corn was warehoused in Marietta and various depots scattered along the W&A. Wofford appreciated the corn but worried that, during transport, it might be captured by lawless bands of thieves and deserters. The railroad between Cassville and Dalton was still inoperable, and the only way to distribute the corn was through the use of horse-drawn wagons. Those caravans required armed guards in order to fend off potential attackers. Wofford wanted his forces to supervise the distribution of this much needed corn, but to do so might attract the suspicions of nearby the nearby Union army. To avoid any confrontation, the general traveled to Dalton where he met with Brigadier General Henry M. Judah to gain the enemy's permission to escort those wagons. At that meeting, Judah permitted Wofford to send wagons behind federal lines to supply starving families. In exchange, the Confederate general agreed to keep his main forces south of the Etowah River.

Wofford and Judah's meeting in Dalton occurred three days after General Robert E. Lee surrendered the Army of Northern Virginia. The Department of North Georgia remained active for a time, receiving orders from the Army of Tennessee and the fleeing Confederate government. Judah wanted Wofford to surrender as soon as possible, but the general delayed that action since so many lawless groups still roamed the region and because Johnston's army remained in the field. On April 21, the commander received word that

Johnston had surrendered in North Carolina. He promptly dispatched a courier to Judah with a message proposing to arrange a peace conference in Resaca on May 8. "I would have proposed an earlier day," explained Wofford, "but I am en route to one of the upper counties, where I have an appointment to meet some men who have been bushwhacking, to the terror and injury of our unfortunate people."[77]

On May 2, Wofford surrendered the Department of North Georgia to Judah. On May 12, the opposing generals met at the McCravey-Johnson house in Kingston where the formal surrender was tendered. Wofford called on all soldiers currently living in the region, whether or not they were actively serving with a Confederate army, to travel to Kingston to be paroled. By May 20, approximately 4,000 soldiers made their way to Kingston. A soldier described the scene:

> The day of the parole, I saw the motliest crew I have seen before or since. These so-called scouts were strutting around with broad-rimmed hats, long hair and jingling spurs. You could see the old "moss back" who had crept out of his cave. You would find groups of sad-looking men who had followed Lee, Jackson, Johnston, and Wheeler through the war. Some of them carried mud and dust of 5 or 6 states on their old clothes. From all over north Georgia and north Alabama they gathered at Kingston.[78]

Most soldiers lacked shoes, food, and money. The Union army distributed rations to the men and provided many with temporary employment repairing the damaged W&A.[79]

The Civil War had ended, much to the relief of many Bartow Countians, but the area still needed protection from lawless bands of outlaws. Wofford telegraphed Thomas requesting that Judah leave a portion of his army in the county to protect civilians from further attacks. The commander consented to the request and stationed regiments in Adairsville, Kingston, Cartersville, and Cassville. As Reconstruction began, civilians embarked on a new era of struggle and deprivation as they rebuilt their tattered lives and communities.

CHAPTER
7

BOTTOM RAIL STILL ON BOTTOM

Confederate defeat thrust Bartow County, like the rest of the South, into a postbellum world that in some ways resembled the old order while in other facets represented a clear break from past traditions. While the Atlanta Campaign and the violence that followed during the remaining months of the war scarred the county both physically and emotionally, those who endured Reconstruction and the last decades of the nineteenth century collected new wounds that overshadowed wartime memories. Emancipation and the threat it posed to white supremacy and white intra-class unity perhaps instilled greater fears in the hearts and minds of local whites than Sherman's army ever did. In addition to freedpeople who demanded to be treated as citizens and free laborers, Confederate veterans, especially those from non-elite households, faced postwar challenges that rivaled their wartime hardships. Many veterans experienced a permanent decline in their personal health, often due to military service, and an inability to achieve any form of upward social and economic mobility, particularly among farmers. Unstable economic conditions among veterans, poor whites, and freedpeople led many to vent their frustrations at the ballot box in support of a number of independent or opposition movements that challenged the elite-dominated Georgia Democratic Party. Brief overtures into biracial political coalitions further pushed the county away from its antebellum past. Bitter divisions among white men continued and left freedpeople stuck in the middle of a hostile battle for home rule among a fractured Democratic Party. As it did during the antebellum period, white supremacy provided the healing elixir that cured mounting white tensions and prevented class tensions from boiling over. By the final decades of the nineteenth century, with the addition of rising Confederate memorial movements, the ascent of "Lost Cause" mythology, and persistent poverty, Bartow County, like other postwar southern communities, remained tethered to an antebellum conservative order that limited prospects for change.[1]

After surviving a near fatal bout of dysentery while imprisoned at Camp Chase, Ohio, John King of the 40th Georgia Infantry Regiment returned to Bartow County. He discovered that "Sherman's force of invading plunderers had swept over the beautiful valley and green hills of my native land and . . . left utter ruin and desolation." King's father had left home prior to the Atlanta Campaign, having located a nook in nearby Canton. For months, he heard nothing about his son's condition besides learning that Union soldiers had captured him near Sevierville, Tennessee. Since two neighbors had sons who died as prisoners-of-war, he too expected the worst. So when his son appeared early one March morning, the father wept as he praised God.[2]

But all was not well. "The year eighteen hundred and sixty-five," John King remembered, "will be ever memorable among the citizens of northwest Georgia, as one of privation and suffering." Shortly after his homecoming, King's father and several former slaves returned to Bartow County. Near Cassville, John King saw destitute inhabitants combing "the camp grounds of the enemy and [feeding] upon the corn and fragments of food left" behind. Despite being late in the planting season, he tried to plant a corn crop, but his poor health and broken down draft horses thwarted his efforts. The future seemed bleak.

John King later claimed that his former slaves seemed willing to work for him in exchange for cash and a share of the crop. Following the perceived intrusion of the Freedmen's Bureau, however, "the negro," he wrote, became a "willing tool of their malice" toward former slaveholders such as himself. He complained that bureau agents convinced the freedpeople that the Federal government would provide each head of household a forty acre farm, a mule, farming utensils, and one year's supply of provisions. They also told the freedpeople that the property of their former masters would be divided into lots to be redistributed among their slaves. King never believed that the government would "carry out the nefarious plan," but, "the poor deluded negro was jubilant in expectation of his fortune, and at once became utterly demoralized as a farm laborer."

John King described a Reconstruction whose characters included carpetbaggers, freedpeople, scalawags, and Radical Republicans who acted in a concerted fashion to yoke white southerners to a "tyrannical" wagon of oppression. Unable to tolerate further abuses, he introduced the final cast of characters, the Ku Klux Klan, who resisted the "miserable 'Carpet Bagger.'" King described Klansmen as virtuous citizens determined to defend southern white manhood at all costs.

King published his reminiscences of the Civil War era almost four decades after the conflict. His account portrays the frustrations of an aging former slaveholder and Confederate veteran living in a progressive era filled with a "younger generation of negroes. . . . [Whose] acts of brutality shock . . . the moral sense of civilized society, [and] are constantly coming and appear to increase as the generations are farther removed from the regime that gave civilization to their ancestors." Bartow Countians, like many southern communities, remembered Reconstruction as a period of great despair filled with corrupt Republicans, ignorant freedpeople, and honorable Klansmen. Indeed, King's memories reflect how many modern-day Bartow Countians still remember Reconstruction.[3]

Veterans and their families, especially those from non-elite households, bore the brunt of the Confederacy's defeat. While many veterans suffered from a similar range of postwar problems, yeomen farmers and poor whites generally fared worse than planters. Despite losing millions of dollars in personal property as a result of wartime emancipation, postbellum veterans from antebellum planter families held onto their real property and continued to hold a disproportionate percentage of the total wealth of all county veterans. For example, by 1870 planters, who accounted for about 5 percent all of local soldiers who served in the Confederate army, controlled approximately 54 percent of the total value of real property held by all of the county's veterans. Most planters emerged from the war with most of their prewar estates intact. Many spent the late 1860s distributing large tracts of land to their sons to aid their transition into establishing independent households. Lewis Tumlin, one of the region's wealthiest antebellum landholders, for example, dispersed over $50,000 in land to his sons ensuring that most of his prewar wealth would remain in family hands for at least another generation. Not only did planters retain a disproportionate share of the county's total wealth but they also continued to dominate local politics winning over 90 percent of all local, state, and national elections. Most continued to identify themselves publicly by their Confederate military officer's rank to remind voters of their veteran status.

Yeomen farmers and poor whites who served in the Confederate army fared worse economically following the war than their planter contemporaries in nearly every distinguishable category. At the start of the war, roughly 65 percent of 1861 volunteers belonged to a household that owned at least 50 acres of land. Less than one quarter of those volunteers were tenant farmers and about 5 percent identified themselves as farm laborers. One decade later, less than 40 percent of 1861 volunteers owned any real estate and nearly half were tenant farmers. While many white households experienced an economic decline in the years following the Civil War, Confederate veterans seemed to have suffered at a higher rate than society as a whole. Veterans and their dependents truly "drank the bitter dregs" of defeat.[4]

Many Confederate soldiers never returned home. Those civilians whose husbands and sons died in arms endured tremendous postwar hardships. Calculating an exact number of Bartow County's war dead is impossible since the whereabouts of soldiers listed as missing in battle frequently cannot be verified. Approximately, 33.2 percent of the nearly two thousand Bartow men identified from the 1860 census as having served in the Confederate military died as a result of wounds received, diseases contracted, and, in at least one case, as a result of a train accident. One out of three Bartow County soldiers—37 percent of them married men—died during the Civil War.[5]

Bartow County's extensive kinship networks ensured that most families suffered from the impact of casualties. The Hite family sent three men off to war in June 1861. Less than one year later, two had died, one from disease and the other from an unknown cause. The remaining family member received a permanent discharge after suffering a severe wound to his chest and left hip. Bailey and Cannon Barton volunteered in March 1862. Seven months later both died from measles in Knoxville, Tennessee, in an epidemic that killed at least twenty-four Bartow soldiers. Two pairs of brothers, Joseph and Samuel Branton and Abram and Robert Barron, succumbed to the disease within days of one another. The Brantons, Barrons, Abernathys, Bartons, Dysarts, Woffords, Sheats, Jolleys, Dodds, Murphys, and numerous other extended kin networks supplied the Confederacy with the manpower needed to fight the war, but, ultimately, their decisions threatened their domestic stability. Sarah Dysart watched as three of her sons—Americus, James, and Levi—volunteered in 1861. One year later, she received word that Americus, age seventeen, had died from a camp disease. In January 1863, Levi, age eighteen, passed away at General Hospital Number Sixteen at Richmond. Despite the death of two brothers, James—the oldest of the three—remained with the army throughout the war and surrendered at Appomattox. The Dysarts's sacrifice was surpassed by the Jackson family who lived near Stilesboro. None of the four men who volunteered for military service survived the war. Two died from disease, one was killed in action, and a fourth passed away in a hospital one month after being wounded.[6]

Bartow County's veterans provide a glimpse into the physical and emotional tensions experienced by locals as they bore the brunt of the Confederacy's defeat. Many of the men who escaped death carried internal and external scars that would haunt them for the remainder of their lives. Sergeant William Sharpe faithfully served in the 22nd Georgia Infantry Regiment from the summer of 1861 through the winter of 1865. While Lee's army remained heavily entrenched around Petersburg, Virginia, Sharpe was wounded when a shell fragment struck his leg. Surgeons amputated above the knee in order to save his life. Physicians transferred the wounded soldier to Jackson Hospital in Richmond, where he fell into enemy hands following the Confederate evacuation. He remained in Richmond as a prisoner-of-war until May 28. Like Sharpe, approximately 200 Bartow soldiers who volunteered in 1861 and 1862 returned home as invalids, most of whom lived the rest of their lives without the use of one or more limbs.[7]

Surviving Georgia Confederate Pension Records indicate that many veterans and their families struggled to overcome physical disabilities for the rest of their lives. Louis Young, Co. B 40th Georgia Infantry, Army of Tennessee, contracted consumption during the spring of 1863 while marching for days on wet roads with little food or rest. His lungs never recovered. Upon returning home, he lacked the physical strength and cardiovascular endurance necessary to work. After the war, Sarah, his wife, and his young children struggled to survive working as tenant farmers and picking up work at a nearby lime kiln. Due to a disability acquired in service to the Confederacy, Young, the son of a yeomen farmer, never managed to escape the cycle of poverty that trapped so many poor veterans. All of Young's sons and grandsons would work as tenant farmers until the family quit farming in the 1940s.[8]

Louis Young represented just one of thousands of Confederate veterans in Georgia who suffered the lifetime effects of a wartime disability or wound. Confederate pension applications in Georgia during the final decade of the 1800s show that lingering health problems were a statewide phenomenon that likely impacted not only the lives of veterans and their families but the overall productivity of a significant part of an entire generation of state farmers. A sample of 150 pension applications filed by Bartow County veterans reveals much about the poor postwar conditions that many soldiers faced. On average, these men were in their early 20s when they joined the Confederate army. Few joined in 1861 whereas a majority enlisted following the enactment of the Confederate conscription acts. All reported long-term health complications originating from ailments contracted or wounds received during the war. Of the 150 soldiers surveyed, only 15 (10 percent) managed to own any real estate after the war. Most of these men identified themselves as farmers in the 1870 and 1880 federal censuses. About 90 percent were either tenants or sharecroppers. Few lived better lives than their parents. Whereas 90 percent of these veterans were tenants and sharecroppers in the postwar years, about 60 percent of their parents had owned land prior to the war. The Confederate veteran generation in Bartow County saw their wealth decline and opportunity for upward social mobility vanish in the postbellum economy. With little help coming from the state and local government, disabled veterans rarely managed to improve their wealth for the remainder of their lives.[9]

The poor health of disabled veterans also impacted the lives of their children. Among the 150 Confederate veterans from Bartow County who applied for a pension, 55 percent of them had an older son living in his parents' household well beyond the age of thirty. Apparently, the strains placed upon the household brought on by their father's inability to perform rigorous manual labor often kept older sons at home for longer periods than might have been expected prior to the war. In 1860, for example, only 11 percent of households in which the father was identified as the head of household had a son at home beyond the age of thirty. For disabled veterans, that number climbed sharply between 1870 and 1880 as older sons must have felt some pressure to postpone any plans to start their own families. To be sure, declining economic conditions generally in the region kept many children at home longer than prior to the war, but it would appear that the sons of disabled veterans were disproportionately impacted.[10]

Emotionally, the memory of the carnage that accompanied battle and the loss of dear friends and loved ones evoked strong feelings years after the war ended. While living as an expatriate in Brazil, George Barnsley wrote an unpublished memoir documenting his memories of the Civil War. Three decades had passed, yet he recalled the sound of a volley striking his advancing line during the First Battle of Manassas and the horror as a man in front of him collapsed to the ground laying completely still as if frozen. He remembered how he watched as his comrades searched the battlefield for their fallen friends and family members.[11]

Most families that lost loved ones during the war never recovered the body and usually had only a vague notion of where those remains might be buried. The federal government's refusal to locate, identify, and relocate Confederate dead upset grieving families. Locally, governments lacked funds to help families recover their loved ones remains. What little money local governments raised in the postwar years usually went directly toward rebuilding public buildings, repairing roads and bridges, and providing immediate relief to destitute families. Local women had to look elsewhere for help. Women across the South, especially in northern Virginia, created associations to help Confederate families locate missing remains. These associations placed advertisements in northwest Georgia newspapers soliciting donations to help their noble cause. Left destitute by the war, only a handful of locals could financially support such an endeavor and generally abandoned any hope of bringing their loved one home for a proper burial.[12]

Unable to mourn for their dead loved ones by visiting their gravesite, many women across the South adopted the gravesites of Confederate soldiers buried in their communities. An article that appeared in the Rome newspaper articulated the feelings of many southern women. "The grave of many a gallant soldier has never been visited by loving wife, affectionate mother or fond sister, but there is a sweet consolation in the reflection, that upon the same day and hour, when you are engaged in paying mournful tribute to the memory of strangers the remains of your dear loved ones are receiving similar attentions from the fair hands of those unknown to you." The writer urged women to embrace the "bonds of sacred sisterhood" to honor their Confederate heroes.[13] In Bartow County, hundreds of Confederate soldiers, mostly from the Army of Tennessee, died while either receiving treatment in one of the county's numerous hospitals or from wounds received in battle during the Atlanta and Nashville campaigns. Hundreds of unidentified Confederate graves could be found in Cassville, Kingston, and Cartersville. Thousands more were scattered across north Georgia, some in cemeteries, others in hastily prepared graves. Organizers worked to relocate thousands of graves in the region consolidating scattered burials into organized cemeteries. Cassville and Cartersville cemeteries received the remains of dozens of relocated Confederate burials. Meanwhile, women such as Mary Green, worked tirelessly in communities throughout northwest Georgia to establish permanent Confederate cemeteries in Resaca, Marietta, Dalton, and Rome. The issue of providing public funds to maintain these cemeteries was raised on a number of occasions in the Bartow County Superior Court sessions. Decades later, southern congressmen lobbied the federal government to dedicate funds for maintaining Confederate cemeteries and marking individual unknown-soldier graves.[14]

In Bartow County, as well as across the South, cemeteries became the first sites for erecting memorials, holding commemorations, and exalting the "Lost Cause." During the final weeks of the Civil War, Kingston Soldiers' Aid Society, who in 1864 had formed to help tend to sick and wounded soldiers, turned their attention toward honoring the 250 plus dead that had been buried in their city cemetery. With the help of federal soldiers who occupied the town, these women gathered flowers and evergreens and led a small procession of mourners onto the burial grounds where the unmarked graves had been organized into rows. The Kingston cemetery also contained the remains of several Union soldiers. On that first decoration day, Confederate women also marked those graves as a sign of respect for all who had died in this great struggle. The following spring, memorial day commemorations spread across the South in response to a letter written by Mary Ann Williams of Columbus, Georgia, printed in regional newspapers that urged southerners to set aside April 26, the date that General Joseph E. Johnston surrendered the last major Confederate field army, as a day to remember Confederate dead. As Kingston prepared to repeat their previous year's events, other decoration day traditions began in Cassville and Cartersville. In 1867, Cassville women formed the Ladies' Memorial Association to direct commemoration activities. This small group, exclusively comprised of elite women, used their social and political connections to lobby government officials to support maintaining cemeteries, holding annual events, and erecting proposed memorials. Women's groups in Kingston, Cassville, and Cartersville collaborated by creating an annual calendar of commemorative fundraisers to support their work. These women hosted bake sales, auctions, concerts, picnics, speeches, and other activities to raise funds and increase awareness of the need to honor those who died to preserve the "Lost Cause." Compared to veterans reunions and commemorations held in the late nineteenth and early twentieth century, Bartow County's Reconstruction-era decoration days drew smaller crowds and attracted less attention.[15]

Northwest Georgia women laid the foundation for how future generations of locals would remember the Civil War. From its inception, annual decoration and memorial day commemorations mourned not only the loss of life that transpired during the war but equally important reminded those who survived or future generations that the war had extinguished an antebellum civilization and had given birth to a new unwelcome age of change. The ladies' organizations evidenced that despite suffering military defeat, enemy occupation, and black emancipation, postbellum southern society remained tethered to its antebellum past. Elite women dominated postwar ladies' organizations. Nearly 100 percent of the women identified in newspapers as organization members belonged to families that had owned slaves prior to the war. Almost as many of those women were related to veterans who had served as either Confederate officers or elected officials. As might be expected, none of the women who joined these groups came from Unionist households. None of the women were poor. All were white. Weakened by the loss of property resulting from emancipation and wartime property damage, these women nonetheless represented the persistent influence that antebellum elite maintained after the war.[16]

Commemorative events depicted a unified South that fought to resist northern aggression. Initially, commemorations placed greater emphasis upon the sacrifices of southern society as a whole rather than the acts of individual soldiers. Speakers also omitted any reference of Unionists, bushwhackers, deserters, or stories about the anarchy that befell the area following the end of federal occupation. Nor did such speeches remind audiences of the hundreds of local men who received exemptions that kept them out of the Confederate army. White Bartow Countians, like others across the

South, seemed eager to put their past behind them so that they could move forward with a fabricated memory that contained only the best parts of what they wanted others to see. Unionists in Bartow County had a difficult time challenging the predominant pro-Confederate narrative. Elsewhere in north Georgia, Unionists countered the pro-Confederate narrative by holding meetings and organizing groups of Union army veterans to celebrate Independence Day. However, even in areas that contained a large Unionist presence, such as Chattooga and Fannin counties, the pro-Confederate narrative became the region's official memory.[17]

Audiences that learned little about the real Civil War from postwar commemorations might have received a far better education had they witnessed Bartow County Superior Court sessions. In each session, an appointed committee delivered reports documenting the state of the county. This information was used by officials to determine funding needs and to prepare new ordinances. Many reports referenced the "unfortunate and demoralizing influences that pervaded our section during the war" when the people "presented the appearance of an angry and disturbed swarm of bees." Long after the last Confederate soldier laid down his arms, poverty continued to plague county residents. Report after report told the court of dire conditions across the county. Families living in squalor without adequate food and unable to work. Debtors unable to pay taxes or loans forced to throw themselves at the mercy of collectors. County leaders made some effort to alleviate conditions by extending tax payment deadlines, exempting some households from payment, or offering alternative payment methods such as working on a county road crew. After the war, the county created a pauper farm where landless white and black families could find shelter and work a common plot of land to raise funds that might rescue them from poverty. The farm, however, was an insufficient effort to confront a problem too large for local government to manage. The Civil War's impact cast a long shadow forward as many people, especially veterans, found little time or comfort in commemorations.[18]

In October 1865, former Confederate Vice-President Alexander Stephens sat quietly as his southbound train moved toward Atlanta along the Western & Atlantic Railroad. The Georgian had witnessed firsthand the destruction that had occurred throughout northern Virginia, but now as he traveled through his home state, he felt a sickness in his stomach that he had not felt before. "War has left a terrible impression on the whole country to Atlanta. The desolation is heart-sickening. Fences gone, fields all a-waste, houses burnt," wrote Stephens. His train likely stopped for water and fuel in Kingston. During the 1860 presidential election, he had visited there where he delivered a series of popularly attended political speeches. The town that had graciously welcomed him five years ago now bore little resemblance to its former state.[19]

Prior to the Civil War, Bartow County had experienced a period of economic growth that gave many farmers hope that slavery and cash crop production might provide opportunities for upward social mobility. The war shattered those aspirations. Farmers entered a prolonged period of economic decline that led many to doubt whether or not their elite leaders had their best interests at heart.

At the end of the war in the spring of 1865, many Bartow Countians were financially insolvent due to wartime debts, worthless Confederate investments, overdue taxes, crop failures, federal devastation, and the loss of many men between the ages of 18 and 35. In addition, the county seat was in ruins, transportation networks were in a state of disrepair, and starvation threatened local stability. Their economy failed to quickly recover after the war due a sporadic drought that ruined several consecutive harvests. Despite dwindling land prices, tenancy rates increased from their antebellum high of 35 percent to nearly 50 percent in 1869. Farmers large and small continued to plant substantial amounts of cotton, but the drought ruined much of that crop. In 1869, the county only produced 2,833 bales of cotton—1,574 fewer than in 1859. As shown in Table 8, the county's overall agricultural production, except wheat, declined sharply when compared to its antebellum numbers.

The decline in agricultural production combined with the property damage suffered during the war convinced many residents to migrate westward. Poor whites looked toward the Freedmen's Bureau to help provide their transportation. In 1866, bureau agent W. H. Pritchett recommended that his agency pay for the relocation of 172 indigent families living in the county. He sent many to Arkansas, Texas, and Indiana. Attempting to aid in providing for the poor, the county promised the Freedmen's Bureau that they would build a poor house for the remaining destitute families if they would remove

Table 8
Selected Agricultural Products of Bartow County, 1870

Wheat (bu.)	% Change from 1860	Corn (bu.)	% Change from 1860	Swine (No.)	% Change from 1860	Cotton (bales)	% Change from 1860
139,647	+2.2	239,197	-44.4	11,794	-48.0	2,833	-36.0

Source: Manuscript Census, Bartow County, Georgia, 1860, 1870, Schedule II.

those 172 families.[20] The Cartersville *Express* reported that many residents had left because the county had become unlivable.[21] About 15 percent of the county's 1860 head of households left between 1860 and 1870. Economics directly influenced out-migration; at the same time a smallpox outbreak in the county during the spring and summer of 1865 perhaps played a role in out-migration.[22]

Those who remained faced a sizable challenge. From 1864 until 1870, severe drought ruined much of the county's crops, preventing many farmers from being able to pay their taxes. "If there is a general drought," wrote Cassville resident William Chunn, "we never miss it, and a special drought is always got up and specially dedicated to this ruined desolate and God-forsaken country."[23] The list of insolvent taxpayers for the county during those years grew with each passing season and quickly became filled with names of residents who had left for the West. The Bartow County Superior Court grew concerned that if the scarce amount of wheat raised in the county were to be sold to distant markets that locals might starve. The court contemplated raising funds to purchase the local wheat crop to be used to feed farm families whose crops had failed. Reports of speculators and farmers trying to gouge prices to profit from the drought concerned the court's officers and raised tensions.[24]

Without adequate provisions, many residents sought charity from benevolent associations and rations from the Freedmen's Bureau. In the months following the war, the bureau distributed more supplies in Bartow County to destitute whites than to freedpeople's families. Area newspapers even reported that most black households had more provisions than their white neighbors.[25] Some elites scoffed at the sight of their fellow ex-Confederates reduced to begging for food. Rome resident physician Robert Battey commented during a trip through Kingston that "large numbers of those who draw could feed themselves had they the manliness to sacrifice their property in place of their honor."[26] Others appreciated the bureau's generosity as those rations helped to relieve part of the lingering resentment that existed within the hearts of many Confederate veterans.[27] The state of Georgia eased the situation when it allocated $200,000 to purchase and transport corn into north Georgia. In Bartow County, however, local officials distributed the corn solely to white families which upset Freedman Bureau agents and freedpeople.[28]

When the Bartow County Superior Court reconvened during the closing months of the Civil War, its officials dedicated almost all of the county's limited resources to providing for indigent families—particularly widows of fallen Confederate soldiers with children—and rebuilding the tattered local economy. Solving postwar crises necessitated raising new taxes that placed new burdens upon farmers. During the winter of 1866, the court compiled a list of disabled soldiers, soldiers' widows, and wives who lacked sufficient provisions. After an extensive search, officials concluded that 189 households of Confederate veterans, or about 761 persons, did not have adequate food and supplies. The county agreed to provide 4,000 bushels of corn to support those families until the next harvest. That same year, the court petitioned Governor Charles J. Jenkins for additional support. The governor responded by delivering a large shipment of corn from the state's southwestern counties. Due to the combined efforts of the state of Georgia, Bartow County, the Freedmen's Bureau, and the Federal army, only a handful of reported incidences of death by starvation occurred in the county.[29]

Prior to the war, the county had experienced significant growth due to the completion of the railroad. Now, the county looked toward possible transportation improvements as a key to revitalizing the region. Repairing more than one dozen damaged bridges was one of the superior court's biggest priorities. In addition to bridge work, the court commissioned district road superintendents to organize road crews to service existing thoroughfares.[30]

The superior court also enacted measures designed to restore law and order throughout the war torn county. Union soldiers had burned the county courthouse and jail that left them without a court to prosecute criminals nor prison cells to house convicts. Until a new prison could be built, the sheriff had to transport inmates to Floyd County for temporary holding. The court eventually passed a resolution funding the erection of a new courthouse and jail in Cartersville.[31]

Beyond the mere physical effects of postbellum life, some residents undoubtedly experienced a period of psychological shock and emotional readjustment. Some felt a sense of debilitating helplessness that made everyday life difficult to endure. "I feel satisfied," William Chunn wrote in 1867, "that if I stay here I will make nothing or be nothing all of my life.... I almost wish that I were dead." After returning to Cassville following his service with the 40th Georgia, the sight of the charred remains of what had been his family home as well as the desecrated grave of his beloved father brought him to tears.

In 1866, he had tried to make a crop, but it failed due to the drought. The following year's crop befell a similar fate. "If we can remove the remains of my dear lamented father," he wrote, "I will be satisfied that my eyes may never rest upon the spot again. I would give anything that I had never seen it since its destruction."[32]

Chunn had been proud of Cassville prior to the war, but, now, much of what he remembered was gone. If Cassville could be restored to its former state, he proclaimed, he would have no problem remaining here forever. Cassville, however, never recovered from its wartime wounds. In 1867, residents voted to relocate the county seat to the growing railroad town of Cartersville, where the new courthouse and jail would rise. Only a handful of the town's antebellum residents rebuilt their homes and farms. Less than 50 percent of the town's 1860 inhabitants remained in Cassville or Bartow County. Hoping to attract new settlers, Cassville organized a land raffle to redistribute the bulk of abandoned lands in and around the town. What had once been referred to as the prettiest village in Georgia now became the region's largest ghost town.[33]

The Civil War and emancipation also damaged planters' fortunes. Large planters such as Lewis Tumlin lost as much as $150,000 in personal property. Even small slaveholders who owned one to three slaves suffered the loss of a few thousand dollars, a tremendous setback during Reconstruction. The average planter lost approximately fifteen thousand dollars—a sum that far exceeded their 1870 average personal property holdings. On the whole, area planters forfeited an estimated $2.5 million worth of slave property.[34]

Without slaves, elite farmers sought alternative labor practices but maintained their dependence on cash crop agriculture. In 1869, ex-planters cultivated approximately 65 percent of all of the cotton grown in Bartow County. Much like the late antebellum period, almost all of these men set aside large portions of their improved lands to planting cotton and significantly fewer acres for corn. Only a handful of elite farmers achieved self-sufficiency during Reconstruction. Rising taxes and a need for cash made it necessary for farmers to engage in the market economy.[35]

No elite family in Bartow County illustrates the physical, emotional, and psychological turmoil of Reconstruction better than the Barnsleys. Their voluminous correspondence reflect such postbellum themes as emasculation, deprivation, and an overall sense of hopelessness. Reconstruction further altered the family's inner dynamics, as Julia Barnsley continued her wartime role as household matriarch and, due to necessity, assumed a greater place within their estate's public sphere. The Barnsleys' postbellum lives seemed foreign compared to their antebellum past.

Between the fall of 1863 and the spring of 1864, while serving as the Confederate provost marshal at Kingston, Captain James Baltzelle married Julia Barnsley. During the final months of the war, she credited her husband with saving her life after he persuaded her to leave Woodlands prior to the start of the Atlanta Campaign, thus avoiding the potential "ravages" of federal soldiers. "All we have saved is due to Capt. B's energy," she wrote, "there are few people like [him]. His energy and patience were superhuman."[36]

Julia Baltzelle adored her husband, whose strong masculine presence came as a welcomed change from what she had witnessed from her father and two brothers during the war. Despite James Baltzelle's best efforts, conditions at Woodlands worsened. "There never was any one living in a populous country like this, that kept themselves as secluded as we do now," wrote Baltzelle. Soon after George's departure, he discovered that producing a market crop such as wheat or cotton required more labor than his household could provide. Securing labor plagued the estate's recovery. Many freedpeople in the area either refused to work for him or demanded a higher wage than he could pay. Poor whites also wanted too much money. He used the profits earned through the sale of distilled liquor to hire day laborers. These workers, however, proved difficult to work with since they frequently refused to show deference toward their employer. Hired laborers required close supervision that distracted his attention from other household matters. Baltzelle typically hired four laborers, a number he felt could adequately work the land if every one of them put in a hard day's labor.

In the fall of 1866, Woodlands had one of its poorest harvests ever recorded. The drought that plagued William Chunn affected Woodlands as well. "This place did not plant much cotton," wrote Godfrey Barnsley, "and only makes about a bale to 7 ½ acres and does as well as most others in this section. [This has been] the worst summer for agriculture ever known, arising from nearly three months of drought."[37] James Baltzelle needed the cash from that crop to pay for the next planting season's laborers. Godfrey attempted to borrow some money but could not secure a loan. Faced with no other option, Baltzelle began "to make some arrangements with my men to crop with me, an arrangement I detest and look upon as equivalent to doing almost nothing but in such a case I would be compelled to do something of the kind."[38]

James Baltzelle's daily interaction with freedpeople further heightened his demoralized condition. Initially, despite his reservations, sharecropping worked well for him. For a brief moment, it seemed as if he had been transported back in time prior to the war when slaves were expected to show deference to their white masters. In the summer of 1867, however, Freedmen's Bureau agents in nearby Kingston registered black voters and encouraged them to participate in a series of state and local elections. Baltzelle reacted badly. "Every law," he bitterly complained, "the Radicals have made had been more binding upon the southern man. . . . free negroes are getting to feel their importance and doubtly will want a great many privileges in our social and political arena." Confident in his belief in white supremacy, he vowed never again to employ freedpeople since they seemed intent upon asserting their equality.

Elite families, such as the Barnsleys, left behind an abundant record of their postwar hardships. Those problems however were relative. Compared to yeomen and poor white households, elites fared quite well in the postbellum era. Despite losing millions of dollars in slave property, planters still accounted for nearly 80 percent of the county's personal property. Planters complained about taxes and labor shortages, yet most plantations expanded following the war. Political power too remained firmly in elite hands. Nonetheless, emancipation reminded planters daily that what they had lost could not be measured in mere dollars.[39]

Freedpeople were agents of change who made strategic choices while pursuing multiple paths they hoped would lead to autonomy, security, and prosperity. When former slaves refused to act like slaves, their ex-masters found themselves in unfamiliar circumstances. Emancipation provided freedpeople with an opportunity to redefine their lives and fundamentally alter the world they knew.

In 1860, Bartow Countians owned 4,282 slaves who comprised about 27.2 percent of the county's total population. One decade later, the county's black population had increased by roughly 10 percent. By 1880, the county's black population had outpaced the growth of the white population growing to 6,271 or about 33.6 percent of the populace. Bartow County's black population rose following the Civil War because African Americans could find work in the rapidly growing city of Cartersville. Black communities, such as Noble Hill in Cassville, also attracted new black residents to the county. Noble Hill had several black landholders who hired day laborers and contracted with tenants plus a popular black church. Also, compared to the rest of northwest Georgia, the level of white-on-black violence in Bartow County was low.[40]

Many freedpeople exercised their newfound freedom by moving. Sarah Jane Patterson witnessed the devastation that the war had upon her former master's plantation. Some of John Patterson's slaves voluntarily remained on the plantation working as wage laborers, but Sarah Jane left because she believed his crop would fail due to the drought. Slaves from neighboring plantations told her that they were moving to Arkansas where unspoiled and inexpensive land was supposedly in great abundance. A few months after first receiving word that she was free, she boarded a wagon train headed for Arkansas.[41]

The bonds between a slave and the white church dissolved. During the Civil War, church records noted that many of their congregation's slaves had runaway and fled to federal lines. In 1863, Nance's Creek Church recorded only five slave members. After the war, few freedpeople attended white churches. A member of Euharlee Presbyterian Church, for example, commented in its membership rolls that since the war "all [slaves had] departed from our communion. Scattered in various parts of the county and state and have never attended divine service since 1865." Meanwhile, at Raccoon Creek Baptist Church, white members allowed local freedpeople to hold independent services in the church as long they kept the building in good order. Freedpeople joined Macedonia Baptist Church as late as 1869 but entirely disappeared from the rolls by 1871. Freedpeople began forming their own churches separate from their former masters and local whites. The creation of postbellum black churches throughout the South stands as one of the hallmark achievements of Reconstruction and formed a lasting foundation for the region's African American population.[42]

Ex-slaveholders who faced crippling labor shortages frequently offered their former slaves employment. Slaves had to choose whether they wanted to remain with their former masters or seek better opportunities elsewhere. Callie Elder stayed despite the brutal punishments her master doled out among his slaves. After emancipation, she remained, despite his continued abuses, because he offered her a wage of ten dollars per month. In 1863, when federal troops threatened Henry Harris's Louisa County, Virginia farm, he sent his slave Rosanna and her family to Bartow County. After weathering the federal occupation, Rosanna looked forward to the end of fighting when she could return home. In August of 1865, she requested the Freedmen's Bureau's help to pay for the cost of transporting her family to Virginia where she wanted to reunite with her former master. Many of the freedpeople that Elder knew had left her former master's plantation to search for missing family members.[43]

Likewise, during the early 1850s, Eveline Cooper worked at Mark A. Cooper's Etowah Iron Works alongside her two sons, Henry and Isaiah. In 1852, her master sold her to a Texas planter; her two children remained at Etowah. Shortly after the Civil War, she wrote the Bartow County bureau agent requesting information concerning the whereabouts of her children. Months later, much to her surprise, she received a letter from Cooper informing her that her two sons were alive. Isaiah lived in Briarfield, Alabama, and Henry worked as a wheelwright in Atlanta.[44]

The Freedmen's Bureau's experiences in Bartow County illustrate the frustrations that many freedpeople and bureau agents felt as they endured the "unfinished revolution." The county fell under the jurisdiction of the Rome sub-district. Cartersville resident and wartime Unionist W. H. Pritchett served as the county's first bureau agent. His tenure ended sometime during the spring of 1866 when he was replaced by former United States Colored Troops officer E. B. Blacker. His replacement, William Moffitt, remained at his post until the bureau's removal from Bartow County during the winter of 1868 and 1869. The bureau placed its primary post in Cartersville, but it distributed large amounts of rations at the Kingston rail depot. Poor whites also gathered their rations at Kingston; whites actually received more rations from the bureau than did freedpeople.[45]

The Union military maintained a small presence in the county. Soldiers stationed there primarily distributed bureau supplies at the Kingston Depot. Bureau agent Blacker routinely asked his superiors for additional forces, but his requests were ignored. Consequently, the local bureau usually lacked the manpower to enforce its policies.[46]

Local Freedmen's Bureau agents served in a variety of roles, ranging from labor contract negotiators to legal guardians of orphaned children. Their duties placed them in conflict with local whites who predominately supported the restoration of home rule. At times, local officials such as judges, sheriffs, and residents, cooperated with bureau officials, but their aid proved unreliable. Ultimately, limited funding, local resistance, and lackluster support from northern benevolent societies minimized the bureau's presence in Bartow County.

Bureau agents frequently served as arbitrators resolving freedpeople's child custody suits. The biological and adopted parents of children routinely squabbled over whom would assume permanent guardianship. Adolescent Ann Elizabeth Freeman lived with freedman Robert Dowell for over two years following her emancipation. One afternoon, an elderly man arrived at Dowell's doorstep claiming to be the girl's grandfather. Reluctant to surrender custody to a complete stranger, he requested help from bureau agent C. B. Blacker. After a brief investigation, the agent ordered Dowell to release the child to the care of her grandfather. Initially, he refused to do so, but once Blacker threatened to use force to take the child, Dowell relinquished his protest.[47]

Sometimes, child custody battles erupted between the biological mother and father. Several years had passed since Katy Hawks saw her mother. During that period, she lived with her father, Robert Akins. When Louisa Hawks returned to Bartow County in July 1867, she visited Akins and demanded that the child be returned to her. After his refusal, she traveled into Cartersville to solicit aid from agent C. B. Blacker. The bureau had received many complaints similar to the one she presented and therefore established a uniform policy to resolve such conflicts. In a letter written to Akins, Blacker demanded that he immediately return the child since "the law gives the mother the guardianship of her child in preference to the father."[48]

Other freedpeople took advantage of the Freedmen's Bureau's authority. Sometime during the winter of 1866, Rock Hamilton used the agency to gain custody of fourteen-year-old Benjamin Hamilton, whom he claimed was his biological son. The following summer, while scouring local farms searching for missing family members, William Hamilton stumbled upon his nephew living with a man who was not his father. Rather than directly confronting Rock, William requested C. B. Blacker to serve as a mediator between the two parties. In Hamilton's case, the agent contacted the local sheriff who supervised the transfer of guardianship.[49]

On rare instances, C. B. Blacker supervised the unofficial adoption of freedpeople's children by their former white masters, despite the protests of their biological parents. An unidentified girl ran away from her mother and returned to her former master requesting permanent shelter citing that "her mother had no money or place to stay." The child's mother found her the following morning, but, despite her protests, the child refused to leave her former master. Frustrated by the child's behavior, as well as the master's demeanor, she sought protection from the Freedmen's Bureau. At first, the agent sided with the mother and requested the child's return but after reading a letter from the girl urging him to allow her to remain, he reversed his initial decision.[50]

In addition to reuniting freedpeople families, Freedmen's Bureau agents aided local efforts to create, staff, and fund schools. Few Bartow County African Americans attended school during Reconstruction. Funding problems, as well as lackluster support from benevolent organizations such as the American Missionary Association, severely limited the area's educational opportunities.

Securing funds and teachers were major hurdles that impeded instruction. By October 1867, the county contained only two black schools. The county operated both in Cartersville, making them virtually inaccessible to the county's predominately rural black population. In June 1867, that city's African Methodist Episcopal Church opened a normal and Sabbath school. The building lacked a furnace and chinking between its hewed logs, which forced the cancellation of classes during the winter. Freedman Charles Edwards served as the school's teacher, but according to the local bureau agent, he could barely read or write and possessed few qualities found among competent instructors. The seventy pupils who attended the school lacked adequate clothing, shoes, food, supplies, and textbooks. Nearly seven months after its inception, the AME School suffered a devastating catastrophe when a powerful storm toppled the aging building. Edwards made a concerted effort to continue the school by finding temporary quarters in private dwellings and stables. Despite his attempts, average attendance fell below twenty students.[51]

The county's second school for blacks, the Union School, opened in February 1867 without sufficient financial support. Their first teacher, a freedman named Edward Milner, could only recite the alphabet. C. B. Blacker wrote several letters to the American Missionary Association (AMA) organizers requesting instructors. The AMA refrained from sending teachers to the county due to financial limitations and perceived white resistance. Undeterred, Blacker searched the county for a literate freedwoman capable of handling a large number of students under adverse conditions while receiving minimal compensation. The hiring of F. J. Harris provided the school with a "competent female teacher." Under her guidance, several dozen children received regular tutelage sharply increasing the number of literate freedpeople residing in the county.[52]

Even with dedicated supporters such as Blacker, Harris, and Edwards, the county's freedpeople schools ultimately failed to educate large percentages of the local black population. Cassville, for example, did not open a black school until 1881. Freedpeople formed several education associations to promote their cause, but apathy among the white population and northern charities thwarted those measures. The Union School, for example, held classes in a small log cabin owned by freedman Robert Parrish, who allowed the students to occupy his cramped home while he was working during the day. Students lacked textbooks, and, ultimately, as stated by Blacker, "all educational associations have failed because people were too poor . . . and [they] never received aid."[53]

While Bartow County freedpeople petitioned for better educational opportunities, some local whites resorted to violence and intimidation to derail their efforts. Freedman Peter Rogers emerged from the Civil War penniless and desperate for work. Unable to migrate elsewhere or find another employer, he entered into a labor contract with his former master, Bryant Leake. Per their arrangement, Rogers earned a monthly allowance of corn in addition to his daily wage. In July of 1867, his employer demanded that he pay for the corn he had consumed. When Rogers protested, the man withheld $18.50 in back wages as payment for the corn. Rogers contacted bureau agent Blacker who provided him with a note demanding that his employer turn over the money. Rogers handed the man the note and returned to his cabin to await payment. Late that night, several masked men stormed into his home awakening Rogers from his sleep. They carried him outside and brutally beat him. Before leaving, the attackers purposely broke one of Rogers' legs, preventing him from earning any additional wages that season. Blacker wanted to prosecute Rogers' employer, but the local sheriff failed to make an arrest citing insufficient evidence. The bureau ordered Leake to pay the freedman his back wages—a request he defiantly ignored.[54]

Throughout the fall of 1867, a group of white men who identified themselves as Regulators waged a wider war of intimidation upon the freedpeople of northern Bartow County, especially targeting landholders. The "Regulators" broke into their "homes swearing and tearing up things generally threatening to blow out their brains." Their terror attacks continued largely unchecked because the bureau lacked the necessary manpower to patrol the large region, and local officials turned a blind eye.[55] Sometimes, however, the Freedmen's Bureau learned of planned attacks upon freedpeople and prevented their execution. According to sworn testimony, on September 11, 1866, a freedman followed a "young white girl" home, allegedly making inappropriate sexual gestures toward her and eventually kissing her against her will. When she arrived home, her father responded to her story by forming a vigilante group to avenge his daughter's mistreatment. The group included local leader Reverend Charles W. Howard as well as several others only identified as leading men of the Kingston. Blacker somehow learned of the plot and arrested Howard before the group could act. The reverend explained that the men only intended to whip the freedman. "If he did it," argued Howard, "why not whip him?"[56]

Starting in 1868, the Ku Klux Klan launched a campaign of terror that targeted black families across northwest Georgia. While Klan violence was commonplace in neighboring Floyd, Polk, Gordon, and Cobb counties, Bartow County, according to Rome attorney and Republican Party organizer Zachariah B. Hargrove, witnessed significantly fewer episodes. Newspapers reported the existence of a number of Democratic Clubs in Bartow County whose members may have been responsible for some of the white-on-black violence that surrounded the 1868 election. The *Cartersville Express*, the county's most popular newspaper, endorsed the Klan by publishing a warning to "Scalawags and Carpetbaggers" and those it referred to as "trembling stinkees who are redolent of the perfumes acquired by the recent contact with the aromatic Nig" that Klansmen would visit them in the dead of night if they did not halt their resistance to the Democratic Party.[57] Klan violence in Bartow County likely remained low because the most prominent Democratic Party leaders in the area, General William T. Wofford and General P. M. B. Young, both condemned the terrorist group and worked instead to forge peaceful relations with black voters—both men hoped to attract black voters into the Democratic Party fold. Klan activity also likely slackened in Bartow County following an 1872 conviction of three Klansmen men for murdering a black man.[58]

Almost all white-on-black acts of violence and intimidation revolved around disputes over earned wages. After demanding $120 in owed wages from his employer, a large party of white men attacked Lewis Covington later that evening severely wounding his chest. Likewise, when Samuel Donaldson attempted to collect his son's wages from Charles Smith of Euharlee, the employer "shot him in the thigh with a shotgun." After Donaldson complained to the Freedmen's Bureau, Smith "was made to pay the doctor's bill plus $25.00."[59]

Black domestic servants became frequent targets for white violence. Lucinda Hays worked for John Crawford from January 1866 until September 1867. In January 1867, she tried to quit her job citing that her employer had physically assaulted her and refused to pay any wages. When she went to Kingston to find another job, Crawford tracked her down and lured her into returning by promising higher wages. Hays, a freedwoman with two children and no husband, felt she had no other option but to endure his continued abuses.

By September of 1867, Hays had grown tired of Crawford's unwillingness to pay her two dollars per month wage. Unable to compel him to distribute those wages, she reported his mistreatment to bureau agent C. B. Blacker, who supplied her with a note that threatened to seize portions of his harvest if he continued to ignore her demands. When she delivered the note to her sixty-eight-year-old employer on September 26, 1867, Crawford attacked her with a large stick, fracturing several ribs and wounding her left arm.

When Blacker learned of the attack, he forced the sheriff to arrest Crawford for assault and battery. A Bartow County justice court convened in Kingston where John Crawford was put on trial to answer Hays' allegations. During the trial, several freedwomen who worked for Crawford testified that they too had witnessed and endured his mistreatment. An overly confident Crawford took the stand swearing under oath that his actions had been necessary due to the woman's licentious allegations. After a few minutes of deliberation, the court's justices T. S. Harris and T. R. Couch returned a not guilty verdict and ordered Hays to pay Crawford $8.20 to cover his court expenses. In Hays's case, as in numerous others, the actions of the Freedmen's Bureau did nothing to secure justice for the county's freedpeople.[60]

Negotiating labor contracts remained the Freedmen's Bureau's primary task in Bartow County. The report of assistant commissioner Brevet Major General Davis Tillson illustrates the problems confronting freedpeople as laborers: "Many whites refused to pay laborers a decent wage and allow them to migrate freely, arresting citizens from other counties who sought their labor."[61] In 1870, fewer than 5 percent of freedpeople heads of households owned any real property. Approximately, 37 percent of the county's black population lived in white headed households working primarily as domestic servants and laborers. The overwhelming majority of freedpeople identified themselves as day laborers or farm laborers; some worked as blacksmiths, wheelwrights, and iron workers. Roughly, 78 percent of black households were identified by the Freedmen's Bureau as "very destitute."[62]

Poor harvests combined with abusive labor contracts hampered freedpeople who worked as farmers. They rarely owned their land, animals, and equipment. According to bureau reports, many Reconstruction-era African American worked on shares or as tenants. Sharecropping was a dangerous gamble for freedpeople. "There are quite a number of freedpeople," reported C. B. Blacker, "who has worked on shares this year with white people the people not owning the land have rented it. . . . with a promise of a certain part of the crop. . . . freedpeople will be robbed out of their years work" unless the bureau seizes the owner's personal property.[63] White farmers commonly swindled black sharecroppers. Once the crop was gathered, whites sold the crop at market and frequently pocketed the entire profit. Sometimes, white farmers moved westward following a season's harvest never distributing the farm's income.

Working as a farm laborer proved just as risky as sharecropping. White employers routinely withheld wages or threatened such actions in order to exert additional control over their freedmen workers. Freedman Virgil Allen remained in Bartow County following the Civil War, choosing to work for his former master in exchange for housing and a small monthly wage. His employer still treated him as if he was enslaved. A relative told Allen that if he moved to Macon, he would find him a higher paying job. When Allen informed his employer that he wanted to move and needed to collect his wages, the former slaveholder told him that moving required his permission and that if he moved, he would surrender his back wages. Allen reported his employer's threats to C. B. Blacker, who wrote the employer a letter demanding payment, but, as usual, the owner defied the bureau's flimsy authority.[64]

Labor conditions worsened in the fall of 1867 and 1868 when hundreds of freedpeople went to the polls to exercise their new civil liberties. Many whites used force and intimidation to curb the black vote. When Levi Hall learned that several of his freedmen laborers had voted the Republican ticket during a local election, he fired all of them and withheld over $200 in wages. The workers complained to agents at the bureau who responded by arresting Hall for violating General Order Number Twenty, which specifically forbade employers from inhibiting freedmen voting rights. Bureau arrests, however, were few and far between.[65]

Frustrated by poor working and living conditions, some freedpeople violently retaliated against their white employers. Freedman James Sumter mortally wounded his former employer with a musket following a disagreement over unpaid wages. A local court arrested, tried, convicted, and hung Sumter in Cartersville on November 1, 1867. In a similar incident, freedman H. H. Kinnabrue cut the throat of a white man near Kingston after exchanging some harsh words. He eluded capture by hiding out in the woods around Cassville. When the white man recovered from the near fatal wound, local authorities uncharacteristically abandoned their manhunt.[66]

Acts of violence toward whites were infrequent occurrences, but rumors of supposed insurrectionary plots kept them in a state of constant fear. According to a bureau report, when local freedmen learned that the government would not redistribute land in Bartow County in time for the 1867 planting season, they began to exhibit their mounting frustrations toward whites. Many whites believed that local freedpeople were plotting a "mass uprising" to be launched on either Christmas or New Year's Day. Worst of all, they thought that bureau agents were secretly providing freedpeople with arms to carry out their rebellion. The Freedmen's Bureau never distributed weapons among the freedmen, and the 1867 holiday season passed without incident. Nevertheless, myth and rumor had a strange way of becoming fact during Reconstruction.[67]

Although fears of black insurrection concerned white citizens, their greatest worries stemmed from black access to the ballot box. Unlike other parts of north Georgia, the Republican Party posed little threat to the dominant Democratic Party in Bartow County. While wartime Unionists existed in the county, their numbers were too small to challenge the Democratic majority without substantial black support. Nonetheless, several statewide Republican leaders hailed from Bartow County. These men made overtures to the black community soliciting votes and forging the first interracial coalitions. Cartersville attorney Henry Farrow played an instrumental role in organizing Georgia's Republican Party. Farrow had opposed secession in 1861 but was conscripted into the Confederate army against his will the following year. For most of the war, Farrow served as superintendent of the Georgia district of the Confederate Nitre and Mining Bureau and ably managed Kingston's salt peter cave. After the war, Farrow remained opposed to secession and saw his involvement in the Republican Party as a chance to remake the South. He served as state party secretary, attended numerous national Republican meetings where he gained a reputation as a southern party leader, and launched several unsuccessful gubernatorial campaigns. Familiar with Bartow County, Farrow courted black voters, reached out to white Unionists, and tried to connect Republicans there with party organizers in Rome, Atlanta, and Dalton. Farrow called party meetings in Kingston where Bartow County's black men first participated in political debates about the organization's platform and candidates.[68]

In 1867, Farrow and local black leaders, including the county's first black landholder, formed a Union League in Cartersville to recruit Republican supporters. When the league marched in the streets calling attention to their party and shouting demands for local reform ranging from public schools to voting procedures, Democrats accused them of forming a secret militia that threatened white residents. The league organized rallies, registered voters, and escorted black men to the polls in masse to protect against white mobs. League activities attracted the ire of local Klansmen who in 1868 targeted organizers in the months leading up to the presidential election. In the face of white violence, league members persevered and remained the loudest voice in support of Republican candidates in the county.[69]

Bartow County Republicans failed to win elections. In the spring 1868 election, Republican gubernatorial candidate Rufus Bullock received 1,000 fewer votes in Bartow County than General John B. Gordon, his Democratic Party challenger. While Bullock won the statewide election receiving over 83,000 votes, Bartow County remained in the Democratic Party column. Republicans lost every election in the county. In the 7th Congressional District election, a fourteen county district that included Bartow County and stretched across northwest Georgia, General P. M. B. Young soundly defeated his Republican opponent James Atkins. In Bartow County, Young outpaced his opponent by a 2:1 majority. As during the antebellum period, Bartow County remained a Democratic Party stronghold.[70]

Republicans faced insurmountable challenges in Bartow County. African American voters only comprised about 30 percent of the electorate. Unionists, whose numbers are difficult to estimate, likely totaled about 15 percent of all white voters. In northeast Georgia, Republican candidates managed to win a number of elected offices thanks to large numbers of white unionists and low numbers of African Americans. Republicans there, as well as throughout the Appalachian region, did not need as many black votes in order to win elections and thus made little effort to form the kind of interracial voting block that northwest Georgia Republicans required. Most of Georgia's Republican strongholds were in south central and coastal areas that contained black majorities.[71]

In Bartow County, many white men, even those who disliked the Democratic Party, could not bring themselves to support an interracial Republican Party. The party tried to appeal to white farmers by supporting the inclusion of a homestead exemption in the 1867 Georgia Constitution. The exemption was intended to help small farmers struggling with mounting debts by placing $2,000 in real property and $1,000 in personal property out of the reach of creditors. Bartow farmers, such as Chunn, supported the exemption but by

1870 a growing number of farmers no longer owned the land they worked and gained no advantage from the law. Even Republican promises to support public school initiatives failed to attract enough poor white voters to form a majority. Republican leadership's compromise measures allowing Democrats to impose a poll tax upon all voters also undermined their chances of building a base among poor white farmers.[72] Regional newspapers berated white Republican voters often accusing them of betraying their race. "173 white men who voted the Radical ticket!" exclaimed the *Rome Weekly Courier*. "Poor deluded creatures, we pity them from the bottom of our heat, and would advise them to keep this act of their as still as possible, and never do so any more." Editorials urged white Republicans to abandon their "folly" and return to the "White Man's or Democratic party."[73] Editorials also suggested that white Republicans belonged to the same "lower class" of people that had abandoned the Confederacy during the war.[74]

At best even a unified white-black Republican coalition in Bartow County lacked enough votes to defeat Democratic candidates. Also, a small number of black voters, perhaps as many as 5 percent, voted Democrat. Some of those black Democrats had been courted by moderate leaning Democrats such as General William T. Wofford. Others had sold their votes on Election Day in exchange for alcohol and barbecue provided by Democrats. Most black voters who joined the Democratic fray only did so after being intimidated by armed bands of white men stationed at the polls that tracked black voting activities. Since Bartow County, like most of the South, still used an open ballot box that required voters to publicly cast ballots in front of witnesses, voter intimidation was commonplace.[75]

By the end of the 1860s, many northwest Georgia farmers had grown dissatisfied with the Democratic Party because they appeared to have forgotten the "little man." In Bartow County, General William T. Wofford, William Chunn, and William H. Felton actively promoted a series of local reforms intended to improve the daily lives of farm families. They urged local businesspersons to invest their profits into community projects, such as churches, schools, and agricultural societies. Felton and Chunn played instrumental roles in forming a Bartow County chapter of The Patrons of Husbandry, or The Grange, a national movement formed to improve farmer education and advocate on behalf of the social and political needs of American farmers. Chunn helped Bartow County farmers to organize a collective buying movement and encouraged locals "to adapt themselves strictly to the new order of things, and drive entirely from their minds the happy retrospections."[76]

Like Chunn, General William T. Wofford tried to help farmers adjust to the "new order of things." His actions during Reconstruction laid a foundation for subsequent Independent Democrat movements in northwest Georgia. After commanding the surrender of north Georgia Confederate forces at Kingston, Wofford returned to civilian life hopeful of resuming his antebellum legal practice. When veterans who had once served in his command returned home from northern Virginia to discover that many of their homes and farms had been destroyed, they turned to Wofford for relief. Renowned for his charity toward widows and indigent families, the general had little money or provisions for his veterans. In need of supplies, Wofford telegraphed Union General George H. Thomas and requested 30,000 bushels of corn to be distributed throughout the county. The general granted his plea and personally guaranteed the corn's delivery.[77]

Wofford also strongly encouraged his former soldiers and local residents to submit to the oath of allegiance. He pleaded with individuals who maintained animosity toward the Federals and freedpeople to abandon their hatred in favor of rebuilding their communities. Freedpeople too trusted Wofford. On several occasions, they approached him during various labor contract disputes with some of his white neighbors imploring him to speak to their employers on their behalf. The testimony of several freedpeople included in the local Freedmen's Bureau records evidence that he publicly advocated for the voting rights of freed slaves and seemed willing to intercede on their behalf during disputes with other whites. Perhaps, Wofford, a lifelong Democrat with Whiggish leanings, supported black voting rights to persuade freedmen to join an independent anti-Bourbon movement that he supported within the larger Georgia Democratic Party. Likewise, some black conservative voters were also interested in forging ties with the Democratic Party.[78]

Like many Bartow County voters, Wofford urged moderation during Reconstruction. He proudly recalled his days as a brigade commander in the "world's finest army," the Army of Northern Virginia, and retold numerous stories of interactions with Robert E. Lee, J. E. B. Stuart, Jefferson Davis, and numerous other Confederate leaders. His fond recollections, however, did not include positive memories of the secession winter of 1861 when he rejected immediate secession on three sequential ballots. Until his death, he believed that emotionalism had trumped rationalism during that crisis and had dearly cost his beloved home of Cassville. During the congressional elections of 1865, veterans urged Wofford to enter the race to represent their concerns ranging from railroad reform to currency valuation. The 7th Congressional District campaign included H. G. Cole of Atlanta, who had been a leading Unionist during the war, and James P. Hambleton, whose rhetoric resembled that of an unreconstructed fire-eater. Reluctant to enter the political contest, Wofford's candidacy benefited from the strong backing of a loud coalition of independent-minded Democrats who distrusted state Democratic Party leadership and entertained options for building a potential biracial political coalition as a means to ending Reconstruction.[79] Without the aid of a single campaign speech, his reputation and local dissatisfaction with state Democratic leadership swept him into office carrying more than 65 percent of the votes cast. A few months later, however, Congressional Republicans denied Wofford and the rest of the Georgia congressional delegation, including former Confederate Vice-President Alexander H. Stephens and Senator Herschel V. Johnson, their seats.

Wofford harbored no visible feelings of ill will toward the northern congressional members who overturned his election. Instead, he used his brief time in Washington to lobby northern Democrats for relief for his beleaguered county. He met with aid societies in Baltimore engaged in soliciting funds to send food supplies into north Georgia. Through his efforts, Bartow's indigent received additional provisions from allocations made by the House Ways and Means Committee, the Federal army, and the state of Kentucky. Wofford hoped that Congress would seat the southern representatives so he could introduce legislation to provide immediate support for north Georgia's poor. His efforts earned him a reputation among area farmers as a leader who cared about the "little man." After spending a few months in Washington, a discouraged Wofford returned to Cassville.[80]

Back in Cassville, Wofford donated funds to help erect the county's first monuments dedicated to the service of Confederate dead buried at the Kingston and Cassville cemeteries. He contributed thirty dollars per year to ensure that the grass at the Cassville cemetery was cut on a regular basis. Always a favorite among veterans, he fought to secure state funding to provide pensions and relief for their indigent families and widows. He protested the prison lease system as inhumane calling it "worse than any slavery the south ever had."[81] Along with fellow Bartow Countian William H. Felton, Wofford strongly criticized Bourbon leaders because their brand of politics ignored the state's suffering families.

During the spring 1868 election, in response to the growing uncertainty among northwest Georgia farmers, the first Independent Democratic candidates appeared on the ballot. Independents were Democratic Party supporters who disagreed with Bourbon Democratic leaders on a number of issues ranging from the candidate nomination process to economic policy. Most Independents had supported secession and the Confederate government but questioned the South's leadership. During the war, many had favored Unionist gubernatorial candidate Joshua Hill and other candidates that clashed with Governor Joseph E. Brown. After the war, these same men criticized the party's nomination process as "undemocratic." The party selected candidates through executive sessions or conventions held locally and attended by party appointed delegates. These sessions enabled state party leaders to screen candidates and nominate men loyal to the executive leadership. Men seeking office who either lacked political connections or had previously run afoul with Democratic leaders routinely found themselves shut out of these meetings. In most counties, between 20 and 60 handpicked delegates controlled who ran for office as a Democrat.

County conventions also highlighted another rising trend in postbellum Georgia. After the Civil War, towns and cities gained social, economic, and political power as rural areas declined. The antebellum South had revolved around plantations and created a system that privileged large rural farms over neighboring towns. Planters held a disproportionate amount of the region's power, status, and wealth. Emancipation and the plantation economy's decline motivated many planters to diversify their economic practices by opening merchant stores and other businesses located in town. As rural farmers became even less self-sufficient due to increased cotton cultivation and more dependent upon merchants to provide credit to purchase farm supplies, household goods, and food, an elite class of townspeople, with direct ties to agricultural planters, ascended into the ranks of a new provincial aristocracy. In Bartow County, Cartersville merchants and entrepreneurs slowly joined planters as the primary community power brokers.[82]

Bourbon Democrats developed a platform that benefited the interests of town and planter elite. During Reconstruction, Bourbons led the fight to oust federal authorities and worked tirelessly to destroy the nascent Republican Party. Led by a host of former Confederate veterans and leaders, Bourbons kept one foot entrenched in the past while the other thrust forward creating the persistent image of the New South. New South Bourbons promoted commerce and industry and protected the interests of large landholders while ignoring the plight of smaller farmers and poor whites. Mindful that they needed poor white votes to maintain power, Bourbons stressed the need for white unity and reminded all white men that African American agency was the single greatest threat to southern prosperity. Bourbons embraced the "Lost Cause," vilified Republicans, distrusted poor whites, and placed democracy in the hands of a select few. By the mid-1870s, critics such as Robert Toombs complained that "there are 150 politicians who rule the state and hold its offices as absolutely in fee as if they had received a title to the property."[83] Political corruption, white supremacy, and one-party politics dominated Georgia politics.

Without a viable second party to challenge Bourbon rule, a group of north Georgia Democrats bolted from the party throughout the 1870s and launched a series of Independent campaigns. Bartow County planter, Methodist minister, physician, and politician William H. Felton emerged as the movement's most vocal leader. Felton, a former Whig who supported secession, had lost a great deal during the Civil War. When he and his wife, Rebecca Felton, left their Cartersville farm to seek refuge in Macon in the months leading up to the Atlanta Campaign, two of the couple's young children died from disease. By the end of the war, Felton became critical of Confederate leadership and sorry that he had endorsed secession. A powerful orator and passionate minister, Felton represented, according to Steven Hahn, an "emerging constituency of small producers disenchanted with the social relations and economic consequences of commercial agriculture."[84] Felton became the spokesperson for small farmers who felt abandoned by Bourbon Democrats and abused by rising taxes, mounting debts, inadequate schools, escalating transportation costs, declining crop prices, and stagnant wages. Furthermore, the minister accused Bourbon leaders of building an aristocracy whose corrupt practices lined the purses of its exclusive leaders as poor farmers begged for scraps.

Geography also played a part in the Independent movement's rise in Bartow County. Remnants of Republicanism remained in the county's Appalachian subregion. In the mountains, removed from existing transportation routes, white farmers' antebellum hardships carried over into the postbellum period. These men were already suspicious, if not outright hostile, toward Bourbon leaders because of the latter's role in the Confederacy. They were equally suspect of town businessmen and politicians who ruled the county. Republicans understood that their best chance to win elections and influence politics was by forming alliances with dissident Democrats.

Independents found abundant support among Piedmont farmers. Since the end of the Civil War, Piedmont farmers had seen their wealth decline with little hope for a future rebirth. Dwindling cotton prices, rising railroad shipping costs, and a town-centered monopoly on supplies and credit left landholding farmers teetering on the brink of financial ruin. Large numbers of tenant and sharecropper farms were also located in the Piedmont. Many of these farmers worked on lands owned by town merchants and planters. Riddled by debts accumulated to raise crops and support their families, these poor white men disliked the Bourbons but needed a leader to unite them under an actionable political platform of demands.

In the valley, Independents found a critical base of potential support as well as their most vocal critics. Cartersville had flourished since 1865. The bustling town was filled with new stores, trains, and large landholders who built new town homes far from their rural land holdings. Felton accused the *Cartersville Express*, the county's leading newspaper, of being an "organ of the cotton ring." For years, Felton's critics in Cartersville, Rome, and Marietta—the region's three largest towns—slandered his reputation. At one point, they described him as a "boisterous, ranting, egotistical, demagogical" radical bent on appealing to "prejudice and ignorance of negroes and weak minded white men" to attain political office.[85] Felton's overtures to court black voters angered town elite. The Bourbon's worst fears were that a charismatic leader such as Felton might align the interests of poor white and black voters. Not only had towns evolved into major centers of commerce and trade, but they also became the permanent home for thousands of ex-slaves who left the countryside to come to the city in search of work. If Felton could build a coalition of mountain Republicans, Upcountry Yeomen, and town freedpeople, he could defeat the "piratical crew" running Georgia affairs.[86]

The 1874 Georgia 7th U.S. Congressional District race revealed the racial and class tensions that permeated postbellum northwest Georgia society. When incumbent Bourbon Democrat General P. M. B. Young got caught up in a series of scandals, district convention delegates began searching for a new candidate to replace the three-term congressman. Felton made himself available but lacked the statewide connections delegates wanted. The convention ignored Felton's candidacy, instead favoring Colonel L. N. Trammell. Trammell, a Dalton attorney and regional Klan leader, was a Confederate veteran with extensive connections within the state and national Democratic Party. In addition to representing the region at several national Democratic events, Trammell counted Joseph E. Brown as a close friend and mentor. Before Trammell received the nomination, however, allegations appeared in newspapers connecting the Dalton attorney to a railroad bonds scandal. Fearful of nominating a candidate connected to a railroad scandal during a period when anxious voters had grown tired of political corruption, the nominating convention thrust Rome attorney Colonel William H. Dabney into the campaign. Scandalous rumors surrounded Dabney, too. Incensed that convention delegates had overlooked him twice in favor of two corruptible yet well connected Democratic Party insiders further confirmed Felton's complaints that the party was more interested in exercising political influence than serving their constituents. With his wife's support and at the urging of several friends, Felton defied the Bourbons and entered the race as an independent candidate.

Bourbon Democrats' condemnation of Felton's campaign revealed the fragile condition of postbellum relations among white men. *Rome Courier* editors accused Felton of throwing "discord into the ranks of the white people of the district." Democrats worried that Felton might either win outright or worse yet siphon off enough votes to allow Republicans to earn a narrow victory. Felton's critics tended to overstate the Republican Party's chances in the election in the hopes of driving independent-minded supporters back into the Bourbon fold. Republicans were initially unsure about Felton. During the summer of 1874, newspaper reports accused Felton of holding secret meetings with Republican organizers in Atlanta. Critics claimed that Felton had brokered a deal with north Georgia Republican leader Major Zachariah B. Hargrove that his candidate, N. P. Harbin, would quietly urge Republicans to vote independent. While it is unclear whether or not Felton and Republican leaders coordinated efforts, Republican voters with or without instruction began showing up and cheering the minister on wherever he campaigned.[87]

Felton's campaign threatened Bourbon Democrats statewide because if he managed to win, his actions might inspire other Democrats to launch independent bids. During the summer of 1874, Felton conducted a vigorous campaign as he canvased the large fourteen-county district. His speeches portrayed Georgia Democrats as undemocratic masters of an increasingly oligarchical political machine. Felton cast himself as a struggling farmer and family man who like many of the region's farmers had been negatively impacted by government malfeasance. The Bourbons, Felton declared, had forgotten the little man. If elected, Felton promised to be the farmer's representative in Washington. Farmers likely found Felton's direct knowledge of their specific problems to be appealing. He clearly saw himself as one of them. In speeches Felton promised to use his office to address credit and transportation reform. Felton's intention to end the abusive convict lease system and not to oppose the federal Civil Rights Act made him a viable choice among Republicans. For most Republicans, Felton's policies did not matter as long as he continued to contrast himself with the much maligned Bourbons. His campaign gave northwest Georgia Republicans their first realistic chance of gaining representation in Congress.

As the November election approached, Bourbons increased their attacks upon Felton and began sending popular speakers into northwest Georgia in the hopes of stemming the independent tide. Newspapers hoped to damage Felton's chances among white farmers by focusing on the minister's "negro" supporters. U.S. Senator General John B. Gordon, a leading Bourbon politician, traveled to Rome to condemn Felton's campaign. Gordon accused Felton of breaking up the Democratic Party and urged him to abandon the race. Bourbons alleged that Felton had manipulated "weak minded white men" who had forgotten that Republicans were the greatest threat to democracy. Felton's critics called upon all white men to do their "patriotic" duty and serve "the interests of their race." Speakers reminded audiences that, if elected, Felton would be a political outsider in Georgia so despised by Bourbon leaders that he would never be able to accomplish any of his campaign promises. The campaign's intensity led many observers to refer to Felton's district as the "Bloody Seventh."[88]

Felton's black supporters defended the minister and launched their own efforts to damage the reputation of Bourbon Democrats. In Cartersville, a black Republican organizer by the name of Crumley, who had traveled from his home in Rome to join Felton at the rally, "made a bitter speech against [Felton's Democratic opponent], denouncing him as the candidate of an odious party of outrages and Ku Kluxism . . . [and] spoke strongly in favor of Dr. Felton." Felton then told the mixed race crowd that if elected he would defend the freedman's right to vote and to participate in fair elections. The minister's intent to clean up Georgia elections would have appealed to both Republicans and white farmers who carried concerns about the validity of elections held under Bourbon rule. During the final weeks of the campaign, a black band of musicians often serenaded Felton's supporters. Felton also accepted invitations from black leaders in Cedartown, Buchanan, Marietta, and Dalton to speak.[89]

In 1874, despite Bourbon efforts to sully Felton's reputation and manipulate white racial prejudices, the minister won a narrow eighty plus vote majority. Election returns from across Felton's northwest Georgia district reveal several trends. Felton dominated the region's major towns of Rome, Cartersville, Calhoun, and Dalton where substantial numbers of black voters defied Bourbon threats of violence and intimidation by supporting an independent candidate. Republican leaders acknowledged after the election that most of their members voted for Felton. In rural areas throughout the district, Felton did well in some places and poorly in others. A majority of white farmers continued to support Bourbon Democrats, but Felton managed enough votes from this class to secure victory. In Bartow County, Felton won handily in every precinct. These returns spread deep concerns among Bourbon leaders that the independent movement might spread elsewhere in Georgia.[90]

Felton proved that Bourbon candidates could be defeated by candidates who built an interracial coalition of Republicans and white farmers. "Democratic hegemony," according to Steven Hahn, "appeared to be shaken in the countryside." Two years later, Felton won reelection by a wide margin despite Bourbon attempts to smear his reputation in newspapers and in speeches statewide. Felton remained the sole Independent Georgia Congressman until the election of 1878 when Henry Parsons, Emory Speer, and Alexander Stephens successfully challenged Bourbon rule in their districts. His campaigns increasingly incorporated Republican Party issues and unlike his Bourbon opponents refrained from using race as a means to divide the Georgia electorate.

Although Felton never championed the cause of black equality, he implicitly supported black civil rights through his partnership with Republican leaders. Independent candidate pledges to respect black access to the polls, clean up corrupt elections, end the convict lease system, and fund black schools appealed to many black voters who were left with little alternative as the Republican Party declined and Bourbons assaulted black voting rights.

In 1878, Bourbon Democrats tried to wave the "bloody shirt" to unseat Felton. Although Felton had supported secession, his military career had been brief and unnoteworthy. He also spent the last years of the war with his family. Bourbons nominated Confederate veteran George N. Lester, a Blue Ridge Circuit Court Judge from Marietta, to challenge Felton. Lester had lost his right arm at the Battle of Perryville. During the campaign, Lester and his supporters claimed that "unpatriotic" and "lesser" men such as Felton had damaged the Confederate cause and now sought to bring down the "white men's democracy." Lester constantly reminded voters of his wartime wound and meritorious Confederate service. White farmers ignored Lester's "Lost Cause" rhetoric and went to the polls in mass providing Felton with a decisive victory.[91]

In 1880, Independents across Georgia urged Felton to run for governor to challenge Alfred Colquitt, the powerful member of the so-called "Bourbon Triumvirate." Felton's health had declined by this point. He refused the nomination and focused his attention on his own 7th District reelection bid. By this point, Felton's relationship with Republican leaders in Atlanta had become more of a liability than a strength. Newspapers accused Felton of collaborating with Republicans in Atlanta and Washington. Bourbons portrayed Independent candidates as racial liberals intent on undermining the South's most cherished institution, white privilege. Democrats also increased their efforts to control who accessed the polls. On Election Day in 1880, white men representing Democrat clubs manned the polls and stationed armed supporters outside. Felton supporters heading to the polls received physical threats and were occasionally assaulted. In the weeks prior to the election, bands of white men terrorized black communities in a fashion reminiscent of the defunct Ku Klux Klan. Meanwhile, Bourbon state legislators entertained all sorts of proposals designed to reduce the number of voters statewide by raising poll taxes and creating new qualifications that disqualified poor and uneducated voters. Bourbon Democrats targeted Felton from the start of the 1880 campaign season. Judson C. Clements of Walker County was handpicked by Bourbon leaders because of his Confederate ties and strong friendship with Gordon. Clements usually avoided direct assaults upon Felton's character. Instead, the "young fire brand" played upon white fears of Radical

Republican rule and black civil equality. Reports of escalating black crime filled newspapers raising fears that the political success of Felton Republicans had created an increasingly lawless black populace. Physically exhausted from years of fending off character attacks and constant travel to and from Washington, an aging Felton stopped delivering stump speeches. On Election Day, Clements achieved an 800 vote majority thus ending Felton's three-term run as Georgia's first independent congressman.[92]

High tide for Independent Democrats in Georgia receded during the early 1880s. Following the 1880 election, Felton tried unsuccessfully on two occasions to regain his seat. Undeterred, Felton returned to the political stage winning a seat in the Georgia General Assembly where he served three terms until he left the office in 1890 to launch a new congressional bid as the district's Populist nominee. Statewide Independents lost their elected offices throughout the early 1880s as Bourbons rebounded from earlier losses and implemented new strategies to silence Republicans and white farmers. Independent political candidates, however, influenced the next generation of Bourbon dissidents as many former Independents cast ballots in favor of a wave of Populist candidates throughout the final decades of the nineteenth century.[93]

At a moment when Bartow Countians, black and white, appeared to have lost faith in the Bourbon's New South vision, many white farmers were inundated with constant reminders of the "Lost Cause." Prior to 1882, local Confederate veteran meetings had been largely confined to attending annual memorial day commemorations. Officers, such as John Maddox and J. W. Wofford, often spoke at such gatherings, and free picnic lunches gave veterans added incentive to attend. Several Bartow County veterans, most notably General P. M. B. Young, became active members of the Survivors' Association of Confederate Soldiers. In 1882, the 18th Georgia Infantry Regiment, General William T. Wofford's first command, organized its first reunion. The 18th Georgia held annual reunions until after World War I. Groups of Confederate veterans also met monthly at the Bartow County courthouse throughout the late nineteenth and early twentieth centuries.

When the United Confederate Veterans formed in 1890, members elected General Young as its first Georgia division commander. Young traveled widely attending reunions across the South and lobbied elected leaders to provide funds to erect Confederate memorials and support aging veterans. Confederate monuments also began appearing across Bartow County. These memorials stood as a constant reminder of the Confederacy's long shadow and continuing relevance to contemporary life. In 1874, the Ladies Memorial Association of Kingston dedicated a large stone obelisk in "honor of our southern heroes" at that town's Confederate cemetery. Four years later the women of Cassville unveiled their Confederate cemetery monument. Large celebrations that included lavish barbecues and processions of Confederate veterans marked the unveiling of each memorial.

Records fail to indicate how many Bartow County Confederate veterans attended reunions and commemorations. Newspaper announcements often appeared asking veterans to send their contact information to reunion organizers. Sometimes the announcements would place asterisks beside the names of veterans who had attended recent reunions. In the case of the 18th Georgia Infantry Regiment, it appears that fewer than 20 percent of their veterans attended reunions. Undoubtedly many veterans moved great distances away from Bartow County after the war and were unable to make the long trip for these annual events. Others, however, remained in the area but for one reason or another kept their distance from these Confederate celebrations.[94]

Several Bartow County veterans played major roles in organizing statewide veteran reunions. General Young routinely served on organizing committees. George W. Maddox, 18th Georgia Infantry, also worked on numerous committees and attended reunions across the South to generate interest in Georgia activities. Dalton native Judge Joseph Bogle, who spent most of his teenage years working for his uncle in Bartow County before joining the 40th Georgia Infantry Regiment, used his political connections to lobby state leaders for financial support for reunions and benefits for Confederate veterans. One of the most colorful veteran organizers was Cartersville mayor David B. Freeman. Born in Gilmer County, two weeks before his 11th birthday, Freemen snuck into Camp Felton in Bartow County and enlisted in the 6th Georgia Cavalry Regiment. After serving in the cavalry for the duration of the war, Freeman returned to northwest Georgia where he edited several newspapers and held a handful of local political offices. During the late 1880s, Freeman moved to Cartersville to edit the *American Courant* alongside his close friend William H. Felton. By the late nineteenth century, Freeman had gained notoriety by claiming to be the youngest Confederate soldier in that army's history. Freeman became a bit of a celebrity figure—the subject of numerous articles in local, state, and national publications and a popular speaker at Confederate reunions. In 1905, Cartersville voters elected Freeman mayor. As mayor Freeman understood that reunions were good for local businesses. During reunions town businesses profited from the large influx of out of town customers who spent nights in local hotels, dined at area restaurants, and generally uplifted the town's economy. With help from Henry Grady and other southern city boosters, Freeman revitalized interest in state Confederate reunions by convincing host cities that promoting such events could reap huge economic rewards. Freeman, like many reunion organizers, was also heavily influenced by the "Lost Cause" and believed that younger generations of white southerners could benefit morally from coming in close proximity to mass gatherings of Confederate heroes. Statewide reunions grew and persisted for many years in part due to Freeman's advocacy.

By the end of the nineteenth century, the "Lost Cause" mythology and Bourbon Democratic regime had taken hold of most white Bartow County residents. Even individuals who had once resisted Bourbon rule by entertaining biracial political coalitions now distanced themselves from those ideas and espoused a new brand of racial prejudice and disdain toward African Americans. The failures of the Independent and Populist movements had created a wide chasm between black and poor white voters. Party leaders, such as Thomas B. Watson, reversed their efforts to forge biracial political coalitions by adopting white supremacist rhetoric to divide black and poor white voters. Like Watson, Rebecca Felton, wife and political advisor of William H. Felton, continued her dislike of Bourbon politicians and outright hatred of General John B. Gordon, who she referred to as "the consummate liar." Her disdain for African Americans, however, trumped the disgust she felt for state Democratic leaders. She expressed sincere doubts that African Americans could ever gain anything through education except for basic vocational skills. Felton believed that African Americans lacked the sincerity and intellect required to become good citizens and educated voters. When reformers sought to change Georgia's child labor laws to rescue young children from the state's textile mills, Felton opposed the idea out of fear that black workers would take the jobs that white children held. A popular speaker and leading advocate for women's suffrage, controversy followed Felton wherever she spoke. At an 1897 meeting of the Georgia State Agricultural Society, Felton appealed to the worst fears of white rural southerners declaring that black rapists posed the greatest threat to white farm women. Felton told the audience that "If it requires lynching to protect women's dearest possession from ravening, drunken human beasts, then I say lynch a thousand negroes a week, if it is necessary."[95]

Felton's opinions of poor whites were equally biased. Whereas her husband had once sought to uplift farmers out of poverty through public policy and education reform, Felton believed that poor whites could not escape "hopeless poverty" because they were "enslaved by their own apathy and adverse conditions." By the end of her life, Felton doubted whether African Americans and poor whites should even participate in American democracy.[96]

Felton's words echoed the fears and prejudices of most white Bartow Countians. The 1890s saw the rise of the Jim Crow South and the nadir of southern race relations. Locally, the growing city of Cartersville became increasingly segregated racially as it expanded. African Americans tended to live on the outskirts of the city far from the opulent neighborhoods that rose along Erwin Street. In this segregated environment, a small black middle class emerged comprised of ministers, merchants, teachers, barbers, and physicians. Many of this class sent their children north to be educated at some of the greatest universities in America. Those who returned spent decades challenging white supremacy as their Reconstruction-era ancestors had done.

In 1933, Cartersville resident Lucy Cunyus published the first history of Bartow County. Cunyus was an amateur historian related to one of the first white families to settle in Bartow County. As a child raised in the Methodist Church, she encountered William H. Felton, Rebecca Felton, the popular evangelist Sam Jones, and numerous Confederate veterans. She lived in a city where rural farmers came to town to buy goods and sell cotton. She developed a strong relationship with Wilbur Kurtz, the historian who consulted with producers during the filming of Margaret Mitchell's classic *Gone With the Wind*. She and Kurtz spent hours traveling the routes of Confederate and Federal armies that had moved through Bartow County during the 1864 Atlanta Campaign. With her help, Kurtz wrote the first series of state historical markers that continue to identify major sites scattered throughout the county. Perhaps no one knew more about Bartow County than Cunyus.

Cunyus's history exalted the "Lost Cause" and evidenced the collective amnesia that twentieth-century residents contracted when they reflected on the county's nineteenth-century past. Like the dozens of historical markers erected in the county, Cunyus's book fails to mention that a sizable number of white men opposed not only secession but the Confederate government. Of the many families that she profiles in the book, most owned slaves, none were black, and all were Confederate supporters. The chaotic struggle that ensued in Bartow County following the withdrawal of federal troops in the fall of 1864 goes without mention. Republicans also fail to make an appearance. Klansmen come and go quickly in the book without much comment about their efforts to intimidate black voters. Although most of the farmers she would have seen on the streets of Cartersville were tenants and sharecroppers who owned no real estate, they and the backwards economic system that had trapped them in a cycle of perpetual poverty fail to appear. By 1933, the "Lost Cause" myth of the Old South and its failure to recognize any consequences of secession and Confederate defeat beyond emancipation had taken hold of the county's collective memory.

As a child reared in Bartow County, I spent many hours riding a yellow school bus from my home on Euharlee Road to Kingston Elementary

School and later Adairsville Middle and High School. Each day, I passed the Reynolds Plantation located along the Etowah River. Its Greek Revival columns and stories of Union soldier atrocities committed in the home during the war sparked my imagination. In school, an annual trip to the Kingston Confederate Cemetery was commonplace. My beloved 5th grade teacher was so infatuated with *Gone With the Wind* that we stopped class for days so she could display her massive doll collection and watch the classic film repeatedly. A field trip to a Civil War memorabilia store owned by a renowned white supremacist accounted for the bulk of my understanding of the Civil War. On Saturday afternoons, my family routinely encountered Klan members sheathed in white robes handing out recruitment brochures in downtown Acworth. In 8th grade, I likely knew for the first time that I wanted to be a historian when the stately Mrs. Casey brought me to tears as she described Pickett's Charge and recounted how the Federals had burned nearby Cassville. Later in high school, I grew jealous of many friends who had Confederate battle flags placed on their senior rings. All that time, I never stopped to think if another side to the Civil War existed. Even in the 1980s and 1990s, the "Lost Cause" continued to hold the imagination of most Bartow County residents. It was not until my days as an undergraduate student in an Old South course taught by Dr. Kenneth W. Noe and after reading Wayne K. Durrill's *War of Another Kind* that the world from which I came suddenly became more complicated. May my contribution to the history of Bartow County complicate the past in ways that I could have never imagined as a child reared in the long shadow of Bartow County's Civil War.

APPENDIX
A

Methodology

Many of the statistics presented in the text were derived from a database containing over 13,000 heads of households and 2,100 household dependents gathered from the following sources:

Federal Manuscript Census, Cass County, Georgia, 1830, Population Schedule
    Every head of household entered

Federal Manuscript Census, Cass County, Georgia, 1840, Population Schedule
    Every head of household entered

Federal Manuscript Census, Cass County, Georgia, 1850, Population Schedule
    Every head of household entered
        Real estate values for every head of household entered
        Place of birth entered for every head of household
        Number of dependents entered for every head of household
        Age of head of household entered for every household
        Occupation of head of household entered for every household

Federal Manuscript Census, Cass County, Georgia, 1850, Slave Schedule
    Name of every slaveholder entered and cross-referenced with heads of households gathered from population schedule
    Age and gender of every slave entered

Federal Manuscript Census, Cass County, Georgia, 1850,
Agriculture Schedule
- Name of every farmer entered
    - Cotton production for every farm entered
    - Corn production for every farm entered
    - Wheat production for every farm entered
    - Livestock holdings for every farm entered
    - Home manufacturers for every farm entered

Federal Manuscript Census, Cass County, Georgia, 1860,
Population Schedule
- Every head of household entered
    - Real estate values for every head of household entered
    - Place of birth entered for every head of household
    - Number of dependents entered for every head of household
    - Age of head of household entered for every household
    - Occupation of head of household entered for every household

Federal Manuscript Census, Cass County, Georgia, 1860, Slave Schedule
- Name of every slaveholder entered and cross-referenced with heads of households gathered from population schedule
- Age and gender of every slave entered

Federal Manuscript Census, Cass County, Georgia, 1860,
Agriculture Schedule
- Name of every farmer entered
    - Farm Value for every farm entered
    - Improved and unimproved acreage for every farm entered
    - Cotton production for every farm entered
    - Corn production for every farm entered
    - Wheat production for every farm entered
    - Livestock holdings for every farm entered
    - Home manufacturers for every farm entered

Federal Manuscript Census, Bartow County, Georgia, 1870,
Population Schedule
- Every head of household entered
    - Real estate values for every head of household entered
    - Place of birth entered for every head of household
    - Number of dependents entered for every head of household
    - Age of head of household entered for every household
    - Occupation of head of household entered for every household
    - Race of head of household entered for every household

Federal Manuscript Census, Bartow County, Georgia, 1870, Agriculture Schedule
    Name of every farmer entered
        Farm value for every farm entered
        Improved and unimproved acreage for every farm entered
        Cotton production for every farm entered
        Corn production for every farm entered
        Wheat production for every farm entered
        Livestock holdings for every farm entered
        Home manufacturers for every farm entered

Georgia State Militia Census, Bartow County, 1864
    Names on militia census entered and cross-referenced with 1860 population census

Compiled Confederate Service Records, Georgia
    Names of soldiers enlisted in companies raised in Bartow County entered and cross-references with 1860 population census

Using this database, I calculated:
    tenancy rates
    persistence rates
    military enlistment rates

The database's goal was to provide an exhaustive and complete statistical rendering of Bartow County life between 1830 and 1870. Census records provide historians with an invaluable glimpse into the lives of ordinary people who failed to leave behind manuscript records. Only a small percentage of Bartow Countians left behind written records or appear in official documents. My database is an effort to recreate the world they lived in as much as possible. Rather than sample these sources, I decided to build an exhaustive database that enabled me to pull an enormous amount of data to draw as precise conclusions as possible.

Tenancy Rates

Tenancy rates measure land ownership among farmers. Land ownership can be measured using the population and agriculture schedules for the 1850, 1860, and 1870 censuses. Using the household as the basic unit of measurement, I entered every head of household in Bartow County in the 1850, 1860, and 1870 population census. Fortunately, genealogists in Bartow County had created a complete index of all heads of households between 1850 and 1870. Using this index as my base, I checked each entry for accuracy and recorded additional information for each household, such as occupation, real property, birthplace, age, size of household, and number of dependents. Since the 1850 census did not include a household's personal property, I omitted it from the 1860 and 1870 entries. I then matched up the households when possible with corresponding entries in the agricultural schedules (Schedule II). For each farm, I recorded farm value, the amount of improved and unimproved acreage, cotton production, corn, production, wheat production, numbers of livestock, and home manufacturers. Matching every farm listed in the agriculture schedule with a corresponding household in the population schedule proved impossible. Ultimately, I was able to find matches for 83 percent of all farms. Using the slave schedule for 1850 and 1860, I then matched the names of slaveholders recorded on Schedule III with households identified in Schedule I. I was able to match 92 percent of slaveholders listed on Schedule III with a Schedule I household.

Using methods described by Frederick A. Bode and Donald E. Ginter that have been adopted by numerous southern historians, I then applied criteria for dividing head of household occupations into nine categories, in order to differentiate tenants among self-described "farmers":

Category	Occupation
1	"Farmer"; Landowner
2	"Tenant": "Renter"
3	"Farmer": No real property listed on Schedule I, but acreage and farm value on Schedule II. Probable Tenant
4	"Farmer": Real property listed on Schedule I, not appearing on Schedule II. Probably landowner
5	"Farmer": No real property on Schedule I, not appearing on Schedule II. Probable tenant
6	Laborer
7	Professional/Businessman
8	Craftsman/Skilled Worker
9	No Occupation/Housekeeper/Matron

Persistence Rates

Persistence rates—a measure of how long a head of household or their white dependents remained in the county—is an important indicator of economic opportunity and community membership. Antebellum families moved frequently, especially poor whites. Persistence rates are measured by tracking heads of households in a particular area, in this case a county, across multiple census enumerations, in this case 1840, 1850, 1860, and 1870. Locating individuals in multiple census enumerations can be difficult. Census takers sometimes missed individuals or misspelled their names. Gathering a complete data set for all heads of households in a county is impossible; however, my database was able to track substantial numbers across time. For example, of the 1,145 heads of households listed in the 1840 Federal Manuscript Census for Bartow County, 872 (approximately 75 percent) were located in the 1850 Federal Manuscript Census in Bartow County or another location where they had moved. Ancestry.com search engines and numerous genealogical websites significantly aided locating individuals who had moved away from Bartow County. Out of the 1,712 heads of households found in Bartow County in 1850, 1,455 (approximately 85 percent) were located in the 1860 Federal Manuscript Census in either Bartow County or elsewhere. In 1860, 2,086 heads of households were listed in that year's Federal census enumeration. Only 1,236 (approximately 60 percent) of those individuals could be located in the 1870 Federal Manuscript Census. The lower findings from the 1870 census was due in part to civilian and military casualties suffered during the Civil War and the massive waves of outmigration that occurred throughout northwest Georgia in the years immediately following the war. Tracking heads of households who moved to western territories, such as Colorado, Nevada, Arizona, and New Mexico, proved difficult. Overall, I was able to track 1,234 heads of households from 1840 through 1870.[1]

Enlistment Rates

Estimating how many Bartow County men served in the Confederate army was difficult. While several companies were raised in the county, many local men enlisted in neighboring counties and vice-versa. The database containing the names of all heads of households listed in Schedule I of the 1860 Manuscript Census was an enormous help. First, I cross-referenced the 1860 head of household list with Lillian Henderson's *Roster of the Confederate Soldiers of Georgia, 1861–1865*, Confederate Service Records for companies raised in Bartow County, and the 1864 Georgia State Militia Census. Using Ancestry.com search engines, I then searched for household dependents who appeared in these military service records. Thankfully, several Bartow County genealogists, United Daughters of the Confederacy chapters, and Sons of Confederate Veterans chapters had compiled large lists of local veterans. Contemporary newspapers also provided many lists of Bartow County soldiers, especially those who died in combat, deserted, or attended postwar reunions. Public interest in identifying Civil War veterans helped to identify names that I later verified using available service records. Through a combination of sources, I identified 2,136 men listed in Schedule I of the 1860 Federal Manuscript Census that served in the Confederate army. Unfortunately, I encountered an additional 274 names of Confederate soldiers suspected of hailing from Bartow County that I could not positively locate in the 1860 Federal Manuscript Census.

Notes

Introduction

1. Bartow County, Georgia, was created in 1832 and originally named Cass County in honor of Senator Lewis Cass of Michigan. In 1862, following the death of Colonel Francis S. Bartow, a Savannah attorney, at the Battle of First Manassas, the Georgia General Assembly renamed the county Bartow County. Throughout the introduction, I will refer to the county as Bartow County to avoid confusion. Bartow County is located in northwest Georgia roughly halfway between the cities of Chattanooga, Tennessee, and Atlanta, Georgia. The county is situated in the Great Appalachian Valley at the far southern point of the Appalachian Mountain region. The southwestern portion of the county resembles the geographic features, rolling hills and valleys, commonly found in the Piedmont region—a region in Georgia that stretches north of Atlanta southward to the Fall Line cities of Columbus, Macon, and Augusta. The northeastern portions of Bartow County contain geographic features such as rocky ridges and hilly terrain commonly found along the borderlands of southern Appalachia.
2. The use of white supremacist rhetoric to foster unity among white men is sometimes referred to as the "white men's democracy." Anthony Gene Carey, *Parties, Slavery, and the Union in Antebellum Georgia* (Athens: University of Georgia Press, 1997); William Cooper, *The South and the Politics of Slavery, 1828–1856* (Baton Rouge: Louisiana State University Press, 1978); John M. Sacher, *A Perfect War of Politics: Parties, Politicians, and Democracy in Louisiana, 1824–1861* (Baton Rouge: Louisiana State University Press, 2003); Donald B. Cole, *A Jackson Man: Amos Kendall and the Rise of American Democracy* (Baton Rouge: Louisiana State University Press, 2004); Sean Wilentz, *The Rise of American Democracy: Jefferson to Lincoln* (New York: W. W. Norton, 2005); Mark V. Wetherington, *Plain Folk's Fight: The Civil War and Reconstruction in Piney Woods Georgia* (Chapel Hill: University of North Carolina Press, 2005); J. Mills Thornton, III, *Politics and Power in a Slave Society: Alabama, 1800–1860* (Baton Rouge: Louisiana State University Press, 1978); Lacy K. Ford, *Deliver Us From Evil: The Slavery Question in the Old South* (New York: Oxford University Press, 2009). While Ford does not specifically use the term white men's democracy, he describes a growing reliance among antebellum southern proslavery advocates of adopting the

language of white supremacy to strengthen broad support for slavery among all white men.
3. Carey, *Parties, Slavery, and the Union in Antebellum Georgia*, xix. For a different interpretation of Georgia's secession winter, see Michael Johnson, *Toward a Patriarchal Republic: The Secession of Georgia* (Baton Rouge: Louisiana State University Press, 1977). Johnson argues that secession represented a struggle over who would rule at home as planters sought to protect slavery and elite dominance from other white southerners.
4. Watson W. Jennison skillfully argues that poor whites in Georgia worked tirelessly to pass legislation that enabled the expansion of slavery into the interior. Such efforts promised to shift political power from the coastal elite to smaller farmers who maximized frontier profits while constructing a new society that was also built on the foundation of racial hierarchy. Many Bartow County settlers experienced significant upward social mobility, sometimes moving from the yeoman class to the planter class in less than a decade. The frontier combined with advances in transportation networks provided unparalleled economic opportunities for many yeomen farmers in northwest Georgia that were impossible elsewhere in the state. Watson W. Jennison, *Cultivating Race: The Expansion of Slavery in Georgia, 1750–1860* (Lexington: University Press of Kentucky, 2012).

Relations among white men in Bartow County seemed to differ from conditions in Southampton County, Virginia. Daniel Crofts argues that in Southampton—while a broad consensus existed among white households—tension and conflict remained. Daniel W. Crofts, *Old Southampton: Politics and Society in a Virginia County, 1834–1869* (Charlottesville: University Press of Virginia, 1992). Stephanie McCurry, *Masters of Small Worlds: Yeoman Households, Gender Relations, and the Political Culture of the Antebellum South Carolina Low Country* (New York: Oxford University Press, 1995). Bartow County yeomen shared much in common with those who lived in the South Carolina low country. As McCurry asserts, yeomen-planter relations were shaped by a shared patriarchal culture buttressed by an Evangelical faith that justified the domination of women, children, and other dependents by white male heads of households. However, whereas McCurry sees great tensions existent among southern whites, the cultural connections that she describes in South Carolina seemed to have bolstered white relations in Bartow County, especially when economic and political factors are added to the mix.

The best study of antebellum common whites remains Cecil Fronsman's *Common Whites*. In this groundbreaking study, Fronsman argues that while planters and common whites shared much in common, their relationship declined in areas that increased market relations. Like the North Carolina common whites that Fronsman examines, Bartow County poor whites experienced similar tensions during the 1850s as rising property values and declining wages created by rising numbers of slaves forced many to relocate. Another excellent look at antebellum poor whites is Charles Bolton, *Poor Whites of the Antebellum South: Tenants and Laborers in Central North Carolina and Northeast Mississippi* (Durham: Duke University Press, 1993). Mark Wetherington's *Plain Folk's Fight* examines counties located in Georgia's Piney Woods region, located more than 150 miles south of Bartow County. Wetherington argues that race trumped class in the antebellum South as plain folk threw their support behind planter class leadership because of their shared values. Wetherington's account of the Piney Woods region shares much in common with Bartow County where large numbers of yeomen and common whites rallied behind secession, the Confederate army, and the Confederate government's elite leaders. The solidarity of race helped unite men rich and poor while reducing potential hostilities among them. Wetherington, *Plain Folk's Fight*. David Williams offers a dramatically different account of antebellum and Civil War era relations among white households. He sees class division and conflict as central to understanding relations among white men before, during, and after the Civil War. In Bartow County, differences in wealth distinguished farmers, but these differences failed to create class identify. David Williams, *Rich Man's War: Class, Caste, and Confederate Defeat in the Lower Chattahoochee Valley* (Athens: University of Georgia Press, 1999).

5. W. Todd Groce, *Mountain Rebels: East Tennessee Confederates and the Civil War* (Knoxville: University of Tennessee Press, 1999); Kenneth W. Noe, *Southwest Virginia's Railroad: Modernization and the Sectional Crisis* (Urbana: University of Illinois Press, 1994); Durwood Dunn, *Cade's Cove: The Life and Death of a Southern Appalachian Community, 1818–1937* (Knoxville: University of Tennessee Press, 1988); David F. Weiman, "Farmers and the Market in Antebellum America: A View from the Georgia Upcountry," *Journal of Economic History* 47:3 (Sept. 1987), 627–47; Donald E. Davis, *Where There Are Mountains: An Environmental History of the Southern Appalachians* (Athens: University of Georgia Press, 2000), 141; Bruce W. Elman, *Entrepreneurs in the Southern Upcountry: Commercial Culture in Spartanburg, South Carolina, 1845–1880* (Athens: University of Georgia Press, 2008); John Fowler, *Mountaineers in Grey: The Nineteenth Tennessee Volunteer Infantry Regiment, C.S.A.* (Knoxville: University of Tennessee Press, 2004); Wilma Dunaway, *The First American Frontier: Transition to Capitalism in Southern Appalachia, 1700–1860* (Chapel Hill: University of North Carolina Press, 1996); John Inscoe, *Mountain Masters, Slavery, and the Sectional Crisis in Western North Carolina* (Knoxville: University of Tennessee Press, 1989).

6. A number of studies have documented the regional and national networks that connected southern communities to a broader world. See Dunn, *Cade's Cove*; Wilma Dunaway, *The First American Frontier: Transition to*

Capitalism in Southern Appalachia, 1700–1860 (Chapel Hill: University of North Carolina Press, 1996); Noe, *Southwest Virginia's Railroad*; Kevin Oshnock, "The Isolation Factor: Differing Loyalties of Watauga and Buncombe Counties during the Civil War," *North Carolina Historical Review* 90:4 (Oct. 2013), 385–413. Other historians have interpreted local factors and a community's isolation from external markets as central factors in a locale's history. See, Robert C. Kenzer, *Kinship and Neighborhood in a Southern Community: Orange County, North Carolina, 1849–1881* (Knoxville: University of Tennessee Press, 1987; Martin Crawford, *Ashe County's Civil War: Community and Society in the Appalachian South* (Charlottesville: University Press of Virginia, 2001); Brian D. McKnight, *Contested Borderland: The Civil War in Appalachian Kentucky and Virginia* (Lexington: University Press of Kentucky, 2006).

7. Appalachian scholars have long acknowledged the significant differences between economic conditions in valley areas and more mountainous sections of the region. During the 1850s, these differences were intensified by the construction of railroads in many southern Appalachian valleys. Because most of Bartow County, Georgia, was located in several valleys, its history shares much in common with other mountain valley regions such as those described by W. Todd Groce, John D. Fowler, and Kenneth W. Noe. See W. Groce, *Mountain Rebels*; Noe, *Southwest Virginia's Railroad*; Fowler, *Mountaineers in Grey*.

8. For a detailed description of Bartow County, Georgia, soil types, see G. L. Fuller and H. H. Shores, *Soil Survey of Bartow County, Georgia* (Washington: USDA, Bureau of Chemistry and Soils, 1926).

9. James L. Roark, *Masters Without Slaves: Southern Planters in the Civil War and Reconstruction* (New York: W. W. Norton, 1977); C. Vann Woodward, *The Origins of the New South*; Andrew Slap, ed., *Reconstructing Appalachia: The Civil War's Aftermath* (Lexington: University Press of Kentucky, 2010). In Appalachia, Robert Tracy McKenzie and Martin Crawford have documented that the poor became measurably poorer between 1860 and 1870. The decline of American yeomen and tenant farmers following the Civil War was a national trend. For a discussion of declining economic wealth of Midwestern yeomen and tenants, see Mary Eschelbach Hansen, "Land Ownership, Farm Size, and Tenancy after the Civil War," *Journal of Economic History* 58:3 (Sept. 1998), 822–29. Throughout this book, I use the terms planter, yeoman, and common or poor whites to differentiate white households of varying degrees of wealth. A planter is a landholding farmer who owns twenty or more slaves. In Bartow County, the largest planters owned more than 150 slaves and were among the wealthiest slaveholders in southern Appalachia and Piedmont Georgia. A yeoman owns a farm that is at least 50 acres in size. In Bartow County, many yeomen farmers owned slaves and sometimes owned farms that exceeded the size of neighboring

planters. Some of the wealthiest men in Bartow County prior to the Civil War were slaveholding yeomen farmers. Common whites or poor whites by-and-large did not own any real property and typically worked as day laborers for area yeomen and planters. Some common whites owned small farms, less than 50 acres. In Bartow County, a small number of common whites owned one or two slaves. In such cases it appears that these men invested in slaves rather than land and rented out these slaves or worked alongside them in exchange for cash wages. While an enormous range of wealth existed separating the richest planter from the poorest wage laborer, these households shared much in common including kinship, religion, and notions of racial supremacy.

10. Mary Ella Engel, "Gathering Georgians to Zion: John Hamilton Morgan's 1876 Mission to Georgia," in Slap, *Reconstructing Appalachia*, 185–210; Leonard J. Arrington, "Mormon Beginnings in the American South," *Task Paper in Latter-day Saints History*, no. 9 (Salt Lake City: Historical Department of the Church of Jesus Christ of Latter-day Saints, 1976).

11. The connection between an area's geography and wealth and politics has been established by a number of Appalachian historians. In *A Separate Civil War*, Jonathan Sarris argues that northeast Georgia counties that had extensive trade relations with Piedmont Georgia communities tended to support the Confederate government whereas counties that lacked extensive external trade networks usually remained staunchly Unionist. Martin Crawford's *Ashe County's Civil War* documented similar findings in western North Carolina where Union devotees were usually farmers located in areas isolated from regional markets. Todd Groce's *Mountain Rebels* argued that pro-Confederates in east Tennessee tended to be connected to the area's major trade and transportation centers. The further one lived from markets and railroads, Groce discovered, the more likely that household opposed the Confederacy. John Williams' *Appalachia* notes similar discrepancies in wealth between those who lived in the region's valleys and those who resided on less productive hills and ridges. Sarris, *A Separate Civil War*; Groce, *Mountain Rebels*; Martin Crawford, *Ashe County's Civil War: Community and Society in the Appalachian South* (Charlottesville: University of Virginia Press, 2001). Noe's *Southwest Virginia's Railroad* also documents differences in wealth and market relations between valley residents and their mountain neighbors. Noe, *Southwest Virginia's Railroad*. In contrast, Durwood Dunn's *Cade's Cove* documents that despite the cove's geographic isolation its residents did not live in isolation from the economy and culture of the rest of the country. A cove is a small valley surrounded by steep ridges. Along the valley, agricultural production is significantly higher than the surrounding ridge land. Durwood Dunn, *Cade's Cove: The Life and Death of a Southern Appalachian Community, 1818–1937* (Knoxville: University of Tennessee Press, 1988). Kevin Oshnock, "The Isolation Factor:

Differing Loyalties of Watauga and Buncombe Counties during the Civil War," *NCHR* 90:4 (Oct. 2013), 385–413.
12. This study disputes the desertion estimates for Georgia Confederate soldiers found in Mark A. Weitz's *A Higher Duty: Desertion among Georgia Troops during the Civil War* (Lincoln: University of Nebraska Press, 2000). Weitz argues that approximately 3,368 Georgia soldiers deserted their units between December 1, 1863, and December 31, 1864, in response to calls from their families to return home. Weitz asserts that a soldier's duty to their homes and families superseded any loyalties to the Confederate cause. While my work can only comment on what happened in Bartow County, it is clear in this community that a vast majority of soldiers remained with their units, even during the height of the Atlanta Campaign as the Army of Tennessee retreated through the area and left their homes vulnerable to the pursuing Federal armies. Keith Bohannon's essay "'Witness the Redemption of the Army': Reenlistments in the Confederate Army of Tennessee, January–March 1864," argues that Confederate morale remained high among units serving in the Army of Tennessee, high enough that a large percentage of men reenlisted for the duration of the war despite their army's military setbacks. Keith Bohannon, "'Witness the Redemption of the Army': Reenlistments in the Confederate Army of Tennessee, January–March 1864," in John Inscoe and Lesley Gordon, eds., *Inside the Confederate Nation: Essays in Honor of Emory M. Thomas* (Baton Rouge, Louisiana State University Press, 2005), 111–27.

Chapter 1

1. Throughout this book, the term yeoman farmer is used to describe a landholding farmer who owned at least fifty acres of property. Many yeomen farmers owned slaves. Those who owned between one and nineteen slaves were identified as yeomen. Some yeomen farmers, especially those with more than ten slaves and large landholdings, were as wealthy as their planter neighbors. While the term yeomen is useful for historians to describe a broad group of people, the term lacked any meaning during this period and yeomen did not express any form of class identity. Yeomen comprised a majority of Cass County's population throughout the period discussed in this book, 1830–1880.
2. A market economy is an economy in which Bartow County farmers made decisions regarding investment, production, and distribution based upon supply and demand created by expanding opportunities to local, regional, and long distance trade enabled by the construction of the Western and Atlantic Railroad. Historians have far too often drawn too harsh a distinction between subsistence and market production. Many Bartow County farmers, as did other farmers across the southeast, produced enough goods to provide for most of their household needs and created additional surpluses and

staple crops to sell at market. When crop prices were high and profits could be had at the market, farmers shifted resources toward the market but did not abandon subsistence. This strategy was employed frequently by yeomen households and less often by tenant farmers and planters, both of whom tended to grow larger percentages of cash crops.
3. Manuscript Census, Cass County, Georgia, 1860, Schedule I, II, and III. In 1860, Cass County residents combined real and personal property totaled to about $9.1 million. Out of the 11,442 free persons living the county, about 5,500 lived in the valley subregion. Those 5,500 free persons owned approximately $6.4 million in real and personal property. The monetary value of slaves owned by valley residents represented about 80 percent (or $4 million) of their personal property. Subregion estimates of wealth were calculated by dividing the sum of the total real property and personal property values for the entire county by the sum of the total real property and personal property values for identified valley households. Valley households were identified as households recorded in the 1860 Population Schedule in Cass County that resided in one of the following census enumeration districts: Cartersville, Cassville, Kingston, Adairsville, District 4 (Cartersville area), District 17 (Stilesboro area), and District 16 (Kingston area).
4. Wilma Dunaway, "Slavery and Emancipation in the Mountain South: Sources, Evidence and Methods," Virginia Tech, Online Archives (accessed January 6, 2015), www.scholar.lib.vt.edu/faculty_archives/slavery/index.htm. Lewis Tumlin, J. S. Rowland, and J. W. Harris were the wealthiest planters in antebellum Cass County and northwest Georgia. Throughout this book, the term planter is used to describe a landholding slaveowner who owned twenty or more slaves. Only a handful of planters in Cass County owned more than 100 slaves. The majority of local planters owned less than fifty slaves. The vast majority of county planters lived in one of the area's fertile river valleys.
5. No copies of the original 1860 Cass County Federal Census Enumeration Map have been located. The 1860 Cass County Federal Census Enumeration District Map included in this book was created by cross-referencing post-1860 Census District Maps and pre-1860 Land Lottery District Maps with 1860 Population Census returns. In 1860, the Federal census used a combination of town boundaries, Land Lottery District, and Georgia Militia District designations to create fourteen enumeration districts. In postwar census enumerations, Land Lottery District designations were replaced by new Georgia Militia District designations. In Cass County, Land Lottery Districts 4 (Cartersville), 21 (Allatoona), 16 (Kingston), and 17 (Stilesboro) were replaced by new militia districts. These postwar militia districts largely maintained the boundaries of the previous Land Lottery Districts and thus an educated reconstruction of those 1860 Census District boundaries can be created.

6. Manuscript Census, Cass County, Georgia, 1850, Schedule I, II, and III; Manuscript Census, Cass County, Georgia, 1860, Schedule I, II, and III.
7. Ibid. The monetary value of slaves owned by Appalachian residents represented about 10 percent (or $90 thousand) of their personal property. Sub-region estimates of wealth were calculated by dividing the sum of the total real property and personal property values for the entire county by the sum of the total real property and personal property values for identified Appalachian households. Appalachian households were identified as households recorded in the 1860 Population Schedule in Cass County that resided in one of the following census enumeration districts: Allatoona, Militia District 1041, Militia District 827, Militia District 856, and Militia District 936.
8. Manuscript Census, Cass County, Georgia, 1850, Schedule I, II, and III; Manuscript Census, Cass County, Georgia, 1860, Schedule I, II, and III. Farmers of all socioeconomic groupings wanted to grow cotton to sell in the region's booming cotton market. Between 1850 and 1860, significant numbers of yeomen and nearly all planters planted cotton on larger percentages of their improved acreage.
9. Tim Alan Garrison, *The Legal Ideology of Removal: The Southern Judiciary and the Sovereignty of Native American Nations* (Athens: University of Georgia Press, 2002); William L. McLoughlin, *Cherokee Renascence in the New Republic* (Princeton: Princeton University Press, 1986); Theda Perdue and Michael D. Green, eds. *The Cherokee Removal: A Brief History with Documents* (Boston: St. Martin's Press, 1995); Numan V. Bartley, *The Creation of Modern Georgia* 2nd ed. (Athens: University of Georgia Press, 1990); Izumi Ishii, *Bad Fruits of the Civilized Tree: Alcohol & the Sovereignty of the Cherokee Nation* (Lincoln: University of Nebraska Press, 2008).
10. David F. Weiman, "Peopling the Land by Lottery? The Market in Public Lands and the Regional Differentiation of Territory on the Georgia Frontier," *Journal of Economic History* 51:4 (Dec. 1991): 835; John Alexander Williams, *Appalachia: A History* (Chapel Hill: University of North Carolina Press, 2002), 79.
11. Weiman, "Peopling the Land by Lottry?," 835–60; U. B. Phillips, *American Negro Slavery: A Survey of the Supply, Employment and Control of Negro Labor as Determined by the Plantation Regime* (Baton Rouge: Louisiana State University Press, 1960), 179–80; James E. Davis, *Frontier America, 1800–1840: A Comparative Demographic Analysis of the Settlement Process* (New York: Arthur H. Clark, 1981), 81–83; David F. Weiman, "The First Land Boom in the Antebellum United States: Was the South Different?," in Erik Alerts et al., eds., *Structures and Dynamics of Agricultural Exploitations: Ownership, Occupation, Investment, Credit, Markets, Studies in Social and Economic History*, vol. 5 (Leuven: Leuven University Press), 27–39.
12. Using Silas Emmett Lucas's *The Cherokee Land Lottery* (Vidalia: Georgia Genealogical Reprints, 1968), I compiled a list of all successful drawers who

drew land lots in the 5th District, 3rd Section of what would become Cass County, Georgia. Of the 388 successful drawers whose names I located, I was able to positively identify 324 of these individuals in 1840 U.S. Census Population Schedule returns for Georgia. The lottery records provided the country of origin for these drawers as of 1832. Using an Ancestry.com search engine, I was able to identify 324 individuals who either remained in their place of origin after the lottery or relocated to Cass County sometime between 1832 and 1840. Out of those 324 individuals, only 65 (or 20 percent) individuals settled on the land they received during the 1832 land lottery by 1840. Local histories of many of the counties where these drawers originated were also consulted to make use of their extensive genealogical resources. These local histories often helped me confirm the identities of the individuals listed in land lottery records. Cunyus, *History of Bartow County*, 12–13; *New Georgia Encyclopedia*, s.v. "Land Lottery System" (by Jim Gigantino), http//:newgeorgiaencyclopedia.org/ (accessed May 15, 2006); Farris W. Cadle, *Georgia Land Surveying History and Law* (Athens: University of Georgia Press, 1991).

13. 1834 State Census, Bartow County File, Telamon Cuyler Collection, Hargrett Rare Books and Special Collections, University of Georgia, Athens.

14. For an extended description of economic conditions in antebellum South Carolina, see Lacy K. Ford, *Origins of Southern Radicalism: The South Carolina Upcountry, 1800–1860* (New York: Oxford University Press, 1988); Orville Vernon Burton, *In My Father's House Are Many Mansions: Family and Community in Edgefield, South Carolina* (Chapel Hill: University of North Carolina Press, 1985).

15. By cross-referencing the names of the head of households listed in the 1834 state census with the 1830 U.S. Census Population Schedule, I identified the place of origin for 235 families listed in both enumerations. A closer inspection using genealogical sources and possible manuscript materials might reveal some errors in my sample caused by mistaken identity, since individuals with common names such as Robert Henderson and William West might have been misidentified due to multiple census listings. Ancestry.com search engines greatly aided my research. While the search engine does not always return exact results, it significantly reduced the amount of time spent pouring through census return pages searching for household surnames. Manuscript Census, Cass County, Georgia, 1830, Schedule I.

16. Manuscript Census, Cass County, Georgia, 1840, Schedule I.

17. John Rowland, Manuscript Census, Cass County, Georgia, 1840, Schedule I, 849th Dist., 98. By 1860, Rowland owned 145 slaves and had accumulated a total wealth valued at more than a quarter of a million dollars, which made him one of the ten wealthiest planters in southern Appalachia.

18. Lewis Tumlin (misspelled as Tumblin by enumerator), Manuscript Census, Cass County, Georgia, 1840, Schedule I, 822nd Dist., 6; Manuscript Census,

Cass County, Georgia, 1850, Schedule II; Dunaway, "Slavery and Emancipation in the Mountain South," Table 1.9.

19. Manuscript Census, Cass County, Georgia, 1840, Schedule I. On the geographic mobility of southern planters, see James Oakes, *The Ruling Race: A History of American Slaveholders* (New York: Knopf, 1982), 77–78.

20. Several dozen Cass County, Georgia, 1840 head of households were men whose mother was Cherokee and father was Scots-Irish. These men used their wealth to purchase lottery draws from successful drawers following the 1832 Cherokee Land Lottery. All of these men had family members who lost land and were removed to Oklahoma. The connections between those who remained in Cass County and those who were removed remained. Between 1840 and 1860, some of the Adairs who had initially stayed in Cass County moved westward to reunite with family members. During the Civil War, members of the Adair and Wofford families who were born in Cass County but removed to Oklahoma returned to Cass County to enlist in the Confederate army with the extended white kin.

21. Charles Orville Walker, *Cherokee Footprints: Cherokee Names Remain in Georgia* (Jasper, GA: Private Publication), 165.

22. Manuscript Census, Walker, Gilmer, Paulding, and Murray counties, Georgia, 1840, Schedule I; Thomas W. Brandon, Manuscript Census, Cass County, Georgia, 1840, Schedule I, 951st Dist., 113.

23. Abstract of the Last Will and Testament of John C. Aycock, 1836–1885 Will Book A Abstracts, Probate Court, Probate Court Records Room, Bartow County, Georgia.

24. Sarris, *A Separate Civil War*, 17–19.

25. Ernest M. Lander, Jr., "The Iron Industry in Ante-Bellum South Carolina," *Journal of Southern History* 20:3 (Aug. 1954), 337–55; Ethel Armes, *The Story of Coal and Iron in Alabama* (Birmingham: Chamber of Commerce, 1910), 65. Jacob Stroup came to Cass County, Georgia, in 1836 after being recruited by a group of local investors who wanted to help finance a blast iron furnace in the iron ore rich hills that surrounded Stamp Creek. His brother Moses joined him in 1843. Jacob Stroup died on October 8, 1846.

26. Wilma A. Dunaway, *Slavery in the American Mountain South* (Cambridge: Cambridge University Press, 2003), 127.

27. For an account of antebellum iron manufacturing practices, see Charles B. Dew, *Bond of Iron: Master and Slave at Buffalo Forge* (New York: W. W. Norton, 1994); Mark Cooper III and J. Donald McKee, *Mark Anthony Cooper: The Iron Man of Georgia* (Huntsville: Graphic Publishing, 2000).

28. Sarah Conley Clayton, *Requiem for a Lost City: Memoir of Civil War Atlanta and the Old South* (Macon: Mercer University Press, 1999), 32–33. The Barnsley Family Papers also mention tensions between poor whites and elites. Godfrey Barnsley openly referred to poor whites as "crackers" and blamed them for interfering with slaves owned by their social superiors.

29. Lacy K. Ford, *Origins of Southern Radicalism: The South Carolina Upcountry, 1800–1860* (Oxford: Oxford University Press, 1988), 42.
30. Ibid, 42; William M. Mathew, *Edmund Ruffin and the Crisis of Slavery in the Old South: The Failure of Agricultural Reform* (Athens: University of Georgia Press, 1988).
31. The sampling included 235 Cass County heads of households included on the 1843 State Census and/or 1840 Federal Census who were identified as natives of South Carolina. The sampling was limited due to the time-consuming genealogical research required to conclusively identify each household's place of origin. The 1840 Federal Census did not ask residents to provide their state of origin. Determining an individual's birthplace required consulting several additional resources. Foremost, if that person was included in the 1850 Federal Census—the first to ask respondents to identify their place of birth—than their place of origin could be determined. Several genealogical resources were also consulted including a few online genealogical list serves that helped me trace previously unidentifiable surnames through local records which I did not directly consult. For examples of online genealogical resources consulted, see Surname Search, Access Genealogy, http//:www.accessgenealogy.com (accessed on September 15, 2005); World Family Tree, Ancestry.com, http//:www.ancestry.com (accessed on November 12, 2005). Landownership estimates were compiled using a variety of manuscript and online resources. The website www.GenWeb.com provides access to deed indexes and wills for several western South Carolina counties. Using this resource, in combination with several local county histories, I was able to determine the percentage of 1834 and 1840 heads of households who had previously owned land in South Carolina. These estimates do not account for individuals who might have lost their land prior to their move to Cass County. For example, a landholder may have owned land in 1830 but might have lost title to it by the time he moved in 1833. Nevertheless, these estimates provide a general sense of the wealth of a sampling of Cass County settlers.
32. Jane Turner Censer, "Southwestern Migration among North Carolina Planter Families: 'The Disposition to Emigrate,'" *JSH* 57:3 (Aug., 1991), 417–20; Carolyn Earle Billingsley, *Communities of Kinship: Antebellum Families and the Settlement of the Cotton Frontier* (Athens: University of Georgia Press, 2004), 1; John Mack Faragher, *Sugar Creek: Life on the Illinois Prairie* (New Haven: Yale University Press, 1986), 56–60.
33. Manuscript Census, Cass County, Georgia, 1850, Schedule I; Manuscript Census, Cass County, Georgia, 1860, Schedule I; Faragher, *Sugar Creek,* 56; Ronald D. Eller, *Miners, Millhands, and Mountaineers: Industrialization of the Appalachian South, 1880–1930* (Knoxville: University of Tennessee Press, 1982), 8; Gene Wilhelm, Jr., "Folk Settlements in the Blue Ridge Mountains," *Appalachian Journal* 5 (1978): 207, 240; Dwight Billings, Kathleen Blee, and

Louis Swanson, "Culture, Family, and Community in Preindustrial Appalachia," *Appalachian Journal* 13 (1986): 154–70.

34. Manuscript Census, Cass County, Georgia, 1850, Schedule I; Manuscript Census, Cass County, Georgia, 1860, Schedule I; Cunyus, *History of Bartow County*, 102–04. In Ashe County, North Carolina, Martin Crawford found that marital alliances strengthened local ties and promoted a family's long term standing in the community. Crawford also found a great number of cooperative efforts among locals who pitched in at times to help out friends and neighbors. These interactions reinforced community bonds while enabling larger number of settlers to remain in the areas for longer periods. Martin Crawford, *Ashe County's Civil War: Community and Society in the Appalachian South* (Charlottesville: University Press of Virginia, 2001), 22–23.

35. Stephanie McCurry, *Masters of Small Worlds*; McCurry, "The Two Faces of Republicanism: Gender and Proslavery Politics in Antebellum South Carolina," *JSH* 78 (1992): 1245–64. Eugene D. Genovese argued that upcountry yeomen remained loyal to the slave South because they rejected the outside world that threatened their culture and material interests. He drew a distinction between upcountry and Black Belt yeomen. Black Belt yeomen, according to Genovese, saw themselves as aspiring planters and thus supported a system that provided an avenue for their future economic advancement. In Bartow County, Georgia, many upcountry yeomen supported the slave South because slavery and the production of staple crops for broadening regional, national, and international markets was a means of upward social mobility that had been attained by many of their family, friends, and neighbors. All that a local yeomen had to do was to look around their immediate environment to discover a significant number of other yeomen who were doing better than they were a decade earlier. Eugene D. Genovese, "Yeomen Farmers in a Slaveholders' Democracy," *Agricultural History* 49:2 (April 1975), 336, 340–41.

36. Inventory and Appraisals, Court of the Ordinary, Cass County, Georgia, microfilm, drawer 167:9, Georgia Department of Archives and History, Morrow; Sam B. Hilliard, *Hog Meat and Hoecake: Food Supply in the Old South, 1840–1860* (Carbondale: Southern Illinois University Press, 1972); Testimony of Sarah Jane Patterson, *Slave* 10 (a): 286–91; Testimony of William Mead, *Slave* 1 (4): 428–32; Eller, *Miners, Millhands, and Mountaineers*, 18–19.

37. For an extended discussion of the formation of Evangelical communities in Georgia, see Frederick A. Bode, "The Formation of Evangelical Communities in Middle Georgia: Twiggs County, 1820–1861," *JSH* 60:4 (Nov. 1994), 171–48. In Twiggs County, according to Bode, Evangelical communities adopted the prevailing sentiment that all white men were created equal and given the right to exercise enormous authority over women and slaves. Bode

argues that white equality among worshipers reflected their broader world religious views. These ideals also instructed wealthier white men to promote the welfare of the community by extending charity and services, such as loaning out slaves, to their poorer white neighbors.

38. Manuscript Census, Cass County, Georgia, 1850, Schedule I; Manuscript Census, Cass County, Georgia, 1860, Schedule I.
39. Wayne Flynt estimated that 25 percent of Alabamians were church members during the antebellum period. Mark V. Wetherington estimated that 33 percent of wiregrass region inhabitants in the counties he sampled were church members. Flynt, *Alabama Baptists*, 79; Wetherington, *Plain Folk's Fight*, 34–7. Ronald D Eller has stated, "Politics and religion were the two major opportunities for mountain residents to engage in organized community life, but these institutions were themselves organized along kinship lines." Eller, *Miners, Millhands, and Mountaineers*, 9.
40. Clent Coker, *Barnsley Gardens at Woodlands: The Illustrious Dream* (Atlanta: The Julia Company, 2000).
41. Sarah Conley Clayton, *Requiem for a Lost City: A Memoir of Civil War Atlanta and the Old South* (Macon: Mercer University Press, 1999), 30. Sarah Conley Clayton attended the Spring Bank School during the years immediately preceding the Civil War. During the 1850s, Howard published the *South Countryman*, a periodical with a statewide readership that provided farming advice. Howard also published a number of articles in newspapers across the state distilling his farming expertise.
42. Plantation Journal, George S. Barnsley Papers, #1521, Subseries 3.1, Southern Historical Collection, University of North Carolina at Chapel Hill; Dunaway, *Slavery in the American Mountain South*, 127.
43. Testimony of Easter Brown, *Slave* 12 (a): 136–40; Testimony of Callie Elder, *Slave* 12 (a): 306–15; Testimony of Julia F. Daniels, *Slave* 4 (a): 273–77. For a discussion of clandestine slave religious practices, see Noel Leo Erskine, *Plantation Church: How African American Religion was Born in Caribbean Slavery* (New York: Oxford University Press, 2014), 134.
44. Estimates gathered from membership rolls of Euharlee Presbyterian Church, 1853–1900; Macedonia Baptist Church, Raccoon Creek Baptist Church, microfilm, Northwest Georgia Document Preservation Program, Shorter College Museum and Archives, Rome. Two hundred and thirty-four church members were identified in these records. Of those 234 members, 198 were located in the 1860 Federal Manuscript Census returns. Donald G. Mathews, *Religion in the Old South* (Chicago: University of Chicago Press, 1977) 26, 109, 47–48, 102, 112; Flynt, *Alabama Baptists*, 40–42.
45. Flynt, *Alabama Baptists*, 40–42.
46. Manuscript Census, Cass County, Georgia, 1860, Schedule I and II.
47. Plantation Journal, George S. Barnsley Papers, #1521, Subseries 3.1, SHC, University of North CarolinaChapel Hill; Dennis Johnson Farm Journal,

MS# 2500, University of Georgia, Athens. The Young and Leake Family Papers also include numerous references to the leasing out of slaves to area yeomen and tenants. Young Family Papers, Bartow History Museum, Cartersville; Leake Family Papers, Bartow History Museum, Cartersville.
48. Martin E. Marty, *Pilgrims in their Own Land: 500 Years of Religion in America* (New York: Penguin Press, 1984), 238; Mathews, *Religion in the Old South*, Preface.
49. Euharlee Presbyterian Church, Minutes, 1853–1900, Macedonia Baptist Church, Minutes, microfilm, NGDPP, Shorter College Museum and Archives, Rome. For a detailed description of slave religion, see Albert J. Raboteau, *Slave Religion: The "Invisible Institution" in the American South* 2nd ed. (New York: Oxford University Press, 1980). Mathews, *Religion in the Old South*, 136–84.
50. Euharlee Presbyterian Church, Minutes, 1853–1900, Macedonia Baptist Church, Minutes, microfilm, NGDPP, Shorter College Museum and Archives, Rome.
51. Ibid.; Cunyus, *History of Bartow County*, 81–82.
52. Nance Creek Baptist Church Minutes, microfilm, NGDPP, Shorter College Museum and Archives, Rome. Peter Kolchin, *American Slavery: 1619–1877* 2nd. ed. (New York: Hill and Wang, 2003), 145–56; John B. Boles, ed. *Masters & Slaves in the House of the Lord: Race and Religion in the American South, 1740–1870* (Lexington: University Press of Kentucky, 1988), 2, 10.
53. Nance Creek Baptist Church Minutes, microfilm, NGDPP, Shorter College Museum and Archives, Rome.
54. Evidence of slaves preaching in white churches exists throughout the antebellum South. Perhaps, slave preachers did the same in Cass County, but the surviving records fail to mention it.
55. Cassville Masonic Lodge, MS # 1714, University of Georgia, Athens; Barbara Bell Canaday, *Georgia Freemasons, 1861–1865* (Atlanta: Georgia Lodge of Research, 2001), 88, 110, 134.
56. Manuscript Census, Cass County, Georgia, 1860, Schedule I and II; "Agricultural Society Meeting," Cassville *Standard*, March 3, 1857; Feb. 5, 1858; Sept. 15, 1858, microfilm, Bartow County Public Library, Cartersville. In 1860, the Cassville *Standard* had 562 subscribers and the Cartersville *Express* had 600.
57. Milton S. Heath, *Constructive Liberalism: The Role of the State in Economic Development in Georgia to 1860* (Cambridge: Harvard University Press, 1954), 143–48; *New Georgia Encyclopedia*, "Bartow County," (By Chantal Parker) (accessed on November 5, 2005), http//:www.newgeorgiaencyclopedia.org; Ulrich Bonnell Phillips, *A History of Transportation of the Eastern Cotton Belt* (New York: Octagon, 1968), 304–06; James H. Johnston, *Western and Atlantic Railroad of the State of Georgia* (Atlanta: Stein Printing, 1932), 27; Cunyus, *History of Bartow County*, 167; *Southern Railway Museum: Georgia's*

Official Transportation History Museum, "Western & Atlantic: 'Crookedest Road Under the Sun," (By Joseph Bogle), http//:www.srmduluth.org/ (accessed on November 5, 2005); James A. Ward, *J. Edgar Thomson: Master of Pennsylvania* (Westport, CT: Greenwood Press, 1980), 40–42; Thornton, *Politics and Power*, 268–80; Hahn, *The Roots of Southern Populism*, 34–38; Wallenstein, *Slave South to New South*, 38–39. Hahn overstates the level of economic and ideological opposition that upcountry farmers expressed against the railroad; James A. Ward, "A New Look at Antebellum Southern Railroad Development," *JSH* 39:3 (Aug. 1973), 409–20; Eugene Alvarez, *Travel on Southern Antebellum Railroads, 1828–1860* (Tuscaloosa: University of AL Press, 1974).

58. Cunyus, *History of Bartow County*, 19–21; *The Standard* (Cassville), April 8, 1852, microfilm, Special Collections Library, BCPL, Cartersville.
59. Calculated from the *Seventh Census of the United States, 1850* (Washington: Robert Armstrong, 1853), 225 and the *Eighth Census of the United States, Agriculture, 1860* (Washington: Government Printing Office, 864), 365.
60. Manuscript Census, Cass County, Georgia, 1850, Schedule I; Manuscript Census, Cass County, Georgia, 1860, Schedule I. The total percentage of the population that was enslaved in Cass County exceeded the southern Appalachian regional average. According to Wilma Dunaway, in 1860, 15.2 percent of the total population in the southern Appalachian region were enslaved. In Cass County, slaves accounted for 27.2 percent of the total population. Cass County also exceeds the average of Appalachian counties in Georgia. Dunaway, "Slavery and Emancipation in the Mountain South," Table 1.3.
61. Manuscript Census, Cass County, Georgia, 1860, Schedule II and III.
62. Manuscript Census, Cass County, Georgia, 1850, Schedule I and II; Manuscript Census, Cass County, Georgia, 1860, Schedule I and III.
63. Cassville *Standard*, March 11, 1855, microfilm, BCPL, Cartersville.
64. Manuscript Census, Cass County, Georgia, 1850, Schedule I and III; Manuscript Census, Cass County, Georgia, 1860, Schedule I and III.
65. Frederick A. Bode and Donald E. Ginter, *Farm Tenancy and the Census in Antebellum Georgia* (Athens: University of Georgia Press, 1986), 130.
66. Manuscript Census, Cass County, Georgia, 1850, 1860, Schedule III.
67. Persistence rates among day laborers and tenant farmers were lower than comparable rates among planters, slaveholders, and non-slaveholding yeomen between 1850 and 1860.
68. Manuscript Census, Cass County, Georgia, 1850, Schedule I and III; Manuscript Census, Cass County, Georgia, 1860, Schedule I and III; Bartow County, Probate Court, Deed Book A, Georgia Archives, Morrow. In Cass County, most tenants worked property that either joined or was adjacent to the landowner's larger property and household. The 1860 agricultural census reflects neighborhood patterns throughout the county because the

enumerator by-and-large traveled door to door in a given militia district. The listings of farms in the agricultural census and the listings of households in the free white population census are usually mirror images of one another, at least in the 1860 censuses compiled in Cass County.

69. Plantation Journal, George S. Barnsley Papers, SHC, University of North Carolina at Chapel Hill.
70. Nathan Land to Mona Land, 1860, Chunn/Land Family Papers, Box 1, Folder 12, AC 44–101M, Georgia Archives, Morrow.
71. Manuscript Census, Cass County, Georgia, 1850, 1860, Schedule I; Hahn, *Roots of Southern Populism*, 64; Also see Rebecca Latimer Felton, *Country Life in Georgia in the Days of My Youth* (Atlanta: Index Printing Company, 1919), 52–53. To identify extended family connections across Cass County, I consulted a number of genealogical sources such as Cunyus, *History of Bartow County* and family files archived at the Bartow County Genealogical Society, Inc., Bartow History Museum, Etowah Valley Historical Society, Georgia Archives, Rome Family History Center, Bartow County Public Library-Cartersville Branch, Bartow County Public Library-Euharlee Branch, Kingston War Between the State Museum, and Rome (Floyd County) Family History Center.
72. Manuscript Census, Cass County, Georgia, 1850, 1860, Schedule II.
73. Manuscript Census, Cass, Catoosa, Gilmer, Whitfield, Gordon, Floyd, Polk, Cherokee, Walker counties, Georgia, 1860, Schedule II; Dunaway, "Slavery and Emancipation in the Mountain South," Table 1.3, Table 5.15.
74. Manuscript Census, Cass, Catoosa, Gilmer, Whitfield, Gordon, Floyd, Polk, Cherokee, Walker counties, Georgia, 1860, Schedule II Lewis Cecil Gray, *History of Agriculture in the Southern United States to 1860* (Gloucester, MA: Smith, 1958), 876, 884.
75. David F. Weiman, "The Economic Emancipation of the Non-Slaveholding Class: Upcountry Farmers in the Georgia Economy," *Journal of Economic History* 47:3 (Sept. 1987), 628–29. Some farmers accepted enormous risks when they elected to plant 80 percent of more of their improved lands in cotton. A majority of yeomen who owned between 100 and 200 acres in property tended to practice a safety-first brand of agriculture that devoted enough land for crops that would be consumed by their household annually to survive and plant the rest in cotton.
76. Manuscript Census, Cass County, Georgia, 1860, Schedule III; Principle Articles of Transportation from Stations Ending in September 1860, Western and Atlantic Freight and Income Expenses, 1848–1868, RG# 18–5-28, Vol. 3–8952, F3, R11, U11, S-1, 3329–01, Box 1, GDAH, Morrow.
77. Manuscript Census, Cass County, Georgia, 1850, Schedule I, II, and III; Manuscript Census, Cass County, Georgia, 1860, Schedule I, II, and III.
78. Principle Articles of Transportation from Stations Ending in September 1850, 1851, 1852, 1853, 1854, 1855, 1856, 1857, 1858, 1859, and 1860, Western

and Atlantic Freight and Income Expenses, 1848–1868, RG# 18-5-28, Vol. 3–8952, F3, R11, U11, S-1, 3329–01, Box 1, GDAH, Morrow; Bartow County Historical Database. The Cassville *Standard* published a list of regional and international cotton prices in each issue. The newspaper also published numerous editorials about fluctuations in the cotton market because such movements concerned its readers. Cassville *Standard* Jan. 17, 1858; Feb. 14, 1858; March 3, 1858; Bartow County Public Library-Cartersville.

79. Principle Articles of Transportation from Stations Ending in September 1860, Western and Atlantic Freight and Income Expenses, 1848–1868, RG# 18-5-28, Vol. 3–8952, F3, R11, U11, S-1, 3329–01, Box 1, GDAH, Morrow.

80. Harold Woodman, *King Cotton and His Retainers: Financing and Marketing the Cotton Crop of the South, 1800–1925* (Columbia: University of South Carolina Press, 1990), 28.

81. Plantation Journal, George S. Barnsley Papers, SHC, University of North Carolina at Chapel Hill; Woodman, *King Cotton*, 48.

82. Manuscript Census, Cass County, Georgia, 1850, Schedule I and III; Manuscript Census, Cass County, Georgia, 1860, Schedule I and III; Sam Bowers Hilliard, *Hog Meat and Hoecake*, 4.

83. United States Census Office, *Agriculture of the United States in 1860: Compiled from the Original Returns of the Eighth Census* (Washington, DC: U.S. Govt. Printing Office, 1864), 30–33.

84. Robert William Fogel and Stanley L. Engerman, *Time on the Cross: The Economics of American Negro Slavery* 2nd ed. (New York: W. W. Norton, 1995), 95.

85. Manuscript Census, Cass County, Georgia, 1850, Schedule I and III; Manuscript Census, Cass County, Georgia, 1860, Schedule I and III.

86. Several historians have pointed out that scholars have tended to exaggerate the distinctions between subsistence and market-oriented agriculture. According to David Weiman, farmers did not have to be one or the other, but in everyday practice tended to balance both interests well. When market conditions allowed for an expansion in production for outside sale and consumption, farmers adjusted to the market and made efforts to meet those demands. Most farmers in Cass County appear to have practiced safety-first forms of agricultural production. They tended to plant enough crops for household consumption to ensure that if market conditions declined they would still be able to feed their families from their own crops. The rest of their improved acreage would be dedicated to raising staple crops for market. If the market proved especially profitable, however, these safety first growers could adjust and grow more market goods and less household food. Farmers were well connected to the market and understood both the risks and rewards that were involved in staple crop production. David F. Weiman, "Farmers and the Market in Antebellum America: A View from

the Georgia Upcountry," *Journal of Economic History* 47:3 (Sept. 1987), 627–47; Gavin Wright, *Old South, New South: Revolutions in the Southern Economy since the Civil War* (New York: W. W. Norton, 1986), 39–43; Wright, *Political Economy of the Cotton South* (New York: W. W. Norton, 1978), 68–74.

87. Dennis Johnson Farm Journal, MS# 2500, University of Georgia, Athens. My findings for Cass County yeomen agricultural practices rely heavily upon Dennis Johnson's farm journal. After years of searching, Johnson's and James Washington Watts' farm journals were the only ones that could be located that documented antebellum practices. Johnson and Watts, however, were typical yeomen landholders at least in terms of their landholdings, crop production, and slave property. Their farms are representative examples of hundreds of similar farms that existed in late antebellum Cass County.

88. Numan V. Bartley, *The Creation of Modern Georgia*, 2nd ed. (Athens: University of Georgia Press, 1990), 25. In Ashe County, North Carolina, Martin Crawford discovered similar declines in food production throughout the late antebellum period. These declines, unlike those in Cass County, appeared to have been the result of declining arable lands and poor farming techniques rather than shifts in market participation. Crawford, *Ashe County's Civil War*, 33–34.

89. United States Census Office, *Agriculture of the United States in 1860: Compiled from the Original Returns of the Eighth Census* (Washington, DC: U.S. Govt. Printing Office, 1864), 30–33. For similar examples of a decline in self-sufficiency accompanied by a rise in cash crop production, see Lacy K. Ford, "Yeoman Farmers in the South Carolina Upcountry: Changing Production Patterns in the Late Antebellum Period," *Agricultural History* 60 (1986): 17–37; Noe, *Southwest Virginia's Railroad*, 31–32; Williams, *Appalachia*, 91–92; Paul Salstrom, *Appalachia's Path to Dependency: Rethinking a Region's Economic History, 1730–1940* (Lexington: University Press of Kentucky, 1994), xii–xxiii, 11–19, 41–59; Robert D. Mitchell ed., *Appalachian Frontiers: Settlement, Society, and Development in the Pre-industrial Era* (Lexington: University Press of Kentucky, 1990).

90. Manuscript Census, Cass County, Georgia, 1850, Schedule I, II, and III; Manuscript Census, Cass County, Georgia, 1860, Schedule I, II, and III.

91. Manuscript Census, Cass County, Georgia, 1850, Schedule I, II, and III; Manuscript Census, Cass County, Georgia, 1860, Schedule I, II, and III; Confederate Service Records (CSR).

92. James W. Watts, Diary and Account Book, 1853–58, microfilm, drawer 28:74, GDAH, Morrow.

93. Historian Richard K. MacMaster argued that western Virginia herdsmen were complete capitalists. Richard K. MacMaster, "The Cattle Trade in Western Virginia, 1760–1830," in *Appalachian Frontiers: Settlement, Society*

& *Development in the Preindustrial Era*, ed. Robert D. Mitchell (Lexington: University Press of Kentucky, 1991).
94. James W. Watts, Diary and Account Book, 1853–1858, microfilm, drawer 28:74, GDAH, Morrow.
95. James W. Watts, Diary and Account Book, 1853–1858, microfilm, drawer 28:74, GDAH, Morrow.
96. James C. Bonner, *A History of Georgia Agriculture, 1732–1860* (Athens: University of Georgia Press, 1964), 187.
97. Hahn, *Roots of Southern Populism*, 55.
98. Plantation Journal, George S. Barnsley Papers, SHC, University of North CarolinaChapel Hill; James Washington Watts Farm Diary, Cass County, 1854–1855, James Washington Watts Papers, GDAH, Morrow.
99. *James Sproull v. State of Georgia*, 1854, Georgia Supreme Court, 1854, GDAH, Morrow.
100. Plantation Journal, George S. Barnsley Papers, SHC, University of North CarolinaChapel Hill; James Washington Watts Farm Diary, Cass County, 1854–1855, James Washington Watts Papers, GDAH, Morrow.

Chapter 2

1. *Federal Union* (Milledgeville), Oct. 13, 1840, Oct. 17, 1843, Nov. 10, 1844, Oct. 23, 1844, Oct. 16, 1845, Oct. 17, 1847, Nov. 12, 1848, Oct. 16, 1849.
2. Turner Hunt Trippe was born on Feb. 28, 1801, near Sparta, Georgia. In 1822, he graduated from Franklin College and passed the bar exam the following year. In 1824, he married Mary Ann Gatewood. In 1839, he was elected to the post of Cherokee Superior Court judge and moved to Cassville. A devoted Whig, who at times supported Union Democrats and Know Nothings, served as one of three state secession convention delegates in 1861. During the Civil War, Trippe served in a local militia unit. In 1867, he passed away and was buried in the Cassville City cemetery.
3. In Lumpkin County, Georgia, Jonathan Sarris argues that market-oriented farmers and miners in that county tended to support political issues that could potentially expand local access to wider markets. Bartow County voters too seemed drawn to political debates that concerned the local economy. Sarris and other Appalachian scholars have often interpreted the increasing interest of mountaineers in statewide and regional economic debates as a sign of their expanding connections with other parts of the American South. Such an argument disputes earlier accounts of Appalachia as a land cut off from regional markets that also lacked interest in market driven expansion. Sarris, *A Separate Civil War*, 30.
4. Numan Bartley, *Rise of the Modern South*; Anthony Carey, *Parties, Slavery, and the Union in Antebellum Georgia* (Athens: University of Georgia Press, 1997), 84–92, 134–38; William H. Freehling, *The Road to Disunion: Volume 1: Secessionists at Bay, 1776–1854* (New York: Oxford University Press, 1991), 461.

5. *Federal Union* (Milledgeville), Oct. 9, 1853. The increase in voter participation in the 1849 gubernatorial race was the largest in the county's history between successive elections.
6. Lewis Tumlin was among the wealthiest men in southern Appalachia and north Georgia. With a large plantation that stretched along the banks of the Etowah River, Tumlin amassed over 150 slaves and regularly grow more cotton that any farmer in the region. A strong supporter of the Western & Atlantic Railroad, as well as a number of other economic issues, Tumlin likely chided secessionists for their rhetoric because of the damage that a political separation of the state of Georgia would have upon his own personal fortune. Cass County was experiencing an economic boom that lifted the fortunes of many locals. Secession threatened to halt that growth. In 1844, Tumlin hosted Lieutenant William T. Sherman during the young officer's trip from Charleston, South Carolina, to Jackson County, Alabama. The two men enjoyed viewing the prosperity of the Etowah Valley from atop the largest of several Mississippian-period American Indian mounds. Sherman gathered a lot of information about the area and took great interest in its topography and resources. During the Atlanta Campaign, Sherman again paid a visit to the Tumlin plantation. George Magruder Battey, *A History of Rome and Floyd County, State of Georgia, United States of America, Volume 1* (Rome: Webb and Vary, 1922), 103.
7. William T. Wofford was a member of one of the pioneering families that settled Cass County during the 1830s. Born in 1823 in Habersham County, Georgia, Wofford's father died when he was 3 years old. Members of his family moved to Cass County during the late 1820s prior to the 1832 land lottery. In 1839, Wofford attended Franklin College in Athens. There he developed a lifelong friendship with Herschel Johnson. He studied law, opening a private practice in Cassville in 1845. Wofford supported the construction of the Western and Atlantic Railroad during the 1840s. During the Mexican War, Wofford served in the Georgia Mounted Volunteers. He also served two terms in the state legislature 1849–1850 and 1851–1852. Locals remembered his generosity and communal spirit. As a leader, he attracted the respect of party loyalists and opponents.
8. Richard Harrison Shyrock, *Georgia and the Union in 1850*, reprint (New York: AMS Press, 1968), 225.
9. Ibid., 225–27; Gerald J. Smith, *"One of the Most Daring Men": The Life of Confederate General William T. Wofford* (Murfreesboro, TN: Southern Heritage Press, 1997), 7; Carey, *Parties in Antebellum Georgia*, 84–92.
10. The alliance between Black Belt and Upcountry Georgians represented one of many moves made on the part of upcountry politicians to align their local interests with those of a broader statewide political body that both protected the interests of slavery and promoted interregional economic developments. William B. Wofford was William T. Wofford's uncle. William B. had many relatives living in Cass County.

11. Shyrock, *Georgia and the Union in 1850*, 215–63.
12. Carey, *Parties in Antebellum Georgia*, 165–68.
13. *The Standard* (Cassville), Nov. 12, 1850.
14. Carey, *Parties in Antebellum Georgia*, 168.
15. Ibid., 171–74; Harry Watson, *Liberty and Power: The Politics of Jacksonian America* (New York: Hill and Wang, 1990).
16. *The Standard* (Cassville), March 4, 1852. The Cassville *Standard* defined democracy in the terms of independence from external forces and entities that threatened the overall preservation of the white men's democracy. Most of the time the paper's editors portrayed large segments of the northern population and politicians as anti-democratic. John W. Burke saw Southern Rights Party members as extremists whose actions threatened the South's existing status within the Union and most notably as being responsible for splintering a the Democratic Party both statewide and nationally.
17. Carey, *Parties in Antebellum Georgia*, 174–75.
18. *The Standard* (Cassville), Sept. 23, 1852; *Southern Banner* (Athens), Sept. 23, 1852; Carey, *Parties in Antebellum Georgia*, 177; John E. Talmadge, "The Origin of the Tugalo Party's Name," *GHQ* 36 (1952): 328–35; "Howell Cobb Papers," *GHQ* 6 (1909): 39.
19. Biographical Sketch of William H. Stiles, MacKay-Stiles Papers, microfilm, drawer 70:67, GDAH, Morrow.
20. Ibid.
21. *The Standard* (Cassville), November 11, 1852; Carey, *Parties in Antebellum Georgia*, 178.
22. *Federal Union* (Milledgeville), Sept. 6, 1853, Sept. 20, 1853; Carey, *Parties in Antebellum Georgia*, 180–83.
23. *The Standard* (Cassville), April 26, 1855, May 31, 1855.
24. *The Standard* (Cassville), Feb. 22, 1855.
25. Cassville *Standard*, Aug. 23, 1855.
26. Cassville *Standard*, Oct. 4, 1855.
27. Cassville *Standard*, Sept. 19, 1855; *Southern Statesman* (Calhoun), Sept. 19, 1855.
28. Ibid.
29. *Federal Union* (Milledgeville), Oct. 11, 1859.
30. Ibid.
31. A. J. Cone, *The Rock: A Story of the War* (Atlanta: Private, 1913), 1–3.
32. Charles W. Howard, "Cherokee Baptist College Address," July 11, 1860, microfilm, drawer 310:11, GDAH, Morrow.
33. "Douglas at Twenty—An Example for Young Men," *Standard* (Cassville), Aug. 30, 1860.
34. *Standard* (Cassville), Sept. 6, 1860.
35. Thomas E. Schott, *Alexander H. Stephens of Georgia: A Biography* (Baton Rouge: Louisiana State University Press, 1996), 279.

36. Groce, *Mountain Rebels*. Groce's study of east Tennessee found that mountaineers living in the region's towns and nearest to its railroad were more likely to support the Confederate government than others who lived in the hills and further from the railroad.
37. United Daughters of the Confederacy, *Confederate Reminiscences and Letters*, Volume 21, GDAH, Morrow, 102.
38. Mahan, *Cassville*, 125; Cunyus, 126; Smith, *The Life of Confederate General William Tatum Wofford*, 18–19. Wykle and William T. Goldsmith and Samuel H. Smith's business relationship severed due to the strains of late antebellum politics. These men, however, remained members of the Cartersville Freemason Lodge No. 101. The lodge contained numerous members who openly supported secession such as Peter H. Larey, J.C. Tumlin, Robert M. Young, James Washington Watts, and James Milner as well as individuals such as Wykle and J. R. Parrott who opposed secession. Barbara Bell Canaday, compiler, *Georgia Freemasons: 1861–1865* (Georgia Lodge of Research, 2001), 88–89; Mahan, *Cassville*, 101; Cunyus, *History of Bartow County*, 124.
39. Carey, *Parties in Antebellum Georgia*, 226–27.
40. Ibid.
41. *Daily Telegraph* (Macon), Nov. 8, 1860. Stephen A. Douglas failed to win in Cass County despite the popularity of William T. Wofford. Douglas did win majorities in three Georgia counties: Richmond (Augusta), Elbert, and Warren County. John C. Breckinridge won a more lopsided victory in Cobb and Gordon County in comparison to Cass County. In both of those counties Breckinridge received more than double the amount of votes than either John Bell or Douglas. In fact, in Gordon County, Douglas managed only 97 votes despite brief stops at the county seat Calhoun. In Cobb County, Douglas received 54 votes. *The Standard* (Cassville), Nov., 15, 1860. During the 1859 gubernatorial election, Cass County lawyer Warren Akin lost in a landslide to Joseph E. Brown both statewide and locally. During the 1856 presidential election, a majority of Cass County voters voted for Democrat James Buchanan.
42. Tom Dowtin, Cassville, to, Mother, Unidentified, Nov. 12, 1860, Confederate Miscellany Files, 1B, #20, Item #2, Dowtin, Emory University, Decatur.
43. Ibid.
44. United Daughters of the Confederacy, *Confederate Reminiscences and Letters*, Volume 21, GDAH, Morrow, 102.
45. Carey, *Parties in Antebellum Georgia*, 230. The total number of votes cast in Cass County during the secession convention vote is unknown.
46. Testimony of James McGee, Southern Claims Commission, NARA-SE.
47. Exact returns from Cass County could not be located, however, the Rome *Tri-Weekly Courier* reported on January 5, 1861 that the election in Cass County had been decided by about 100 votes, see "Result of Election for Delegates," *Tri-Weekly Courier* (Rome), January 5, 1861.

48. Allen Candler, *The Confederate Records of Georgia*, Volume 1, 218; Cunyus, *The History of Bartow County*, 95–6, 209. Manuscript Census, 1860, Cass County, Georgia.
49. Manuscript Census, 1860, Cass County, Georgia, 828th District, 15, Schedules I, II, III; Cunyus, *The History of Bartow County*, 126.
50. Bobby Gilmer Moss, *The Patriots at Cowpens* (Greenville, SC: B.G. Moss Press, 1979): 241; Bobby Gilmer Ross, *Roster of South Carolina Patriots in the American Revolution* (Baltimore: Genealogical Publishing: 1978): 1009; *History of Spartanburg County*, 220–39; Lyman C. Draper, *King's Mountain and Its Heroes: History of the Battle of King's Mountain, October 7th, 1780, and the Events Which Led to It* (Marietta, GA: Continental Book, 1954), 181–83; Carl Flowers, Jr. "The Wofford Settlement on the Georgia Frontier," *GHQ* 61 (1977): 258–67.
51. *Standard* (Cassville), June 5, 1858.
52. Trippe does not appear in the 1860 Slave Census, however, his surrounding family members have seemingly assumed his slave property due, perhaps, to his advanced age. Nevertheless, Trippe did not sell-off his slaves between 1850 and 1860. He owned slaves but they were now working and residing at the residences' of various family members.
53. Manuscript Census, Cass County, Georgia, 1850, Schedules I, II, III; Manuscript Census, Cass County, Georgia, 1860, Schedules I, II, III.
54. Manuscript Census, Cass County, Georgia, 1850, Schedules I, II, III; Manuscript Census, Cass County, Georgia, 1860, Schedules I, II, III.
55. Carey, *Parties in Antebellum Georgia*, 242.
56. Allen D. Candler, *The Confederate Records of the State of Georgia*, Vol. 1 (Atlanta: C. P. Byrd, 1909–11): 256–60; *The Heritage of Polk County, Georgia, 1851–2000* (Marceline, M.O.: Walsworth, 2000); *Pickens County, Georgia Heritage, 1853–1998* (Waynesville, NC: Don Mills, 1998); Frances Terry Ingmire, *Citizens of Pickens County, Georgia, 1860 Census Index* (St. Louis: F. T. Ingmire, 1986).
57. *The Heritage of Cherokee County, Georgia, 1831–1998* (Cherokee County, Ga.: Cherokee County Heritage Book Committee, 1998); Sarah Blackwell Gober, *The First Hundred Years: A Short History of Cobb County, in Georgia* (Atlanta: Walter W. Brown, 1935); George Magruder Battey, *A History of Rome and Floyd County, State of Georgia, United States of America; including numerous incidents of more than local interest, 1540–1922* (Atlanta: Webb and Vary, 1922); *The Heritage of Paulding County, Georgia, 1832–1999* (Dallas, Ga.: Paulding County Historical Society, 1999).
58. Candler, *Confederate Records*, Vol. 1, 256–60; Lulie Pitts, *History of Gordon County, Georgia* (Calhoun, Ga.: Press of the Calhoun Times, 1933); Burton J. Bell and Lulie Pitts, *1976 Bicentennial History of Gordon County, Georgia* (Calhoun, Ga.: Gordon County Historical Society, 1976); Jewell B. Reeve, *Stories of Gordon County and Calhoun, Georgia*, 2nd Ed., (Easley, SC: Southern Historical Press, 1979).

59. James L. Huston's *Calculating the Value of the Union: Slavery, Property, Rights, and the Economic Origins of the Civil War* (Chapel Hill: University of North Carolina Press, 2003).
60. Candler, *Confederate Records*, Vol. 1, 115–17.
61. Ibid., 231.
62. Ibid., 232.
63. Ibid., 272, 274, 281. William T. Wofford enlisted in the 18th Georgia Infantry Regiment months after the secession convention vote. He eventually rose to the rank of brigadier general and remained with the Confederate army until the end of the war. Hawkins F. Price also served the Confederate government helping the state and national governments round up men who avoided conscription and encouraging others to join the army.
64. Tom Dowtin, Cass County, to, Miss Nanie L. Dowtin, Rocky Hill, Jan. 24, 1861, Confederate Miscellany Files, 1B, #20, Item #2, Dowtin, EU, Decatur.
65. Testimony of Shem Carnes, Southern Claims Commission, NARA-SE.
66. For an account of Rome's celebration, see "Secession Jubilee," *Tri-Weekly Courier* (Rome), Jan. 24, 1861.
67. Rebecca Latimer Felton, *My Memoirs of Georgia Politics* (Atlanta: Index Printing, 1911), 25–26.
68. Pierce Manning Butler Young to Joseph E. Brown, Feb. 6, 1861, Pierce Manning Butler Young Papers, Miscellaneous Papers, GDAH, Morrow. At West Point, Young developed a close friendship with his roommate George Armstrong Custer. Custer and Young would meet in battle during the Gettysburg Campaign.
69. Lynwood Mathis Holland, *Pierce M. B. Young: The Warwick of the South* (Athens: University of Georgia Press, 1964), 24.
70. Reply to a Circular Letter Sent to Former Confederate Soldiers Residing in Brazil, George S. Barnsley Papers, #1521, Series 3.1, Box 2: 26, SHC, University of North Carolina at Chapel Hill.
71. J.S. De Roulhac Hamilton, "Three Centuries of Southern Records, 1607–1907," *JSH* 1 (1944), 12–13; Theodore H, Jack, "The Preservation of Georgia History," *NCHR* 4 (1927), 240.
72. May Spencer Ringold, "Robert Newman Gourdin and the '1860 Association,'" *GHQ* 4 (1971), 504.
73. Candler, *Memoirs of Georgia*, Vol. 1, pp. 296–97; Susan J. Howard, Kingston, to, Joseph E. Brown, Milledgeville, 1863, Executive Department, Governor's Incoming Correspondence, MS 104, GDAH, Morrow.
74. Agatha M. Mayer to Elizabeth M. Stiles, Jan. 20, 1861. MacKay-Stiles Papers, microfilm, drawer 231:45, GDAH, Morrow.
75. William Henry Stiles held a lifelong friendship with ardent secessionist Francis S. Bartow of Savannah. Bartow's views concerning secession closely mirrored those held by Stiles. When Stiles purchased real estate in Cass County several decades earlier, he tried to convince Bartow to build

a summer home there, but Bartow turned down his friend's invitation. The Stiles's Cass County home was known as Etowah Bluffs and overlooked the county's principle waterway the Etowah River. Eliza Mackay had once been courted by Robert E. Lee. The two maintained a lifelong friendship and correspondence.

76. Felton, *Georgia Politics*, 35.
77. Ibid, 35.

Chapter 3

1. James M. McPherson, *Battle Cry of Freedom: The Civil War Era* (New York: Ballentine Books, 1998), 273–74; William K. Scarborough, ed., *The Diary of Edmund Ruffin*, Vol. 1: *Toward Independence*, October 1856–April 1861 (Baton Rouge: Louisiana State University Press, 1972), 542; Coleman, *History of Georgia*, 188.
2. Manuscript Census, Cass County, Georgia, Schedule I, 1860; CSR.
3. Manuscript Census, Cass County, Georgia, Schedule I, 1860; CSR.
4. Hahn, *Roots of Southern Populism*, 116–17; Bryant, *How Curious a Land*, 85.
5. Manuscript Census, Cass County, Georgia, Schedule I, 1860; CSR.
6. Groce, *Mountain Rebels*; Fowler, *Mountaineers in Grey*; Noe, *Southwest Virginia's Railroad*; Keith S. Bohannon, "The Northeast Georgia Mountains during the Secession Crisis and Civil War," (PhD diss., Pennsylvania State University, 2001), iii.
7. Cass County has much in common with the Tazewell County, Virginia, communities Ralph Mann examined. Cass, like Tazewell, contained different communities that responded to various issues distinctively rather than as a unified county. Some communities, even those within the same county, were more isolated than others and thus were more likely to oppose Confederate governance. Ralph Mann, "Diversity in the Antebellum Appalachia South: Four farms Communities in Tazewell County, Virginia," in *Appalachia in the Making*, 132–62.
8. The Army of Northern Virginia did not exist in 1861. It received its name when Robert E. Lee took command during the Peninsula Campaign. Those Army of Northern Virginia soldiers served in the Army of the Shenandoah and other armies that were later combined under Lee's command.
9. James I. Robertson Jr, *Soldiers Blue and Gray* (Columbia: University of South Carolina Press, 1988).
10. William A. Chunn to Delila Land Chunn, Sept. 8, 1861, Chunn-Land Papers, Box 1:5, GDAH, Morrow; James M. McPherson, *For Cause and Comrades: Why Men Fought in the Civil War* (New York: Oxford University Press, 1997), 23; Stephen Berry's *All That Makes a Man: Love and Ambition in the Civil War South* (New York: Oxford Press, 2003) persuasively argues that notions of masculine duty led many white Southern males to enlist in the Confederate army. Letters gathered from Cass County soldiers support

Berry's conclusions. Berry's research was strongly influence by Bertram Wyatt-Brown's seminal work *Southern Honor: Ethics and Behavior in the Old South* (New York: Oxford Press, 1983). Wyatt-Brown argues that southern male and female behavior were governed by a shared notion of honor that was especially present among the region's social elite. Certainly, gender roles and expectations played a major role in pushing many young men into military service.

11. William A. Chunn to Delila Land Chunn, Sept. 8, 1861, Chunn-Land Papers, Box 1:5, GDAH, Morrow; Quoted in Warren Wilkinson and Steven E. Woodworth, *A Scythe of Fire: A Civil War Story of the Eight Georgia Infantry Regiment* (New York: Harper Collins, 2002), 43; John W. Bentley to Father and Mother, July 31, 1861, John W. Bentley Collection, Georgia Historical Society, Savannah.
12. United Daughters of the Confederacy, *Confederate Reminiscences and Letters 1861–1865*, vol. 13, 168.
13. John F. Milhollin to Wife, Aug. 1862, John F. Milhollin Letters, microfilm, drawer 57:65, GDAH, Morrow.
14. *Confederate Reminiscences and Letters 1861–1865*, Vol. 15, 143–144, GDAH, Atlanta; Rebecca Rainey Hood Papers, microfilm, MSS325, reel 1, EU, Decatur.
15. Mark A. Cooper to Jefferson Davis, May 13, 1861, Jefferson Davis Letters, MS #5, Series II, Box 1:1, Woodson Research Center, Fondren Library, Rice University, Houston.
16. Steven E. Woodworth, *While God is Marching On: The Religious World of Civil War Soldiers* Modern War Studies (Topeka: University of Kansas Press, 2001), 28. See Jason Phillips, "Religious Belief and Troop Motivation: 'For Smiles of My Blessed Savious,'" in *Virginia's Civil War*, ed. Peter Wallenstein and Bertram Wyatt-Brown (Charlottesville: University of Virginia Press, 2005), 101–13; Randall M. Miller, Harry S. Stout, and Charles Reagan Wilson, eds., *Religion in the American Civil War* (New York: Oxford University Press, 1998); Christine Leigh Heyrman, *Southern Cross: The Beginnings of the Bible Belt* (Chapel Hill: University of North Carolina Press, 1997); Robertson, *Soldiers Blue and Gray*; Richard E. Beringer, Herman Hattaway, Archer Jones, and William N. Still Jr, eds., *Why the South Lost the Civil War* (Athens: University of Georgia Press, 1986).
17. John F. Milhollin to Wife, Sept. 15, 1861, Milhollin Letters, microfilm, drawer 57:65, GDAH, Morrow; McPherson, *For Cause and Comrades*, 27; Milhollin died during a skirmish in September 1863 while serving with General J. E. B. Stuart. He left behind a wife and six children.
18. George S. Barnsley Papers, M#1521, Series 4, microfilm, SHC, University of North Carolina-Chapel Hill.
19. Ibid.
20. Ibid.; Barnsley Family Papers, M#201, microfilm, reel 1, TSA, Nashville.

21. Tom Dowtin to Mother, June 23, 1861, Confederate Miscellany Files, 1B, #20, Item #2, Dowtin, EU, Decatur; John W. Bentley, Manuscript Census, Cassville, Cass County, Georgia, 1860, 11.
22. John W. Bentley to Father, July 31, 1861, John W. Bentley Papers, GHS Society, Savannah.
23. Pope and McKee, *Mark Anthony Cooper*, 171–72. *Minutes of the Cherokee Baptist Convention*, NGDPP, BCPL, Cartersville.
24. John W. Bentley to Father, July 31, 1861, John W. Bentley Papers, GHS Society, Savannah.
25. Cunyus, *History of Bartow County*, 57.
26. Quoted in Cunyus, *History of Bartow County*, 212. Peter H. Larey to Joseph E. Brown, March 27, 1861, Incoming Executive Department Correspondence, GDAH, Morrow.
27. John F. Cooper to Joseph E. Brown, Jan. 3, 1861, Incoming Executive Department Correspondence, GDAH, Morrow.
28. Mark E. Cooper to Joseph E. Brown, April 21, 1861, Incoming Executive Department Correspondence, GDAH, Morrow.
29. John F. Cooper to Joseph E. Brown, April 27, 1861, Incoming Executive Department Correspondence, GDAH, Morrow.
30. Dana Davis, *Tomorrow is Better: The Story of the Kingston Woman's History Club, 1861-Tomorrow* (University Press of America, 2007), 3–4.
31. Cunyus, *History of Bartow County*.
32. Leon Litwack, *Been in the Storm So Long: The Aftermath of Slavery* 2nd. ed. (New York: Knopf Doubleday Printing, 2010), 47.
33. Sarah Conley Clayton, *Requiem for a Lost City: Memoir of Civil War Atlanta and the Old South* (Macon: Mercer University Press, 1999), 33–35; *Daily Intelligencer* (Atlanta), 10 May 1861; *Augusta Daily Constitutionalist* (GA), Aug. 31, 1864.
34. Thomas, *The Confederacy as a Revolutionary Experience*, 10.
35. Ralph W. Donnelly, "The Bartow County Confederate Saltpetre Works," *GHQ* 54 (1970), 305–19.
36. Mark A. Cooper to Joseph E. Brown, March 14, 1861, Incoming Executive Department Correspondence, GDAH, Atlanta.
37. Pope and McKee, *Iron Man of Georgia*.
38. Robert C. Black III, *The Railroads of the Confederacy* (Chapel Hill: University of North Carolina, 1952), 23.
39. George Barnsley to Lucien Barnsley, April 24, 1861, Godfrey Barnsley Family Papers, MSS13, Box 1:7, EU, Decatur.
40. Ibid.
41. CSA Bonds, Godfrey Barnsley Family Papers, MSS13, Box 3:1, EU, Decatur.
42. E.V. Johnson to Godfrey Barnsley, Feb. 25, 1861, June 1861, Godfrey Barnsley Family Papers, MSS13, Box 1:7, EU, Decatur.

43. In late May and early June of 1861, several companies from counties around the state were organized as the 8th Georgia Infantry Regiment. The regiment was mustered into Confederate service in June at Camp Bartow located outside of Richmond, Virginia. The regiment became part of General Joseph Johnston's Army of the Shenandoah.
44. George S. Barnsley to Godfrey Barnsley, July 14, 1861, Godfrey Barnsley Family Papers, MSS13, Box 1:9, EU, Decatur.
45. Ibid.
46. C. W. Howard to Godfrey Barnsley, June 20, 1861, Godfrey Barnsley Family Papers, MSS13, Box 1:8, EU, Decatur.
47. Diary of George S. Barnsley, Sao Paulo, Brazil, forwarded along with a letter to, Godfrey Emerson Barnsley, Woodlands, July 6, 1915, George Scarborough Barnsley Papers, M#1521, Series 4, microfilm, SHC, University of North Carolina at Chapel Hill.
48. Ibid.
49. Ibid.
50. Ibid.
51. Ibid.
52. Ibid.
53. James M. McPherson, *Ordeal by Fire: The Civil War and Reconstruction*, 2nd Ed. (New York: McGraw-Hill, Inc., 1992), 212–13.
54. Pope and McKee, *Iron Man of Georgia*, 175–77; *Eighth United States Census*, Cass County, Georgia, M653–114, 765.
55. C.W. Howard to Godfrey Barnsley, July 23, 1861, Godfrey Barnsley Family Papers, MSS13, Box 1:9, EU, Decatur.
56. Julia Barnsley to George S. Barnsley, July 8, 1861, George Scarborough Barnsley Papers, M# 1521, Series 1.3, Folder 7, SHC, University of North Carolina at Chapel Hill.
57. Julia Barnsley to George S. Barnsley, Nov. 4, 1861, George Scarborough Barnsley Papers, M# 1521, Series 1.3, Folder 7, SHC, University of North Carolina at Chapel Hill.
58. Lucien Barnsley to George S. Barnsley, Nov. 4, 1861, George Scarborough Barnsley Papers, M# 1521, Series 1.3, Folder 7, SHC, University of North Carolina at Chapel Hill.
59. Ibid.
60. Ibid.
61. Lucien Barnsley to George S. Barnsley, Dec. 21, 1861, George Scarborough Barnsley Papers, M# 1521, Series 1.3, Folder 7, SHC, University of North Carolina at Chapel Hill.
62. Woodworth, *A Scythe of Fire*, 116.
63. Mark A. Cooper to Jefferson Davis, May 1862, Lynda L. Crist, Mary S. Dix, Kenneth H. Williams, eds., *The Papers of Jefferson Davis*, Volume 8 (Baton Rouge: Louisiana State University Press, 1995), 82.

64. John W. Brantley to Father, July 31, 1861, John W. Brantley Papers, GHS, Savannah.
65. Ramseur to Brown, Joseph E. Brown Papers, University of Georgia, Athens.
66. Prior to the Civil War, local elites often suspected poor whites to be guilty of plotting to arm slaves. During the war, Georgia Governor Joseph E. Brown received many letters from across the state penned by local elites concerned that poor whites might be plotting slave rebellions.
67. Ramseur to Brown, Joseph E. Brown Papers, University of Georgia, Athens.
68. Cunyus, *History of Bartow County*, 33–34.

Chapter 4

1. Lucien Barnsley to George Barnsley, Jan. 3, 1862, Jan. 9, 1862, George S. Barnsley Papers, MS# 1521, Series 1, Subseries 1.3, Folder 10, SHC, University of North Carolina at Chapel Hill.
2. Manuscript Census, Cass County, Georgia, 1860, Schedule I; CSR; Bartow County Historical Database. About 2,074 Bartow County men served in the Confederate army between 1861 and 1865. These numbers include about 274 men who joined a Confederate regiment and at some point in the war returned home and joined either a local home guard unit or state militia company. The 2,074 are men who I was able to locate in both Confederate military service records and either the 1860 or 1870 manuscript census returns. Of the 2,074 Bartow County soldiers identified in Confederate muster rolls and found in either the 1860 or 1870 manuscript census, only 62, or 3 percent, were identified as deserters prior to the spring of 1864. Exemption estimates based on 1864 Georgia Militia Census returns that identify men in the county who claimed a military service exemption.
3. Lila Chunn to William Chunn, Jan. 4, 1862, Chunn-Land Family Papers, AC# 44–101, GDAH, Morrow.
4. Rome *Weekly Courier*, July 16, 1862.
5. Manuscript Census, Cass (Bartow) County, Georgia, 1860, 1870, Schedule I. There was an approximate 40 percent increase in the number of children between the ages of 9 and 13 listed in white households found in the 1870 census returns compared to the 1860 returns. The expansion in the number of births between 1861 and 1865 was likely the result of the increased number of marriages during that same period.
6. William A. Chunn to Lila L. Chunn, March 1862, Chunn Family Papers, AC# 44–101, GDAH, Morrow.
7. Emma Hardin to William Hardin, Sept. 14, 1864, William Castleberry Hardin Collection, GDAH, Morrow.
8. Delilah Land Chunn to William Augustus Chunn, March 14, 1862, Chunn Family Papers, AC# 44–101, GDAH, Morrow; Julia Barnsley to George Barnsley, June 14, 1862, George S. Barnsley Papers, Series 1.3, Folder 8, SHC, University of North Carolina at Chapel Hill; Noble John Brooks to Father

and Family, May 24, 1862, *Confederate Reminiscences*, Vol. 10, GDAH, Morrow.
9. Godfrey Barnsley to Lucien Barnsley, July 7, 1862, MS# 1521, Series 1, Subseries 1.3, Folder 10, SHC, University of North Carolina at Chapel Hill.
10. Warren Akin to Joseph E. Brown, Dec. 2, 1862, Executive Office Incoming Correspondence, Joseph E. Brown, GDAH, Morrow.
11. John F. Mihollin to Wife, Jan. 1862, John F. Milhollin Letters microfilm, drawer 57:65, GDAH, Morrow.
12. Charles W. Howard to Joseph E. Brown, Nov. 29, 1862, Executive Office Incoming Correspondence, Joseph E. Brown, GDAH, Morrow.
13. William Chunn to Lila Chunn, Feb. 18, 1863, William Augustus Chunn Letters, EU, Decatur. Many of William Chunn's letters to his wife include a description of how nice it was to see "soldier X" receive a package from home. He frequently described the items included in that shipment, regularly ending the letter with a fleeting suggestion that his family should engage in such activities more often. Chunn seemed to feel that people on the home front were hoarding food and supplies from him and his fellow soldiers. In reality, his family had little to spare.
14. Smith, *The Life of General William Tatum Wofford*, 35.
15. Ibid.
16. George S. Barnsley Memoirs, MS# 1521, Series 1, Subseries 1.3, Folder 10, SHC, University of North Carolina at Chapel Hill.
17. Noble John Brooks to Father and Family, May 24, 1862, *Confederate Reminiscences*, Vol. 20, 231, GDAH, Morrow.
18. John W. Brantley to Sister, Jan. 26, 1862, John W. Brantley Papers, GHS, Savannah.
19. William Chunn to Mother, Nov. 14, 1863, Chunn Family Papers, AC# 44–101, GDAH, Morrow.
20. Petition from Ladies of Bartow County, Oct. 10, 1862, Cuyler Collection, Georgia Governor Papers, Joseph E. Brown, MS 1170, Box # 58, University of Georgia. Governor Brown received similar petitions from ladies aid organizations across Georgia.
21. Manuscript Census, Cass County, Georgia, 1860, Schedule I, II. The names of the women who signed the petition were located in the 1860 manuscript census. I was able to determine if their household owned any slaves by cross-referencing the head of household listed in the manuscript census with the names of slaveowners identified in the 1860 slave census. *Rome Weekly Courier*, July 18, 1862.
22. Mary Carter to George Carter, 1862, George Carter Papers, Private Collection of George Carter, Calhoun, Georgia.
23. *Tri-Weekly Courier* (Rome), April 5, 1862, Special Collections, Rome Public Library.
24. Charles Howard to Joseph Brown, Jan. 1862, Executive Office Incoming Correspondence, Joseph E. Brown, GDAH, Morrow; Sarris, *A Separate Civil*

War; Bohannon, *The Northeast Georgia Mountains During the Secession Crisis and Civil War.*

25. George Carter to C.W. Carter, Feb. 11, 1862, George Carter Papers, Private Collection of George Carter, Calhoun, Georgia.
26. Eliza Stiles to William Stiles, Feb. 3, 1863, microfilm, GDAH, Morrow.
27. Cunyus, *History of Bartow County*, 216–17.
28. Ibid.; Joseph B. Mahan Jr. "A History of Old Cassville 1833–1864," (MA Thesis, University of Georgia, 1950), 82; Nathan Land to William Chunn, Nov. 17, 1863, Chunn Family Papers, AC# 44–101, Box 2:01, GDAH, Morrow.
29. Testimony of Sarah F. Scott, Barton County, SCC [Allowed], Claim Number 2295, 1877, NARA-ATL. Claims Commission records misidentified Bartow County as Barton County.
30. *Tri-Weekly Courier* (Rome), Oct. 18, 1862.
31. *Weekly Courier* (Rome), Oct. 24, 1862.
32. Charles W. Howard to Joseph Brown, Jan. 1862, Executive Office Incoming Correspondence, Joseph E. Brown, GDAH, Morrow.
33. *Tri-Weekly Courier* (Rome), April 5, 1862, Special Collections, Rome Public Library.
34. Ibid. Charles W. Howard's decision to recruit an infantry company attracted the private condemnation of Barnsley family members. Godfrey Barnsley, in particular, questioned Howard's military credentials as well as his age. He also felt that Howard was too much of a dreamer to ever effectively lead a unit into battle nor demand the respect of his subordinates. Lucien and George Barnsley likewise were envious of Howard's efforts. George had once hoped to raise a company equipped by his father's fortune with him at command. Now he realized that his friend Jett Howard, Charles W. Howard's son, might receive such an opportunity. But like his father, he falsely believed that the Howard family lacked the resourcefulness and energy necessary to raise a company.
35. Ibid. Howard was not the only local leader to encounter great difficulty in recruiting an infantry company. J. W. Goldsmith informed Governor Brown in February 1862 that he "[found] it impossible to get men at this time to volunteer." Some men Goldsmith encountered wanted to delay their enlistment until after the government made its final decision regarding conscription. Once men were confronted with the option of either volunteering or submitting to a policy of conscription, he speculated, would they voluntarily enlist rather than face the disreputable distinction of being drafted? J. W. Goldsmith to Joseph Brown, February 10, 1862, Executive Office Incoming Correspondence, Joseph E. Brown, GDAH, Morrow.
36. Godfrey Barnsley to Lucien Barnsley, Jan. 1863, MS# 1521, Series 1, Subseries 1.3, Folder 10, SHC, University of North Carolina at Chapel Hill.
37. David Williams argues that a planter oligarchy exploited enslaved blacks and poor whites in the Chattahoochee Valley of Georgia and Alabama thereby creating a hostile class conflict that significantly contributed to

Confederate defeat. His argument has been challenged by Gary Gallagher, who argues that class conflict or internal pressures did not determine the Confederacy's fate. Mark Wetherington also argues that in the Piney Woods of Georgia, plain folk actively supported the interests of the planter class and Confederate government. David Williams, *Rich Man's War: Class, Caste, and Confederate Defeat in the Lower Chattahoochee Valley* (Athens: University of Georgia Press, 1998); Gary Gallagher, *The Confederate War* (Cambridge: Harvard University Press, 1997); Mark Wetherington, *Plain Folk's Fight*.

38. P. M. B. Young, Yorktown, Virginia, to Dr. Robert M. Young, Cass County, GA, April 11, 1862, Young Family Papers, 2010.60.28, Bartow History Museum, Cartersville, GA; P. M. B. Young, Fredericksburg, Virginia, to Dr. Robert M. Young, Cass County, GA, May 14, 1862, Young Family Papers, 2010.60.23, Bartow History Museum, Cartersville, GA.
39. George Carter to Family, Aug. 18, 1862, George Carter Papers, Private Collection of George Carter, Calhoun, GA.
40. Ibid.
41. Rome *Weekly Courier* 20 February 1863; Sarris, *A Separate Civil War*.
42. Clarence L. Mohr, *On the Threshold of Freedom: Masters and Slaves in Civil War Georgia* (Baton Rouge: Louisiana State University Press, 1986), 155.
43. Manuscript Census, Cass County, Georgia, 1860, Schedule I, II, III; CSR. The estimates of slaveholding soldier casualties in Bartow County were derived by compiling a database of over 1,800 soldiers who served in the Confederate army between 1861 and 1863. These soldiers were matched with their 1860 Federal census households to determine their wealth. Compiled Confederate service records were then consulted to determine how many soldiers died in service during this period. Since many slaveholding soldiers became officers in their companies and regiments and tended to lead their units into battle thus placing themselves before the enemy at the head of their men, their casualty rates were generally higher as a group than privates who tended to also be from poorer families.
44. Manuscript Census, Cass County, Georgia, 1860, Schedule I, II, III. Estimates for slaveholders among Confederate troops who surrendered were based upon lists recorded at Appomattox Courthouse, Goldsboro, or Kingston. I was able to locate 80 percent of the 625 Bartow County soldiers who remained with their units until the final surrender in the 1860 Federal population and slave censuses. Of the 500 soldiers identified, 46 percent of them either owned slaves or belonged to a household that owned slaves in 1860.
45. Kenneth W. Noe, *Reluctant Rebels: The Confederates Who Joined the Army after 1861* (Chapel Hill: University of North Carolina Press, 2010). Noe discovered similar trends among later enlisting Confederates.
46. John W. Brantley to Sister, March 31, 1862, John W. Brantley Papers, GHS, Savannah.

47. Godfrey Barnsley to Lucien Barnsley, November 2, 1862, MS# 1521, Series 1, Subseries 1.3, Folder 10, SHC, University of North Carolina at Chapel Hill; P.M.B. Young, Fredericksburg, Virginia, to Dr. Robert M. Young, Cass County, Georgia, May 14, 1862, Young Family Papers 2010.60.23, Bartow History Museum, Cartersville, GA.
48. Russell S. Bonds, *Stealing the General: The Great Locomotive Chase and the First Medal of Honor* (Yardley, PA: Westholme Publishing, 2006).
49. Ibid.
50. John S. Rowland to Joseph E. Brown, April 13, 1862, Executive Office Incoming Correspondence, Joseph E. Brown, GDAH, Morrow.
51. *Standard* (Cassville), January 7, 1862; *Georgia Weekly Telegraph* (Macon), Aug. 1, 1862.
52. Julia Barnsley to Lucien Barnsley, Aug. 3, 1862, MS# 1521, Series 1, Subseries 1.3, Folder 10, SHC, University of North Carolina at Chapel Hill.
53. Godfrey Barnsley to Lucien Barnsley, Dec. 27, 1862, MS# 1521, Series 1, Subseries 1.3, Folder 10, SHC, University of North Carolina, Charlotte.
54. William A. Chunn to Lila Chunn, Feb. 18, 1863, AC# 44–101, Box 3:1, Chunn Family Papers, GDAH, Morrow.
55. Michael B. Ballard, *Vicksburg: The Campaign that Opened the Mississippi* (Chapel Hill: University of North Carolina Press, 2004), Chapter 13.
56. Confederate Service Records; Henderson, *Roster*, 351–417.
57. Manuscript Census, Cass/ Bartow County, Georgia, 1860, 1870, Schedule I. About 2,074 Bartow County men served in the Confederate army between 1861 and 1865. These numbers include about 274 men who joined a Confederate regiment and at some point in the war returned home and joined either a local home guard unit or state militia company. The 2,074 are men who I was able to locate in both Confederate military service records and either the 1860 or 1870 manuscript census returns. Of the 2,074 Bartow County soldiers identified in Confederate muster rolls and found in either the 1860 or 1870 manuscript census, only 62, or 3 percent, were identified as deserters prior to the spring of 1864. Exemption estimates based on 1864 Georgia Militia Census returns that identify men in the county who claimed a military service exemption.
58. James M. McPherson, *Battle Cry of Freedom: The Civil War Era* (New York: Ballantine Books, 1988), 675–678.
59. Ibid.
60. William A. Chunn to Lila Chunn, Dec. 6, 1863, William Augustus Chunn Letters, 1837–1879, MSS018, Box 2:7, EU, Decatur.
61. McPherson, *Battle Cry of Freedom*, 681.
62. William A. Chunn to Lila Chunn, Dec. 6, 1863, William Augustus Chunn Letters, 1837–1879, MSS018, Box 2:7, EU, Decatur.
63. Historians offer contrasting depictions of the Army of Tennessee's morale following the loss of Chattanooga. Keith S. Bohannon argues that "the

reenlistments that took place in the Army of Tennessee in the months of January through March 1864 suggest that the majority of men retained a high level of morale and confidence in their leadership." Mark A. Weitz, in contrast, claims that the Army of Tennessee's morale had plunged into its deepest recesses following the debacle at Missionary Ridge. Sources are critical to understanding these varying interpretations. Whereas Bohannon uses reenlistment pronouncements in conjunction with a number of soldier correspondences to construct his argument, Weitz's use of estimated desertion figures and soldier correspondences portrays a different story. Thomas L. Connelly argued that following Missionary Ridge Confederate commanders "exaggerated assertions of high morale in the army." In February, the army recovered when Johnston gained the army's "confidence." When placed into synthesis, their works ultimately suggest that soldiers in the Army of Tennessee held an assorted array of mixed opinions regarding the future success of their nation and army. See Keith S. Bohannon, "'Witness the Redemption of the Army': Reenlistments in the Confederate Army of Tennessee, January–March 1864," in Lesley J. Gordon and John C. Inscoe, eds. *Inside the Confederate Nation: Essays in Honor of Emory M. Thomas* (Baton Rouge: Louisiana State University Press, 2005), 111–27, quotation located on 122; Weitz, *A Higher Duty*. Connelly, *Autumn of Glory: The Army of Tennessee, 1862–1865*, quotation located on 291.

64. William A. Chunn to Lila Chunn, Dec. 12, 1863, Chunn Family Papers, AC# 44–101, GDAH, Morrow.
65. Critics of General Robert E. Lee, following his loss of West Virginia, referred to him as the king of spades because of his reluctance to engage the enemy in combat. Godfrey Barnsley believed that General Joseph E. Johnston lacked the fortitude to fight and preferred to retreat when confronted by the enemy.

Chapter 5

1. Testimony of Robert S. Montgomery, SCC, [Allowed], Claim # 2895, Barton County, microfilm, NARA-ATL. The Southern Claims Commission Allowed records incorrectly list Bartow County as Barton County.
2. Manuscript Census, Cass County, Georgia, 1860, Schedule I.
3. J. P. Baltzelle to Col. E. J. Harris, March 27, 1864, Barnsley Papers, microfilm, #204, TSA, Nashville.
4. Manuscript Census, Cass County, Georgia, 1860, Schedule I; CSR.
5. J. P. Baltzelle to Col. E. J. Harris, April 15, 1864, Barnsley Papers, microfilm, #204, TSA, Nashville.
6. Manuscript Census, Cass County, Georgia, 1860, Schedule I, II, III; Manuscript Census, Bartow County, Georgia, 1870, Schedule I and II; CSR.
7. Nancy J. Cornell, Compiler, *1864 Census for Re-Organizing the Georgia Militia* (Atlanta: Genealogical Publishing, 1990), 18–34; William R. Scaife and William Harris Bragg, *Joe Brown's Pets: The Georgia Militia, 1861–1865* (Macon, GA: Mercer University Press, 2004), 4–5.

8. A. J. Neal to Ma, Feb. 3, 1864, Bartow County Vertical File, GDAH, Atlanta.
9. Talmadge, *Rebecca Latimer Felton*, 21; Karen Hamilton, "The Union Occupation of Bartow County, Georgia: 1864–1865" (Master's Thesis: State University of West Georgia, 1998), 14; Sally May Akin, "Refugees of 1863," *GHQ* 31 (1947): 113; Godfrey Barnsley to Captain R. S. Page, Jan. 6, 1864, Godfrey Barnsley Papers, Box 14:3, University of Georgia, Athens; William A. Chunn to Nathan Land, March 1864, Chunn-Land Papers, AC# 1401, Box 1:4, GDAH, Morrow.
10. Frances Thomas Howard, *In and Out of the Lines* (Cartersville, GA: Etowah Valley Historical Society, 1998), 5.
11. Testimony of James McGee, SCC, [Allowed], Claim # 1155, microfilm. NARA-ATL.
12. Testimony of William Collins, SCC, [Allowed], microfilm, NARA-ATL.
13. *Tri-Weekly Courier* (Rome), Jan., Feb., 1864; Warren Akin to Mary Akin, Dec. 18, 1864; Jan. 10, 1865; Jan. 11, 1865; Jan. 13, 1865; Jan. 23, 1865; Jan. 26, 1865; Mary Akin to Warren Akin, Jan. 15, 1865; Bell Irvin Wiley, ed. *Letters of Warren Aiken Confederate Congressman*, 42, 73, 76, 78, 93, 99, 121; Mrs. William A. Chunn to Mrs. E. W. Chunn, Nov. 14, 1864, Chunn-Land Papers, AC# 1401, Box 4:02, GDAH, Morrow.
14. *Confederate Reminiscences and Letters 1861–1865*, Vol. 21, 103–104, GDAH, Morrow; Cunyus, *History of Bartow County*, 71. Anne Elizabeth Johnson was the wife of Kingston businessman Erastus V. Johnson.
15. Felton, *Country Life in Georgia In the Days of My Youth*, 89.
16. *Confederate Reminiscences and Letters 1861–1865*, Vol. 21, 103–104; Cunyus, *History of Bartow County*, 71.
17. Nathan Land to William Chunn, March 21, 1864, Chunn-Land Papers, GDAH, Morrow; Hamilton, "The Union Occupation of Bartow County," 14.
18. William Chunn to Judge Nathan Land, March 1864, Chunn-Land Papers, GDAH, Morrow.
19. Ibid.
20. Ibid.; William Chunn's confidence in the leadership of General Joseph E. Johnston was not shared by many of his comrades serving in the Army of Tennessee. See Larry Daniel, *Soldiering in the Army of Tennessee* (Chapel Hill: University of North Carolina Press, 1991).
21. Albert Castel, *Decision in the West: The Atlanta Campaign of 1864* (Lawrence: University Press of Kansas, 1992), 125.
22. Robert A. Doughty, *American Military History and the Evolution of Warfare in the Western World* (Lexington, MA: D. C. Heath, 1996), 208; McPherson, *Battle Cry of Freedom*, 744–45; Castel, *Decision in the West*, 121–186.
23. H. E. Sterkx, ed., "The Autobiography and Civil War Letters of Joel Murphree of Troy, Alabama: 1864–1865," *Alabama Historical Quarterly* 19 (1957): 176–77.
24. Castel, *Decision in the West*, 195–96.

25. Sam R. Watkins, *"Co. Aytch" A Side Show of the Big Show* (New York: Touchstone, 1997), 149–50; *War of the Rebellion: Official Records of the Union and Confederate* Armies (Washington: Government Printing Office, 1891), Ser. 1, 38: 65, 91, 191; O. P. Hargis, *Thrilling Experiences of a First Georgia Cavalryman in the Civil War* (n.p.: n.d.), 19. Colonel Francis T. Sherman's brigade bore the brunt of the fight at the Octagon House. During the early morning hours of May 18, 1864, the 73rd Illinois Infantry Regiment destroyed the Octagon House by setting it on fire. The Army of the Cumberland sustained approximately 200 casualties during engagements fought while moving through Adairsville. "Octagon House," Wilbur Kurtz Collection, MS 130, 37:1. Kenan Research Center and Archives, AHC, Atlanta.
26. Kenneth W. Noe, ed., *A Southern Boy in Blue: The Memoir of Marcus Woodcock 9th Kentucky Infantry (U.S.A.)* (Knoxville: University of Tennessee Press, 1996), 285; Castel, *Decision in the West*, 197.
27. Ibid.
28. Howard, *In and Out of the Lines*, 5; Cunyus, *History of Bartow County*, 223; Testimony of Sarah Jane Patterson, *Slave* 10, (a): 286–91. Cunyus and Howard both note that Hardee's Corps passed Spring Bank at 4:00 a.m.
29. Howard, *In and Out of the Lines*, 5.
30. Ibid, 7; *War of the Rebellion*, Ser. 1, 38: 102–103, 191, 465–71.
31. A discrepancy exists regarding the specific time that Union soldiers first appeared at Spring Bank. Francis Howard recalled that Union soldiers entered her family's property around 5:00 a.m. or one hour after William Hardee's Corps passed their plantation. Historian Wilbur Kurtz argued that Howard's memory of when the first Union soldiers arrived was full of discrepancies. He argued that remnants of Union cavalry and infantry skirmishers probably did not arrive at Spring Bank until that afternoon. A discrepancy also exists pertaining to the number of cavalry companies dispatched by Colonel John T. Wilder to cut the telegraph lines north of Kingston. Brigadier General Kenner Garrard's report, located in the *Official Records*, states that "four companies of the Seventeenth Indiana" was dispatched toward Kingston. Wilbur Kurtz's research notes state that Garrard's reports were inaccurate and that six companies were sent to cut the wire. Research Notes, Wilbur Kurtz Collection, MS-130, 25:7, Kenan Research Library and Archives, AHC, Atlanta.
32. *Official Record of the War of the Rebellion*, Series 1, 38: 806.
33. "Henry Albert Potter to Morris H. Palmer, May 22, 1864," http://freepages.genealogy.rootweb.com/~mruddy/letters5.htm (accessed July 15, 2005).
34. *O. R.*, Series I, 38: 828; 811; "Springbank," Wilbur Kurtz Collection, MS-130, 33:10, Kenan Research Library and Archives, AHC, Atlanta.
35. Jane Howard to George Barnsley, Sept. 17, 1864, George Scarborough Barnsley Papers, M# 1521, SHC, University of North Carolina at Chapel Hill; Cunyus, *History of Bartow County*, 223; Howard, *In and Out of the*

Lines, 7; Coker, *The Illustrious Dream*, 118–28; Charles W. Wills, *Army Life of an Illinois Soldier Including Day-by Day Records of Sherman's March to the Sea* (Evansville: Southern Illinois Press, 1996), 243.

36. Cunyus, *History of Bartow County*, 395. The 2001 edition of Cunyus's *History of Bartow County* contains some correspondence between the author and historian Wilbur Kurtz. According to Kurtz, "Garrard reached Barnsley's some hours ahead of Logan and McPherson and the Garrard troopers were the ones who got the worst of the running fight on that old back-bone road that runs directly from Barnsley's to Kingston." *O.R.*, Ser. 1, 38: 191, 188.

37. Willis, *Army Life of an Illinois Soldier*, 243. The death of Colonel Richard Earle has been a constant source of fascination for local historians and residents. The valiant depictions of precisely how the colonel fell widely vary. Clent Coker, who has spent most of his life studying the Barnsley family, wrote that "Colonel Earle was shot and killed by a federal sharpshooter listed as: T. H. Bonner of Company "A" 98th Illinois Infantry Volunteers." Unfortunately, Coker's book does not contain endnotes documenting his primary sources; however, the Wilbur Kurtz Collection, housed at the Atlanta History Center, contains several articles written by Kurtz that also list "Boner" as the soldier who shot down Earle. Lucy Cunyus commented that Earle was "shot near the house by the mounted infantry of Wilder's brigade." She did not provide any detailed account of the circumstances that surrounded his death. Frances Thomas Howard provided one of the most dramatic accounts of Earle's death. "[Earle] had sworn never to be captured, and when surrounded and ordered to surrender, he shot the man issuing the order. Of course he was instantly killed." Howard's sister, Jane Howard wrote a lengthy ten-page letter to George Barnsley in September of 1864 that detailed the events that occurred at Woodlands on May 18. Her account fails to mention any dramatic struggle between Earle and the Federals. She simply mentions in passing that he had died. Recently, while talking to historian Keith Bohannon, I learned, second hand, that a military antiques collector owned a rifle that had belonged to a Federal cavalryman. The butt of this rifle contained a large gash made perhaps by Earle's sword during a moment of hand-to-hand combat between the colonel and the enemy. Earle's relationship with the Barnsley family also remains cloudy. Coker asserted that Earle chose to warn the family because of a prior relationship/friendship that he had with Godfrey Barnsley. While such a relationship was entirely possible given Barnsley's wide circle of friends and Earle's Jacksonville, Alabama, origins, the accounts provided by Jane and Frances Howard, as well as George Barnsley, fail to mention any longstanding relationship between Barnsley and Earle. Howard, *In and Out of the Lines*, 7.

38. Jane Howard to George Barnsley, Sept. 17, 1864, George S. Barnsley Papers, M# 1521, SHC, University of North Carolina at Chapel Hill. Howard

commented that Godfrey Barnsley escaped much of the devastation that other local families endured. Barnsley's letters celebrate the fact that the Federals did not damage his beloved garden.

39. Castel, *Decision in the West*, 198; O.R., Ser. 1, 38: 65, 628–30.
40. Howard, *In and Out of the Lines*, 8–10.
41. Ibid.
42. Ibid.
43. Ibid, 18–19; Coker, *Barnsley Gardens at Woodlands*, 125–27.
44. Howard, *In and Out of the Lines*, 17–21; Coker, *Barnsley Gardens at Woodlands*, 125–27.
45. Lila Chunn and William A. Chunn, May 23, 1864, William A. Chunn Papers, Box 1:7, EU, Decatur.
46. Hamilton, "The Union Occupation of Bartow County," 19.
47. William K. Watson, 150th New York Volunteer Infantry Diary, microfilm, 199:75, GDAH, Morrow.
48. Watkins, *Co. Aytch*, 169. "It was like going to a frolic or wedding. Joy was welling up in every heart. We were going to whip and rout the Yankees."
49. Castel, *Decision in the West*, 200–202.
50. O. R., Ser. 1, 38: 222.
51. Castel, *Decision in the West*, 204. Anyone interested in observing Hood's position can do so by climbing the steep grade at the Cassville Cemetery. Atop that hill, the position of the Federal artillery can be plainly seen. The Cassville Female Seminary no longer exists. It was burned by Federal troops in the fall of 1864. While many of Hood's depictions of the Atlanta Campaign have undergone intense scrutiny, anyone can see that his position at Cassville could have been compromised by Federal artillery. Johnston chose a poor site to make a defensive stand.
52. Ibid., 204–6; O. R., Ser. 3, 38: 616; 4:723–26; John B. Hood, *Advance and Retreat*, 105–16; French, *Two Wars*, 196–98.
53. Sydney C. Kerksis, *The Atlanta Papers* (Dayton, OH: Morningside, 1980), 101–103.
54. O.R., Ser. 1, 38: 92.
55. Lewis N. Wynne and Robert A. Taylor, eds., *The War So Horrible: The Civil War Diary of Hiram Smith Williams* (Tuscaloosa: University of Alabama Press, 1993), 73–74.
56. *Two Germans in the Civil War*, 119–20
57. Ibid.; Testimony of Harriet Collins, SCC, [Allowed], microfilm, NARA-ATL. In 1871, Collins received $175.00 from the SCC for the loss of her mule. Testimony of Sarah Jane Patterson, *Slave* 10, (a): 188–93; Testimony of Callie Elder, *Slave* 12, (a): 306–15; Testimony of Easter Brown, *Slave* 12, (a): 136–40. Callie Elder and Easter Brown lived in neighboring Floyd County. Their experiences, however, were representative of slaves living in Bartow County.
58. K. Jack Bauer, *Soldiering: Diary Rice C. Bull: The Civil War Diary of Rice C. Bull* (New York: Presidio, 1995), 101–3; Sherman, *Atlanta Campaign*, 39–40.

Chapter 6

1. Maggie Branson to Mildred, July 22, 1864, Box 1, Folder 35, Confederate Collection, EU.
2. Stephen V, Ash, *When the Yankees Came: Conflict & Chaos in the Occupied South, 1861–1865* (Chapel Hill: University of North Carolina Press, 1995), 21–22.
3. O. P. Hargis, *Thrilling Experiences of a First Georgia Cavalryman in the Civil War: Three Months Inside the Federal Lines in rear of Sherman* (Atlanta: n.p., 1910), 26.
4. *O.R.* vol. 38, pt. 4, 492; vol. 38, pt. 5, 245; vol. 38, pt 2, 494–97.
5. T. Conn Bryan, *Confederate Georgia* (Athens: University of Georgia Press, 1953), 242; Gaines, "We Begged to Hearts of Stone:" The Wartime Journal of Cassville's Lizzie Gaines," edited by Frances Josephine Black, *Northwest Georgia Historical and Genealogical Quarterly* 20 (1988), 6; Hamilton, "Union Occupation of Bartow County," 17; Cunyus, *History of Bartow County*, 125.
6. Ash, *When the Yankees Came*, 77.
7. Petition of Rebecca R. Hood, SCC, (Disallowed), Claim # 2845, NARA-ATL; Jones, 264; Jones, 264.
8. Thomas A. Scott, ed., *Cornerstones of Georgia History: Documents that Formed the State* (Athens: University of Georgia Press, 1995), 97–98.
9. Gaines, "We Begged to Hearts of Stone," 3–4.
10. Benjamin Devor Dean, *Recollections of the 26th Missouri Infantry in the War for the Union* (Lamar, MO: Southwest Missourian Office, 1892), 33.
11. Howard, *In and Out of the Lines*, 58–59, 62.
12. Gaines, "We Begged to Hearts of Stone," 5. The men asked for the location of Oliver Vaughn's home. Warren Akin identified Vaughn as a member of the home guard that was formed during the occupation. Vaughn probably left the county when the Union army ended its occupation, and the region returned to Confederate control.
13. *O.R.*, vol. 38, pt. 4, 634.
14. Gaines, "We Begged to Hearts of Stone," 6.
15. Howard, *In and Out of the Lines*, 82–83.
16. *Daily Chronicle and Sentinel* (Macon), Sept. 13, 1864.
17. Howard, *In and Out of the Lines*. Howard refers to the Murchison sisters as the McDonald sisters.
18. Howard, *In and Out of the Lines*, 50; Jones, 262.
19. Gaines, "We Begged to Hearts of Stone," 5.
20. Ralph W. Donnelly, "The Bartow County Saltpetre Works," *GHQ* 54 (1974), 305–19; Clarence L. Mohr, *On the Threshold of Freedom: Masters and Slaves in Civil War Georgia* (Athens: University of Georgia Press, 1986): 88, 151–55.
21. Howard, *In and Out of the Lines*, 34, 37; Gaines, "We Begged to Hearts of Stone," 6; G. Barnsley to Alfred A. Marsh, March 3, 1865, Godfrey Barnsley Papers, MS# 1737, Box 14: 3, University of Georgia, Athens.

22. Mohr, *On the Threshold of Freedom*, 60, 90–91, 321.
23. Ibid., 92–93.
24. Hamilton, "Union Occupation of Bartow County," 14.
25. Testimony of Willis McDow, SCC, (Allowed), Claim # 14920, NARA-ATL; Testimony of Nancy Russell, SCC, (Allowed), Claim # 6058, NARA-ATL.
26. Manuscript Census, Cass County, Georgia, 1860, Schedule I.
27. Testimony of William Collins, SCC, (Allowed), NARA-ATL.
28. Testimony of Sarah Crow, SCC, (Allowed), Claim # 71941, NARA-ATL. Crow's brother and two nephews eventually deserted the Confederate army and enlisted with the Union army in east Tennessee.
29. Testimony of Edmund S. Cook, SCC, (Allowed), NARA-ATL. Cook deserted from the Army of Tennessee following the debacle at Missionary Ridge.
30. Testimony of Mary McDonald, SCC, (Allowed), Claim # 1232, NARA-ATL.
31. Testimony of Samuel McDow, SCC, (Disallowed), Claim # 14919, NARA-ATL.
32. Testimony of William F. Corbin, SCC, (Disallowed), Claim # 3996, NARA-ATL; Groce, *Mountain Rebels*.
33. Testimony of William D. Law, SCC, (Disallowed), Claim # 17825, NARA-ATL.
34. Testimony of Grandison Vaughan, SCC, (Allowed), Claim # 520, NARA-ATL.
35. Testimony of Nancy Russell, SCC, (Allowed), Claim # 6058, NARA-ATL.
36. Ash, *When the Yankees Came*, 76–107.
37. Gaines, "We Begged to Hearts of Stone," 4.
38. Howard, *In and Out of the Lines*, 57–58.
39. Hargis, *Thrilling Experiences*, 24.
40. Ibid., 25.
41. Howard, *In and Out of the Lines*, 158–64.
42. Wiley, *Letters of Warren Akin*, 28.
43. Jones, 228, 234, 243–44, 253.
44. Lloyd G. Marlin, *The History of Cherokee County* (Atlanta: Walter W. Brown, 1932), 75.
45. *O. R.* I, vol. 39, I, 748.
46. *O. R.* I, vol. 39, I, 748–66.
47. *O. R.* I, vol. 39, I, 764.
48. *O. R.* I, vol. 39, I, 765.
49. Ibid.
50. Williams, *Rich Man's War*, 74–75; Mahan, *Cassville*, 104–5; Bell Wiley, ed., *The Letters of Warren Akin*, 30; Wills, 112, Gaines, "We Begged to Hearts of Stone," 6.
51. Mrs. William A. Chunn to Mrs. E. W. Chunn, Nov. 14, 1864, Chunn-Land Papers, M# 44–101, Box 4:2, GDAH, Morrow; Gaines, "We Begged to Hearts of Stone," 6.

52. *O. R.* I, vol. 39, pt. 3, 513.
53. The fire destroyed the Bartow County courthouse which contained the county's antebellum court records. Fire destroyed the superior court's records. Fortunately, the inferior court clerk removed the court's records prior to the Atlanta Campaign. After the war, the court paid B. O. Crawford $169.00 for saving these records. Bartow County, Inferior Court Minutes 1865–1868, microfilm, drawer 166:54, GDAH, Morrow.
54. Gaines, "We Begged to Hearts of Stone," 6; Wiley, ed. *The Letters of Warren Akin*, 54; Howard, *In and Out of the Lines*, 173.
55. Gaines, "We Begged to Hearts of Stone," 6; Hamilton, "Union Occupation of Bartow County," 75.
56. Hamilton, "Union Occupation of Bartow County," 76–77; Mahan, *Cassville*, 109; Cunyus, *History of Bartow County*, 83.
57. Wiley, ed. *Letters of Warren Akin*, 61; Testimony of Berry Houk, SCC, (Disallowed), Claim # 802, GDAH, Morrow.
58. Styles Porter Diary, Ohio Historical Society; Kennett, *March to the Sea*, 228–33; Castel, *Atlanta Campaign*, 554.
59. *Southern Banner* (Athens), Dec. 14, 1864.
60. Wiley, ed. *The Letters of Warren Akin*, 48; Hamilton, "Union Occupation of Bartow County," 78.
61. Wiley, ed. *The Letters of Warren Akin*, 65, 138.
62. Hamilton, "Union Occupation of Bartow County," 85; Cunyus, *History of Bartow County*, 248; Smith, *The Most Daring of Men*, 140.
63. Howard, *In and Out of the Lines*, 153; Hamilton, "Union Occupation of Bartow County," 85.
64. Manuscript Census, H.M. Prior Household, Polk County, Georgia, 1860, Schedule I; Battey, *A History of Rome and Floyd County*, 206–8; Gordon D. Sargent, "Bloody Legacy in Polk: A Frontier Family and Some Prior Commitments," *North Georgia Journal* (1995), 36–43; Cunyus, *History of Bartow County*, 248–49; Hamilton, "Union Occupation of Bartow County," 86. J. Woodville Baker assumed command of Abraham Tate's scouts following their leader's resignation.
65. Testimony of Richard Chitwood, Southern Claims Commission, (Disallowed), Claim # 121, NARA-ATL.
66. Ibid.; *Southern Banner* (Athens), Feb. 15, 1865; Marlin, *The History of Cherokee County*, 73–77.
67. Smith, *The Most Daring of Men*, 132.
68. Weitz, *A Higher Duty*, 79.
69. Smith, *The Most Daring of Men*, 133.
70. Wiley, *Letters of Warren Akin*, 148; Smith, *The Most Daring of Men*, 133; Hamilton, "Union Occupation of Bartow County," 89.
71. Smith, *The Most Daring of Men*, 135.
72. *O. R.* I, vol. 46, pt. 3, 1356.

73. O. R. I, vol. 46, pt. 3, 1355.
74. McPherson, *Battle Cry of Freedom*, 820–21. On desertion in the Army of Tennessee during this time, see Pete Daniel, *Soldiering in the Army of Tennessee*, 107, 114, 136–38; and Mark A. Weitz, *A Higher Duty*.
75. Ralph Mann argued "The national and professional orientations of Confederate officers, reinforced by class and cultural biases, precluded their understanding these men, and so they lost them—just as, on a larger scale, a failure to understand the power of localism was fatal to the Confederacy." In his study of Sand Lick, Virginia, Mann discovered that localism trumped nationalism in the minds of many Confederate soldiers when their homes came under attack from real and perceived threats. Localism certainly influenced many deserters' decisions to serve in Wofford's command rather than remain with their original companies. Ralph Mann, "'Ezekiel Counts's Sand Lick Company: Civil War and Localism in the Mountain South," in Kenneth W. Noe and Shannon H. Wilson, eds. *The Civil War in Appalachia: Collected Essays* (Knoxville: University of Tennessee Press, 1997), 78–103, quote located on 98–99.
76. O. R. I, vol. 49, II, 396, 456, 469.
77. O. R. I, vol. 49, II, 488.
78. Hamilton, "Union Occupation of Bartow County," 90; Robert MaGill, *Personal Reminiscences of a Confederate Soldier Boy* (Milledgeville: Boyd, 1993), 66.
79. Hamilton, "Union Occupation of Bartow County," 90; Smith, *The Most Daring of Men*, 145–46; O. R. I, vol. 49, II, 723–24.

Chapter 7

1. Mark Summers, *The Ordeal of the Reunion: A New History of Reconstruction* (Chapel Hill: University of North Carolina Press, 2014).
2. Megan Kate Nelson, *Ruin Nation: Destruction and the American Civil War* (Athens: University of Georgia Press, 2012).
3. John H. King, *Three Hundred Days in a Yankee Prison: Reminiscences of War Life, Captivity, Imprisonment at Camp Chase, Ohio* (Atlanta: Confederate Soldiers' Home, 1904), 99–114; William Archibald Dunning, *Reconstruction: Political and Economic, 1865–1877* reprint edition (New York: Harper, 1962) ; Walter L. Fleming, *Civil War and Reconstruction in Alabama* reprint edition (Gloucester, MA: Peter Smith, 1949); C. Mildred Thompson, *Reconstruction in Georgia: Economic, Social, and Political, 1865–1872*, reprint edition (Gloucester, MA: Peter Smith, 1964); Michael Fitzgerald, *Urban Emancipation: Popular Politics in Reconstruction Mobile, 1860–1890* (Baton Rouge: Louisiana State University, 2002); Michael Perman, *Reunion without Compromise: The South and Reconstruction: 1865–1868* (Cambridge: Cambridge University Press, 1973).
4. Manuscript Census, Bartow County, Georgia, 1860, Schedule I and III; Manuscript Census , Bartow County, Georgia, 1870, Schedule I and III

5. Aggregate data from Manuscript Census, Georgia, Bartow County, Schedule I, 1860, 1870 and CSR. This dataset only includes soldiers who fought with regular units that were commissioned into service by the Confederate States of America. Many of the soldiers who served in home guard or irregular units had at one time or another served in a commissioned Confederate company. This dataset also excludes Bartow County men who served in the Union army.
6. Ibid; Mary Branton Pension Application, Confederate Pension Applications, Bartow County, Georgia, microfilm, drawer 271, Box 14. According to Mary Branton's application her husband, Samuel, and brother-in-law, Joseph, died of measles while stationed near Knoxville, Tennessee, in June of 1862. Both brothers died only three months after their initial enlistment.
7. Aggregate data from CSR and Georgia Confederate Pension Records; Guy R. Hasegawa, *Mending Broken Soldiers: The Union and Confederate Programs to Supply Artificial Limbs* (Carbondale: Southern Ill. University Press, 2012); Brian Craig Miller, *Empty Sleeves: Amputation in the Civil War South* (Athens: University of Georgia Press, 2015).
8. Lewis Young, Manuscript Census, Georgia, Bartow County, Schedule I, 58.
9. Jeffrey W. McClurken, *Take Care of the Living: Reconstructing Confederate Veteran Families in Virginia* (Charlottesville: University of Virginia Press, 2009); James Marten, *Sing Not War: The Lives of Union and Confederate Veterans in Gilded Age America* (Chapel Hill: University of North Carolina Press, 2011). Bartow County's Confederate veteran experience differs from the Confederate veterans portrayed in Paul Cimbala, *Veterans North and South: The Transition from Soldier to Civilian after the American Civil War* (New York: Praeger, 2015).
10. Aggregate data from Manuscript Census, Bartow County, Georgia, Schedule I, 1860, 1870, 1880 and GCPR.
11. George Barnsley Diary, EU.
12. *Tri-Weekly Courier* (Rome), Sept. 18, 1866.
13. *Weekly Courier* (Rome), April 26, 1867.
14. *North Georgia Citizen*, Jan. 4, 1906; *North Georgia Citizen*, Jun. 18, 1903; *Dalton Daily Citizen*, July 11, 2015; Superior Court Records, Bartow County, Georgia, 1865 microfilm, drawer # 166: 54, GDAH, Morrow; David N. Wiggins, *Georgia's Confederate Monuments and Cemeteries* (Charleston: Arcadia Publishing, 2006), 102; William A. Blair, *Cities of the Dead: Contesting the Memory of the Civil War in the South, 1865–1914* (Chapel Hill: University of North Carolina Press, 2011).
15. *Rome Weekly Courier*, Sept. 6, 1867; *Express* (Cartersville), April 15, 1869.
16. Manuscript Census, Cass County, Georgia, 1860, Schedule I; Cunyus, *History of Bartow County*, 252; *Rome Weekly Courier*, Sept. 6, 1867; *Express* (Cartersville), April 15, 1869.
17. Sarris, *A Separate Civil War*, 162.

18. Superior Court Records, Bartow County, Georgia, 1865–1970, microfilm, drawer # 166: 54, GDAH, Morrow
19. Quotation in David W. Blight, *Race and Reunion: The Civil War in American Memory* (Cambridge, MA: Belknap Press, 2001), 33.
20. Report of W. H. Pritchett, Sept. 25, 27, and Oct. 7, 1866, Registered Letters Received, BRFAL microfilm, M# 798, reel # 11, p. 401–2. NARA-ATL.
21. *Express* (Cartersville), March 17, 1870.
22. Manuscript Census, Bartow County, Georgia, 1860, 1870, Schedule I; Superior Court Records, Bartow County, Georgia, 1865, microfilm, drawer # 166: 54, 30–31, GDAH, Morrow. The persistence rates include heads of households who died during the war. Therefore, the actual number of migrants was slightly smaller than the percentage suggests.
23. William A. Chunn to Elizabeth W. Chunn, July 7, 1867, Chunn-Land Family Papers, GDAH, Morrow; Quoted in Alexa Ilene Claremont, "Creators of Community: Cassville, Georgia, 1850–1880," [Master's thesis, University of Georgia, 2005], 48.
24. Superior Court Records, Bartow County, Georgia, 1865, microfilm, drawer # 166: 54, GDAH, Morrow.
25. *Rome Weekly Courier*, June 15, 1865.
26. Mills Lane, ed. *Georgia History Written by Those Who Lived It* (Savannah: Beehive Press, 1995), 195.
27. Smith, *The Most Daring of Men*, 149–69. General William T. Wofford believed that Freedmen's Bureau supplies would help heal the wounds of war.
28. Report of Brevet Major General Davis Tillson, 1867, Reports Relating to Operations and to Murders and Outrages, 1865–1868, BRFAL, microfilm, M# 798, reel # 32, NARA-ATL.
29. Superior Court Records, Bartow County, Georgia, 1866, microfilm, drawer # 166:54, GDAH, Morrow.
30. Superior Court Records, Bartow County, Georgia, 1865, 1866, microfilm, drawer # 166:54, GDAH, Morrow.
31. Ibid.
32. William A. Chunn to Mother, July 7, 1867, Chunn-Land Family Papers, M# 44–101, GDAH, Morrow.
33. Claremont, "Creators of Community: Cassville, Georgia, 1850–1880," 62.
34. Manuscript Census, Cass County, Georgia, 1860, Schedule I, II, and III; Manuscript Census, Bartow County, Georgia, 1870, Schedule I and II.
35. Manuscript Census, Bartow County, Georgia, 1870, Schedule I and II; Hahn, *Roots of Southern Populism*, 182.
36. Julia Barnsley Baltzelle to George S. Barnsley, June 9, 1864, George S. Barnsley Papers, MS# 1521, Series 1, Subseries 1.3, Folder 10, SHC, University of North Carolina at Chapel Hill.
37. Godfrey Barnsley to John Gardner, Oct. 26, 1866, Barnsley Family Papers, 1825–1904, M# 1165, reel 1, Box 1, Folder 1, TSA, Nashville; Julia Barnsley to

Lucien Barnsley, Feb. 23, 1866, George Scarborough Barnsley Papers, MS# 1521, Series 1, Subseries 1.1, Box 1, Folder 12, SHC, University of North Carolina at Chapel Hill.
38. James P. Baltzelle to Lucien Barnsley, February 10, 1866, Barnsley Family Papers: 1825–1904, M# 1165, reel 1, Box 1, Folder 1, TSA, Nashville.
39. Manuscript Census, Cass County, Georgia, 1860, Schedule I; Manuscript Census, Bartow County, Georgia, 1870, Schedule I
40. Manuscript Census, Cass County, Georgia, 1860, Schedule I, II, and III; Manuscript Census, Bartow County, 1870, Schedule I and II; Manuscript Census, Bartow County, 1880, Schedule I and II.
41. Testimony of Sarah Jane Patterson, *Slave* 10: (a): 286–91.
42. Euharlee Presbyterian Church, Minutes, 1853–1900; Raccoon Creek Baptist Church, Minutes, 1837–1900, microfilm, NGDPP, Shorter College Museum and Archives, Rome.
43. WPA Slave Narrative Project, GA Narratives, Vol. 4, Part 1, Callie Elder, 306.
44. O. E. Pratt to W. H. Pritchett, Sept. 17, 1866, Register of Letters Received, BRFAL, microfilm, M# 798, reel # 11, 400, NARA-ATL; Mark A. Cooper to W. H. Pritchett and Eveline Cooper, Oct. 8, 1866, Register of Letters Received, BRFAL, microfilm, M# 798, reel # 11, 401, NARA-ATL.
45. Paul A. Cimbala, *Under the Guardianship of the Nation: The Freedman's Bureau and the Reconstruction of Georgia, 1865–1870* (Athens: University of Georgia Press, 1997), 64; Lane, *Georgia History Written by Those Who Lived It*, 193–204; Freedman Bureau Station Agents: Cartersville, GA, Records of the Field Offices for the State of GA, BRFAL, microfilm, M# 1903, Roll # 55, NARA-ATL. W. H. Pritchett served as the Cartersville station agent from April 1865 to March 1867. C. B. Blacker served as the Cartersville agent from April 1867 to Dec. 1868.
46. C. B. Blacker to Hiram Miller, Sept. 3, 1867, Records of the Field Offices for the State of Georgia, BRFAL, microfilm, M# 1903, Roll # 55, 23, NARA-ATL. Blacker reported that "local whites and freedmen are anxious to see some U. S. soldiers stationed in their county."
47. C. B. Blacker to Robert Dowell, Aug. 28, 1867, Records of the Field Offices for the State of GA, BRFAL, microfilm, M# 1903, reel # 55, 30, NARA-ATL.
48. C. B. Blacker to Robert Akins, Aug. 1867, Records of the Field Offices for the State of GA, BRFAL, microfilm, M# 1903, reel # 55, 39, NARA-ATL.
49. C. B. Blacker to Rock Hamilton, Sept. 30, 1867, Records of the Field Offices for the State of GA, BRFAL, microfilm, M# 1903, reel # 55, 32, NARA-ATL.
50. C. B. Blacker to Joe Pearson, Oct. 19, 1867, Records of the Field Offices for the State of GA, BRFAL, microfilm, M# 1903, reel # 55, 38, NARA-ATL.
51. C. B. Blacker Report, Nov. 1, 1867, Registered Letters Received, BRFAL, microfilm, M# 798, reel # 12, 32, NARA-ATL; C. B. Blacker Report, Oct. 4, 1867, Records of the Field Offices for the State of GA, BRFAL, microfilm, M# 1903, reel # 55, 36, NARA-ATL.

52. C. B. Blacker School Report, Oct. 4, 1867, Records of the Field Offices for the State of GA, BRFAL, microfilm, M# 1903, reel # 55, 36, NARA-ATL, Atlanta; C. B. Blacker School Report, Jan. 1868, Records of the Superintendent of Education for the State of GA, BRFAL, microfilm, M# 799, reel # 16, NARA-ATL. C. B. Blacker School Report, C. B. Blacker School Report, Jan. 1868, Registered Letters Received, BRFAL, microfilm, M# 798, reel # 12, 32, NARA-ATL.
53. C. B. Blacker School Report, Jan. 1868, Records of the Superintendent of Education for the State of GA, BRFAL, microfilm, M# 799, reel # 16, NARA-ATL.
54. C. B. Blacker to Bryant Leake, July 1867, Records of the Field Offices for the State of GA, BRFAL, microfilm, M# 1903, reel # 55, 73, NARA-ATL.
55. Report Received by C. B. Blacker, Sept. 3, 1867, Records of the Field Offices for the State of GA, BRFAL, microfilm, M# 1903, reel # 55, 23, NARA-ATL.
56. C. W. Howard to C. B. Blacker, Sept. 11, 1866, Register of Letters Received, BRFAL, microfilm, M# 798, reel # 11, 216, NARA-ATL.
57. Quoted in Claremont, "Creators of Community: Cassville, Georgia, 1850–1880," 52.
58. Ibid., 54.
59. C. B. Blacker Report, Oct. 1867, Records of the Field Offices for the State of GA, BRFAL, microfilm, M# 1903, reel # 55, 69, NARA-ATL; Samuel Donaldson, 1867, List of Freedmen Murdered or Assaulted, BRFAL, microfilm, drawer 159:61, GDAH, Morrow.
60. C. B. Blacker Report, Nov. 18, 1867, Register of Letters Received, BRFAL, microfilm, M# 798, reel # 12, 36, NARA-ATL; C. B. Blacker Report, Sept. 1867, Records of the Field Offices for the State of GA, BRFAL, microfilm, M# 1903, reel # 55, 29, NARA-ATL; C. B. Blacker to John Crawford, Sept. 26, 1867, Records of the Field Offices for the State of GA, BRFAL, microfilm, M# 1903, reel # 55, 30, NARA-ATL.
61. C. B. Blacker to C. Sibley, Dec. 6, 1867, Records of the Field Offices for the State of GA, BRFAL, microfilm, M# 1903, reel # 55, 68, NARA-ATL.
62. Manuscript Census, Bartow County, Georgia, Schedule I, 1870.
63. C. B. Blacker to C. Sibley, Dec. 6, 1867, Records of the Field Offices for the State of GA, BRFAL, microfilm, M# 1903, reel # 55, 68, NARA-ATL.
64. C. B. Blacker to Major C. T. Watson, Sept. 17, 1867, Records of the Field Offices for the State of GA, BRFAL, microfilm, M# 1903, reel # 55, 27, NARA-ATL.
65. C. B. Blacker to Levi Hall, Oct. 30, 1867, Records of the Field Offices for the State of GA, BRFAL, microfilm, M# 1903, reel # 55, 41, NARA-ATL.
66. List of Freedmen Murdered or Assaulted, BRFAL, microfilm, drawer 159:61, GDAH, Morrow.
67. Carter, *When the War Was Over*, 201.
68. Olive Hall Shadgett, *The Republican Party in Georgia: From Reconstruction Through 1900* (Athens: University of Georgia Press, 1964), 5; James Alex

Baggett, *The Scalawags: Southern Dissenters in the Civil War and Reconstruction* (Baton Rouge: Louisiana State University Press, 2004), 52.
69. *Express* (Cartersville), Aug. 23, 1867; Charles Flynn, *White Land, Black Labor: Caste and Class in Nineteenth-Century Georgia* (Baton Rouge: Louisiana State University Press, 1983), 51.
70. *Rome Weekly Courier*, May 1, 1868.
71. Williams, Appalachia, 181–84; Sarris, *A Separate Civil War*, 150–52.
72. Bartley, *Creation of Modern Georgia*, 55–57.
73. Ibid.
74. *Express* (Cartersville), May 1, 1868.
75. Bartley, *Creation of Modern Georgia*, 63.
76. Claremont, "Creators of Community," 62.
77. Smith, *The Most Daring of Men*, 149. During the war Wofford lost two children from disease. On Aug. 19, 1865, his young daughter Laura died of diphtheria. Only one of his four daughters, Helena, would survive to adulthood.
78. Hahn, *Roots of Southern Populism*, 213–14; Stephen Robinson, "To Think, Act, Vote, and Speak for Ourselves": Black Democrats and Black "Agency" in the American South after Reconstruction," *Journal of Social History* 48:2 (Winter 2014): 363–82.
79. Sidney Andrews, *The South Since the War* (Boston: Houghton Mifflin, 1971), 329–30; Smith, *The Most Daring of Men*, 151.
80. Burkley, Margaret Nola, "Floyd County, Georgia, during the Civil War Era," (PhD Diss.: FSU, 1998), 393; *Weekly Express* (Cartersville), June 12, 1866; *Tri-Weekly Courier* (Rome), Oct. 16, 1866.
81. Smith, *The Most Daring of Men*, 159.
82. Bartley, *Creation of Modern Georgia*, 103–26; Hahn, *Roots of Southern Populism*, 204
83. Quoted in Bartley, *Creation of Modern Georgia*, 82.
84. Hahn, *Roots of Southern Populism*, 228.
85. *Tri-Weekly Courier* (Rome), Sept. 26, 1876.
86. *Atlanta Weekly Constitution*, Oct. 6, 1874.
87. *Tri-Weekly Courier* (Rome), Sept. 26, 1874.
88. *North Georgia Citizen*, Sept. 3, 1874, Sept. 24, 1874; *Tri-Weekly Courier* (Rome), Sept. 3, 1874, Sept. 10, 1874, Sept. 17, 1874, Sept. 26, 1874, Oct. 3, 1874; *Express* (Cartersville), June 10, 1874, June 17, 1874, July 1, 1874, July 22, 1874, Oct. 21, 1874; George L. Jones, "William H. Felton and the Independent Democratic Movement in Georgia, 1870–1890," (PhD diss.: University of Georgia, 1971), 76–77, 173–85; Robinson, "To Think, Act, Vote, and Speak for Ourselves," 363–82.
89. Quoted in Hahn, *Roots of Southern Populism*, 233.
90. Jones, "William H. Felton and the Independent Democratic Movement in Georgia, 1870–1890," 173–85; *Tri-Weekly Courier* (Rome), Nov. 12, 1874, Nov. 19, 1874, Nov. 26, 1874; *Express* (Cartersville), Nov. 19, 1874.

91. *New York Times*, Feb. 6, 1882.
92. Ibid.; Jones, "William H. Felton and the Independent Democratic Movement in Georgia, 1870–1890," 173–85.
93. Cunyus, *History of Bartow County*, 164–65; Hahn, *Roots of Southern Populism*, 237-38.
94. *Courant American* (Cartersville), March 16, 1888, March 30, 1888, Feb. 2, 1901; *North Georgian Citizen* (Dalton), June 16, 1892 Dec. 10, 1908.
95. Robert W. Thurston, *Lynching: American Mob Murder in Global Perspective* (Burlington, VT: Ashgate, 2011), 104; Christopher Waldrep, ed., *Lynching in America: A History in Documents* (New York: NYU Press, 2006), 140–43; Bartley, *Creation of Modern Georgia*, 122.
96. Quoted in Hahn, *Roots of Southern Populism*, 121.

Appendix

1. For an excellent discussion of changing persistence rates in American history since 1830, see James P. Allen, "Changes in the American Propensity to Migrate," *Annals of the Association of American Geographers* 67:4 (Dec. 1977), 577–87; James I. Stewart, "Economic Opportunity or Hardship? The Causes of Geographic Mobility on the Agricultural Frontier, 1860–1880," *Journal of Economic History* 69:1 (March 2009): 238–68; Randolph B. Campbell, "Population Persistence and Social Change in Nineteenth-Century Texas: Harrison County, 1850–1880," *Journal of Southern History* 48:2 (May 1982): 185–204; Joseph P. Ferrie, "Up and Down or down and out? Immigrant Mobility in the Antebellum United States," *Journal of Interdisciplinary History* 26:1 (Summer 1995): 33–55; Jonathan Wiener, "Planters Persistence and Social Change: Alabama, 1850–1870," *Journal of Interdisciplinary History* 7:2 (Autumn 1976): 235–60.

Bibliography

Primary Sources

Manuscripts

Alabama Department of Archives and History, Montgomery.
    Zillah Haynie Brandon Diary, 1823–1871

Bartow History Museum, Cartersville, Georgia
    Yeoman Farm Journal [Author Unknown]

Young Family Papers
Kenan Research Library and Archives, Atlanta History Center
    Warren Akin Letter
    Wilbur Kurtz Collection

Baker Library, Harvard Business School, Boston, Mass.
    R. G. Dun & Company Collection, Georgia

Special Collection, Bartow County Public Library, Cartersville
    Northwest Georgia Document Preservation Project (microfilm)

Robert W. Woodruff Library, Emory University, Atlanta
    Confederate Miscellany Files
    George Scarborough Barnsley Papers (microfilm)
    Godfrey Barnsley Family Papers
    Rebecca Rainey Hood Papers (microfilm)
    William Augustus Chunn Letters
    William H. Stiles Papers

Georgia Department of Archives and History, Atlanta
    Bartow County Vertical File
    Bartow County Maps
    Cass County Deeds (microfilm)
    Cass County Superior Court Minutes (microfilm)
    Charles W. Howard Cherokee Baptist College Address
    Cherokee Baptist College Commencement Address, 1860 (microfilm)
    Cherokee Baptist Convention Minutes (microfilm)
    Chunn-Land Family Papers
    Confederate Reminiscences and Letters, 1861–1865

Cooper Family Vertical File
Family Genealogical drawer
Etowah Mill Journal (microfilm)
Executive Department Correspondence (Incoming)
Executive Department Correspondence (Outgoing)
Macedonia Baptist Church Minutes (microfilm)
Mackay-Stiles Family Papers (microfilm)
Mark A. Cooper Papers (microfilm)
John F. Milhollin Letters (microfilm)
Noble John Brooks Letters (microfilm)
Summary Reports of Southern Claims Commission (microfilm)
James W. Watts Farm Journal (microfilm)
William K.Watson Diary (microfilm)
Western and Atlantic Railroad
William Hardin Papers
Wofford Family Vertical File

Georgia Historical Society Archives, Savannah
Godfrey Barnsley Papers
John W. Bentley Collection

Huntingdon Library, San Marino, California
Godfrey Barnsley Papers

National Archives and Records Administration, Southeast Region, Atlanta
Southern Claims Commission (Allowed)
Bureau of Freedmen, Refugees, and Abandoned Lands Records, Georgia

National Archives and Records Administration, Washington, DC.
Manuscript Censuses, Georgia, Cass, Floyd, Gordon, Cobb, Polk, Cherokee Counties, Schedules I, II, III, IV, 1850, 1860
Manuscript Censuses, Georgia, Bartow County, Schedule I, 1870
Record Group 56, General Records of the Department of the Treasury, Records of the Commissioners of Claims (Southern Claims Commission), 1871–80, Microfilm Publication 87
Record Group 217, Records of the U.S. General Accounting Office, Allowed Cases Files of the Southern Claims Commission
Record Group 233, Records of the U.S. House of Representatives, Barred and Disallowed Claims of the Southern Claims Commission

Ohio Historical Society, Columbus, Ohio
Styles Porter Diary

Southern Historical Collection, Library of the University of North Carolina at Chapel Hill
George Scarborough Barnsley Papers
Mackay-Stiles Family Papers

Shorter College, Rome, Georgia
  Northwest Georgia Document Preservation Project (microfilm)
    Macedonia Baptist Church Minutes
    Raccoon Creek Baptist Church Minutes Tennessee State Archives, Nashville
  Barnsley Family Papers (microfilm)
University of Georgia, Hargrett Rare Books and Special Collections Library, Athens
  Telamon Cuyler Collection
Woodson Research Center, Fondren Library, Rice University, Houston
  Jefferson Davis Letters

Journals, Magazines, and Newspapers
New York Times
Southern Cultivator
The Confederate Veteran
The Courant American (Cartersville)
The Daily Chronicle and Sentinel (Macon)
The Daily Telegraph (Macon)
The Express (Cartersville)
The Federal Union (Milledgeville)
The North Georgia Citizen (Dalton)
The Southern Banner (Athens)
The Southern Statesman (Calhoun)
The Standard (Cassville)
The Standard and Express (Cartersville)
The Tri-Weekly Courier (Rome)

Published Primary Sources
Bauer, K. Jack. *Soldiering: The Civil War Diary of Rice C. Bull.* New York: Presidio Press, 1995.
Black, Frances Josephine, ed. "'We Begged to Hearts of Stone': The Wartime Journal of Cassville's Lizzie Gaines." *Northwest Georgia Historical and Genealogical Quarterly* 20 (Winter: 1988): 6–16.
Candler, Allen D. *The Confederate Records of the State of Georgia: Volume One.* Atlanta: C. P. Byrd, 1909.
Cone, A. J. *The Rock: A Story of the War.* Atlanta: n.p., 1913.
Dean, Benjamin Devor. *Recollections of the 26th Missouri Infantry in the War for the Union.* Lamar, Missouri: Southwest Missourian Office, 1892.
DeBow, J. D. B. *A Statistical View of the United States: A Compendium of the Seventh Census.* Washington: Beverly Tucker, 1864.
Felton, Rebecca Latimer. *Country Life in Georgia in the Days of My Youth.* Atlanta: Index Printing, 1919.

Hargis, O. P. *Thrilling Experiences of a First Georgia Cavalryman in the Civil War: Three Months Inside the Federal Lines in Rear of Sherman.* N.p., 1910.

Howard, Frances Thomas. *In and Out of the Lines.* Cartersville, GA: Etowah Valley Historical Society, 1998.

"Howell Cobb Papers." *Georgia Historical Quarterly* 6 (1909): 23–49.

Jones, Joseph. *First Report to the Cotton Planters' Convention of Georgia on the Agricultural Resource of Georgia.* N.p.: 1860.

Kerksis, Sydney, ed. *The Atlanta Papers.* Dayton, OH: Morningside, 1980.

McGill, Robert. *Personal Reminiscences of a Confederate Soldier Boy.* Milledgeville: Boyd, 1993.

Noe, Kenneth W., ed. *A Southern Boy in Blue: The Memoir of Marcus Woodcock 9th Kentucky Infantry (U.S.A.).* Knoxville: University of Tennessee Press, 1996.

Scarborough, William K., ed. *The Diary of Edmund Ruffin, Volume One: Toward Independence.* Baton Rouge: Louisiana State University Press, 1972.

Scott, Thomas A., ed. *Cornerstones of Georgia History: Documents that Formed the State.* Athens: University of Georgia Press, 1995.

Sterkx, H. E., ed. "The Autobiography and Civil War Letters of Joel Murphree of Troy, Alabama: 1864–1865." *Alabama Historical Quarterly* 19 (1957): 176–77.

United Confederate Veterans. *Minutes of the Annual Meeting and Reunion of the United Confederate Veterans.* New Orleans: Hopkins' Printing Office, 1889.

War of the Rebellion: Official Records of the Union and Confederate Armies. Washington: Government Printing Office, 1891.

Watkins, Sam R. *"Co. Aytch" A Side Show of the Big Show.* New York: Touchstone, 1997.

"Whites with Indian Families." *Bartow County Genealogical Society and Family Research Library,* No. 10 (2001): 20–21.

Wiley, Bell Irvin, ed. *Letters of Warren Aiken Confederate Congressman.* Athens: University of Georgia Press, 1964.

Wills, Charles W. *Army Life of an Illinois Soldier Including Day-by-Day Records of Sherman's March to the Sea.* Evanston: Southern Illinois Press, 1996.

Wynne, Lewis N. and Robert A. Taylor, eds. *The War So Horrible: The Civil War Diary of Hiram Smith Williams.* Tuscaloosa: University of Alabama Press, 1993.

Secondary Sources

Books and Articles

Akin, Sally Mary. "Refugees of 1863." *Georgia Historical Quarterly* 31 (1947): 113–20.

Ash, Stephen V. *The Black Experience in the Civil War South.* Santa Barbara: Praeger, 2010.

———. *When the Yankees Came: Conflict & Chaos in the Occupied South, 1861–1865.* Chapel Hill: University of North Carolina Press, 1995.

Athey, Lou. "Loyalty and Civil Liberty in Fayette County During the Civil War." *West Virginia History* 55 (1996): 1–24.
Ayers, Edward L. *What Caused the Civil War? Reflections on the South and Southern History.* New York: Norton, 2005.
Barron, Hal S. *Those Who Stayed Behind: Rural Society in Nineteenth-Century New England.* Cambridge: Cambridge University Press, 1984.
Battey, George Magruder. *A History of Rome and Floyd County, State of Georgia, United States of America.* Atlanta: Webb and Vary, 1922.
Beringer, Richard E., Herman Hattaway, Archer Jones, and William N. Still Jr, eds. *Why the South Lost the Civil War.* Athens: University of Georgia Press, 1986.
Billingsley, Carolyn Earle. *Communities of Kinship: Antebellum Families and the Settlement of the Cotton Frontier.* Athens: University of Georgia Press, 2004.
Black, Robert C. III. *The Railroads of the Confederacy.* Chapel Hill: University of North Carolina Press, 1952.
Blair, William A. *Cities of the Dead: Contesting the Memory of the Civil War in the South, 1865–1914.* Chapel Hill: University of North Carolina Press, 2011.
Bode, Frederick A. "The Formation of Evangelical Communities in Middle Georgia: Twiggs County, 1820–1861." *Journal of Southern History* 60 (1994): 711–48.
Bonner, James C. *A History of Georgia Agriculture, 1732–1860.* Athens: University of Georgia Press, 1964.
Bryan, Charles T. Jr. "Tories' Amidst Rebels: Confederate Occupation of East Tennessee, 1861–1863." *East Tennessee Historical Society's Publications* 60 (1988): 3–22.
Bryan, T. Conn. *Confederate Georgia.* Athens: University of Georgia Press, 1953.
Cadle, Farris W. *Georgia Land Surveying History and Law.* Athens: University of Georgia Press, 1991.
Canaday, Barbara Bell. *Georgia Freemasons, 1861–1865.* Atlanta: Georgia Lodge of Research, 2001.
Carey, Anthony Gene. *Parties, Slavery, and the Union in Antebellum Georgia.* Athens: University of Georgia Press, 1997.
Cashin, Edward J. and Glenn T. Eskew, eds. *Paternalism in a Southern City: Race, Religion, and Gender in Augusta, Georgia, 1860–1865.* Athens: University of Georgia Press, 2001.
Castel, Albert. *Decision in the West: The Atlanta Campaign of 1864.* Lawrence: University Press of Kansas, 1992.
Censer, Jane Turner. "Southwestern Migration among North Carolina Planter Families: The Disposition to Emigrate." *Journal of Southern History* 57 (1991): 426–44.
Coker, Clent. *The Illustrious Dream: Barnsley Gardens at Woodlands.* Atlanta: The Julia Company, 2000.
Coleman, Kenneth, ed. *A History of Georgia,* 2nd ed. Athens: University of Georgia Press, 1991.

Corley, Florence Fleming. *Confederate City, Augusta, Georgia, 1860–1865.* Columbia: University of South Carolina Press, 1960.
Coulter, E. Merton. *Old Petersburg and the Broad River Valley of Georgia.* Athens: University of Georgia Press, 1965.
Crawford, Martin. *Ashe County's Civil War: Community and Society in the Appalachian South.* Charlottesville: University Press of Virginia, 2001.
Cunyus, Lucy Josephine. *History of Bartow County, Georgia, Formerly Cass,* 5th reprint. Greenville, SC: Southern Historical Press, 2001.
Daniel, Larry. *Soldiering in the Army of Tennessee.* Chapel Hill: University of North Carolina Press, 1991.
Davis, Donald E. *Where There Are Mountains: An Environmental History of the Southern Appalachians.* Athens: University of Georgia Press, 2000.
Davis, Robert S. "Forgotten Union Guerrillas from the North Georgia Mountains." *North Georgia Journal* (1998): 30–49.
———. "Memoirs of a Partisan War: Sion Darnell Remembers North Georgia, 1861–1865." *Georgia Historical Quarterly* 80 (1996): 93–116.
———. "The North Georgia Moonshine War of 1876–77." *North Georgia Journal* (1989): 41–46.
———. "White and Black in Blue: The Recruitment of Federal Units in Civil War North Georgia." *Georgia Historical Quarterly* 85 (2001): 347–74.
Davis, Natalie Zemon. *Society and Culture in Early Modern France,* 4th ed. Stanford: Stanford University Press, 1975.
Demos, John. *Past, Present, and Personal: The Family and Life Course in American History.* New York: Oxford University Press, 1988.
Donnelly, Ralph W. "The Bartow County Confederate Saltpetre Works." *Georgia Historical Quarterly* 54 (1970): 305–19.
Dorgan, Howard. *Giving Glory to God in Appalachia: Worship Practices of Six Baptist Subdenominations.* Knoxville: University of Tennessee Press, 1987.
Drake, Richard B. "Slavery and Antislavery in Appalachia." *Appalachian Heritage* 14 (1986): 25–33.
Draper, Lyman C. *King's Mountain and Its Heroes: History of the Battle of King's Mountain, October 7, 1780, and the Events Which Led to It.* Marietta, GA: Continental Book, 1954.
Dunaway, Wilma. *Slavery in the American Mountain South.* Cambridge: Cambridge University Press, 2003.
Dunn, Durwood. *Cade's Cove: The Life and Death of a Southern Appalachian Community. 1818–1937.* Knoxville: University of Tennessee Press, 1988.
Durrill, Wayne K. *War of Another Kind: A Southern Community in the Great Rebellion.* New York: Oxford University Press, 1990.
Edwards, Stewart C. "'To do the manufacturing for the South': Private Industry in Confederate Columbus." *Georgia Historical Quarterly* 85 (2001): 538–54.
Elman, Bruce W. *Entrepreneurs in the Southern Upcountry: Commercial Culture in Spartanburg, South Carolina, 1845–1880.* Athens: University of Georgia Press, 2008.

Faragher, John Mack. *Sugar Creek: Life on the Illinois Prairie.* New Haven: Yale University Press, 1986.
Felton, Rebecca Latimer. *My Memoirs of Georgia Politics.* Atlanta: Index Printing, 1911.
Fisher, Noel C. *War at Every Door: Partisan Politics and Guerrilla Violence in East Tennessee, 1860–1869.* Chapel Hill: University of North Carolina Press, 1997.
Flowers, Carl Jr. "The Wofford Settlement on the Georgia Frontier." *Georgia Historical Quarterly* 61 (1977): 258–67.
Flynt, Wayne. *Alabama Baptists: Southern Baptists in the Heart of Dixie.* Tuscaloosa: University of Alabama Press, 1998.
Ford, Lacy K. *Origins of Southern Radicalism: The South Carolina Upcountry, 1800–1860.* Oxford: Oxford University Press, 1988.
———. "Yeoman Farmers in the South Carolina Upcountry: Changing Production Patterns in the Late Antebellum Period." *Agricultural History* 60 (1986): 17–37.
Fowler, John D. *Mountaineers in Grey: The Nineteenth Tennessee Volunteer Infantry Regiment, C.S.A.* Knoxville: University of Tennessee Press, 2004.
Gallman, Robert. "Self-Sufficiency in the Cotton Economy of the Antebellum South," *Agricultural History* 44 (1970): 5–23.
Gardner, Sarah E. *Blood and Irony: Southern White Women's Narratives of the Civil War, 1861–1937.* Chapel Hill: University of North Carolina Press, 2003.
Garrison, Tim Alan. *The Legal Ideology of Removal: The Southern Judiciary and the Sovereignty of Native American Nations.* Athens: University of Georgia Press, 2002.
Genovese, Eugene D. and Elizabeth Fox-Genovese. "The Religious Ideals of Southern Slave Society," *The Georgia Historical Quarterly* 70 (1986): 1–16.
Genovese, Eugene D. "Yeomen Farmers in a Slaveholders' Democracy," *Agricultural History* 49:2 (April 1975): 331-42.
Gober, Sarah Blackwell. *The First Hundred Years: A Short History of Cobb County, in Georgia.* Atlanta: Walter W. Brown, 1935.
Grimsley, Mark. *The Hard Hand of War: Union Military Policy Toward Southern Civilians, 1861–1865.* Cambridge: Cambridge University Press, 1995.
Groce, W. Todd. *Mountain Rebels: East Tennessee Confederates and the Civil War, 1860–1870.* Knoxville: University of Tennessee Press, 1999.
Hahn, Steven. *The Roots of Southern Populism: Yeoman Farmers and the Transformation of the Georgia Upcountry, 1850–1890.* New York: Oxford University Press, 1983.
Hamilton, J.S. De Roulhac. "Three Centuries of Southern Records, 1607–1907." *Journal of Southern History* 1 (1944): 12–13.
Harris, William C. "East Tennessee's Civil War Refugees and the Impact of the War on Civilians." *Journal of East Tennessee History* 64 (1992): 3–19.
Hasegawa, Guy R. *Mending Broken Soldiers: The Union and Confederate Programs to Supply Artificial Limbs.* Carbondale: Southern Illinois University Press, 2012.

Heyrman, Christine Leigh. *Southern Cross: The Beginnings of the Bible Belt.* New York: A. A. Knopf, 1997.
Hilliard, Sam Bowers. *Hog Meat and Hoecake: Food Supply in the Old South, 1840–1860.* Carbondale: Southern Illinois Press, 1972.
Holland, Lynwood Mathis. *Pierce M. B. Young: The Warwick of the South.* Athens: University of Georgia Press, 1964.
Horton, Paul. "Submitting to the 'Shadow of Slavery': The Secession Crisis in Alabama's Lawrence County." *Civil War History* 44 (1998): 111–36.
Huston, James L. *Calculating the Value of the Union: Slavery, Property, Rights, and the Economic Origins of the Civil War.* Chapel Hill: University of North Carolina, 2003.
Inscoe, John, ed. *Appalachians and Race: The Mountain South From Slavery to Segregation.* Lexington: University of Kentucky Press, 2001.
Inscoe, John. *Mountain Masters: Slavery and the Sectional Crisis in Western North Carolina.* Knoxville: University of Tennessee Press, 1989.
Inscoe, John C. and Gordon B. McKinney. *The Heart of Confederate Appalachia: Western North Carolina in the Civil War.* Chapel Hill: University of North Carolina Press, 2000.
Iobst, Richard W. *Civil War Macon: The History of a Confederate City.* Macon: Mercer University Press, 1999.
Isbell, Mrs. Luther. *Col. William Wofford, R.S., 1812, Nathaniel Wofford, 1812, Gen. William Tatum Wofford, C.S.A.* (N.p.: Mrs. Luther Isbell, 1960.
Jack, Theodore H. "The Preservation of Georgia History." *North Carolina Historical Review* 4 (1927): 230–45.
Janney, Caroline E. *Remembering the Civil War: Reunion and the Limits of Reconciliation.* Chapel Hill: University of North Carolina Press, 2013.
Johnson, Michael P. *Toward a Patriarchal Republic: The Secession of Georgia.* Baton Rouge: Louisiana State University Press, 1977.
Johnson, Whittington B. *Black Savannah, 1788–1864.* Fayetteville: University of Arkansas Press, 1996.
Johnston, James H. *Western and Atlantic Railroad of the State of Georgia.* Atlanta: Stein, 1932.
Klotter, James C. "The Black South and White Appalachia." *Journal of American History* 66 (1980): 832–49.
Landrum, J. B. O. *History of Spartanburg County: Embracing an Account of Many Important Events and Biographical Sketches of Statesmen, Divines and Other Public Men, and Names of Many Others Worthy of Record in the History of their County.* Atlanta: Franklin, 1900.
Linden, Fabien. "Economic Democracy in the Slave South." *Journal of Negro History* 31 (1946): 140–89.
Malone, Henry Thompson. *Cherokees of the Old South: A People in Transition.* Athens: University of Georgia Press, 1956.
Mann, Ralph. "Mountains, Land, and Kin Networks: Burke's Garden, Virginia, in the 1840s and 1850s." *Journal of Southern History* 58 (1992): 411–34.

Marlin, Lloyd G. *The History of Cherokee County.* Atlanta: Walter W. Brown, 1932.
Mathews, Donald G. *Religion in the Old South.* Chicago: University of Chicago Press, 1977.
Marten, James. *Sing Not War: The Lives of Union and Confederate Veterans in Gilded Age America.* Chapel Hill: University of North Carolina Press, 2011.
McCauley, Deborah Vansau. *Appalachian Mountain Religion.* Urbana: University of Illinois Press, 1995.
McClurken, Jeffrey W. *Take Care of the Living: Reconstructing Confederate Veteran Families in Virginia.* Charlottesville: University of Virginia Press, 2009.
McCurry, Stephanie. *Masters of Small Worlds: Yeoman Households, Gender Relations, and the Political Culture of the Antebellum South Carolina Low Country,* 2nd ed. New York: Oxford University Press, 1997.
McGuire, Robert, and Robert Higgs. "Cotton, Corn, and Risk in the Nineteenth Century: Another View," *Explorations in Economic History* 14 (1977): 167–82.
McKenzie, Robert Tracy. *One South or Many? Plantation Belt and Upcountry in Civil War-Era Tennessee.* New York: Oxford University, 1994.
McKnight, Brian D. *Contested Borderland: The Civil War in Appalachian Kentucky and Virginia.* Lexington: University Press of Kentucky, 2012.
McLoughlin, William G. *Cherokees and Missionaries: 1789–1839.* New Haven: Yale University Press, 1984.
———. *Cherokee Resistance in the New Republic.* Princeton: Princeton University Press, 1986.
McPherson, James M. *Battle Cry of Freedom: The Civil War Era.* New York: Ballentine, 1998.
———. *For Cause and Comrades: Why Men Fought in the Civil War.* New York: Oxford University Press, 1997.
———. *Ordeal by Fire: The Civil War and Reconstruction.* New York: Knopf, 1982.
Melton, Brian. "'The Town that Sherman Wouldn't Burn': Sherman's March and Madison, Georgia, in History, Memory, and Legend," *Georgia Historical Quarterly* 86 (2002): 201–30.
Miller, Brian Craig. *Empty Sleeves: Amputation in the Civil War South.* Athens: University of Georgia Press, 2015.
Miller, Randall M., Harry S. Stout, and Charles Reagan Wilson, eds. *Religion and the American Civil War.* New York: Oxford University Press, 1998.
Mitchell, Robert D., ed. *Appalachian Frontiers: Settlement, Society, and Development in the Pre-industrial South.* Lexington: University Press of Kentucky, 1990.
Mohr, Clarence. *On the Threshold of Freedom: Masters and Slaves in Civil War Georgia.* Athens: University of Georgia Press, 1986.
Moss, Bobby Gilmer. *Roster of South Carolina Patriots in the American Revolution.* Baltimore: Genealogical Publishing, 1978.
———. *The Patriot at Cowpens.* Greenville, SC: B.G. Moss Press, 1979.
Neely, Mark E. *The Civil War and the Limits of Destruction.* Cambridge, MA: Harvard University Press, 2007.

Nelson, Megan Kate. *Ruin Nation: Destruction and the American Civil War.* Athens: University of Georgia Press, 2012.
Noe, Kenneth W. "Appalachia Before Mr. Peabody: Some Recent Literature on the Southern Mountain Region." *Virginia Magazine of History and Biography* 110 (2002): 5–35.
———. *Reluctant Rebels: Later Enlisting Confederate Soldiers.* Chapel Hill: University of North Carolina Press, 2011.
———. *Southwest Virginia's Railroad: Modernization and the Sectional Crisis in the Civil War Era.* 2nd ed. Tuscaloosa: University of Alabama Press, 2003.
Noe, Kenneth W. *Reluctant Rebels: The Confederates Who Joined the Army after 1861.* Knoxville: University of Tennessee Press, 1997.
Norgren, Jill. *The Cherokee Cases: The Confrontation of Law and Politics.* New York: McGraw-Hill, 1996.
Oshnock, Kevin. "The Isolation Factor: Differing Loyalties of Watauga and Buncombe Counties during the Civil War," *North Carolina Historical Review* 90:4 (Oct. 2013): 385–413.
Otto, John Solomon. "The Migration of the Southern Plain Folk: An Interdisciplinary Synthesis." *Journal of Southern History* 51 (1985): 183–200.
———. *The Southern Frontiers, 1607–1860: The Agricultural Evolution of the Colonial and Antebellum South.* New York: Greenwood Press, 1989.
Owsley, Frank L. *Plain Folk of the Old South.* Baton Rouge: Louisiana State University Press, 1949.
———. "The Pattern of Migration and Settlement on the Southern Frontier." *Journal of Southern History* 11 (1945): 147–67.
Perdue, Theda, and Michael D. Green, eds. *The Cherokee Removal: A Brief History with Documents.* Boston: Bedford-St. Martin's: 1995.
Phillips, Ulrich Bonnell. *A History of Transportation of the Eastern Cotton Belt.* New York: Octagon, 1968.
———. "The Origin and Growth of the Southern Black Belts." *Journal of Southern History* 12 (1906): 780–99.
Pitts, Lulie. *History of Gordon County, Georgia.* Calhoun, GA: Press of the Calhoun Times, 1933.
Poole, Cary Franklin. *A History of Railroading in Western North Carolina.* Johnson City, TN: Overmountain Press, 1995.
Pope, Mark Cooper II and J. Donald McKee. *Mark Anthony Cooper: The Iron Man of Georgia.* Atlanta: Graphic Publishing, 2000.
Range, Willard. *A Century of Georgia Agriculture, 1850–1950.* Athens: University of Georgia Press, 1954.
Ransom, Roger L., and Richard Sutch. *One Kind of Freedom: The Economic Consequences of Emancipation.* Cambridge: Cambridge University Press, 1977.
Reed, John Shelton. *The Enduring South: Subcultural Persistence in Mass Society.* Lexington, Mass.: Heath, 1972.

Reeve, Jewell B. *Stories of Gordon County and Calhoun, Georgia*. 2nd Edition. Easley, SC: Southern Historical Press, 1979.
Ringold, May Spencer. "Robert Newman Gourdin and the '1860 Association.'" *Georgia Historical Quarterly* 4 (1971): 500–12.
Robertson, James I., Jr. *Soldiers Blue and Gray*. Columbia: University of South Carolina Press, 1988.
Robinson, Stephen. "To Think, Act, Vote, and Speak for Ourselves": Black Democrats and Black "Agency" in the American South after Reconstruction." *Journal of Social History* 48:2 (Winter 2014): 363–82.
Raboteau, Albert J. *Slave Religion: The "Invisible Institution" in the Antebellum South*. 2nd ed. New York: Oxford University Press, 1980.
Rodgers, Michelle Amie Spinks, and Scott Thompson. *Architecture of Bartow County, Georgia*. Cartersville, GA: Bartow History Center, 2003.
Rubin, Anne Sarah. *Through the Heart of Dixie: Sherman's March and American Memory*. Chapel Hill: University of North Carolina Press, 2014.
Sacher, John A. *A Perfect War of Politics: Parties, Politicians, and Democracy in Louisiana, 1824–1861*. Baton Rouge: Louisiana State University Press, 2003.
Salstrom, Paul. *Appalachia's Path to Dependency: Rethinking a Region's Economic History, 1730–1940*. Lexington: University Press of Kentucky, 1994.
Sarris, Jonathan. *A Separate Civil War: Communities in Conflict in the Mountain South*. Charlottesville: University Press of Virginia, 2006.
———. "Anatomy of an Atrocity: The Madden Branch Massacre and Guerrilla Warfare in North Georgia, 1861–1865." *Georgia Historical Quarterly* 77 (1993): 679–710.
Scaife, William R. and William Harris Bragg. *Joe Brown's Pets: The Georgia Militia, 1861–1865*. Macon, GA: Mercer University Press, 2004.
Schwarze, Edmund. *History of the Moravian Missions among the Southern Indian Tribes of the United States*. Bethlehem, PA: Times Publishing, 1923.
Sensing, Thurman. *Champ Ferguson: Confederate Guerrilla*. Nashville: Vanderbilt University Press, 1942.
Shyrock, Richard Harrison. *Georgia and the Union in 1850*. Reprint edition. New York: AMS Press, 1968.
Smith, Gerald J. *"One of the Most Daring of Men": The Life of Confederate General William Tatum Wofford*. Journal of Confederate History Series 16. Murfreesboro, TN: Southern Heritage Press, 1997.
Sutherland, Daniel E., ed. *Guerillas, Unionists, and Violence on the Confederate Home Front*. Fayetteville: University of Arkansas Press, 1999.
Talmadge, John E. *Rebecca Latimer Felton: Nine Stormy Decades*. Athens: University of Georgia Press, 1960.
———. "The Origin of the Tugalo Party's Name." *Georgia Historical Quarterly* 36 (1952): 328–35.
Thomas, Emory. *The Confederacy as a Revolutionary Experience*. Columbia: University of South Carolina Press, 1991.

Thornton, J. Mills, III. *Politics and Slavery in a Slave Society: Alabama, 1800–1860.* Louisiana State University Press, 1978.
Turner, William H., and Edward J. Cabbell. *Blacks in Appalachia.* Lexington: University Press of Kentucky, 1985.
Walker, Robert Sparks. *Torchlight to the Cherokees: The Brainerd Mission.* New York: MacMillan, 1931.
Wallenstein, Peter, and Bertram Wyatt-Brown, eds. *Virginia's Civil War.* Charlottesville: University of Virginia Press, 2005.
Ward, James A. *J. Edgar Thomson: Master of Pennsylvania.* Wesport, CT: Greenwood Press, 1980.
Watson, Harry L. *Liberty and Power: The Politics of Jacksonian America.* New York: Hill and Wang, 1990.
Weiman, David F. "Farmers and the Market Economy in Antebellum America: A View from Georgia's Upcountry." *Journal of Economic History* 47 (1987): 627–47.
Weitz, Mark A. *A Higher Duty: Desertion Among Georgia Troops during the Civil War.* Omaha: University of Nebraska Press, 2000.
Wetherington, Mark V. *Plain Folk's Fight: The Civil War in Piney Woods Georgia.* Chapel Hill: University of North Carolina Press, 2005.
Whites, LeeAnn. *Gender Matters: Civil War, Reconstruction, and the Making of the New South.* New York: Palgrave: 2005.
Whites, LeeAnn, and Alecia P. Long. *Occupied Women: Gender, Military Occupation, and the American Civil War.* Baton Rouge: Louisiana State University Press, 2009.
Wilentz, Sean. *The Rise of American Democracy: Jefferson to Lincoln.* New York: W. W. Norton, 2005.
Wilkerson, Warren and Steven E. Woodworth. *A Scythe of Fire: A Civil War Story of the Eighth Georgia Infantry Regiment.* New York: HarperCollins, 2002.
Williams, David. *Rich Man's War: Class, Caste, and Confederate Defeat in the Lower Chattahoochee Valley.* Athens: University of Georgia Press, 1998.
Williams, David. *The Georgia Gold Rush: Twenty-niners, Cherokees, and Gold Fever.* Columbia: University of South Carolina Press, 1993.
Williams, John Alexander. *Appalachia: A History.* Chapel Hill: University of North Carolina Press, 2002.
Woodworth, Steven E. *While God is Marching On: The Religious World of Civil War Soldiers.* Lawrence: University of Kansas Press, 2001.
Wright, Gavin. *Old South, New South: Revolutions in the Southern Economy since the Civil War.* Baton Rouge: Louisiana State University Press, 1986.
Wyatt-Brown, Bertram. *Southern Honor: Ethics and Behavior in the Old South.* New York: Oxford University Press, 1982.

Unpublished Dissertations and Theses
Bohannon, Keith S. "The Northeast Georgia Mountains during the Secession Crisis and Civil War." PhD diss., Pennsylvania State University, 2001.

Burkley, Margaret Nola. "Floyd County, Georgia, during the Civil War Era." PhD diss., Florida State University, 1998.
Claremont, Alexa Ilene. "Creators of Community: Cassville, Georgia, 1850–1880." Master's thesis, University of Georgia, 2005.
Edwards, Stewart C. "River City at War: Columbus, Georgia, in the Confederacy." PhD diss., Florida State University, 1998.
Hebert, Keith S. "A Case Study of a Nineteenth-Century Rural Physician: Robert T. Ellett, M.D." Master's thesis, Virginia Tech, 2001.
Hamilton, Karen. "The Union Occupation of Bartow County: 1864–1865." Master's thesis, State University of West Georgia, 1998.
Jones, George L. "William H. Felton and the Independent Democratic Movement in Georgia, 1870–1890." PhD diss., University of Georgia, 1971.
Kleit, David H. "'We wanted the land': Cherokee County during the Era of Removal and Resettlement." PhD diss., Duke University, 2003.

Index

Adair, Samuel, 14–15
Adairsville, 65, 125
Addington, John, 105, 109
African Methodist Episcopal Church, 188
Akin, Warren, 51, 95, 100, 120, 155, 162–63
Alfred (slave), 38
Allatoona Pass, 136, 157–59
Allen, Virgil, 192
Alpha Phi Delta, 52–53
African Methodists Episcopal School, 188
American Missionary Association, 189
American Party, 49, 50–51
Andrews, Garnett, 49
Andrews Raiders, 110–12
Antebellum, home manufacturing, 33; intra-racial relations, 38; iron production, 16; kinship, 18
Anti-Democratic Party, 55
Appalachian region; 6–7, 9–12, 16, 19, 26, 28, 30, 35–36, 71–72, 82, 94, 97–99, 102–3, 150, 194, 215n, 218n, 219n, 222n, 223n, 229n, 233–43n; postbellum politics, 199
Army of Tennessee, 113–39, 175
Athens, Georgia, *Southern Banner*, 163
Atkins, James, 194
Atlanta Campaign, 117–39

Baker's Regiment, Georgia Militia Cavalry, 118
Baltzelle, James, 118, 183–84
Baptists, 20, 22–23, 52, 77, 186, 227n, 228n

Barnsley, George, 38, 74, 83–88, 92–93, 101
Barnsley, Godfrey, 20–22, 38, 83–85, 100, 106–7, 183–84
Barnsley, Harold, 66
Barnsley, Julia, 90–91
Barnsley, Lucien, 85. 92–93, 97
Bartering, 6, 17, 26, 37
Bartow, Francis S., 95
Battey, Robert, 181
Battle of Adairsville, 125
Battle of Allatoona Pass, 157–59
Battle of Cassville, 133–37
Battle of First Manassas, 85–90
Beck, A. A., 151
Beck, Josephine, 80
Bentley, John, 74, 77
Blacker, E. B., 186–87
Bogle, Joseph, 55, 205
Brandon, Thomas, 38
Branson, Maggie, 141
Brantley, John, 94, 101
Breckinridge, John C., 55
Brooks, Noble, 101
Broughton, James M., 119
Brown, Easter, 21, 138
Brown, Joseph E., 4, 7, 51–53, 62, 66–67, 70, 72, 78–79, 82, 94–96, 100, 102–3, 106, 112, 119, 138, 148, 197, 200, 236n, 243n, 245n
Bunn, Moses H., 1–2
Burge, Joseph P., 109
Burke, John, 25, 46

California, migration, 5, 27–29, 44
Camp McDonald, 77
Carnes, Shem, 65

Carter, George A., 103–4, 107–8
Cartersville, 55, 81, 104, 108, 117, 120, 142–45, 151–57, 162–65, 170, 177–78, 181–87
Cartersville *Express*, 55–56, 181
Cassville, 20, 178; destruction by Union Army, 161–62; Union Army occupation, 137
Cassville Female Seminary, 134, 160
Cassville *Standard*, 24–25, 27, 38, 46, 50, 54, 56, 59, 231n, 235n, 236n, Standard, 46
Charleston Democratic Convention (1860), 54
Cherokee Baptist Association, 77
Cherokee Baptist College, 52, 160
Cherokee Indians, 13, 81; removal, 15, 18
Chitwood, Richard, 165
Christian Index, The, 22
Chumler, Martin, 156
Chunn, Lila, 98–100, 132
Chunn, William Augustus, 73–74, 98–100, 102, 112, 114–15, 119–20, 122–23, 181–82, 195
Church; baptism, 23; membership, 21, 23
Clayton, Sarah, 17, 81
Coker, Clint, 129
Cole, H. G., 196
Collins, Dossius M., 120
Collins, William, 120, 138
Colquitt, Jack, 165
Compromise of 1850, 48
Cone, Andrew Jackson, 52
Confederate States of America; conscription, 17, 95, 103–8, 115, 141, 151, 175, 238n, 245n; damage to civilian property, 101–2; desertion, 113, 118, 168, 220n, 248n, 256n; enlistment patterns, 70–78, 211–14, 220n, 245n, 248n, 257n; women and home front, 99; hospitals, 77, 88–89, 98–99, 104–5, 121, 174–75, 177; military service exemptions, 98, 119; mobilization, 36, 72, 79, 83, 168; nationalism, 70, 75, 95, 256n; resistance to Confederate authority, 94–95, 103, 108; spies, 110–11, 144–46, 150; public relief, 22, 70, 164; veteran reunions, 178, 204–6, 213; veterans, 173–74; war weariness, 95–97, 112–13
Congressional election of 1874, 200–201
Congressional election of 1880, 203
Connelly, John, 32
Connor, Thomas B., 109
Constitutional Unionist Party, 45–46, 54
Convict lease system, 201
Cook, Edmund, 151
Cooper, Eveline, 186
Cooper, James F., 50, 79, 88
Cooper, Mark A., 16, 20, 55, 75, 77
Cooper, Thomas, 93
Cooperationists, 41, 57–63
Corbin, William, 151
Cotton production, 30–32
Couch, T. R., 191
Covington, Lewis, 190
Crawford, John, 38, 191
Crow, Miles, 152
Crow, Sarah, 65, 151
Cunyus, Lucy, 207

Dabney, William H., 200
Daniels, Julia F., 20
Democratic Party; antebellum, 41–68, 171; Bourbon Democrats, 194–206
Denman, Madison, 163
Department of North Georgia (Confederate), 166–70
Douglas, Stephen A., 54–56
Dowtin, Tom, 57, 64, 67
Drought, 6, 112, 115, 180–82, 184–85

Earle, Richard, 129
Edwards, Charles, 188
8th Georgia Infantry Regiment, 74, 76, 85–90
18th Georgia Infantry Regiment, 100, reunions, 204–5
Elder, Callie, 20, 138, 186
Election of 1860, 57–59
Etowah Agricultural Society, 24
Etowah Mining and Manufacturing Company (Etowah Iron Works), 77, 82, 98

Etowah River, 49, 82, 118
Etowah River Valley region, 2, 4–5, 7, 9–11, 14, 26–28, 36, 71, 97–98, 102–3, 199
Euharlee Baptist Church, 185
Euharlee Presbyterian Church, 22
Euharlee, 20, 99, 185, 191, 207

Farrow, Henry, 193
Felton, Rebecca L., 65–66, 206
Felton, William H., 195, 65–66, 198–206
Fifth Congressional District, 43, 49, 51
1st Confederate Infantry Regiment, 78
1st Confederate States of America Regiment, 110
1st Georgia Cavalry, 153–54
Ford, Edward, 118
40th Georgia Infantry Regiment, 112, 118, 175
4th Georgia Cavalry Regiment, 118
14th Georgia Infantry Regiment, 109
Franks, Malinda, 22
Freedmen's Bureau, 180–81, 185, 188
Freedpeople; child custody disputes, 187–88; education, 188–89; migrations, 185; church, 185–86; labor, 192
Freeman, David B., 205–6

Gaines, Lizzie, 142–44, 153, 161
Gatewood, John, 153
General Order No. 2, 145
General Order No. 20, 192
Georgia Land Lottery (1832), 13
Georgia Militia Census (1864), 119
Georgia Platform, 45
Georgia Secession Convention (1860), 59–65
Goldsmith, Turner, 35, 61
Grange, The, 195
Gray, John, 81
Great Appalachian Valley, 71, 97–99
Green, Mary, 177
Guerillas bands, Benjamin McCollum's Band, 166; J. Woodville Tate's Scouts, 162, 165; Abraham Tate's Scouts, 165; Matt Moore's Scouts, 165; John Gatewood's Scouts, 165, John Prior's Scouts, 165; Woody's Scouts, 165; Lilliard's Scouts, 165; Benjamin McCullom's Scouts, 165; Jordan's Gang, 165; Jack Colquitt's Partisans, 165; violence, 153, 156–57, 160–62, 166
Guyton, Nathaniel, 105

Hall, Levi, 192
Hambleton, James P., 196
Hamilton, Rock, 187
Harbin, N. P., 201
Hardin, John, 35
Hardin, Mark A., 61–62
Hardin, William, 99
Hargis, O. P., 155
Hargrove, Zachariah B., 190, 201
Harris, F. J, 189
Harris, Rosanna, 186
Harris, T. S., 191
Hawks, Katy, 187
Hays, Lucinda, 191
Henderson, Washington, 163
Hendricks, Lindsay, 163
H.H.H. Society, 52
Hill, Benjamin H., 51
Hood, John Bell, 101, 125, 133–36, 157
Hood, Rebecca, 74–75, 142, 147
Houk, Berry, 152
Howard, Charles W., 20, 24, 35, 37, 48, 66–67, 89, 108, 120, 190
Howard, Frances, 130–31, 153
Howard, Jane, 130–31
Howard, Jett, 20, 85, 88, 120, 127
Howard, Susan Jett, 20, 120, 127, 132, 149

Independent Democrats, 197; African American support, 202–3
Iron Production, 2, 15–16, 50, 81–82, 130, 186, 192, 224n, 241n

Jackson, Tennessee, *Southern Statesman*, 51
Jenkins, Charles, 45
John Brown's Raid, 52, 62
Johnson, Abda, 55
Johnson, Anne Elizabeth, 121
Johnson, Dennis, 21, 33–35, 38

Johnson, Erastus V., 80, 121
Johnson, Herschel V., 52
Johnson, Lindsey, 49
Johnston, Joseph E., 84–85, 114, 115, 116, 119, 121, 123–26, 130, 133–39, 169, 170, 177
Jones, Jenkins, 156
Judah, Henry M., 169

King, John, 172–73
Kingston Presbyterian Church, 57
Kingston saltpeter cave, 81, 109, 119, 193
Kingston Soldiers Aid Society, 177
Kingston, 20, 48, 56, 99, 104, 108, 170, 196
Kinnabrue, H. H., 193
Know Nothing Party, 51
Ku Klux Klan, 190, 194
Kurtz, Wilbur, 207

Ladies of Bartow County wartime petition, 102–3
Ladies Memorial Association, 178, 204
Land, Nathan, 29, 122
Larey, Peter H., 78
Law, William, 151
Leake, Bryant, 189
Lecompton Constitution, 53
Lester, George N., 203
Livestock, 5–6, 12, 22, 25, 30, 34–37, 66, 121, 127, 137, 160
Lost Cause mythology, 171, 206–7
Lynching, 104, 127, 166, 206

Macedonia Baptist Church, 20, 22–23, 186, 227n
Mackey, Eliza, 47
Maddox, George, 205
Magnis, Lou, 118
Market economy, 35–39, 57, 72, 147, 181, 183–84, 192, 216n, 218–19n; defined, 220n
Masonic Orders, 24, 236n
Maxwell, Joel, 105
McCravey-Johnson House, 170
McDonald, Charles, 45
McDonald, Mary, 151

McDow, James, 65
McDow, John, 150
McDow, Samuel, 166
McDow, Willis, 150
McGee, James, 58, 120
McKelvey House, 136
Merino Sheep, 35
Methodists, 20, 22, 188, 199, 207
Milam, Turner, 22
Milan, Riley, 22
Milhollin, John F., 74–76, 161, 240n
Milledgeville *Federal Union*, 48
Milledgeville *Southern Recorder*, 56
Miller, Emma, 188
Milner, Edward, 189
Missouri Compromise, 48
Moffitt, William, 186
Montgomery, Robert, 117
Morrison, James, 58
Mostetter, David, 105
Murchison Sisters, 153

Nance Creek Baptist Church, 23, 185
Neal, Andrew Jackson, 119
Nisbet, James A., 64
Noble Hill, 185
Northwest Georgia; secession convention voting patterns, 61–62; unionism, 103, 108; wartime violence, 103

Octagon house, 126
Overby, Basil H., 50

Parrish, Robert, 189
Patterson, Sarah Jane, 185
Patton, Will, 152
Peaches, 138, 148
Persistence rates, 28, 211–13n
Phillips Legion, 74
Piedmont region, 5–6, 71; postbellum politics, 199
Pierce, Franklin, 47
Pine Log, 18, 94, 97, 103, 150, 156
Pitts, Jim, 166
Poor whites, 19, 24, 27, 29, 70, 98–99, 101, 107, 110, 173, 195
Populism, 204

Postbellum; debt, 179–80, 184; economy, 183; labor, 180, 186–87; politics, 198–208
Price, Hawkins F., 27, 48, 59
Pritchett, W. H., 180

Quinn, Mary, 120, 131–32, 148

Raccoon Creek Baptist Church, 186, 227n
Refugees, 115, 119–20, 122–23, 132, 141, 146, 149–50, 164
Regulators, 188–89
Republican Party, 54, 56–58, 62, 67, 73, 172–73, 193–94, 199
"Rich Man's War, Poor Man's Fight", 98, 107–9
Rogers, Peter, 189
Rome, 30, 51, 65, 76, 84, 103, 105, 121, 130, 133, 142, 149, 157, 165, 176, 181, 186, 190, 193, 200
Rome *Courier*, 200
Rome *Tri-Weekly Courier*, 103, 105–6, 121
Rome *Weekly Courier*, 195
Rowland Highlanders, 70
Rowland, John, 14, 28, 35, 46–47, 111, 221n, 223n
Ruffin, Edmund, 17
Russell, Nancy, 150, 152

Sampson, Ezekiel, 154
7th Congressional District, 194, 200
Shackleford, Achelles, 44
Sharpe, William, 174
Sherman, William T., 113, 117, 120–70, 234n, 250n
61st Georgia Infantry Regiment, 109
63rd Georgia Infantry Regiment, 100, 127
Slavery; church, 22–24; Civil War, 148; economic significance, 10–15, 22, 26–27, 39, 72; insurrection fears, 16–17, 80, 193; iron production, 16; politics, 44, 63; population increases, 30–32; pro-slavery defense, 52–54; runaways, 38, 63, 148–49, 185; secession, 54, 58–61; Union occupation, 148–49

Small pox, 105, 181
Smith, Charles, 191
Soldier's Aid Society, 80
South Carolina, migration patterns, 19
Southern Claims Commission, 150–51
Southern Rights Party, 45, 58
Spring Bank, 128, 130
Sproull, James, 36–37
Star Fort, 157
Stiles, Benjamin, 85
Stiles, Elizabeth Mackay, 67, 117
Stiles, William H., 38, 47, 104, 123
Stilesboro, 20
Stroup, Jacob, 15
Stroup, Moses, 15
Sumter, James, 192

Tate, Abraham, 162
Taylor, R. H., 22
Tenant farmers; rates, 27–29, 33, 180, 211n
Thomas, George H., 169, 196
Tillson, Davis, 191
Towns, George, 43
Trammell, L.N., 200
Treaty of New Echota, 14
Trippe, Turner H., 46, 59
Tucks, John R., 118
Tugalo Ticket, 47
Tumlin, Lewis, 14, 21, 35, 183, 221n, 234n
22nd Georgia Infantry Regiment, 174
23rd Georgia Infantry Regiment, 103

Underwood, John, 51
Union Army; destruction of private property, 130–32; occupation of Bartow County, 141–70
Union Democratic Party, 44
Union League, 194
Union School, 188
Unionists, 3–4, 65, 94–95, 103, 105, 108, 120–21, 127, 138, 141, 149–53, 165–66, 193
United Confederate Veterans, 204–5

Vaughn, Grandison, 152

Watkins, Sam, 126
Watts, James Washington, 36–37
Western & Atlantic Railroad, 24–26, 49, 50
Wheat, 11–12, 30–35
Wheeler, Joseph, 167
Whig Party, 6, 25, 41–52, 55–56, 59, 199, 233n
White Men's Democracy, 3, 68, 195, 203, 215n, 235n
White Supremacy, 3–4, 9, 16, 19, 39, 69, 108, 171, 184, 198, 207, 216n, 219n
Wilmot Proviso, 43–44
Wofford, Lydia, 18
Wofford, Nancy, 149
Wofford, Nathaniel, 18, 27
Wofford, William B., 47
Wofford, William T., 27, 44, 56, 59, 101, 166–70, 190, 195–97
Wofford's Cross Roads, 19, 97
Wolf Pen, 156
Woodcock, Marcus, 126
Woodlands, 20, 76, 83–84, 88, 90–93, 120, 146, 148–50, 155, 160, 183–84, 251n; cavalry skirmish, 128–31
Woolley, Mary Ann, 80
Woolley's Bridge, 136

Wooten, William, 119
Women; church, 21–23; Confederate memorials, 176–78; freedwomen, 191; interactions with guerrillas, 164; interactions with soldiers, 102, 118, 127, 130–31, 138, 141–52, 155, 161; role in white households, 19, 216n; spies, 153–54; support for Confederacy, 70–73, 102–3, 121; wartime households, 90, 98; wartime organizations, 80
Wright, Augustus, 51
Wykle, James R., 55

Yeoman farmers; agriculture, 31–33; antebellum wealth, 9, 11–14; kinship, 28; material culture, 19; migrations, 17; military enlistment, 70, 108, 110, 118; politics, 25–26, 200, 216–19n, 220–22n; postbellum wealth, 173–75, 185; religion, 19, 23; self-sufficiency, 34; slaveholders, 26, 80, 226n
Young, Louis, 175
Young, Pierce Manning Butler, 55, 66, 107, 190, 194, 200, 204–5
Young, Robert, 35